Formal Languages for Computer Simulation:

Transdisciplinary Models and Applications

Pau Fonseca i Casas
Universitat Politècnica de Catalunya – BarcelonaTech, Spain

Information Science
REFERENCE
An Imprint of IGI Global

Managing Director:	Lindsay Johnston
Editorial Director:	Joel Gamon
Production Manager:	Jennifer Yoder
Publishing Systems Analyst:	Adrienne Freeland
Development Editor:	Myla Merkel
Acquisitions Editor:	Kayla Wolfe
Typesetter:	Erin O'Dea
Cover Design:	Jason Mull

Published in the United States of America by
      Information Science Reference (an imprint of IGI Global)
      701 E. Chocolate Avenue
      Hershey PA 17033
      Tel: 717-533-8845
      Fax: 717-533-8661
      E-mail: cust@igi-global.com
      Web site: http://www.igi-global.com

Library of Congress Cataloging-in-Publication Data

Formal languages for computer simulation : transdisciplinary models and applications / Pau Fonseca i Casas, editor.
    pages cm
  Includes bibliographical references and index.
  Summary: "This book investigates a variety of programming languages used in validating and verifying models in order to assist in their eventual implementation, exploring different methods of evaluating and formalizing simulation models, enabling computer and industrial engineers, mathematicians, and students working with computer simulations to thoroughly understand the progression from simulation to product"-- Provided by publisher.
  ISBN 978-1-4666-4369-7 (hardcover) -- ISBN 978-1-4666-4371-0 (print & perpetual access) -- ISBN 978-1-4666-4370-3 (ebook) 1. Computer simulation. 2. Programming languages (Electronic computers) I. Fonseca i Casas, Pau, 1973-
  QA76.9.C65F66 2014
  005.1--dc23
                    2013011316

British Cataloguing in Publication Data
A Cataloguing in Publication record for this book is available from the British Library.

All work contributed to this book is new, previously-unpublished material. The views expressed in this book are those of the authors, but not necessarily of the publisher.

Table of Contents

Detailed Table of Contents

Chapter 1
   Antoni Guasch, Universitat Politècnica de Catalunya - Barcelona Tech, Spain
   Jaume Figueras, Universitat Politècnica de Catalunya - Barcelona Tech, Spain
   Josep Casanovas, Universitat Politècnica de Catalunya - Barcelona Tech, Spain

Petri nets are used by students as a formal modeling technique before building a working simulation model in Arena or Simio. The Petri net model enables the simulation analyst to build a complete, unambiguous, and readable model of the target process before coding it in the target simulation tool. One of the aims of this chapter is to emphasize the need for formal specification of the simulation model before it is coded in the chosen target simulation environment. Formal specification of the model is of great help throughout the simulation project life cycle, especially in the coding and verification phase.

Chapter 2
   Marisa Analía Sánchez, Universidad Nacional del Sur, Argentina

The purpose of this chapter is to provide an overview of System Dynamics modeling and to highlight its potential as a tool for system´s understanding. Although the work is not intended to cover all the activities involved in a simulation process, the authors present the steps in the modeling process. The authors first summarize the role of Causal Loop diagrams in the modeling process. The authors then introduce Stock-and-flow diagrams and describe how they can be defined using mathematical functions. Along this chapter the authors claim that System Dynamics is an adequate modeling tool for "partially reducible uncertainty" and "irreducible uncertainty" problems. Finally, the authors discuss that in System Dynamics, validity means adequacy with respect to a purpose, and hence it cannot be made in absolute terms and the authors briefly introduce a set of techniques for testing structure and accuracy.

Rhys Goldstein, Autodesk Research, Canada
Gabriel A. Wainer, Carleton University, Canada
Azam Khan, Autodesk Research, Canada

The DEVS formalism is a set of conventions introduced in 1976 for the specification of discrete event simulation models. This chapter explains the core concepts of DEVS by applying the formalism to a single ongoing example. First, the example is introduced as a set of informal requirements from which a formal specification is to be developed. Readers are then presented with alternative sets of modeling conventions which, lacking the DEVS formalism's approach to representing state, prove inadequate for the example. The chapter exploits the DEVS formalism's support for modular model design, as the system in the example is specified first in parts and later as a combination of those parts. The concept of legitimacy is demonstrated on various model specifications, and the relationship between DEVS and both object-oriented programming and parallel computing is discussed.

Alejandro Moreno Astorga, Universidad Nacional de Educación a Distancia,
Spain
José L. Risco-Martín, Universidad Complutense de Madrid, Spain
Eva Besada-Portas, Universidad Complutense de Madrid, Spain
Luís de la Torre, Universidad Nacional de Educación a Distancia, Spain
Joaquín Aranda, Universidad Nacional de Educación a Distancia, Spain

The MIPS simulator is built upon known techniques for discrete event simulation (DEVS). The definition of the MIPS processor within a formal language, such as DEVS, provides completeness, verifiability, extensibility, and maintainability. Moreover, DEVS conceptually separates models from the simulator, making it possible to simulate the MIPS processor and its experimental frame using different simulators working in centralized, parallel, or distributed execution modes. Also, models can be simulated with a simple ad-hoc program written in any language. In this chapter, we start with the MIPS architecture, followed by a brief overview of DEVS explained alongside with the models of the MIPS processor. We continue with a thermal analysis of the MIPS processor using a DEVS simulator. Next, we describe a register reallocation policy based on evolutionary algorithms that notably decreases the resulting register bank temperature. Finally, some conclusions and future views are drawn.

Chapter 5

Designing a new simulation model usually involves the participation of personnel with different knowledge of the system and with diverse formations. These personnel often use different languages, making more difficult the task to define the existing relations between the key model elements. These relations represent the hypotheses that constrain the model and the global behavior of the system, and this information must be obtained from the system experts. A formalism can be a powerful tool to understand the model complexity and helps in the communication between the different actors that participate in the definition of the model. In this chapter we review the use of the "Specification and Description Language," a standard and graphical language that simplifies the model understanding thanks to its modular nature. To do this we present a complete example, representing a simple queuing model that helps the reader to understand the structure and the nature of the language.

Chapter 6

In this chapter, the authors present a formal model of the Anesthesia Unit and Surgical Wards (UAPQ) of a Chilean hospital. The objective was to document and to understand its operation, to assist hospital management and to facilitate its simulation. The model was built with Specification and Description Language (SDL). This methodology was used because it allows the design of a model that represents the system in a graphical, modular, and standard way. Our design contains the following agents: the system, 11 blocks, and 52 processes. The blocks and the processes describe the clinical and administrative activities. The environment of the UAPQ model contains 3 components: clinical services, emergency units, and support units.

To capture and analyze the functional requirements of an information system, UML and the Unified Process (UP) propose the use case and sequence diagrams. However, one of the main difficulties behind the use of UML is how to ensure the consistency of the various diagrams used to model different views of the same system. In this chapter, the authors propose an enriched format for documenting UML2.0 use cases. This format facilitates consistency verification of the functional requirements with respect to the sequence diagrams included in the analysis model. The consistency verification relies on a set of rules to check the correspondence among the elements of the documented use cases and those of the sequence diagrams; the correspondence exploits the implicit semantic relationship between these diagrams as defined in UP. Furthermore, to provide for a rigorous verification, the authors formalize both types of diagrams and their correspondence rules in the formal notation Z. The formal version of the analysis model is then verified through the theorem prover Z/EVES to ensure its consistency.

Chapter 8

Model-based system design is served by a single, multi-layered model supporting all design activities, in different levels of detail. SysML is a modeling language, endorsed by OMG, for system engineering, which aims at defining such models for system design. It provides discrete diagrams to describe system structure and components, to explore allocation policies crucial for system design and to identify design requirements. In this chapter, SysML is used for the model-based design of enterprise information system architecture, supporting a systemic view of such systems, where software and hardware entities are treated as system components composed to create the system architecture. SysML extensions to facilitate the effective description of non-functional requirements, especially quantitative ones, and their verification are presented. The integration of evaluation parameters and results into a discrete SysML diagram enhances requirement verification process, while the visualization of evaluation data helps system engineers to explore design decisions and properly adjust system design. Based on the proposed extensions, a SysML profile was developed. The experience obtained when applying the profile for renovating the architecture of a large-scale enterprise information system is also briefly discussed to explore the potential of the proposed extensions.

Chapter 9

In this chapter, the authors present an approach for developing a simulation-tool-independent description of manufacturing systems and how to convert such a general model into simulation-tool-specific models. They show why we need standards for these discrete processes, what the state of the art is, why SysML has the chance to become a standard in modeling discrete systems, and how to use it. The authors present SysML and explain how to model discrete systems with it. For that, they explain the concept of domain-specific modeling in detail. They furthermore have a look at model-to-model transformations and its validation and verification. Finally, the authors examine different SysML modeling tools and how to improve the usability of SysML tools for engineers.

System models validation is an important engineering activity of the system development life-cycle, usually performed via simulation. However, usability and effectiveness of many validation approaches are hindered by the fact that system simulation is not performed using a system model described by a standardized modeling language as SysML. This requires system simulation models to be recreated from scratch, burdening the engineer and introducing inconsistencies between system and validation models. In this chapter, the authors present how system engineers may effectively perform SysML system model validation utilizing the original SysML model and standards-based simulated related extensions. This is achieved by a framework that exploits MDA concepts and techniques, such as profiling, meta-modeling and formal transformations. This way an open, standards-based, customizable approach for SysML models validation using DEVS simulators is formed. A simple battle system is used as an example throughout the chapter to facilitate the presentation of the proposed approach.

The use of agent-based modelling and simulation techniques in the social sciences has flourished in the recent decades. The main reason is that the object of study in these disciplines, human society present or past, is difficult to analyse through classical analytical techniques. Population dynamics and structures are inherently complex. Thus, other methodological techniques need to be found to more adequately study this field. In this context, agent-based modelling is encouraging the introduction of computer simulations to examine behavioural patterns in complex systems. Simulation provides a tool to artificially examine societies, where a big number of actors with decision capacity coexist and interact. However, formal modelling in these areas has not traditionally been used compared to other fields of science, in particular in their use of formal languages during the modelling process. In this chapter, the authors aim to revise the most relevant aspects on modelling in social sciences and to discuss the use formal languages by social scientists.

Chapter 12

Conceptual modelling is the process of abstracting a model from a real or proposed system into a conceptual model. An explicit conceptual model representation allows the model to be communicated and analysed by the stakeholders involved in a simulation project. A good representation that can be understood by all stakeholders is especially essential when the project involves different stakeholders. The three commonly used paradigms in business applications are discrete-event simulation, agent-based simulation and system dynamics. While the conceptual model representations in discrete-event simulation and system dynamics have been dominated by process-flow and stock-and-flow diagrams, respectively, research into the conceptual model representation in agent-based simulation is relatively new. Many existing representation methods for agent-based simulation models are less friendly to business users. This chapter advocates the use of Business Process Model and Notation (BPMN) diagrams for the agent-based simulation conceptual model representation in the context of business applications. This chapter also demonstrates how the proposed BPMN representation and other methods such as Petri Nets, DEVS and UML are used to represent the well-known SugarScape model.

Preface

Understanding and predicting reality is one of humanity's dreams, perhaps the first and most intricate dream. Nevertheless, reality is sometimes complex and it is therefore difficult to understand all of it without the use of models that simplify its understanding. Models are tools for conceptualizing reality. Therefore, they simplify system compression and analysis. Operations Research (OR) uses models to solve problems and owns a set of methodologies to construct these models.

Simulation is a part of OR in which a set of methodologies is used to understand and analyze a wide range of systems. A good definition for simulation can be "(...) the process of designing a model of a real system and conducting experiments with this model for the purpose of understanding the behavior of the system and/or evaluating various strategies for the operation of the system" (Shannon 1998).

In applying these methodologies, the relationships between different system elements are reproduced and a set of hypotheses can be used, some of them to simplify reality. Simplification hypotheses are not true, from the point of view of the system, but are used in the construction of the model to simplify the modeling process, and sometimes just to make this process possible, due to the inherent complexity of the system. These relationships and hypotheses describe the behavior of the system and an experimental environment that represents the target of the study is created. The various relationships and rules, which are usually mathematical or logical, make up the model, the tool that acquires data and provides answers about the system.

The main interest of this book is to offer the reader a broader view of some of the various alternatives that currently exist for formally representing a simulation model. Not all the alternatives are represented, and please forgive the omission of some other interesting, useful, and powerful alternatives that exist; but, obviously, we need to focus on just a few. The main objective of the alternatives presented here is to introduce the reader to the methodologies of formally representing a simulation model. This book is a first step in understanding the importance of formalizing a simulation model and a starting point for beginning to learn in this area.

The book is structured as follows: the first chapter, "Conceptual Modeling Using PETRI Nets" describes the use of Petri Nets for discrete simulation and provides some examples. As an introductory chapter, it also emphasizes the need to formally represent the simulation model before coding it in the chosen simulation environment.

The second chapter, "Modeling for System's Understanding" describes system dynamics modeling and the main diagrams needed for describing complex systems through this approach.

The third and fourth chapters, "The DEVS Formalism" and "Thermal Analysis of the MIPS Processor Formulated Within DEVS Conventions" describe DEVS formalism. While the third chapter discusses DEVS from a broader perspective, the fourth chapter presents a detailed example of a MIPS processor defined using DEVS.

The fifth and sixth chapters, "Specification and Description Language for Discrete Simulation" and "Modeling a Chilean Hospital Using Specification and Description Language", describe Specification and Description Language (SDL), which is a standard graphical alternative for fully representing a simulation model. The fifth chapter describes SDL from a broader perspective while the sixth chapter presents a detailed example using the language.

The seventh chapter, "Formal Consistency Verification of UML Requirement and Analysis Models" proposes an enriched format for documenting UML 2.0 use cases to verify the consistency of the functional requirements of the sequence diagrams included in the analysis model.

The eighth chapter, "Model-Based System Design Using SysML: The Role of the Evaluation Diagram" presents SysML and proposes some extensions to the language in order to effectively describe non-functional requirements.

The ninth chapter, "Domain Specific Simulation Modeling with SysML and Model-to-Model Transformation for Discrete Processes" presents an approach for developing a simulation model using SysML and how to convert such a general model into a simulation-tool-specific model.

The tenth chapter, "An Integrated Framework to Simulate SysML Models Using DEVS Simulators" presents a framework that joins SysML and DEVS, allowing the validation of SysML models using DEVS simulators.

The eleventh chapter, "Overview on Agent-Based Social Modelling and the use of Formal Languages" presents a review of the most relevant aspects of modeling in the social sciences and discusses the use of formal languages by social scientists.

And last but not least, the twelfth chapter, "Agent-Based Simulation Model Representation Using BPMN" presents the Business Process Model and notation diagrams for representing the agent-based simulation conceptual model for business applications.

I hope that this collection of chapters, which illustrate some of the existing alternatives for formally representing a simulation model, will help the reader understand the complexity of the discipline.

Finally, I wish to thank the hard work performed by the authors of the chapters, the Editorial Advisory Board, the reviewers and the editorial team, all of whom made this book possible.

Enjoy modeling!

Pau Fonseca i Casas
Universitat Politècnica de Catalunya - BarcelonaTech, Spain

REFERENCES

Shannon, R. E. (1998). Introduction to the art and science of simulation. In *Proceedings of the 1998 Winter Simulation Conference*. Washington, DC: ACM.

Chapter 1
Conceptual Modeling Using Petri Nets

Antoni Guasch
Universitat Politècnica de Catalunya - Barcelona Tech, Spain

Jaume Figueras
Universitat Politècnica de Catalunya - Barcelona Tech, Spain

Josep Casanovas
Universitat Politècnica de Catalunya - Barcelona Tech, Spain

ABSTRACT

Petri nets are used by our students as a formal modeling technique before building a working simulation model in Arena or Simio. The Petri net model enables the simulation analyst to build a complete, unambiguous, and readable model of the target process before coding it in the target simulation tool. One of the aims of this chapter is to emphasize the need for formal specification of the simulation model before it is coded in the chosen target simulation environment. Formal specification of the model is of great help throughout the simulation project life cycle, especially in the coding and verification phase.

INTRODUCTION

Petri nets have proved to be a successful tool for modeling logistic and manufacturing systems thanks to a series of properties, including the conciseness with which they embody static structure and dynamics, the availability of mathematical analysis techniques, and the clear graphical nature (Jensen, 1997; Silva & Valette, 1989;

DOI: 10.4018/978-1-4666-4369-7.ch001

Zimmermann, Dalkowski, & Hommel, 1996). Furthermore, Petri nets are very suitable for modeling and visualizing patterns of behavior comprising concurrency, synchronization, and resource sharing, which are key factors in optimizing system performance.

Another key feature that makes Petri nets an ideal choice of conceptual modeling formalism is the ease with which a Petri net model can be mapped into Arena simulation code. From a scientific perspective, this might seem redundant, since Petri net simulators (www.informatik.uni-hamburg.de/TGI/PetriNets/tools/quick.htm) can be used to analyze the model behavior, making the translation to Arena unnecessary. However, classical simulators such as Arena are the standard choice in industry, whereas Petri net simulators are largely confined to academic circles.

This chapter introduces the reader to ordinary Petri nets, which are called Place/Transition nets (PTN), Timed Petri nets (TPN), and Colored Timed Petri nets (CTPN). We explain how basic Petri net structures can be mapped to Arena code. Finally, we present a series of examples that combine the Petri net modeling formalism and Arena coding.

The chapter is intentionally written in an informal style, with the aim of explaining the key concepts through examples and omitting reference to formal specifications where they are not strictly relevant.

PETRI NETS

Petri nets originate from Carl Adam Petri's doctoral thesis of 1962, "Kommunikation mit Automaten" (Petri, 1962), which introduced a new model of information flow in systems. Today, Petri nets are commonly used to model a variety of discrete event systems, such as communication protocols and networks; manufacturing, production and scheduling systems; logistic systems; and the design, specification, simulation and validation of software systems. Petri nets have a number of advantages:

- They capture the precedence relations and structural interactions of concurrent and asynchronous events.
- Their precise graphical formalism simplifies the visualization of complex systems.
- Petri net theory provides an integrated methodology for modeling physical systems and complex decision processes.
- They provide a uniform environment for modeling and formal analysis. The same model supports the construction of discrete event simulators and controllers as well as the formal verification of behavioral properties such as the

precedence relations of events, concurrent operations, appropriate synchronization, freedom from deadlock, and mutual exclusion of shared resources.
- They explicitly represent model states and events.
- Petri net models can be used to implement real-time control systems. They can be used to model or replace Programmable Logic Controllers (PLCs).

Place/Transition Nets (PTN)

A Petri net is a directed bipartite graph that contains places, represented by circles; transitions, represented by bars; and directed arcs that connect places to transitions and transitions to places. Places are used to describe the local system state. Transitions are used to describe events that may modify the system state and arcs specify the relationship between local states and events.

The dynamic nature of the system modeled in a Petri net is represented by the movement of *entities* (referred to as *tokens* in the Petri net literature) through the net. An entity can be either *temporal*, in that it moves through the system, or *permanent*, in that it serves other entities. Permanent entities are also referred to as *resources*.

A PTN can be formally defined as a 5-tuple:

$$PTN = (P, T, A, W, M_0)$$

where

- $P = \{P_1, P_2, P_3, ..., P_{np}\}$ is a finite set of places;
- $T = \{T_1, T_2, T_3, ..., T_{ne}\}$ is a finite set of transitions;
- $A = \{A_1, A_2, A_3, ..., A_{na}\}$ is a finite set of arcs that connect places to events and vice versa;
- $W = A_i \mapsto \{1, 2, 3, ...\}$ $\forall A_i$ is the weight associated with each arc;
- $M_0 = P_i \mapsto \{1, 2, 3, ...\}$ $\forall P_i$ is the initial number of entities in each place (initial marking).

The current location and distribution of entities in a Petri net is called a marking, which defines the state of the system.

A transition can be fired if each transition input has the required number of entities specified by the weight associated with the arc from the place to the transition. Firing the event removes entities from the input places and adds entities to the output places. The number of entities removed or added equals the weight of the associated arc.

In more detail, the following rules are used to govern the flow of entities in a Petri net:

- **Enabling rule:** A transition, T_i, is enabled if each place, P_j, connected to the entrance of the transition has at least $W(P_j,T_i)$ entities. $W(P_j,T_i)$ is the weight of the arc connecting the place P_j with the transition T_i. Therefore, a transition, T_i, is enabled if

$$M\left(P_j\right) \geq W\left(P_j,T_i\right) \quad \forall\ P_j \in I\left(T_i\right)$$

where $M(P_j)$ is the number of entities at place P_j and $I(T_i)$ is the set of input places to transition T_i

$$I\left(T_i\right) = \left\{P_j \in P, \left(P_j,T_i\right) \in A\right\}$$

- **Firing rule:** An enabled transition can be fired at any time. The action of firing an enabled transition is the removal of $W(P_j, T_i)$ entities from each place P_j at the entrance of the transition, T_i, and the addition of $W(T_i, T_k)$ entities to each place at the exit of the transition, T_i.

Figure 1 shows the result of firing transition T1: two entities are removed from P1, one from P2, two from P3; and one entity is added to P4 and three to P5.

Figure 2 models the use of a shared resource. Hereafter, thick arcs represent the flow of temporal entities through the net. These are the entities that are created by T1 and disappear with the firing of T3. The arc weight is assumed to be 1 if no explicit weight is shown. The permanent entity at P5 represents a shared resource since it is needed for firing T2 or T5. T2 and T5 cannot be fired simultaneously since the firing of either one removes the entity from P5.

This basic PTN model is not suitable for modeling many of the systems encountered in logistics, production, communication, flexible manufacturing or information processing. Petri nets describing real systems tend to be complex and extremely

Figure 1. Firing of transition T_1

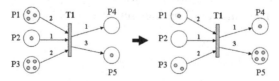

Figure 2. Shared resource

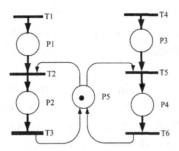

large. Sometimes, it is actually impossible to model the behavior of the system accurately. To overcome this problem, many authors have proposed extensions of the basic PTN model.

Timed Petri Nets (TPN)

The PTN model considered in the previous section does not include the notion of time. However, time is a crucial aspect when dealing with dynamic logistics, manufacturing or transportation processes.

When introducing time into the basic Petri net model, we have to assign time durations (delays) to certain activities in the net. The literature on TPNs describes many locations in a Petri net which may be used to represent time. One option is to associate time with places (Wong, Dillon, & Forward, 1985), so that entities arriving at a place are unavailable for a specified period. However, most authors propose a model in which time is associated with the enabling time of a transition (Molloy, 1981; Ajmone, Balbo, Conte, Donatelli, & Franceschinis, 1985; Ajmone, Balbo, Bobbio, Chiola, Conte, & Cumani, 1995). Each transition in this type of TPN must remain enabled for a specified time before it can fire. In these models, firing is instantaneous.

The firing of a transition in a Petri net corresponds to an event that changes the state of the system. This change of state can have one of two causes:

- The firing of a transition may result from the verification of a logical condition in the system. These types of transitions do not consume time and are called *immediate transitions* (Figure 3(a)), firing as soon as they become enabled. In this chapter, these transitions are represented as thin bars.
- Transitions can be induced by the completion of an activity. In this case, the transitions can be used to model activities, so that transition enabling periods correspond to activity executions and transition firing corresponds to activ-

ity completions. As such, time can be naturally associated with transitions. These transitions are called *timed transitions* and are represented as rectangular boxes in this chapter (Figure 3(b)). A time function, *tf*, specifies the duration of the timed transition.

Looking in more detail at the timed transition shown in Figure 3(b), when an entity is generated in place P1, T1 becomes enabled and the associated timer is set to its initial value—obtained from the time function, *tf*—and starts to count down. The transition T1 fires when the timer reaches the value 0. Thus, the timer associated with a transition can be used to model the duration of an activity whose completion induces the state change that is represented by the change of marking produced by the firing of T1.

It is important to note that the activity is assumed to be in progress while the transition is enabled. This means that as a complex net evolves, an activity may be interrupted if the transition loses its enabling condition before it can fire (Ajmone et al., 1995).

Discrete event models are based on the concepts of events, activities, and delays. In Petri nets, events are associated with the firing of transitions; a timed transition corresponds to an unconditional event and an immediate transition to a conditional event. Thus, unconditional events are associated with the end of an activity and conditional events with the fulfillment of a logical condition.

An activity is a period of time whose duration is known prior to commencement of the activity. Thus, when the period begins, its end can be scheduled. The period can be a constant, a random value from a statistical distribution, the result of an equation, an input from a file, or computed based on the event state. A delay is an indefinite duration that is caused by some combination of system conditions. When an entity joins a queue waiting for a resource, the time that it will remain in

Figure 3. An immediate (a) and a timed (b) transition

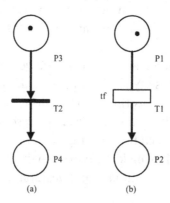

the queue may be unknown initially, since this time may depend on other events that may occur.

Figure 4 models a TPN with a shared resource. Entities are delayed in P1 or P3 if the shared resource is not available. An activity starts as soon as the immediate transition T2 or T5 is fired. The entity remains at P2 or P4 until the end of the activity; that is, the firing of the timed transition T3 or T6. tf1 and tf2 are the time functions that specify the duration of the timed transitions.

A TPN can be formally defined as a 6-tuple:

$$TPN = (P,T,A,W,M_0,TF)$$

where TF is a time function associated with each transition. The time function value for immediate transitions is zero.

One of the limitations of PTN and TPN is that they demand a large number of places and transitions to represent complex systems. As the net expands, the general view of the modeled system gradually becomes compromised. In addition, entities often represent objects or resources in the modeled system; these objects may have attributes, which are not easily represented by a simple entity.

Colored Timed Petri Nets (CTPN)

Many authors have extended the previous net models with the addition of colored or typed entities (Zervos, 1977; Peterson, 1980; Jensen, 1997). In these models entities have a value, often referred to as a 'color' or attribute in discrete event simulation. The association of color sets with entities and transitions, and the definition of functions associated with the net arcs, allows a very concise and readable representation of complex models (Alla, Ladet, Martinez & Silva, 1984).

A CTPN can be specified as a 9-tuple:

Figure 4. Timed petri net of a shared resource

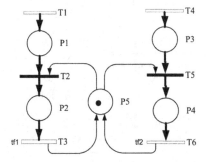

CTPN = (Σ,P,T,A,C,G,E,I,TF)

where

- Σ is a finite, non-empty set of types, called a color set;
- P = {$P_1,P_2,P_3,.....,P_{np}$} is a finite set of places;
- T = {$T_1,T_2,T_3,.....,T_{ne}$} is a finite set of transitions;
- A = {$A_1,A_2,A_3,.....,A_{na}$} is a finite set of arcs that connect places to events and vice versa;
- C is a color function, defined from P on Σ;
- G is a guard function, defined from T;
- E is a function of arc expression, defined from A;
- I is an initiation function, defined from P;
- TF is a time function, defined from T.

The color set Σ determines the types, operations and functions which can be associated with the expressions used in the net (arc functions, guards, colors, etc). The sets *P, T, A* and *TF* have the same significance as in PTNs or TPNs. Color functions, *C*, map every place in the net, including them in a color set. Guard functions, *G*, map all the transitions in the net, moderating the stream of entities according to Boolean expressions. Arc functions, *E*, map each arc in the net, associating them to an expression compatible with the possible color sets. Finally, initialization functions, *I*, are equivalent to the initial marking, M_0, specified in the previous nets but also initialize the color values of the entities.

Figure 5 shows the CTPN of a shared resource. The size of the net has been reduced by half with respect to the equivalent TPN in the previous section (Figure 4). The color, *ty*, identifies the type of identity. This information is used in the

Figure 5. CTPN of a shared resource

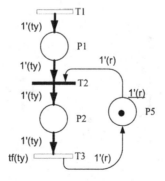

Figure 6. Formal representation of the CTPN of a shared resource

$$\Sigma = \{TY, R\}$$
$$P = \{P1, P2, P5\}$$
$$T = \{T1, T2, T3\}$$
$$A = \{(T1, P1), (P1, T2), (T2, P2), (P2, T3), (T3, P5), (P5, T2)\}$$
$$C(p) = \begin{cases} TY & \text{if } p \in \{P1, P2\} \\ R & \text{if } p \in \{P5\} \end{cases}$$
$$G(t) = \{ \text{true } \forall t \in T \}$$
$$E(a) = \begin{cases} 1`(ty) & \text{if } a \in \{(T1, P1), (P1, T2), (T2, P2), (P2, T3)\} \\ 1`(r) & \text{if } a \in \{(T3, P5), (P5, T2)\} \end{cases}$$
$$I(p) = \begin{cases} 1`(r) & \text{if } p = P5 \\ \varnothing & \text{otherwise} \end{cases}$$
$$TF(t) = \begin{cases} \text{tf(ty)} & \text{if } t = T3 \\ 0 & \text{otherwise} \end{cases}$$

function tf(*ty*) to obtain the process time value for each entity, which depends on the entity type value.

Figure 6 is the formal representation of the same CTPN of a shared resource. Although it is more complete, we prefer the graphical representation as it is easier to read and comprehend.

ELEMENTS OF A SIMULATION MODEL

In this section, we introduce the most significant elements of a simulation model using the CTPN model shown in Figure 7.

Entities

Entities are the sets of system components, such as machines, parts, equipment or clients. Entities can be grouped in two categories:

- **Resources or permanent entities:** As the name indicates, the main characteristic of these entities is that their number does not increase or decrease during the simulation. In general, they are used to describe the means by which activities are executed. A resource defines who or what executes the activity. Examples of resources include machines, transportation units and operators.
- **Temporal entities:** The main characteristic of these entities is that they are created and destroyed throughout the simulation. In general, they are used to describe the objects that are processed in the system, for example the parts, clients or documents.

Figure 7. Simple TPN model

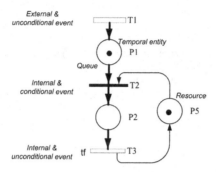

Petri nets do not distinguish explicitly between resources and temporal entities. This is part of the semantics of the net.

The Petri net in Figure 7 models a simple process with one machine and a single queue. The parts (temporal entities) that arrive to be processed wait in a queue and, once processed, leave the system.

Attributes

Attributes (colors in the Colored Petri nets formalism) allow the characterization of the entities. Each attribute corresponds to a property (example.g.,, price, priority, size). Attributes store important information and are essential for controlling the flow of entities through the system.

Activities

Activities are the tasks or actions that take place in the system. One of their essential properties is the duration, which is needed so that the simulator can determine the moment at which the activity will finalize. In the previous example of a simple workstation with one machine, the activity begins whenever the system contains a free resource (machine) and a temporal entity (part) that is available to be processed. Note that the beginning and the end of an activity coincide with the firing of a transition in the Petri net.

Events

In discrete event simulation models, the state variables can only change value as a result of an event. Therefore, an event can be defined as an instantaneous action (i.e., does not consume time) that can change the value of a state variable in the modeled system.

Usually, more than one activity begins or ends with each event. An initial classification allows us to differentiate two types of events:

- **Conditional events:** Events that are activated when one or more conditions are fulfilled.
- **Unconditional events:** Events that are planned for execution and do not depend on logical conditions. They are activated after a specific (usually stochastic) time interval.

Events also can also be classified as:

- **Endogenous or Internal Events:** Events caused by conditions in the model; for example, the end of an operation.
- **Exogenous or External Events:** Events external to the model; for example, the arrival of a part at the model.

In the previous example, three events can be distinguished:

1. **Associated with transition T1:** An *unconditional* and *external* event that describes the arrival of parts at the model.
2. **Associated with transition T2:** A *conditional* and *internal* event whose activation causes the beginning of the activity that processes the part. For this event to be activated, the machine must be free and there must be one or more parts in the queue (P1). Therefore, T2 will be evaluated after the arrival of a part (event related to transition T1) or after the end of the process (event related to transition T3).
3. **Associated with the firing of transition T3:** An *unconditional* and *internal* event activated by the end of the process.

It is very important to bear in mind that the global state of the model, like the state of each of its attributes, can only change in response to an event. This is the characteristic that allows simulators to advance the simulation time and to manage events in such a way that the evolution of state variable values describes the behavior of the system.

Queues

These structures are a collection of entities (in general, temporal entities) ordered in a logical form, for example, clients in a FIFO waiting line. The entities in the queue undergo a delay of unknown duration. In Petri nets, queues do not appear explicitly, but those places occupied by temporal entities that are delayed waiting for restricted resources are usually queues. In the previous example, place P1 can be associated with a queue.

MAPPING TO AN ARENA EXECUTABLE MODEL

Once a Petri net conceptual model has been created and validated, its structure is mapped into an Arena executable model using building modules associated with the use of resources (Seize, Delay and Release), the life cycle of the temporal entities (Create and Dispose) and grouping and splitting batches (Batch and Separate) (Pels & Goossenaerts, 2007).

The typical characteristics exhibited by the activities in a dynamic event-driven system, such as concurrency, decision making, and synchronization, can be modeled effectively by Petri nets (Wang, 2007). These Petri net models can be mapped into equivalent Arena model code:

1. **Sequential Execution:** In Figure 8(a), transition T2 can fire only after the firing of T1. This Petri net construct models the sequential relationship between activities. The place/timed transition pair can be coded in Arena using the Delay module (Figure 8(b)).

2. **Conflict:** Transitions T1 and T2 are in conflict in Figure 9(a): both are enabled but the firing of either one disables the other. Such a situation will arise, for example, when a machine has to choose between part types or a part has to choose between several machines. The resulting conflict may be resolved in a purely non-deterministic way or in a probabilistic way, by assigning appropriate probabilities to the conflicting transitions. The situation in which a part has to choose between several machines can be coded in Arena using the Decide module (Figure 9(b)). This module can resolve the conflict by a deterministic decision—using, for example, color properties (attributes in Arena)—or in a probabilistic way. The Decide module codes conflict resolu-

Figure 8. Sequential execution

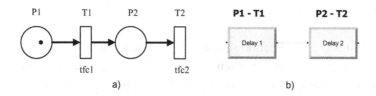

tion over temporal entities (i.e., parts). The situation in which a machine has to choose between part types is coded using priorities.

3. **Concurrency with temporal entities:** In Figure 10(a), the transitions T2 and T3 are concurrent. Concurrency is an important attribute of system interactions. Note that a necessary condition for transitions to be concurrent is the existence of a forking transition that deposits a temporal entity in two or more output places. The Separate module (Figure 10(b)) in Arena deposits temporal entities at two output places.

4. **Synchronization with temporal entities:** It is quite normal in a dynamic system for an event to require multiple entities. The resulting synchronization of resources can be captured by transitions of the type shown in Figure 11(a). Here, T1 is enabled only when each of P1 and P2 receives an entity. The ar-

Figure 9. Conflict

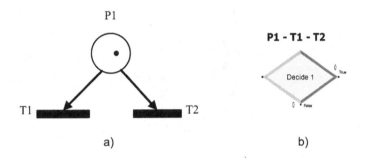

Figure 10. Concurrency

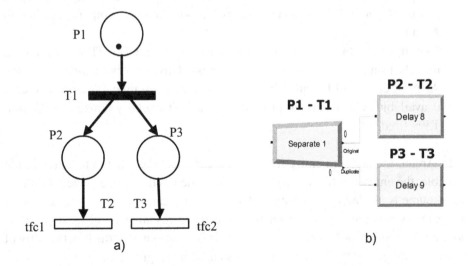

Figure 11. Synchronization

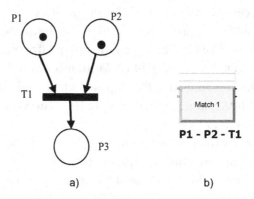

a)   b)

Figure 12. Queue-server model

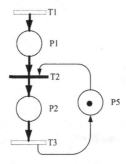

rival of an entity at each of the two places could be the result a potentially complex sequence of operations elsewhere in the Petri net model. The Match module (Figure 11(b)) models the synchronization of temporal entities in Arena.

5. **Concurrency and synchronization with resources:** The TPN in Figure 12 models a single-queue single-server process. This is a classic queuing model. Arriving entities (T1) wait at the queue (P1) for the resource. When the resource is available (T2) it starts to process the entity. The entity remains at P2 until T3 is fired.

In Arena, the arriving entity tries to Seize the resource. If the resource is not available, the entity has to wait in the queue attached to the Arena Seize module. If the resource is available, the entity is delayed for the amount of time, *tf*, specified in the Delay module. Finally, after the time *tf* the resource is released (Release module). The Seize-Delay-Release structure is so common that the functionality of the tree modules is integrated in the Process module (Figure 13).

Figure 13. Seize-delay-release structure

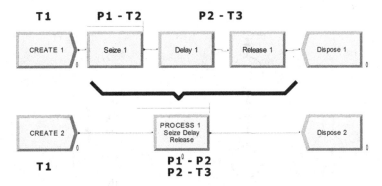

The thick arcs of the Petri nets emphasize the flow of temporal entities through the nets. In Arena, the line connections between modules build the flow of temporal entities through the Arena code. The use of resources is not explicitly shown in Arena code. The same functionality could be achieved by using the Match-Delay-Separate structure in this simple case. However, the use of this structure is not recommended since the mapped Arena code is usually much more complicated and statistics related to resource use will have to be calculated by the user.

Looking back to the shared resource model, Figure 14 shows the TPN and CTPN models and the mapped Arena code. Not that, for a given dynamic system, there is more than one correct model. Both models shown in Figure 14 are correct. It is up to the modeler to decide which is most suitable for his specific needs.

Manufacturing System

This example represents a flexible manufacturing system that processes three types of products with inter-arrival times that are independent exponential random variables with a mean of 9.6 minutes. The system has four manufacturing cells, each one with a certain number of machines. Each type of product has its own sequence of visits (1 to 4) as shown in Table 1. The time to perform an operation at a particular machine is a constant variable with the process time shown in Table 1.

We will use this example to illustrate three conceptually different models. For each model we will show the Petri net and the mapped Arena code. The first model is a TPN model and the second and third are CTPN models. The TPN shown in Figure 15 is very simple; after the arrival of a new product to be processed, the net decides which process it is routed to and the product is processed sequentially. Note that places Pm1, Pm2, Pm3, and Pm4 are depicted twice in the model. This is to make the figure more readable. Pm1 is a place with four free resources; that

Figure 14. Timed (a) and colored timed (b) petri net of a shared resource and the mapped arena code

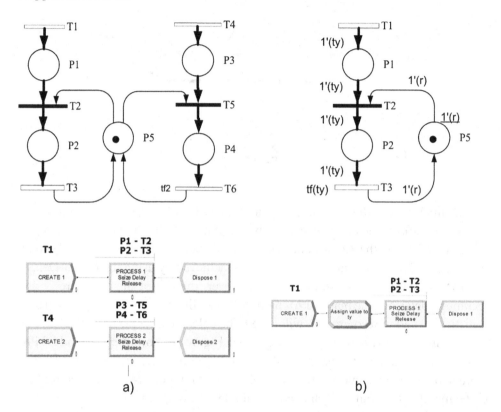

a)   b)

Table 1. Sequences of visits according to process type

Proc. #	Prob.	Visits	Process Time
1	0.24	1, 3, 2	125, 35, 20 min
2	0.44	4, 2	105, 90 min
3	0.32	1, 4, 3	135, 250, 50 min

is, the number of machines at manufacturing cell #1. These four resources are needed for processing product 1 at place P3 and for processing resources of product 3 at place P13. Therefore, resources at Pm1, Pm2, Pm3 and Pm4 are shared resources.

We call this Petri net model a *process-oriented model* as it focuses on the processes and the structure does not resemble the physical layout of the system.

Figure 15. TPN of the manufacturing system

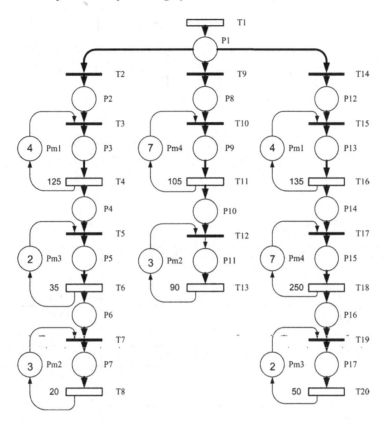

Figure 16 shows the mapped Arena code and Table 2 lists the configuration of each flowchart module. Note that the routing decision (*conflict* structure in Petri nets) is based on probabilities. The decision cannot be based on the attributes of the color set because the entities are untyped.

The spreadsheet Resource data module is used to specify the available resources (m1 to m4) and the capacity of each resource.

Figure 17 shows a CTPN of the manufacturing system. In this new model the color properties are used to simplify the number of places and transitions used to formalize the system. Conflict decisions are used to route products according to their color type values. To route the products, a color, *ty*, that represents the product type is used to determine the next process to take. The guard function

$$G(T2) = \left[ty == 1 \,||\, ty == 3 \right]$$

Figure 16. Arena code mapped from the TPN of the manufacturing system

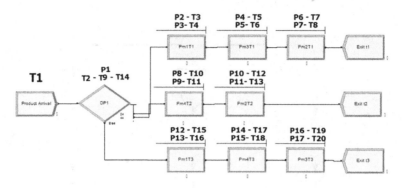

Table 2. Arena flowchart modules

Module	Parameter	Subparameter	Value
CREATE	Name		Product arrival
	Type		Expression
	Expression		Expo(19.2)
	Units		Minutes
DECIDE	Name		DP1
	Type		N-way by Chance
	Percentages		24, 44
PROCESS	Name		Pm1T1
	Action		Seize Delay Release
	Resources		m1, 1
	Delay Type		Expression
	Units		Minutes
	Expression		125
PROCESS	::::::::::::::::::::::::::		
DISPOSE	Name		Exit t1
DISPOSE	::::::::::::::::::::::::::		

Table 3. Arena data modules

Spreadsheet	Parameter	Value
RESOURCE	Name	m1
	Capacity	4
RESOURCE	::::::::::::::::::::::::::	

states that the transition T2 can only be activated if the entity attribute *ty* has the value 1 or 3. Thus, the constraint that limits the flow of entities is coded in the guard function. The arc expression *E(P1,T11)=1`(2)* also constrains the flow of entities through T11.

Figure 18 shows the mapped Arena code. We call this Petri net model a *layout-oriented model* as it focuses on the machine cells and the structure resembles the physical layout of the system.

Figure 17. CTPN of the manufacturing system

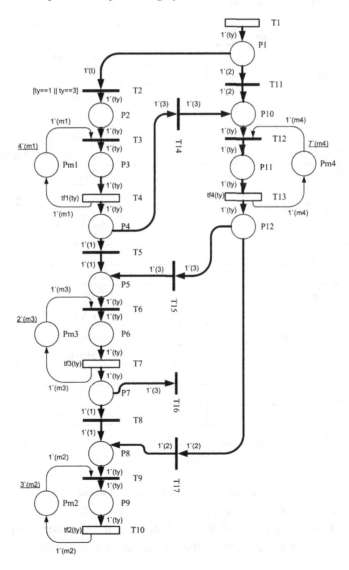

Figure 18. Arena code of the CTPN of the manufacturing system

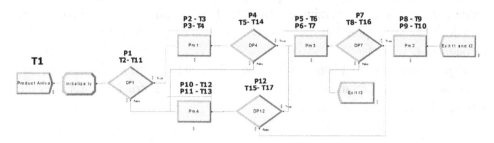

Table 4. Arena flowchart modules

Module	Parameter	Subparameter	Value
CREATE	Name		Product arrival
	Type		Expression
	Expression		Expo(19.2)
	Units		Minutes
ASSIGN	Name		Initialize ty
	Assignment 1	Attribute	ty = DISC(0.24,1,0.68,2,1,3)
DECIDE	Name		DP1
	Type		2-way by Condition
	If		Expression
	Value		ty==1 || ty == 3
DECIDE	::::::::::::::::::::::::::::		
PROCESS	Name		Pm1
	Action		Seize Delay Release
	Resources		m1, 1
	Delay Type		Expression
	Units		Minutes
	Expression		tf1(ty)
PROCESS	::::::::::::::::::::::::::::		
DISPOSE	Name		Exit t1 and t2
DISPOSE	Name		Exit t3

Table 4 lists the configuration of each flowchart module. In this model the rout-ing decision (*conflict* structure in Petri nets) is based on the value of the attribute *ty* initialized from a discrete random variable. Now, the decision can be based on the attributes of the color set because the entities are typed. Implicit routing can be

Table 5. Arena data modules

Spreadsheet	Parameter	Value
RESOURCE	Name	m1
	Capacity	4
RESOURCE	::::::::::::::::::	
VARIABLE	Name	tf1(3)
	Initial Values	125, 0, 135
VARIABLE	::::::::::::::::::	

Figure 19. Compact CTPN of the manufacturing system

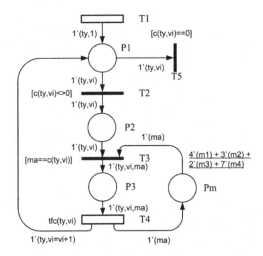

coded in Arena using sequences. However, for educational purposes, we prefer to restrict ourselves to a limited number of Arena modules.

The process time depends on the product type coded in the attribute *ty*. The Variable table tf1(3) coded in the spreadsheet contains the process time value for each product type at the first manufacturing cell (Table 5).

A much more compact model is shown in Figure 19. The main difference with respect to the previous CTPN is that all free machines appear at the Pm. In this model the route decision is taken at P1 and P2 acts as the queue of all processes in the system.

Figure 20 shows the formal specification of this CTPN. To understand its behavior let us look at Table 6 and Table 7. The first table shows which machine is needed for each product type, *ty*, at each visit, *vi*. When a product entity enters the process, the attribute value *vi* is set to 1. This value is incremented by 1 after the product is being process at the machine. The guard function G(T3) stipulates that we want to seize the machine indexed by this table.

The second table gives the time function for each product type, *ty*, at each visit, *vi*.

Figure 20. Formal representation of the CTPN of the manufacturing system

$$
\begin{aligned}
\Sigma \;\; &= \;\; \{TY,VI,MA\} \\
P \;\; &= \;\; \{P1,P2,P3,Pm\} \\
T \;\; &= \;\; \{T1,T2,T3,T4,T5\} \\
A \;\; &= \;\; \{(T1,P1),(P1,T2),(T2,P2),(P2,T3),(T3,P3),(P3,T4),...\} \\[4pt]
C(p) \;\; &= \;\; \begin{cases} (TY,VI) & \text{if } p \in \{P1,P2\} \\ (TY,VI,MA) & \text{if } p = P3 \\ MA & \text{if } p = Pm \end{cases} \\[4pt]
G(t) \;\; &= \;\; \begin{cases} [c(ty,vi) <> 0] & \text{if } t = T2 \\ [c(ty,vi) == 0] & \text{if } t = T5 \\ [ma == c(ty,vi)] & \text{if } t = T3 \\ true & otherwise \end{cases} \\[4pt]
E(a) \;\; &= \;\; \begin{cases} 1`(ty,1) & \text{if } a = (T1,P1) \\ 1`(ty,vi) & \text{if } a \in \{(P1,T5),(P1,T2),(T2,P2),(P2,T3)\} \\ 1`(ty,vi,ma) & \text{if } a \in \{(T3,P3),(P3,T4)\} \\ 1`(ma) & \text{if } a \in \{(T4,Pm),(Pm,T3)\} \\ 1`(ty,vi = vi+1) & \text{if } a = (T4,P1) \end{cases} \\[4pt]
I(p) \;\; &= \;\; \begin{cases} 4`(m1)+3`(m2)+2`(m3)+7`(m4) & \text{if } p = Pm \\ \varnothing & otherwise \end{cases} \\[4pt]
TF(t) \;\; &= \;\; \begin{cases} tf(ty,vi) & \text{if } t = T4 \\ 0 & otherwise \end{cases}
\end{aligned}
$$

Table 6. c function

vity	1	2	3	4
1	m1	m3	m2	0
2	m4	m2	0	0
3	m1	m4	m3	0

Table 7. tfc function

vity	1	2	3
1	125	35	20
2	105	90	0
3	135	250	50

Figure 21. Arena code of the compact CTPN of the manufacturing system

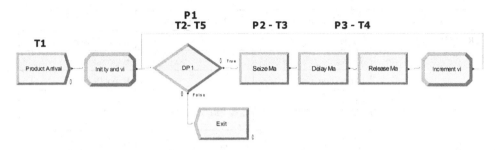

Figure 21 shows the mapped Arena code. The Seize-Delay-Release loop is repeated as many times as needed. This depends on the particular sequence of each product type.

Looking at the Arena flowchart modules in Table 8, it should be emphasized that the Seize module works with a set of four queues, one queue for each machine cell. This simulates the fact that each cell has a separate queue. Moreover, $ma(c(ty,vi))$ in the Seize and Release modules points to the machine that must be seized and released, taking into account the product type, ty, and the visit value, vi.

In the Arena data modules of Table 9 the most relevant modules are the specification of the $ma(4)$ Set of resources and the specification of the $ma.queue(4)$ Advanced Set of queues.

Dining Philosophers

The dining philosophers problem is an illustrative example of a common computing problem in concurrency. It is a classic multi-process synchronization problem. In 1971, Edsger Dijkstra (1971) set an examination question on a synchronization problem in which five computers competed for access to five shared tape drive peripherals. Soon afterwards the problem was reformulated by Tony Hoare as the dining philosophers problem (http://en.wikipedia.org/wiki/Dining_philosophers_problem) (see Figure 22).

Five Chinese philosophers (ph1, ph2, … ph5) are sitting around a circular table. In the centre of the table there is a bowl of rice. Between each pair of philosophers there is one chopstick. Each philosopher alternates between meditating and eating. To eat, the philosopher needs two chopsticks, and he is only allowed to use the two which are situated next to him (on his left and right side). The sharing of chopsticks prevents two neighbors from eating at the same time.

The dining philosophers are often used to illustrate various problems that can occur when many synchronized threads are competing for limited resources. The

Table 8. Arena flowchart modules

Module	Parameter	Subparameter	Value
CREATE	Name		Product arrival
	Type		Expression
	Expression		Expo(19.2)
	Units		Minutes
ASSIGN	Name		Init t and vi
	Assignment 1	Attribute	ty = DISC(0.24,1,0.68,2,1,3)
	Assignment 2	Attribute	vi = 1
DECIDE	Name		DP1
	Type		2-way by Condition
	If		Expression
	Value		c(ty,vi) <> 0
SEIZE	Name		Seize Ma
	Resources 1	Set	ma(c(ty,vi))
	Queue Type	Set	ma.Queue(c(ty,vi))
DELAY	Name		Delay Ma
	Delay Time		tfc(ty,vi)
	Units		Minutes
RELEASE	Name		Release Ma
	Resources 1	Set	ma(c(ty,vi))
ASSIGN	Name		Increment vi
	Assignment 1	Attribute	vi = vi + 1
DISPOSE	Name		Exit

lack of available chopsticks is an analogy of the locking of shared resources in real computer programming, a situation known as concurrency. Locking a resource is a common technique to ensure the resource is accessed by only one program or chunk of code at a time. When several programs are involved in locking resources, deadlock can occur, depending on the circumstances. One approach to prevent deadlock is to impose the condition that both chopsticks (the one on the left and the one on the right) must be simultaneously available to a philosopher.

Figure 23 shows one possible Petri net model. Each philosopher may be represented by three places (M_i, W_i and E_i), which represent the states of meditating, waiting for chopsticks and eating, respectively. Places CS_i represent the available chopsticks. In order to move from the meditating state to the eating state, both chopsticks (the one

Table 9. Arena data modules

Spreadsheet	Parameter	Value
RESOURCE	Name	m1
	Capacity	4
RESOURCE	::::::::::::::::::::	
QUEUE	Name	m1.Queue
QUEUE	Name	m2.Queue
QUEUE	Name	m3.Queue
QUEUE	Name	m4.Queue
SET	Name	ma(4)
	Type	Resources
	Members	m1, m2, m3, m4
EXPRESSION	Name	c(3,4)
	Expression Values	1, 3, 4, 0; 4, 2, 0, 0; 1, 4, 3, 0
EXPRESSION	Name	tfc(3,4)
	Expression Values	125, 35, 20, 0; 105, 90, 0, 0; 135, 250, 50, 0
ADVANCED SET	Name	ma.queue(4)
	Members	m1.Queue, m2.Queue, m3.Queue, m4.Queue

Figure 22. Philosophers' table

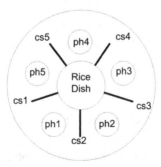

on the left and the one on the right) must be available to a philosopher. A submodel is shown in Figure 24. The complete model has five copies of the same structure. In this example, the meditating time follows a Uniform(1,10) minute distribution and the eating time a Uniform (1,10) minute distribution.

Figure 23. Dining philosophers TPN

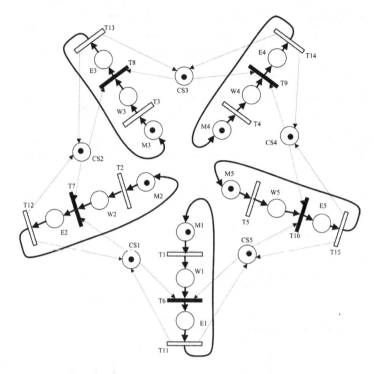

Figure 24. Arena submodel code mapped from the TPN of the philosophers model

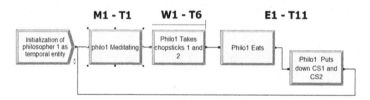

The flowchart and data modules used in the Arena simulation submodel are specified in Tables 10 and 11.

A much more compact representation can be obtained using CTPN, as shown in Figure 25. The key aspect of the CTPN is the guard expression of T2, which indicates that any philosopher of value *ph* who wants to eat needs the chopstick of value *ph* and the chopstick of value *ph+1*, with the exception of philosopher 5, who needs cs5 and cs1. The *fhilonext* function specification is

Function *fhilonext*(ph:PHI):PHI = if ph<5 then ph+1 else 1

Table 10. Arena flowchart modules

Module	Parameter	Subparameter	Value
CREATE	Name		Initialization of philosopher 1 as temporal entity
	Entities per Arrival		1
	Max Arrivals		1
DELAY	Name		philo1 Meditating
	Delay Time		UNIF(1, 10)
	Units		Minutes
SEIZE	Name		Philo1 Takes chopsticks 1 and 2
	Resources 1		CS1
	Resources 2		CS2
DELAY	Name		Philo1 Eats
	Delay Time		UNIF(1, 10)
	Units		Minutes
RELEASE	Name		Philo1 Puts down CS1 and CS2
	Resources 1		CS1
	Resources 2		CS2

Table 11. Arena data modules

Spreadsheet	Parameter	Value
RESOURCE	Name	CS1
	Capacity	1
RESOURCE	::::::::::::::::::::	

The Arena simulation model (Figure 26) is very similar to the previous PTN with respect to the flowchart modules used. A new Assign module is used to specify the value of the attribute *ph* for each philosopher entity.

Looking at the Arena modules in Table 12 and Table 13, the most relevant aspect is the specification and use of the *Chopsticks(5)* Set and *TakeChopsticks.queue(5)* Advanced Set queue. We should also note that the philosophers' temporal entities remain in the model for ever.

Figure 25. CTPN of the dining philosophers problem

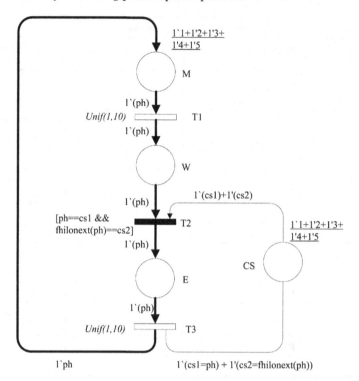

Figure 26. Arena code mapped from the CTPN model of the dining philosophers problem

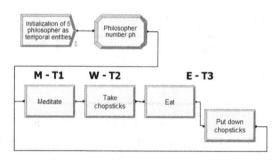

Flexible Manufacturing System

This example is originally described in (Carrie, 1992). The system consists of three machines, a vehicle and twelve local stations, as shown in Figure 27. Each load-unload station is dedicated to particular part type and also serves as a pallet storage

Table 12. Arena flowchart modules

Module	Parameter	Subparameter	Value
CREATE	Name		Initialization of 5…
	Entity Type		Philosopher
	Entities per Arrival		5
	Max Arrivals		1
	First Creation		0
ASSIGN	Name		Philosopher number ph
	Assignment 1	Variable	in = in +1
	Assignment 2	Attribute	ph = in
DELAY	Name		Meditate
	Delay Time		UNIF(1,10)
	Units		Minutes
SEIZE	Name		Take chopsticks
	Resources 1	Set	chopsticks(ph)
	Resources 2	Set	chopsticks(fhilonext(ph))
	Queue	Set	take chopsticks(ph)
DELAY	Name		Eat
	Delay Time		UNIF(1,10)
	Units		Minutes
RELEASE	Name		Put down chopsticks
	Resources 1	Set	chopsticks(ph)
	Resources 2	Set	chopsticks(fhilonext(ph))

location. We will assume that each part requires only one operation and that every pallet is used for only one part type. We will also assume that the vehicle can carry only one pallet at a time. Thus, the main assumptions are as follows:

1. The vehicle has only one load carrying position.
2. Each part requires only one operation.
3. Operations can be performed by any machine.
4. Machines do not break down.
5. Each load-unload station serves only one part type and pallet.

The flow of actions is as follows:

Table 13. Arena data modules

Spreadsheet	Parameter	Value
VARIABLE	Name	fhilonext(5)
	Initial Values	2, 3, 4, 5, 1
RESOURCE	Name	Cs1
	Capacity	1
RESOURCE	::::::::::::::::::::::::::::::::	
SET	Name	Chopsticks(5)
	Members	cs1, cs2, cs3, cs4, cs5
QUEUE	Name	QU_1
QUEUE	Name	QU_2
QUEUE	Name	QU_3
QUEUE	Name	QU_4
QUEUE	Name	QU_5
ADVANCED SET	Name	TakeChopsticks.queue(5)
	Members	QU_1, QU_2, QU_3, QU_4, QU_5

Figure 27. Flexible manufacturing system

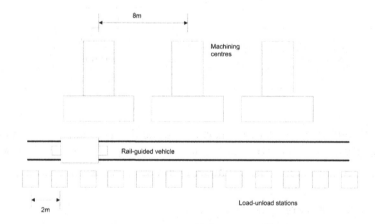

- The operator loads the part on to the pallet placed in the corresponding load-unload station.
- The vehicle moves the pallet with the part to any machine.
- The machine processes the part.
- The vehicle takes the pallet with the part back to the load-unload station.
- The operator unloads the part.

The CTPN of the system shown in Figure 28 has the following resources:

- Machines (ma)
- Load-Unload positions (st)
- Operator (op)
- Vehicle (rgv)

The $G(T2)=[st==pr]$ guard function evaluates to true when the value of the station, *st*, is equal to the value of the part, *pr*.

Figure 21 shows the mapped Arena code. Check the sequence of Seize, Delay and Release modules and compare it to the CTPN (see Figure 29).

The time between arrivals is an exponential distribution whose mean has been obtained from the data in Table 14. This data is also used to compute the discrete probability for each part number.

The operator part loading or unloading time is 3 minutes. The vehicle speed is 40 meters per minute and the vehicle part loading or unloading time is 30 seconds. By performing a simple calculation we can create a worst-case analysis to verify that the vehicle does not have capacity problems. We assume that the complete vehicle cycle takes 3 minutes: 30 seconds for loading, 30 seconds for unloading, and 1 minute for transportation in the worst case. A precise vehicle transportation model can be built but it would require memorizing the vehicle position, the load-

Figure 28. CTPN model of the flexible manufacturing system

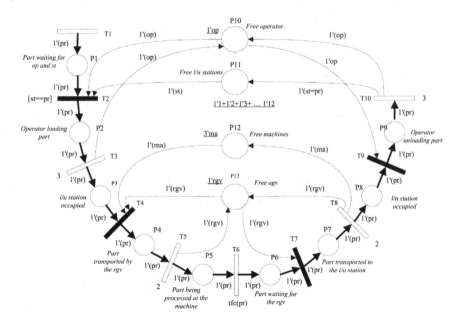

Figure 29. Arena code mapped from the CTPN of the flexible manufacturing system

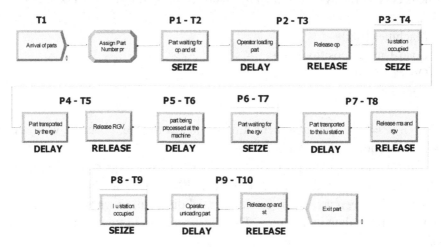

Table 14. Parts monthly forecast

Part Number	Quantity per Month	Machining Time
1	320	18
2	270	60
3	260	36
4	180	40
5	140	36
6	120	24
7	100	32
8	80	28
9	72	20
10	64	20
11	48	30
12	40	32

ing station or machine and the unloading machine or station. Table 15 and Table 16 describe the Arena flowchart data modules for this model.

Table 15. Arena flowchart modules

Module	Parameter	Subparameter	Value
CREATE	Name		Arrival of parts
	Entity Type		Part
	Type		Random(expo)
	Value		17
	Units		Minutes
ASSIGN	Name		Assign Part Number pr
	Assignment 1	Attribute	pr=DISC(0.19,1,0.35,2,0.50,3,0.61,4,0.69,5,0.76,…, 0.98,11,1,12)
SEIZE	Name		Part waiting for op and s
	Resources 1		op
	Resources 2	Set	st(pr)
	Queue	Set	operatorAndStation.queue(pr)
DELAY	Name		Operator loading part
	Delay Time		3
	Units		Minutes
RELEASE	Name		Release op
	Resources 1		op
SEIZE	Name		Part waiting for op and s
	Resources 1		ma
	Resources 2		rgv
DELAY	Name		Part transported by the rgv
	Delay Time		2
	Units		Minutes
RELEASE	Name		Release rgv
	Resources 1		rgv
DELAY	Name		part being processed at the machine
	Delay Time		tfc(pr)
	Units		Minutes
SEIZE	Name		Part waiting for the rgv
	Resources 1		rgv
DELAY	Name		Part transported to the lu station
	Delay Time		2
	Units		Minutes

continued on following page

Table 15. Continued

Module	Parameter	Subparameter	Value
RELEASE	Name		Release ma and rgv
	Resources 1		rgv
	Resources 1		ma
SEIZE	Name		l u station occupied
	Resources 1		op
DELAY	Name		Operator unloading part
	Delay Time		3
	Units		Minutes
RELEASE	Name		Release op and st
	Resources 1		op
	Resources 2	Set	St(pr)
DISPOSE	Name		Exit part

Table 16. Arena data modules

Spreadsheet	Parameter	Value
VARIABLE	Name	tfc(12)
	Initial Values	12, 42, 25, 28, 25, ..., 14, 21, 22
SET	Name	st(12)
	Members	st1, st2, st3, st4, ..., st11, st12
QUEUE	Name	ex1.queue
QUEUE	Name	ex2.queue
QUEUE	Name	ex3.queue
QUEUE	::::::::::::::::::::::::::::::	
QUEUE	Name	ex12.queue
ADVANCED SET	Name	operationAndStation.queue(12)
	Members	ex1.queue, ex2.queue, ..., ex12.queue

CONCLUSION

Consensus exists between those involved in the development and maintenance of simulation models that simple models are preferable to complex models. Despite this, the simulation models used in many projects are large and complex. It is important to emphasize that excessive complexity not only has an impact on computational performance but affects other aspects, such the time needed for development, maintenance, verification, and validation of the model.

A simulation project is dynamic by nature. The results that are obtained as the project develops highlight new problems as well as the inherent limitations of the studied system, which can cause the initial project orientation to be reconsidered. Moreover, the interests of the client can also change during the project cycle, either as a direct consequence of the results obtained or due to the influence of factors external to the project. In order to be successful in such dynamic environment, choosing the right methodology is crucial.

Often, simulation projects focus more on constructing the model than on actually solving the problem in question. Obtaining a running model becomes—erroneously—a high-priority objective. The primary motivation should be understanding the problem and obtaining solutions.

Once the objectives of the simulation project have been specified, we should avoid the temptation to begin construction of the simulation model immediately, as this generally leads to simulation models with multiple omissions that are difficult to maintain. It is therefore advisable to formulate or to specify the simulation model at a higher level of abstraction (conceptual model) to that of the simulation code. The conceptual model specifies the most important structural relations of the system that being simulated. Therefore:

- It is a formal specification of the dynamic process to be simulated.
- It is needed for model verification. The verification consists of checking that the model is executed correctly and according to the conceptual model and associated data.
- It constitutes a means of dialog and coordination between the different departments or groups involved in the operation of the system.

Petri nets are our chosen methodology for conceptual modeling. The main reasons for this choice are as follows:

- Petri nets capture the precedence relations and structural interactions of concurrent and asynchronous events.

- Their precise, graphical formalism simplifies the visualization of complex systems.
- Petri net theory provides an integrated methodology for modeling complex physical systems.
- Petri nets explicitly represent model states and events.
- Petri net structures can be mapped easily into Arena modules.

ACKNOWLEDGMENT

This work has been funded by the Ministerio de Ciencia e Innovación, Spain. Project reference TIN2011-29494-C03-03.

REFERENCES

Ajmone Marsan, M., Balbo, G., Bobbio, A., Chiola, G., Conte, G., & Cumani, A. (1985). On Petri nets with stochastic timing. In *Proceedings of the International Workshop on Timed Petri Nets*. Torino, Italy. IEEE Computer.

Ajmone Marsan, M., Balbo, G., Conte, G., Donatelli, S., & Franceschinis, G. (1995). *Modeling with generalised stochastic Petri nets*. New York: Wiley.

Alla, H., Ladet, P., Martinez, J., & Silva, M. (1984). Modeling and validation of complex systems by coloured Petri nets. In *Proceedings of 5th European Workshop on Applications and Theory of Petri Nets* (pp. 122-140).

Carrie, A. (1992). *Simulation of manufacturing systems*. New York: Wiley.

Dijkstra, E. W. (1971). Hierarchical ordering of sequential processes. *Acta Informatica*, *1*, 115–138. doi:10.1007/BF00289519.

Jan Pels, H., & Goossenaerts, J. (2007). A Conceptual modeling technique for discrete event simulation of operational processes. In Olhager, J., & Persson, F. (Eds.), *IFIP International Federation for Information Processing* (Vol. *246*, pp. 305–312). Boston: Springer.

Jensen, K. (1997). *Coloured Petri nets: Basic concepts, analysis methods and practical use* (Vol. *1-3*). Berlin, Germany: Springer-Verlag. doi:10.1007/978-3-642-60794-3.

Molloy, M. K. (1981). *On the integration of delay and throughput measures in distributed processing models*. PhD thesis, University of California, Los Angeles.

Peterson, J. L. (1980). A note on colored Petri nets. *Information Processing Letters*, *11*, 40–43. doi:10.1016/0020-0190(80)90032-0.

Petri, C. A. (1962). *Kommunikation mit Automaten*. PhD Thesis, University of Bonn, Germany.

Silva, M., & Valette, R. (1989). Lecture Notes in Computer Science: *Vol. 424. Petri nets and flexible manufacturing* (pp. 374–417).

Wang, J. (2007). Petri nets for dynamic event-driven system modeling. In Fishwick, P. (Ed.), *Handbook of Dynamic System Modeling*. CRC Press. doi:10.1201/9781420010855.ch24.

Wong, C. Y., Dillon, T. S., & Forward, K. E. (1985). Timed places Petri nets with stochastic representation of place time. In *Proceedings of the International Workshop on Timed Petri Nets* (pp. 66-103). Torino, Italy. IEEE Computer Society.

Zervos, C. R. (1977). *Coloured petri nets: Their properties and applications*. PhD thesis, University of Michigan, Michigan.

Zimmermann, A., Dalkowski, K., & Hommel, G. (1996). A case study in modeling and performance evaluation of manufacturing systems using colored Petri nets. In *Proceedings of the 8th European Simulation Symposium (ESS '96)* (pp. 282-286). Society for Computer Simulation.

KEY TERMS AND DEFINITIONS

Activity: A task or action that takes place in the system.

Attribute: A property of the entity.

Entity: A set of components of the system. In Petri nets, entities are called *tokens*.

Event: An instantaneous action that can change the value of a state variable in the modeled system. In Petri nets, events are associated with the firing of transitions.

Permanent Entity: Also called a *resource*. An entity that remains in the system and usually serves other entities.

Petri Net: A mathematical modeling formalism for the description of distributed systems.

Temporal Entity: An entity that enters, moves through and leaves the system.

Chapter 2
Modeling for System's Understanding

Marisa Analía Sánchez
Universidad Nacional del Sur, Argentina

ABSTRACT

The purpose of this chapter is to provide an overview of System Dynamics modeling and to highlight its potential as a tool for system´s understanding. Although the work is not intended to cover all the activities involved in a simulation process, the authors present the steps in the modeling process. The authors first summarize the role of Causal Loop diagrams in the modeling process. The authors then introduce Stock-and-flow diagrams and describe how they can be defined using mathematical functions. Along this chapter the authors claim that System Dynamics is an adequate modeling tool for "partially reducible uncertainty" and "irreducible uncertainty" problems. Finally, the authors discuss that in System Dynamics, validity means adequacy with respect to a purpose, and hence it cannot be made in absolute terms and the authors briefly introduce a set of techniques for testing structure and accuracy.

INTRODUCTION

Simulation is a fascinating tool given the wide range of domains of application, the ability to include probabilistic behavior, the flexibility to describe nonlinear relationships, and the scalability for large systems. The complexities of the phenomena in the world force us to use simulation to understand much of anything about them. Complexity may arise from structural or dynamic aspects. Structural complexity refers to the number of components in a system, or the number of combinations one must consider in making a decision. In this case we face the combinatorial explosion

DOI: 10.4018/978-1-4666-4369-7.ch002

problem. In the literature there are many references to this problem which has implications on the amount of resources needed to compute solutions (Pelánek, 2008).

Dynamic complexity arises because systems are dynamic, tightly coupled, governed by feedback, nonlinear, history-dependent, self-organizing, and adaptive (Sterman, 2000). To understand dynamic complexity, consider the evolution of a population. This is a dynamic system whose rules are very simple: the population grows according to a birth rate and decreases according to a death rate. Dynamic complexity is given by the interaction of these rules. If we know the rates with some precision then we can build a model and easily study the evolution of the system over time. On the other hand, if the size of the population varies by factors relevant, but unclear, then we can build a model to test our assumptions about the system's behavior, but we can hardly use it as a forecasting tool. These observations lead us to think that there is a variety of degrees of difficulty when dealing with dynamic systems.

The level of uncertainty with regard to the behavior of a system determines the difficulty in building a model. At one extreme we have the systems whose rules are well known; for example, sales revenues can be estimated with an arbitrary degree of accuracy given enough demand data. If from the analysis of historical data we identify variables that partially explain the behavior of demand, then, we are in the presence of conditioning and unknown information. And hence model building is more challenging. Lo and Mueller analyze the role of quantitative methods in theory and practice (Lo & Mueller, 2010). Based on the classic work of Knight that distinguishes risk from uncertainty (Knight, 1921), Lo and Mueller propose a five-tiered categorization of uncertainty in any system, whether it be physical, economic, or political. The classification ranges from complete deterministic certainty (Level 1), exemplified by Newtonian mechanics, through noisy systems and those that must be described statistically because of incomplete knowledge about deterministic processes (Levels 3 or 4), to "irreducible uncertainty" (Level 5).

The level of uncertainty restricts the set of adequate modeling and analysis tools. A system with "risk without uncertainty" (Level 2) or with "fully reducible uncertainty" (Level 3), may be analyzed using classic probability theory or Monte Carlo simulation. But in the case of systems with "partially reducible uncertainty" (Level 4) or "irreducible uncertainty" (Level 5), we need a theory-building approach, such as System Dynamics.

System Dynamics modeling was developed by Jay W. Forrester and has gained relevance in recent years because of the need to model complex systems. System Dynamics postulates that the behavior of such systems results from the underlying structure of flows, delays, and feedback loops (Forrester, Industrial Dynamics, 1961). There is a tradition in the use of dynamic simulation to study problems in the social sciences. Currently, it is used in public health (Barlas, 2002; Horner &

Hirsch, 2006; Sánchez, 2011; Thompson & Tebbens, 2008), social welfare (Zagonel, Rohrbaugh, & Andersen, 2004), sustainable development (Dudley, 2008), security (Bontkes, 1993), among many others. The methodology is iterative, allowing various stakeholders to combine their knowledge of a problem in a dynamic hypothesis and then, using computer simulation, formally comparing various scenarios on how to lead change (Andersen, Richardson, & Vennix, 1997). The emphasis of system dynamics is not to forecast the future, but in learning how the actions in the present can trigger reactions in the future (Senge, 1990). Even though it is not possible to determine with some degree of certainty the value of constants or change rates, the model is used as a learning tool to determine causal paths and relevant factors. This view is consistent with the systemic thinking Senge calls the "fifth discipline" and considers the dynamics of systems as part of the learning organization (Senge, 1990).

A central aspect of system dynamics is that complex behavior of organizations and social systems are the result of the accumulation -of people, materials, or financial assets- and balance and feedback mechanisms. The first step to develop a dynamic model is to develop a hypothesis explaining the cause of a problem and define a Causal Loop diagram. The diagram is a tool to analyze the problem, to then define a formal model using a set of differential equations that can be analyzed mathematically to determine conditions of convergence. In addition, the model is used to develop simulations that allow numerical experiments and analyze scenarios.

The objective of this chapter is to introduce the key concepts of System Dynamics with special emphasis on the modeling of systems framed in Levels 3 and 4 of uncertainty. The rest of this work is organized as follows. Section 2 presents the running example used through the chapter. The modeling process is introduced in Section 3. Section 4 presents Causal Loop diagrams as the basic notation to use at the start of a modeling project. Section 5 describes the Stocks-and-flow diagrams. Section 6 shows how to derive numerical results using a software package. Section 7 discusses model validation. Finally, Section 8 offers conclusions.

RUNNING EXAMPLE: THE BURDEN OF DIABETES MELLITUS

Motivated by the levels of uncertainty described in the Introduction, we will introduce system dynamics concepts from this perspective. We will illustrate some of the issues involved using a running example of the diabetes mellitus (DM) disease burden. Diabetes is a chronic disease that occurs either when the pancreas does not produce enough insulin or when the body cannot effectively use the insulin it produces. Type 1 diabetes is characterized by deficient insulin production and requires daily administration of insulin. Type 2 diabetes results from the body´s ineffective use of insulin and comprises 90% of people with diabetes. Gestational diabetes is a form of glucose intolerance diagnosed during pregnancy. Diabetes can lead to serious complications such as heart disease and stroke, high blood pressure, blindness, kidney disease, among others. However, people with diabetes can lower the occurrence of these complications by controlling blood glucose, blood pressure, and blood lipids, and by receiving other preventive care practices (Centers for Disease Control and Prevention).

Given the increasing prevalence of diabetes, quantifying the number of people affected by diabetes is very important to allow rational planning and allocation of resources. During the last decades, a variety of mathematical models, statistical methods and computer algorithms have been proposed in order to understand different aspects of diabetes. For example, in (Danaei, Friedman, Oza, Murray, & Ezzati, 2009) the authors estimate undiagnosed diabetes prevalence as a function of a set of health system and socio-demographic variables using logistic regression. This solution fits the "fully reducible uncertainty" (Level-3). Fully reducible uncertainty describes a world in which a single model generates all outcomes, and this model is parameterized by a finite number of unknown parameters that do not change over time and which can be estimated with an arbitrary degree of precision given enough data (Lo & Mueller, 2010).

In Wild, Roglic, Green, Sicree, & King (2004), the authors estimate the prevalence of diabetes for all age-groups worldwide using DisMod software. DisMod is a general model for the assessment of disease epidemiology. It is based on a set of differential equations that describe age specific incidence, remission, case fatality, and "all other causes" of mortality. With total mortality and three transition hazards–incidence, remission, and case fatality–as inputs, the equations are solved numerically using an iterative approximation method, the finite differences method (Barendregt, Van Oortmarssen, Vos, & Murray, 2003). Although it had been reported as being useful it is general and then behaviors peculiar to each disease are missing.

Let us consider the diabetes burden in a more real clinical setting. As pointed out by Kahn (2003) diabetes care is complex if we begin to consider the risk of hypoglycemia, the side effects of medications, the uncertainties of adherence to treatment, hypertension, dyslipidemia, obesity, co morbid conditions, quality of life, among many other factors. The modeling approach should help in representing complex interactions between input variables. The complexity is given by the feedbacks between variables states that may be apparent after a long period of time. In order to better understand the disease we will adopt System Dynamics approach.

System dynamic is widely used to model epidemics. The application of epidemiological models is widely spread for infectious diseases since it is an interesting tool providing conceptual results such as thresholds, basic reproduction numbers, contact numbers, and replacement numbers. However, recently it has been proposed for non-communicable diseases such as diabetes and obesity.

We start with a model of the dynamics of diabetes based on the model proposed by Boutayeb, Twizell, Achouayb, & Chetouani (2004). The population is divided into the following classes: non-diabetics, diabetics with complications, and diabetics without complications. The model parameters to be incorporated are the incidence of diabetes mellitus, the natural mortality rate, the probability of a diabetic person developing a complication, the rate at which complications are cured, the rate at which diabetic patients with complications become severely disabled, and the mortality rate due to complications. We extend the model to consider risk factors and prevention impact on disease evolution. The inclusion of these features increase the complexity of the basic model adding feedback and making possible the analysis of the impact of health interventions.

In what follows, we use the diabetes example to illustrate Causal Loop diagrams, Stock-and-Flow diagrams, and the construction of a simulator. But first, we present an overview of the whole modeling process.

THE MODELING PROCESS

In System Dynamics there are five steps that define an iterative learning process (Morecroft, 2007). The first step (Problem articulation) defines the problem as well as the scope of the factors involved, the time frame and the level of analysis. An active participation of policy makers is expected and given that it is necessary to frame the problem in a feedback systems perspective, Causal Loop diagrams become a mandatory resource. Causal Loop diagrams are quite basic and intuitive in showing what is connected to what and how changes in one part of the system might propagate to others and return (Morecroft, 2007). In addition, Stock-and-flow diagrams are used to distinguish among accumulations (of materials, money, or people) and flows.

In step 2 (Dynamic hypothesis), the Stock-and-flow diagram is converted into algebra and diagnostic simulations are conducted and the result is a dynamic hypothesis of the main interactions and feedback loops that could explain observed or anticipated performance. In this step, some revisions arise and it is necessary to fix some equations or even to come back to the Causal Loop diagram to properly model the intended or observed behavior.

Once we get confidence with the model, we are ready for Step 3 (Formulation) in which a detailed Stock-and-flow diagram is formulated. Each symbol in such a detailed diagram refers to a unique equation in the formal model the diagram represents. Then, the model is transformed into a simulator. Nowadays, this step is supported by simulation environments like Stella™ – an acronym that stands for Structural Thinking, Experiential Learning Laboratory with Animation (Richmond,

1994). In this simulation environment, the modeler concentrates on drawing the Stock-and-flow diagram of the system and the software writes the model equations in the background.

Step 4 (Testing) fixes errors and establishes the validity of the model. In System Dynamics we adopt a different notion of correctness as traditionally used in discrete event simulation or Monte Carlo simulation. We come back to this topic later in the chapter. Finally, Step 5 (Policy formulation and evaluation) shifts attention to policy changes intended to improve performance and the simulator is used as a learning laboratory.

In what follows, we introduce two essential and widely used tools throughout the modeling process: the Causal Loop diagram and the Stock-and-flow diagram.

CAUSAL LOOP DIAGRAMS

This is the basic notation to use at the start of a modeling project. The first step to create a dynamic model is to develop a hypothesis explaining the cause of a problem and define a Causal Loop diagram. A Causal Loop diagram consists of variables connected by arrows denoting the causal influences among the variables. The model consists of causal relationships. The causal relationship $x \to y$ means that the input variable x has some causal influence on the output variable y. A positive influence means "a change in x, being the rest of variables unchanged, causes y to change in the same direction." The symbol + indicates a positive causality. On the other hand, a negative influence means "a change in x, being the rest of variables unchanged, causes y to change in the opposite direction." Exogenous items are items that affect other items in the system but are not themselves affected by anything in the system. Arrows are drawn from these items but there are no arrows drawn to them.

Feedback describes the process wherein one component of the model initiates changes in other components, and those modifications lead to further changes in the component that set the process in motion (McGarvey & Hannon, 2004).

Figure 1 presents the model of the dynamics of diabetes using a Causal Loop diagram. The population is divided into the following classes: non-diabetics (S), and diabetics (D) with and without complications (C). The diagram shows the interactions between the states of the population and the incidence of diabetes mellitus (γ), the natural mortality rate (μ), the probability of a diabetic person developing a complication (τ), the rate at which complications are cured (ρ), the rate at which diabetic patients with complications become severely disabled (θ), and the mortality rate due to complications (π).

As population grows, the incidence rate increases and adds up to the number of diabetics. However, if we consider the role of feedback, increasing prevalence of diabetes may add pressure to reduce incidence and more health prevention campaigns will be arranged, then the incidence rate may decay, and this balances the disease prevalence. Additionally, the balancing loop B7 can be reinforced increasing prevention (i.e., controlling the levels of glucose, blood pressure, and blood lipids); and other preventive care practices for eyes, feet and kidneys). In this way, the population is less prone to develop complications. The model depicts feedback loops not only among preventive actions and the system but in between the various components in the system.

Causal Loop diagrams provide insight into a system's structure. However, it is often difficult to infer the behavior of a system from its casual-loop representation. As pointed out in (Sterman, 2000) an increase in a cause variable does not necessarily mean the effect will actually increase. A variable may have more than one input so a change depends on the combined effect of all input variables. Also, the syntax does not distinguish between sufficient and necessary causes–although differentiating between sufficient causes can possible be difficult at an earlier stage of modeling.

In some of the system dynamics literature, instead of + or – the polarity of a causal link is denoted by "s" or "o," respectively (denoting the same or opposite relationship between independent and dependent variables). Richardson provides strong arguments against the use of "s" and "o" (Richardson, 1976). The + or – notation is less confusing but some caution is necessary when interpreting diagrams. If the incidence rate decrease, the non-diabetic population would not increase as its "-" label suggests (non-diabetics would continue to decrease as more become sick). The link from the *Incidence rate* to the *Diabetic without Complications* population may be misleading: when the incidence rate decreases, the diabetic population does

Figure 1. The dynamics of diabetes (causal loop diagram)

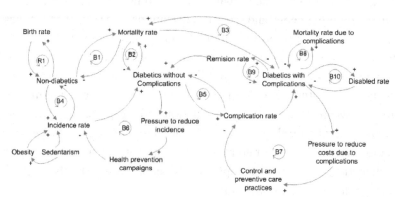

not decrease since the incidence rate always subtracts from the non-diabetic population and adds to the diabetic population. To avoid confusion, Richardson suggests defining links as either additive or proportional influences: a positive arrow from A to B means that A adds to B; a negative link from A to B means A subtracts from B. These alternative definitions may help but the point is that Causal Loop diagrams do not show the difference between the accumulation of resources in a system (stocks) and the rates of change (flows). And hence, it is necessary to develop a more precise representation amenable of execution. In the following section we introduce Stock-and-flow diagrams.

STOCK-AND-FLOW DIAGRAMS

The accumulation of resources in a system (stocks), the rates of change (flows), along with feedback are the central concepts of dynamic systems theory. By 1961 Forrester proposed the Stock-and-flow diagram to model systems. The basic elements are stocks represented by rectangles, inflows and outflows represented by a pipe pointing into or out the stock, valves that control the flows, and clouds representing the sources and sink for the flows originating outside the boundary of the model. A converter represents a process that converts inputs into outputs and is depicted as a circle.

Figure 2 shows a model of the dynamics of diabetes. The population classes defined in the Causal Loop diagram (non-diabetics, diabetics with complications and diabetics without complications) are represented as stocks. Also, since we intend to count the number of severely disabled patients and deaths we include additional stocks. The birth rate is always positive and new born people go into non-diabetics population. The incidence rate subtracts from non-diabetics and adds into diabetics pool. The Causal Loop diagram in Figure 1 includes causal relationships between incidence and some of the main contributors to the disease. To incorporate these relationships into the simulation model it is necessary to quantify, for example, the relative risk of developing diabetes in the presence of obesity. In general, to model the impact of risk factors, we may proceed as follows: given the percentage F_i of population exposed to risk i and the relative risk R_i of developing diabetes, the incidence rate is defined as:

$$F_i * S * R_i * \gamma + \left(1 - F_i\right) * S * \gamma \tag{1}$$

where S represents the non-diabetics population and γ the incidence of diabetes. The number of diabetics generates pressure for health prevention campaigns and this also adjusts the incidence rate.

If the number of diabetic patients with complications is greater than a given threshold, then there exists pressure to reduce costs and the complications rate is adjusted by a factor captured by the Control and prevention converter. The complications rate adds to the number of diabetics with complications pool, and the sum of the remission and disabled rate subtract from it. The death rate depends on the average lifetime, and it is increased when calculating the number of expected deaths of diabetics with complications and diabetics severely disabled individuals.

The stock-and-flow diagram has a precise and unambiguous mathematical meaning. We can always characterize the behavior of stocks and flows using mathematical functions. In discrete time modeling we have a state transition function that gives the information of the state at the next time instant given the current state and input. For differential equations models we do not specify a next state directly, but use a derivative function to specify the rate of change of the state variables (Zeigler, Praehofer, & Kim, 2000). At any particular time, given a state and an input value, we only know the rate of change of the state and with this information the state at any point in the future has to be computed. The structure represented in Figure 2 corresponds to the following integral equation (consider the Non-diabetics stock and its in and outflows) (see Box 1).

Figure 2. Stocks-and-flow diagram (Stella™ model). ©[2012] [isee systems]. Used with permission.

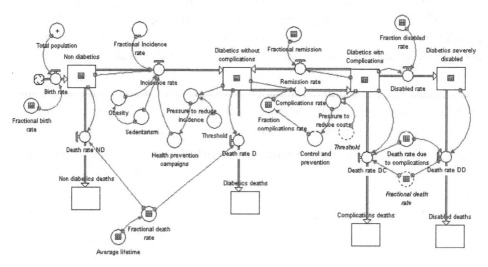

Calculus provides the rules to quantitatively infer the behavior of a system. Stocks accumulate or integrate their net flow, and the net rate of change of any stock is its derivative. Integration and differentiation are the two fundamental operations in calculus. Integration computes the amount added to a stock and differentiation computes the net rate of change. A continuous system simulator solves this integration problem and simulation environments offer several integration methods. Additionally, in modern packages for continuous simulators users are able to work with models independently of the underlying integration method.

System dynamics models are systems of nonlinear ordinary differential equations. For some real world phenomena, in particular, for systems in the social and economic domain, formalizations forces to omit important aspects to preserve tractability. Practical models often do not have tractable analytical solutions. And hence the great contribution of simulation becomes apparent: simulation (also called numerical experimentation) is the only practical way to test these models.

But before turning to simulation we include some reflections about how Causal Loop diagrams are compared to Stock-and-flows diagrams. From a computer science perspective one may expect a translation or refinement mechanism from CLD to stock-and-flows. This is not a minor issue since it would assure that one can go from one level of abstraction to the next preserving semantics. However, there is no such thing between these diagrams and we should appreciate their usefulness from another point of view. In the early stages of a project, CLD are a useful graphical tool to interact with policy makers and discover the hypothesis about dynamic behavior. Causal Loop diagrams are effective for communicating a complex system behavior but they are not appropriate as the basis for a computing model (Morecroft, 2007). On the other hand, the Stock-and-flow diagram reveals the operating detail behind a causal link and hence is proximal to implementation. As stated by Morecroft, the diagrams guide equation formulation and help to ensure that the algebraic model remains consistent with people´s descriptions of how the parts of a complex organization fit together.

Table 1. Some parameter values used in numerical experiments

Parameter	Value (Annual)
τ	0.01
ρ	0 or 0.08
μ	1/75.8
π	0.01
γ	[0.001-,0.04]

Box 1.

$$Nondiabetics\left(t\right) = \int_{t_0}^{t}\left[Birth\,rate\left(s\right) - Incidence\,rate(s)\right]ds + Stock(t_0)$$

where $Birth\,rate(s)$ represents the value of the inflow at any time t between the initial time t_0 and the current time t_1. The net rate of change of the stock is the derivative defined by the following differential equation:

$$d(Nondiabetics)\,/\,dt = Birth\,rate\left(t\right) - Incidence\,rate(t)$$

FROM MODELS TO NUMBERS: SIMULATION

By using Stock-and-flow diagrams as a modeling tool and deriving equations from them we are in conditions of computing numerical solutions. Tools such as ithink™ or Stella™ allow one to build models using a graphical environment and equations are automatically derived from the model. Hence, system dynamics is accessible to a wide range of practitioners who can develop models and perform numerical experiments. There are many techniques for numerical integration of differential equations. The most popular are Runge-Kutta methods. We do not cover numerical integration in this chapter. But readers should consult numerical methods literature and software manuals to decide the integration algorithm and to select the appropriate time step. Tool users should be aware that the use of a finite step and resulting approximation to the average rates over the interval introduce errors. Additionally, round-off errors affect the results.

In building the model depicted in Figure 2, we utilize the graphical in Stella™. The Appendix includes model equations. Several simulation experiments were conducted to analyze scenarios and determine which factors are of greater impact on the prevalence of diabetes. The data sources for this model include census data, and estimates of incidence rates of diagnosed diabetes from 1980 through 2010 in Argentina (see Table 1 for additional parameter values). Key assumptions for the model follow. First, people cannot move from diabetes to non diabetes. Second, the relative risk of death for the diabetic population is constant over time. Although there are no accurate records to validate data, results are close to some forecasts (Wild, Roglic, Green, Sicree, & King, 2004; World Health Organization, 2008). If we assume that incidence remains the same in the next 10 years (2010-2020), then diabetic population growth is smooth. For the year 2020 we estimate a total of 2,617,359 diabetics, which represents a prevalence of 6.5%.

Increase in the incidence rate: We experiment using the same data of the base experiment –except for the incidence rate for the period 2010-2020. Figure 3 plots the number of people with diabetes for different incidence scenarios. For the year 2020, the total diabetic population for incidence rates increments of 0 (no variation with respect to current values), 0.005, and 0.001 are 2,617,359; 2,953,412; and 3,286,254, respectively. The experiments illustrate the consequences of a slight rise of the incidence rate that may be due to changes in risk factors such as obesity, sedentary lifestyle, or eating badly.

Effect of preventive interventions: Preventive interventions have a great impact on the complications rate. Recent studies indicate that strict control of glycemia is crucial to reduce the risk of microvascular complications (UK Prospective Diabetes Study Group, 1998). In order to assess the impact of preventive interventions we conduct a sensitivity analysis. A preventive intervention that would reduce the complications rate in a 25% would reduce the number of diabetics with complications in 7.5% in ten years.

We turn to our discussion about uncertainty. Further research reveals that for each risk factor there are age-, sex-, and ethnicity-specific distributions. This is relatively easy to incorporate into simulations using data on demographic and clinical characteristics. Certain factors are harder to estimate such as the impact of preventive care interventions. On the other hand, there is the chance that the model does not capture every aspect of reality. For example, some years ago it would have been difficult to guess the impact of Internet on child habits and the increment of sedentariness and hence on diabetes incidence. Also, a dramatic social change could invalidate birth or death rates. These examples warn us about the chance that some relevant properties or behaviors maybe unknown to us because we may be dealing with a problem in Level 4 of uncertainty. In Lo & Mueller (2010), the authors state that

Figure 3. Sensitivity analysis, incidence rate changes in the last 10 year. (Increments as follows: 1:0; 2:0.0005; 3:0.001). ©[2012] [isee systems]. Used with permission.

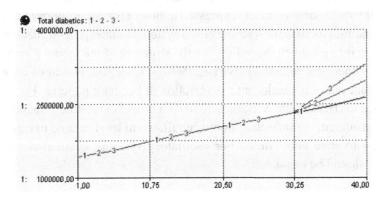

Level 4 includes processes that exhibit the dependence on relevant but unknown and unknowable conditioning information. Lo and Mueller further explain that "under partially reducible uncertainty, we are in a casino that may or may not be honest, and the rules tend to change from time to time without notice." This insight has a practical relevance during validation which is our next topic.

VALIDATION: STRUCTURE, BEHAVIOR AND ACCURACY

Validation is concerned with determining that a model is an accurate representation of the real system. No model is ever totally representative of the system under study, so in practice validation refers to the problem of how one knows whether a model is satisfactory to make decisions about modeled systems. This perspective of validation is consistent with the relativist philosophy of science that argues validity means adequacy with respect to a purpose, and hence it cannot be made entirely objective, formal and quantitative (Barlas, 1996).

Barlas discusses some philosophical and technical issues that support this view of validation. The philosophical arguments say there are no formal tests that one can use in deciding if the structure of a given model is close enough to the real structure (Barlas, 1996). The technical issues refer to the difficulty of designing formal tools that address structure validity. If we discuss the relativist perspective in the context of the level of uncertainty we arrive to similar conclusions. In Levels 1 to 3 a model is assessed to be valid if there are no differences between its output and historical data, and so the problem is mainly solved performing statistical significance testing. On the other hand, Level 4 and 5 deal with incomplete knowledge and the focus is to analyze how systems actually operate. So when dealing with problems above Level 3, no matter which modeling approach is used, absolute validation is unfeasible since a complete specification of system operation is unavailable. When we address the problem of results reliability in the context of software engineering, formal verification is defined as the use of mathematical techniques to ensure that a design conforms to some precisely expressed notion of functional correctness. Since System Dynamics focus on describing how a system operates, the ultimate objective of validation is to establish the validity of the structure of the model ("right output behavior for the right reasons") (Barlas, 1996). Hence, the notion of correctness should include not only results but a description of behavior patterns. For example, as described in (Hekimoglu & Barlas, 2010) if a model exhibiting s-shaped growth is being considered, the inflection points, equilibrium level or time to equilibrium, are relevant to state correctness. For oscillatory systems, oscillation periods or amplitudes should be evaluated.

There are many specific validation techniques for system dynamics models. Perhaps the most comprehensive proposal is the one of Barlas (1996) who proposes to first validate the structure of the model and then start testing the behavior accuracy. He distinguishes between two types of structural tests: direct structure test and structure-oriented behavior tests. Direct structure tests assess the validity of the model structure, by direct comparison with knowledge about real system structure. Examples of techniques are structure confirmation tests; direct extreme condition testing, dimensional consistency that check the correct use of units of measure (Forrester & Senge, Tests for Building Confidence in System Dynamics Models, 1980) (Forrester & Senge, 1980). These tests do not involve simulation.

Structure-oriented behavior tests assess the validity of the structure applying tests to the simulation output. Techniques that fall in this category are extreme condition tests, behavior sensitivity tests (Carson & Flood, 1990), boundary adequacy, phase relationship test, and Turing test (Schruben, 1980).

Once enough confidence has been built in the validity of the model structure, Barlas (1996) propose to address results accuracy. Traditional simulation literature dealing with the comparison of the model input-output transformations to corresponding input-output transformations for the real system is based on point prediction (Banks, Carson, Nelson, & Nicol, 2001). On the other hand, the validation approaches suggested for system dynamics simulations have a broader scope: they consider periods, frequencies, trends, phase lags, and amplitudes. The interested reader may refer to (Sterman, 2000) for a description of these techniques. In Hekimoglu & Barlas (2010), the authors use sensitivity analysis to evaluate behavior patterns´ sensitivity to various model structures or different parameters values.

In order to execute simulations, the input data distributions are typically estimated from real system data. The procedures for analyzing input data from a random sample are discussed elsewhere (Banks, Carson, Nelson, & Nicol, 2001). Unfortunately, in some situations a simulation study must be undertaken when we do not have enough data in which to base input models. In the case of input uncertainty, experiments based on the so-called "what if" scenario analysis make explicit that results are conditional on the specified input distributions (Barton & Schruben, 2001).

Finally, the choice of the right degree of complexity of a conceptual model is a common challenge when adopting a systemic approach and should be addressed during validation. In Chick (2006), the author highlights the importance of the balance between the credibility of a model and its simplicity. Recently, a model that was meant to portray the complexity of American military strategy bounced around the Internet as an example of non-understandable model after General McChrystal remarked "When we understand that slide, we'll have won the war" (Bumiller, 2010). The story advises us of the importance of using common sense when modeling. Sometimes our poor mental models contribute to building complex diagrams. When dealing with an unknown problem it is hard to assess which factors are relevant enough to influence decisions. In this case, sensitivity analysis may help to reduce the number of variables.

CONCLUDING REMARKS

The purpose of this chapter was to provide an overview of System Dynamics modeling and highlight its potential as a tool for system's understanding. Although the work is not intended to cover all the activities involved in a simulation process, we presented the steps in the modeling process. We first summarized the role of Causal Loop diagrams in the modeling process. Although Causal Loop diagrams do not have a precise and formal semantic they provide an appropriate communication tool between domain experts and modelers. At the same time, the modeler should be aware of the main drawbacks that may arise when inferring behaviors for a system from its causal-loop representation. For this reason, we also included some known remarks regarding Causal Loop diagrams interpretation.

We then introduced Stock-and-flow diagrams and described how they can be defined using mathematical functions. There is no system dynamics modeling without stocks and flows: they represent the central concepts of accumulation, the rates of change and feedback. Software simulation environments such as Stella™ or ithink™ provide a graphical interface with the basic building blocks and equations are automatically derived from the model. The software uses standard numerical methods to solve the system of equations that comprise the model. A user with programming skills can also implement his algorithms–having more control over integration and round-off errors.

Validation and verification is always a controversial issue in any computing development. In particular, a System Dynamics approach is mainly used to model systems with "partially reducible uncertainty" or "irreducible uncertainty." The practical implications for validation and verification are that some relevant knowledge about the real system may be unknown; and the oracle problem is exacerbated. An oracle–as it relates to testing–is defined as a means to decide whether a behavior is correct or not. As discussed in Section 7, for any system dynamics study, the notion of correctness should include results and a description of behavior patterns. Therefore, an oracle includes a set of validity tests based on the techniques as described previously. And although this oracle is not sufficient to answer validity in absolute terms, if tests are performed thoroughly they do have a good coverage of relevant behaviors.

The reason why it is not possible to assess validity in absolute terms brings us to the "categorization of uncertainty in a system" issue that began the chapter.

Along this chapter we claimed that Systems Dynamics is an adequate modeling tool for problems in Levels 4 and 5 of uncertainty ("partially reducible uncertainty" or "irreducible uncertainty"). This claim is supported by the following. To model problems with these levels of uncertainty we require an iterative learning process and modeling tools able to deal with incomplete information. System Dynamics embodies an iterative learning process based on the use of two diagrammatic tools that facilitate analyzing causal relationships and the structure that gives rise to dynamic behavior The Causal loop diagram allows the conceptualization of system behavior and its main strength is simplicity making it an adequate tool within policy makers or clients. Stock-and-flow diagrams guide a detailed design and at the same time hide the mathematical model they represent. Finally, in Section 7 we discussed that in System Dynamics validity means adequacy with respect to a purpose, and hence it cannot be made in absolute terms and we mentioned a set of techniques for testing structure and accuracy. This is consistent with a holistic philosophy. System dynamics is a method to enhance learning in complex systems.

REFERENCES

Andersen, D., Richardson, G., & Vennix, J. (1997). Group model building: adding more science to the craft. *System Dynamics Review*, *13*(2), 187–201. doi:10.1002/(SICI)1099-1727(199722)13:2<187::AID-SDR124>3.0.CO;2-O.

Banks, J., Carson, J., Nelson, B., & Nicol, D. (2001). *Discrete-Event System Simulation*. Upper Saddle River, New Jersey: Prentice Hall.

Barendregt, J., Van Oortmarssen, G., Vos, T., & Murray, C. (2003). A Generic Model for the assessment of disease epidemiology: the computational basis of DisMod II. *Population Health Metrics*, *1*(4). PMID:12773212.

Barlas, Y. (1996). Formal aspects of model validity and validation in system dynamics. *System Dynamics Review*, *12*(3), 183–210. doi:10.1002/(SICI)1099-1727(199623)12:3<183::AID-SDR103>3.0.CO;2-4.

Barlas, Y. (2002). System dynamics: Systemic Feedback Modeling for Policy Analysis. In *UNESCO, Knowledge for Sustainable Development - An Insight into the Encyclopedia of Life Support Systems* (pp. 1131–1175). Oxford: UNESCO-Eolss Publishers, Paris, France.

Barton, R., & Schruben, L. (2001). Simulating Real Systems. *In submission*.

Bontkes, T. E. (1993). Dynamics of rural development in southern Sudan. *System Dynamics Review*, *9*(1), 1–21. doi:10.1002/sdr.4260090102.

Boutayeb, A., Twizell, E., Achouayb, K., & Chetouani, A. (2004). A mathematical model for the burden of diabetes and its complications. *Biomedical Engineering Online, 3*(20). PMID:15222886.

Bumiller, E. (2010, 4 26). We have Met the Enemy and He is Powerpoint. *The New York Times*.

Carson, E. R., & Flood, R. L. (1990). Model Validation: Philosophy, Methodology and Examples. *Trans Inst MC, 12*(4), 178–185. doi:10.1177/014233129001200404.

Centers for Disease Control and Prevention. (n.d.). Retrieved February 25, 2010, from http://www.cdc.gov/diabetes/statistics/incidence

Chick, S. E. (2006). Six ways to improve a simulation analysis. *Journal of Simulation, 1*, 21–28. doi:10.1057/palgrave.jos.4250006.

Danaei, G., Friedman, A., Oza, S., Murray, C., & Ezzati, M. (2009). Diabetes prevalence and diagnosis in US states: analysis of health surveys. *Population Health Metrics, 7*(16). PMID:19781056.

Dudley, R. (2008). A basis for understanding fishery management dynamics. *System Dynamics Review, 24*(1), 1–29. doi:10.1002/sdr.392.

Forrester, J. (1961). *Industrial Dynamics*. Massachutses: Pegasus Communications.

Forrester, J., & Senge, P. (1980). Tests for Building Confidence in System Dynamics Models. In Legasto, A., Forrester, J., & Lyneis, M. (Eds.), *System Dynamics*. Amsterdam: North-Holland.

Hekimoglu, M., & Barlas, Y. (2010). Sensitivity Analysis of System Dynamics Models by behavior Pattern Measures. *Proceedings of the 28th International Conference of the System Dynamics Society*. Seul.

Horner, J., & Hirsch, G. (2006). *American Journal of Public Health*, (96): 452–458. PMID:16449591.

Kahn, R. (2003). Dealing with Complexity in Clinical Diabetes. *Diabetes Care, 26*(11), 3168–3171. doi:10.2337/diacare.26.11.3168 PMID:14578256.

Knight, F. (1921). *Risk, Uncertainty, and Profit*. Boston: Houghton Mifflin.

Lo, A., & Mueller, M. (2010). *Cornell University Library*. Retrieved July 20, 2011, from WARNING: Physics Envy May Be Hazardous To Your Wealth!: http://www.arxiv.org/abs/1003.2688

McGarvey, B., & Hannon, B. (2004). *Modeling Dynamic Systems*. Springer.

Morecroft, J. (2007). *Strategic Modelling and Business Dynamics. A feedback systems approach.* Chichester: John Wiley & Sons Inc..

Pelánek, R. (2008). Fighting state space explosion: Review and evaluation. *Proc. of Formal Methods for industrial Critical Systems.*

Richardson, G. P. (1976). Problems with Causal Loop Diagrmas. *System Dynamics Review, 2*(2), 158–170. doi:10.1002/sdr.4260020207.

Richmond, B. (1994). System Dynamics/Systems Thinking: Let's Just Get On With It. *International Systems Dynamics Conference.* Sterling.

Sánchez, M. A. (2011). Using System Dynamics to Assess the Role of Socioeconomic Status in Tuberculosis Incidence. In B. Gilles, A. Pardo, & G. Schneider (Ed.), *Lecture Notes in Computer Science: 9th International Conference on Software Engineering and Formal Methods, Special Track on Modelling for Sustainable Development. 7041*, pp. 464-475. Berlin/Heidelberg: Springer-Verlag.

Schruben, L. W. (1980). Establishing the Credibility of Simulations. *Simulation, 34*(3), 101–105. doi:10.1177/003754978003400310.

Senge, P. (1990). *The fifth discipline: the art and practice of the learning organization.* New York: Doubleday/Curency.

Sterman, J. (2000). *Business Dynamics: Systems Thinking and Modeling for a Complex World.* New York: McGraw-Hill.

Thompson, K., & Duintjer Tebbens, R. (2008). Using system dynamics to develop policies that matter: global management of poliomyelitis and beyond. *System Dynamics Review, 24*(4), 433–449. doi:10.1002/sdr.419.

UK Prospective Diabetes Study Group. (1998). Effect of intensive blood glucose control policy with metformin on complications in type 2 diabetes patients. *Lancet, 352*, 864–865.

Wild, S., Roglic, G., Green, A., Sicree, R., & King, H. (2004). Global Prevalence of Diabetes. Estimates for the year 2000 and projections for 2030. *Diabetes Care, 27*, 1047–1053. doi:10.2337/diacare.27.5.1047 PMID:15111519.

World Health Organization. (2008). *World Health Statistics 2008.*

Zagonel, A., Rohrbaugh, J., & Andersen, D. (2004). Using simulation models to address "What if" questions about welfare reform. *Journal of Policy Analysis and Management, 23*(4), 890–901. doi:10.1002/pam.20054.

Zeigler, B., Praehofer, H., & Kim, T. (2000). *Theory of Modeling and Simulation. Integrating Discrete Event and Continuous Complex Dynamic Systems*. San Diego: Academic Press.

KEY TERMS AND DEFINITIONS

Causal Loop Diagrams: The basic notation used in System dynamics consisting of variables connected by arrows denoting the causal influences among variables.

Continuous Simulation: Continuous simulation refers to the simulation based on a continuous model which defines equations for relationships among state variables. To simulate continuous systems, numerical integration methods are used.

Feedback Loop: A succession of cause and effect relationships that starts and ends with the same variable.

Flows: In a Stock-and-Flow Diagram a flow represents the rate of change of stocks.

Simulation: Simulation is the process of building a mathematical or logical model of a system, and experimenting with the model to obtain insight into the system's behavior or to support a decision-making process.

State Variables: In a Stock-and-Flow Diagram state variables are a collection of variables that are defined to monitor the status of a system.

Stock-and-Flow Diagrams: A notation developed by Jay Forrester to represent systems using stocks or levels, and flows or rates which cause stocks to change.

Stocks: In a Stock-and-Flow Diagram a stock represents accumulations (*e.g.* of materials, people, or money) over time. Stocks represent the state of a system at a time instant *t*.

System Dynamics: System dynamics is a modeling approach that postulates that the behavior of complex systems results from the underlying structure of flows, time delays and feedback loops.

Time Delays: A time duration before a cause can reach its effect.

APPENDIX

Equations

The following equations were derived by Stella™ from the model in Figure 2.

Complications_deaths(t) = Complications_deaths(t - dt) + (Death_rate_DC) * dt

INIT Complications_deaths = 0

   INFLOWS:

Death_rate_DC = Diabetics_with_Complications*(Death_rate_due_to_
complications+Fractional_death_rate)

   INFLOWS:

Diabetics_deaths(t) = Diabetics_deaths(t - dt) + (Death_rate_D) * dt

INIT Diabetics_deaths = 0

   INFLOWS:

Death_rate_D = Diabetics_without_complications*Fractional_death__rate

Diabetics_severely_disabled(t) = Diabetics_severely_disabled(t - dt) + (Dis-
abled_rate - Death_rate_DD) * dt

INIT Diabetics_severely__disabled = 0

   INFLOWS:

Disabled_rate = Diabetics_with_Complications*Fraction_disabled_rate

   OUTFLOWS:

Death_rate_DD = Diabetics_severely__disabled*(Death_rate_due_to_
complications*2+Fractional_death_rate)

Diabetics_with_Complications(t) = Diabetics_with_Complications(t - dt) + (Complications_rate - Death_rate_DC - Remission_rate - Disabled_rate) * dt

INIT Diabetics_with_Complications = 0.0015//Percentage

INFLOWS:

Complications_rate = Diabetics_without__complications*Fraction_complications_rate

OUTFLOWS:

Death_rate_DC = Diabetics_with_Complications*(Death_rate_due__to_complications+Fractional_death__rate)

Remission_rate = Diabetics_with_Complications*Fractional_remission

Disabled_rate = Diabetics_with_Complications*Fraction_disabled_rate

Diabetics_without_complications(t) = Diabetics_without_complications(t - dt) + (Incidence_rate + Remission_rate - Complications_rate - Death_rate_D) * dt

INIT Diabetics_without_complications = 0.0002

INFLOWS:

Incidence_rate = IF(TIME<30)THEN(Non_diabetics*Fractional_Incidence_rate)ELSE(Non_diabetics*(Fractional_Incidence_rate*(Health_prevention__campaigns*Obesity*Sedentarism)))

Remission_rate = Diabetics_with_Complications*Fractional_remission

OUTFLOWS:

Complications_rate = Diabetics_without_complications*Fraction_complications_rate

Death_rate_D = Diabetics_without_complications*Fractional_death_rate

Disabled_deaths(t) = Disabled_deaths(t - dt) + (Death_rate_DD) * dt

INIT Disabled_deaths = 0

 INFLOWS:

Death_rate_DD = Diabetics_severely_disabled*(Death_rate_due_to_complications*2+Fractional_death_rate)

Non_diabetics(t) = Non_diabetics(t - dt) + (Birth_rate - Incidence_rate - Death_rate_ND) * dt

INIT Non_diabetics = 0.9975

 INFLOWS:

Birth_rate = Fractional_birth_rate*Total_population

 OUTFLOWS:

Incidence_rate = IF(TIME<30)THEN(Non_diabetics*Fractional_Incidence_rate)ELSE(Non_diabetics*(Fractional_Incidence_rate*(Health_prevention_campaigns*Obesity*Sedentarism)))

Death_rate_ND = Non_diabetics*Fractional_death__rate

Non_diabetics_deaths(t) = Non_diabetics_deaths(t - dt) + (Death_rate_ND) * dt

INIT Non_diabetics_deaths = 0

 INFLOWS:

Death_rate_ND = Non_diabetics*Fractional_death_rate

Average_lifetime = 75.8

Control_and_prevention = IF(Pressure_to_reduce_costs=1)THEN(0.1)ELSE(1)

Death_rate_due_to_complications = 0.05

Fraction_complications_rate = IF(TIME<30)THEN(0.01)ELSE(Control_and_prevention*0.01)

Fractional_birth_rate = 0.0225

Fractional_death_rate = 1/Average_lifetime

Fractional_Incidence_rate = GRAPH(time)(1.00, 0.002), ..., (40.0, 0.004)

Fractional_remission = 0.001

Fraction_disabled_rate = 0.05

Health_prevention_campaigns = IF(Pressure_to_reduce_incidence=1) THEN(0.25)ELSE(1)

Initial_population = 28093507

Obesity = Sedentarism

Poblacion_total = Total_population*Initial_population

Pressure_to_reduce_costs = IF(Diabetics_with_Complications>Threshold) THEN(1)ELSE(0)

Pressure_to_reduce_incidence = IF(Diabetics_without_complications>Threshold)THEN(1)ELSE(0)

Sedentarism = 1//No observational data

Threshold = 0.5

Total_Complications = (Diabetics_severely_disabled+Diabetics_with_Complications)*Initial_population

Total_diabetics = Total_Complications + Total_Diabetics_without_C + Total_Disabled

Total_Diabetics_without_C = Diabetics_without_complications*Initial_population

Total_Disabled = Diabetics_severely_disabled*Initial_population

Total_Non_diabetics = Non_diabetics*Initial_population

Total_population = Diabetics_with_Complications + Diabetics_without_complications + Non_diabetics + Diabetics_severely_disabled

Chapter 3
The DEVS Formalism

Rhys Goldstein
Autodesk Research, Canada

Gabriel A. Wainer
Carleton University, Canada

Azam Khan
Autodesk Research, Canada

ABSTRACT

The DEVS formalism is a set of conventions introduced in 1976 for the specification of discrete event simulation models. This chapter explains the core concepts of DEVS by applying the formalism to a single ongoing example. First, the example is introduced as a set of informal requirements from which a formal specification is to be developed. Readers are then presented with alternative sets of modeling conventions which, lacking the DEVS formalism's approach to representing state, prove inadequate for the example. The chapter exploits the DEVS formalism's support for modular model design, as the system in the example is specified first in parts and later as a combination of those parts. The concept of legitimacy is demonstrated on various model specifications, and the relationship between DEVS and both object-oriented programming and parallel computing is discussed.

INTRODUCTION

The DEVS (Discrete Event System Specification) formalism is a set of conventions for specifying discrete event simulation models. It was introduced in 1976 with the publication of Bernard Zeigler's *Theory of Modeling and Simulation* (Zeigler, 1976).

DOI: 10.4018/978-1-4666-4369-7.ch003

While the latest edition of that book (Zeigler et al., 2000) provides a comprehensive overview of DEVS theory, here we focus on the application of the core concepts. The chapter is organized around a particular example: the simulation of an automatic lighting system in an office environment. We develop this example from a set of informal requirements to a complete formal specification.

Before we begin, let us clarify the difference between a discrete time simulation and a discrete event simulation. Numerous simulations are implemented with a time variable t that starts at some initial value t_0, and increases by a fixed time step Δt between calculations. The flowchart in Figure 1 outlines the procedure.

This type of simulation is a discrete time simulation, as t is effectively a discrete variable. The approach is simple and familiar, but limited in that the duration between any pair of inputs, outputs, or state transitions must be a multiple of Δt.

DEVS can be applied to discrete time simulation, but it is best suited to the discrete event approach for which it was invented. In a discrete event simulation, time is continuous. Any pair of events can be separated by any length of time, and there is generally no need for a global Δt. Later in the chapter we will present a procedure like that in Figure 1, but suitable for all discrete event simulations.

The adoption of a discrete event approach impacts the model development process. For example, suppose one designs separate models for different parts of a larger system. Ideally, modeling the overall system would be a simple matter of combining these submodels. With discrete time simulation, one would have to choose a single Δt appropriate for every submodel, or invent some scheme by which only certain submodels experience events at any given iteration. With DEVS, two

Figure 1. Discrete time simulation procedure

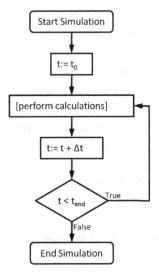

models can be coupled together regardless of how they handle time advancement. The only requirement is that the output values of one model are consistent with the input values of the other.

In this chapter we exploit the DEVS formalism's support for modular model design. First we present an example of a system as a combination of three interacting subsystems. We later specify an atomic model, an indivisible DEVS model, for each of these subsystems. From there we specify a coupled model, a DEVS model composed of other DEVS models, by combining the three atomic models. As we proceed from atomic models to coupled models, we analyze the legitimacy of various specifications. Towards the end of the chapter, we discuss DEVS in the context of object-oriented programming and parallel computing.

AN EXAMPLE

Buildings are believed to be responsible for roughly one third of greenhouse gas emissions worldwide (United Nations Environment Programme, 2009). Understandably, there is a growing interest in technologies that reduce the energy required for building operation.

Consider an automatic lighting system in an office building. At its simplest, such a system consists of a motion detector controlling a lighting fixture for a single workstation. When an office worker is present, the motion detector signals the lighting fixture, and the lighting fixture keeps the workstation illuminated. When the worker leaves, the motion detector signals the lighting fixture again, and the lights may turn off to save energy. We are interested in modeling the overall system; not just the Detector and the Fixture subsystems that compose the Automatic Lighting System, but the Worker as well. Combined, the three subsystems compose the Automatic Lighting Environment as illustrated in Figure 2.

Figure 2 identifies the type of information that can be transmitted to and from each subsystem. This transmitted information is organized into the four sets of values seen in Box 1. We can see, for example, that the Detector may send one of two values to the Fixture: "Still" or "Moving".

The specification we seek must accommodate arbitrary schedules, which indicate whether the Worker is present or absent at any given time. For now, consider a scenario resulting from the specific schedule in Figure 2. At the beginning of the day, the Worker is absent and the light is off. At 9:00 the Worker arrives (*phase* = "Present") and begins typing on the computer (*action* = "Typing"). The Detector observes motion and informs the Fixture (*signal* = "Moving"). The Fixture responds by turning on (*level* = "Light"), and the Worker simply continues typing.

Figure 2. Conceptual model of an automatic lighting environment

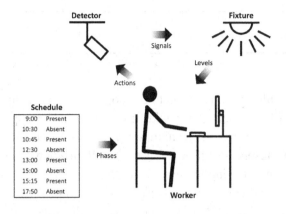

Box 1.

$$Phases = \left\{ \text{"} Absent \text{"}, \text{"} Present \text{"} \right\}$$
$$Actions = \left\{ \text{"} Gone \text{"}, \text{"} Typing \text{"}, \text{"} Reading \text{"}, \text{"} Waving \text{"} \right\}$$
$$Signals = \left\{ \text{"} Still \text{"}, \text{"} Moving \text{"} \right\}$$
$$Levels = \left\{ \text{"} Dark \text{"}, \text{"} Light \text{"} \right\}$$

At 10:30, the Worker is scheduled to leave for a break (*phase* = "Absent"). The Detector will notice that the Worker has left (*action* = "Gone"), and signal the Fixture (*signal* = "Still"). The lights will then turn off (*level* = "Dark"), but not right away. The system is programmed such that there is a delay of Δt_{Saving} between the time when motion is last detected and the time when the lights are turned off to save energy. If Δt_{Saving} exceeds 15 minutes, the workstation will remain lit throughout the Worker's 10:30-10:45 break. Otherwise the Fixture will turn off after Δt_{Saving} elapses, then turn back on again when the Worker returns at 10:45.

Let us revisit 9:00, or shortly thereafter, when the lights are on and the Worker is typing. The Worker is to continue typing for a time of Δt_{Typing}, after which they switch to reading (*action* = "Reading"). They continue reading for a time of $\Delta t_{Reading}$, and then revert to typing for Δt_{Typing}, and then start reading again for $\Delta t_{Reading}$, etc. Relying on motion, the Detector is unable to distinguish between reading and absence. It simply informs the Fixture that there is no motion. Consequently, if Δt_{Saving} is less than $\Delta t_{Reading}$, the Worker may still be present when the Fixture turns off. If that happens, the Worker must make a waving gesture to trigger the Detector (*action* = "Waving"). The Worker resumes reading when the light turns back on.

Box 2.

$$Environment\left(\Delta t_{Saving}, \Delta t_{Typing}, \Delta t_{Reading}\right) = \left[specification\right]$$

An engineer could use simulation to help optimize automatic lighting systems like the one described. Their goal could be to determine an appropriate value for Δt_{Saving}. If Δt_{Saving} is too large, the technology would fail to save much energy when office workers are absent. But if Δt_{Saving} is too small, office workers would become annoyed for frequently having to "wave" the lights back on while reading.

Our goal is to provide a formal specification for a model of the overall system. This Environment model (see Box 2) is a function of the three parameters described above.

We will begin by seeing what makes DEVS appropriate for the task.

REPRESENTATION OF STATE

One aspect of DEVS that sets it apart from other modeling formalisms is its approach to representing state. To understand the impact of how state is represented, let us first consider a formalism that neglects state completely. We will apply this formalism to the Detector, which is the simplest of the three subsystems described in the previous section. Recall that the Detector receives actions as input and sends signals as output. Hence, our formalism will allow us to define inputs, outputs, and a function that maps the former to the latter. See Box 3 for such a formalism, which we call Formalism A.

Box 4 contains a Detector model specified using Formalism A.

There are a couple of things in the specification worth noting. First, we have defined an input port "action$_{in}$" and an output port "signal$_{out}$". A port is a label used to distinguish a particular type of input or output from other types of inputs or

Box 3.

$\langle X, Y, \lambda \rangle$ *is the structure of a Formalism A model specification*

   X *is the set of input values*

   Y *is the set of output values*

   $\lambda : X \to Y$ *is the output function*

Box 4.

$$Detector_{A} = \langle X, Y, \lambda \rangle$$
$$X = \left\{ \left("action_{in}", \ action \right) | action \in Actions \right\}$$
$$Y = \left\{ \left("signal_{out}", \ signal \right) | signal \in Signals \right\}$$
$$\lambda \left(\left("action_{in}", \ action \right) \right) = \left("signal_{out}", \ signal \right)$$
$$\left(action \in \left\{ "Typing", "Waving" \right\} \right) \Rightarrow \left(signal = "Moving" \right)$$
$$\left(action \in \left\{ "Gone", "Reading" \right\} \right) \Rightarrow \left(signal = "Still" \right)$$

outputs. Ports are not strictly necessary for such a simple model, but we will make a habit of using them to help us combine models later on. All inputs and outputs will be defined as (*port, value*) pairs, as done above. Also note the two implications that define the output function. One maps both the "Typing" and "Waving" input actions to the output signal "Moving", and the other maps both "Gone" and "Reading" to "Still".

There is a subtle problem with this specification. If a "Reading" action is received, followed by "Gone", the model will output two consecutive "Still" signals. Or if it receives two consecutive "Typing" actions, it will send two consecutive "Moving" signals. We want the signals "Moving" and "Still" to be output in alternation only. If an input action would produce the same signal as its predecessor, the redundant output should be skipped. This implies that each output will depend not only on the current input, but on previous inputs as well. In other words, the model must have state.

State is generally represented as a group of state variables. State variables are analogous to model parameters in that they are associated with a single model and can affect that model's output. The difference is that model parameters, like Δt_{Saving}, Δt_{Typing}, and $\Delta t_{Reading}$ in our automatic lighting example, remain constant throughout a simulation. State variables may be reassigned.

If we want to simulate the Detector model with Formalism A, we must define the simulation procedure associated with the formalism. Illustrated in Figure 3, the procedure is simple. As always, the time t starts at some initial time t_0. It then advances repeatedly to the time of the next event, which in this formalism is the time of the next input x ($x \in X$). At each event, the output function λ is evaluated to obtain the corresponding output y ($y \in Y$). Note that when the inputs are exhausted, we assume that "[time of next input]" is ∞.

Figure 3. Formalism A simulation procedure

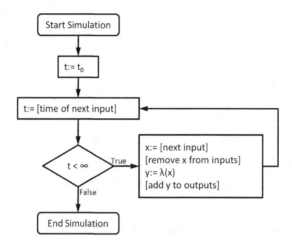

Box 5.

$$\langle X, Y, S, \delta, \lambda \rangle \qquad is\,the\,structure\,of\,a\,Formalism\,B\,model\,specification$$

$X \quad$ *is the set of input values*
$Y \quad$ *is the set of output values*
$S \quad$ *is the set of states*
$\delta : S \times X \rightarrow S \quad$ *is the transition function*
$\lambda : S \times X \rightarrow Y \bigcup \{\varnothing\} \quad$ *is the output function*

As we just discussed, models specified in Formalism A have no state (as the formalism does not have a representation of state). Formalism A models are therefore memoryless. Among other things, this prevents us from avoiding identical consecutive output values (as in our Detector model). To address this issue in a more elegant fashion, let us propose a more complex formalism, called Formalism B.

Formalism B is similar to Formalism A in that events coincide with inputs. However, models now have state. The state of a Formalism B model remains constant between events, but may change during any event. See Box 5 for Formalism B.

There are four differences between this formalism and the previous. First, a set of states S has been added. At any point, a model's state s must satisfy $s \in S$. Second, there is now a transition function δ that can change the model's state. Third, the output function λ now takes s as one of its arguments. Fourth, λ may result in $\varnothing$, indicating that the output is to be ignored.

By giving up Formalism A for Formalism B, we have accepted additional complexity for improved generality. The Detector model specification in Box 6 is lengthier than the previous, but we have introduced behavior that we could not previously describe. The model has one state variable, *signal*, which allows us to now check whether a newly received action would produce the same signal as the preceding action. If so, we now output $\varnothing$ instead of sending redundant information.

Using Formalism B, the Detector specification is that shown in Box 6.

Observe that the transition function δ records the previous output, either "Moving" or "Still", in the state variable *signal*. Likewise, note the changes to the output function λ. The two implications are still there, but now the conditions depend on *signal*. We only output "Moving" if *signal* was previously "Still", and we only output "Still" is *signal* was previously "Moving". There is also a third implication: if the neither of the first two conditions are met, we output $\varnothing$.

Figure 4 shows the simulation procedure associated with Formalism B. Note the inclusion of s, its initial value s_0, its reassignment using δ, and the changes to λ.

Box 6.

$$Detector_B = \langle X, Y, S, \ \delta, \ \lambda \rangle$$
$$X = \left\{ \left("action_{in}", \ action \right) \big| action \in Actions \right\}$$
$$Y = \left\{ \left("signal_{out}", \ signal \right) \big| signal \in Signals \right\}$$
$$S = Signals$$
$$\delta \left(signal, \left("action_{in}", \ action \right) \right) = signal'$$
$$action \in \left\{ "Typing", "Waving" \right\} \Rightarrow \left(signal' = "Moving" \right)$$
$$action \in \left\{ "Gone", "Reading" \right\} \Rightarrow \left(signal' = "Still" \right)$$
$$\lambda \left(signal, \left("action_{in}", \ action \right) \right) = \left("signal_{out}", signal' \right)$$
$$\begin{bmatrix} action \in \left\{ "Typing", "Waving" \right\} \\ signal = "Still" \end{bmatrix} \Rightarrow \left(signal' = "Moving" \right)$$
$$\begin{bmatrix} action \in \left\{ "Gone", "Reading" \right\} \\ signal = "Moving" \end{bmatrix} \Rightarrow \left(signal' = "Still" \right)$$
$$\begin{bmatrix} \text{above conditions} \\ \text{are all false} \end{bmatrix} \Rightarrow \left(y = \varnothing \right)$$

Figure 4. Formalism B simulation procedure

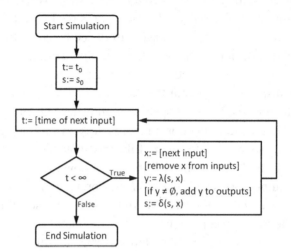

Formalism B appears well suited to the Detector model. However, our modeling requirements are about to get steeper. Consider the Fixture model. After receiving an input signal of "Still", the lights will turn off after a time of Δt_{Saving}. So after Δt_{Saving} elapses, the Fixture model must spontaneously send an output without having received an input at the same time. Such internally triggered outputs are not possible with Formalism B. But Formalism B and others like it have an even more fundamental problem. The problem pertains to how state is represented.

In Formalism B, state remains constant between events. The problem is that the state of a real-world system may change continuously over time. Take the automatic lighting system, for example. After the office worker leaves their workstation, the lighting system is in such a state that it will turn off after a time of Δt_{Saving}. One infinitesimal duration dt later, the lighting system is in an entirely new state: a state in which it will turn off after a time of $\Delta t_{Saving} - dt$. The system passes through an infinite number of states like this one before Δt_{Saving} elapses and the light turns off.

Fortunately, the difference between the constant state of Formalism B and the continuously changing state of a real-world system can be captured by a single variable: the time Δt_e elapsed since the previous event. If we know that Δt_e has elapsed since motion was last detected, we know that the lighting system will turn off after a time of $\Delta t_{Saving} - \Delta t_e$.

Having acknowledged the importance of the elapsed time, we now have a means to represent two types of state. First we have our original type of state, s, which remains constant between events. We will continue to refer to s as "the state", despite the fact that we now have another type of state. The other type is the total state, $(s, \Delta t_e)$, which reflects the continuously changing state of a real-world system. Note that the total state is simply the state (i.e., the first type of state) and the elapsed time, grouped together.

In the DEVS formalism, a model's output values and state transitions can be considered functions of its total state. As mentioned earlier, this approach to representing state sets DEVS apart from other modeling formalisms. It gives DEVS the generality to represent practically any real-world system that varies in time.

DEVS ATOMIC MODELS

It can be convenient to distinguish between atomic models, which are indivisible DEVS models, and coupled models, which are DEVS models composed of other DEVS models. The conventions in Box 7 are typically associated with atomic models. We will later see that, indirectly, they apply to coupled models as well.

The first thing to notice is that instead of one transition function δ, there are two: δ_{ext} and δ_{int}. The external transition function δ_{ext} is invoked whenever an input is received. Observe that one of its arguments is an input value (some $x \in X$). The internal transition function δ_{int} is invoked at the same time as the output function λ, though λ is evaluated before δ_{int} changes the state.

At what simulated time, exactly, are λ and δ_{int} invoked? The answer is provided by the time advance function *ta*. Suppose that an event has just occurred. It may have been an external event coinciding with an input and the evaluation of δ_{ext}, or it may have been an internal event coinciding with an output and the evaluation of λ

Box 7.

$$\langle X, Y, S, \delta_{ext}, \delta_{int}, \lambda, ta \rangle \quad \text{is the structure of a DEVS atomic model}$$

X *is the set of input values*

Y *is the set of output values*

S *is the set of states*

$\delta_{ext} : Q \times X \rightarrow S \quad$ *is the external transition function*

$$Q = \left\{ (s, \Delta t_e) \Big|_{\substack{s \in S \\ 0 \leq \Delta t_e \leq ta(s)}} \right\} \quad \text{is the set of total states}$$

$\delta_{int} : S \rightarrow S \quad$ *is the internal transition function*

$\lambda : S \rightarrow Y \cup \{\varnothing\} \quad$ *is the output function*

$ta : S \rightarrow T \quad$ *is the time advance function*

$T = \left\{ \Delta t_{int} \big| 0 \leq \Delta t_{int} \leq \infty \right\} \quad$ *is the set of time durations* and δ_{int}. Regardless, an internal event will occur after a time of $ta(s)$, provided that no inputs are received beforehand.

We stated earlier that a model's output values and state transitions can be considered functions of its total state. Yet we see in Box 7 that only δ_{ext} takes the total state $(s, \Delta t_e)$ as an argument. The output function and the internal transition function take as their arguments the state s but not the elapsed time Δt_e. It turns out that passing Δt_e into λ or δ_{int} is unnecessary. Whenever λ and δ_{int} are evaluated, Δt_e must be equal to $ta(s)$. So if the total state is needed during an internal event, one simply evaluates the time advance function and obtains the elapsed time.

At the beginning of this chapter, we illustrated the procedure for discrete time simulation and mentioned that we would later present one for the discrete event approach. A discrete event simulation flowchart based on DEVS is shown in Figure 5.

Observe that if an input is received before the time elapsed reaches $ta(s)$, the model experiences an external event during which the input is processed. If on the other hand $ta(s)$ elapses before the next input is scheduled, an internal event occurs and an output may be processed. But what happens if the time of the next input coincides with the elapsing of $ta(s)$? Figure 5 indicates that in the case of a tie, external events take priority over internal events. This convention allows one to use the information provided by an input at the earliest possible stage.

Figure 5. Discrete event simulation procedure using DEVS

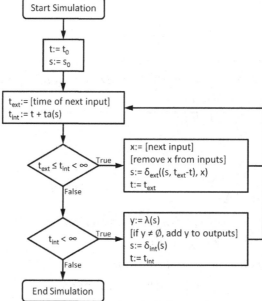

For the time being, as we specify DEVS models for the Detector and the Fixture, we will assume that inputs never coincide with the elapsing of *ta(s)*. Later, once coupled models have been introduced, we will see how to ensure that these two models process their outputs before receiving inputs.

In Box 8 is a specification of the Detector using the DEVS formalism.

Note that the new δ_{ext} looks a lot like the output function of our Formalism B Detector. One difference is that the resulting signal, either "Moving" or "Still" is recorded in a state variable to be output at a later stage. Another difference is that there is no longer a need to output $\varnothing$. Instead, we make use of the new a state variable *sent*, which is either true ($\top$) or false ($\bot$), to avoid unwanted outputs. The following explains how that works.

Box 8.

$$Detector = \left\langle X, Y, S, \ \delta_{ext}, \ \delta_{int}, \lambda, \ ta \right\rangle$$

$$X = \left\{ \left("action_{in}", \ action \right) | action \in Actions \right\}$$

$$Y = \left\{ \left("signal_{out}", \ signal \right) | signal \in Signals \right\}$$

$$S = \left\{ \left(signal, \ sent \right) \middle| \begin{array}{l} signal \in Signals \\ sent \in \{\top, \ \bot\} \end{array} \right\}$$

$$\delta_{ext} \left(\left(\left(signal, sent \right), \Delta t_e \right), \left("action_{in}", \ action \right) \right) = \left(signal', \ sent' \right)$$

$$\left(\begin{array}{c} action \in \{"Typing", "Waving"\} \\ signal = "Still" \end{array} \right) \Rightarrow \left(\begin{array}{c} signal' = "Moving" \\ sent' = \bot \end{array} \right)$$

$$\left(\begin{array}{c} action \in \{"Gone", "Reading"\} \\ signal = "Moving" \end{array} \right) \Rightarrow \left(\begin{array}{c} signal' = "Still" \\ sent' = \bot \end{array} \right)$$

$$\left[\begin{array}{c} above\,conditions \\ are\,all\,false \end{array} \right] \Rightarrow \left(\begin{array}{c} signal' = signal \\ sent' = \top \end{array} \right)$$

$$\delta_{int} \left(\left(signal, \ \bot \right) \right) = \left(signal, \ \top \right)$$

$$\lambda \left(\left(signal, \ \bot \right) \right) = \left("signal_{out}", \ signal \right)$$

$$ta \left(\left(signal, \ sent \right) \right) = \Delta t_{int}$$

$$\neg sent \Rightarrow \left(\Delta t_{int} = 0 \right)$$

$$sent \Rightarrow \left(\Delta t_{int} = \infty \right)$$

If an input is received, then after δ_{ext} updates the state, the time advance function will be evaluated. In the case that δ_{ext} changes the signal from "Still" to "Moving" or from "Moving" to "Still", *sent* is assigned $\perp$ and consequently *ta(s)* is 0. The output therefore occurs immediately. Once the output value $\lambda(s)$ is sent, δ_{int} changes *sent* to $\top$. This causes *ta(s)* to yield ∞, which means nothing happens until the next input arrives.

Suppose that δ_{ext} leaves the signal unchanged (i.e., the "[above conditions are all false]" implication is selected). According to the specification, *sent* must end up $\top$, and thus *ta(s)* will yield ∞. In this case there is no need for λ to yield $\emptyset$, as *ta(s)* = ∞ prevents λ from being evaluated at all.

With the Detector model out of the way, we turn our attention to the Fixture model. Recall that the Fixture emits light in response to a "Moving" signal, and turns the light off in response to a "Still" signal. Also recall that the light only turns off after Δt_{Saving} elapses. See Box 9 for the specification.

There are two important observations here. First note that one of the state variables, Δt_{int}, directly provides the result of the time advance function. This is a very common technique in the specification of DEVS models. The other observation is the use of Δt_e in δ_{ext}.

When the light turns on, δ_{int} indicates that the Δt_{int} state variable is assigned ∞. If the Fixture model then receives a "Still" signal, it must turn the lights off after a time of Δt_{Saving}. Hence there is a case in δ_{ext} that, upon finding $\Delta t_{int} = \infty$, sets Δt_{int} to Δt_{Saving}. Continuing this scenario, suppose that the Fixture model receives another "Still" signal before Δt_{Saving} elapses. (It is true that we previously went to great trouble to prevent the Detector model from outputting two "Still" signals in a row. However, if we want the Fixture model to be reusable in other contexts, its specification should accommodate any sequence of inputs.) Because this is the second consecutive "Still" signal, it is handled by the case in δ_{ext} that requires $\Delta t_{int} \neq \infty$. In this case the Fixture was previously about to turn off after a time of Δt_{int}, but Δt_e has elapsed since then, so now it must turn off after $\Delta t_{int} - \Delta t_e$. This demonstrates the importance of the elapsed time as an argument of the external transition function.

In this section and the previous, we have looked at three formalisms: Formalism A, Formalism B, and DEVS. Each of these formalisms was more complex than the previous, but allowed us to define a larger set of possible models. Extrapolating this trend, one wonders if there are models that cannot be specified with DEVS. When might we require yet another, even more flexible formalism? The answer is hardly ever. True to its name, DEVS is a very general formalism for specifying discrete event simulation models. Incidentally, it can also be used for discrete time simulation, which is really just a special case of the discrete event approach.

To be fair, while DEVS is a plausible option for modeling almost any time-varying system, it may not be the most convenient option for all applications. If the scope

Box 9.

$$Fixture\left(\Delta t_{Saving}\right) = \left\langle X, Y, S, \ \delta_{ext}, \ \delta_{int}, \lambda, \ ta\right\rangle$$

$$X = \left\{\left("signal_{in}", signal\right) \mid signal \in Signals\right\}$$

$$Y = \left\{\left("level_{out}", level\right) \mid level \in Levels\right\}$$

$$S = \left\{\left(level, \Delta t_{int}\right) \left| \begin{array}{l} level \in Levels \\ 0 \leq \Delta t_{int} \leq \infty \end{array}\right.\right\}$$

$$\delta_{ext}\left(\left(\left(level, \Delta t_{int}\right), \Delta t_e\right), \left("signal_{in}", signal\right)\right) = \left(level, \Delta t_{int}'\right)$$

$$\left.\begin{array}{c} signal = "Moving" \\ level = "Dark" \end{array}\right\} \Rightarrow \left(\Delta t_{int}' = 0\right)$$

$$\left.\begin{array}{c} signal = "Still" \\ level = "Light" \\ \Delta t_{int} = \infty \end{array}\right\} \Rightarrow \left(\Delta t_{int}' = \Delta t_{Saving}\right)$$

$$\left.\begin{array}{c} signal = "Still" \\ level = "Light" \\ \Delta t_{int} \neq \infty \end{array}\right\} \Rightarrow \left(\Delta t_{int}' = \Delta t_{int} - \Delta t_e\right)$$

$$\left.\begin{array}{c} \text{above conditions} \\ \text{are all false} \end{array}\right] \Rightarrow \left(\Delta t_{int}' = \infty\right)$$

$$\delta_{int}\left(\left(level, \Delta t_{int}\right)\right) = \left(level', \infty\right)$$

$$\left(level = "Dark"\right) \Rightarrow \left(level' = "Light"\right)$$

$$\left(level = "Light"\right) \Rightarrow \left(level' = "Dark"\right)$$

$$\lambda\left(\left(level, \Delta t_{int}\right)\right) = \left("level_{out}", \ level'\right)$$

$$\left(level = "Dark"\right) \Rightarrow \left(level' = "Light"\right)$$

$$\left(level = "Light"\right) \Rightarrow \left(level' = "Dark"\right)$$

$$ta\left(\left(level, \Delta t_{int}\right)\right) = \Delta t_{int}$$

of a simulation project is both constrained and well understood, other approaches should be considered as well. But especially for large projects, it is reassuring to use a set of conventions like DEVS that can accommodate a wide range of potentially unforeseen model requirements.

Research has shown that for any of a great number of alternative modeling formalisms, any specification written in that formalism can be mapped into a DEVS specification. This generality has led to the description of DEVS as a "common denominator" that supports the use of multiple formalisms in a single project (Vangheluwe, 2000).

LEGITIMACY OF ATOMIC MODELS

Whenever we specify a model using DEVS, we ought to ensure the specification is both consistent and legitimate. For a specification to be consistent, it must contradict neither itself nor the conventions of the formalism. Suppose we have a DEVS model in which Y is the set of positive real numbers. If there exists an $s \in S$ for which $\lambda(s)$ is negative, the specification is inconsistent.

Although ensuring consistency may require considerable effort, the concept is intuitive and its importance is obvious. Legitimacy is more subtle. Even if a DEVS model has a consistent specification, it will not necessarily allow simulated time to properly advance. The problem is not that the simulation procedure stops. Rather, if the specification is not legitimate, an infinite number of events may occur in a finite duration of simulated time.

A DEVS model has a legitimate specification if, in the absence of inputs, simulated time will necessarily advance towards ∞ without stopping or converging. This condition can be written mathematically as it is in Box 10.

The convenient thing about this condition is that, when assessing the legitimacy of an atomic model, one can ignore a large part of the specification. In fact, only S, δ_{int}, and ta are relevant. To demonstrate, let us check whether our Detector model is legitimate. The relevant part of the specification is repeated in Box 11.

We can see that δ_{int} changes the state variable *sent* to $\top$. If *sent* is $\top$, ta yields ∞, so the model is legitimate (see Box 12).

Regardless of what state it is in, the Detector model will experience at most one internal event before it starts waiting for an input. We will leave it as an exercise for the reader to show that the Fixture model behaves similarly, and is therefore legitimate as well. Things are more complicated with the Worker model, which can

Box 10.

$$\sum_{i=0}^{\infty} ta\left(s_i\right) = \infty \quad \text{for all} \quad s_0 \in S \quad \text{where for } i \geq 1, \quad s_i = \delta_{int}\left(s_{i-1}\right)$$

Box 11.

$$
\begin{aligned}
S &= \left\{ (signal, \ sent) \ \middle| \ \begin{aligned} &signal \in Signals \\ &sent \in \{\top, \ \bot\} \end{aligned} \right\} \\
\delta_{int} & \big((signal, \bot) \big) = (signal, \top) \\
ta & \big((signal, sent) \big) = \Delta t_{int} \\
& \neg sent \Rightarrow \big(\Delta t_{int} = 0 \big) \\
& sent \Rightarrow \big(\Delta t_{int} = \infty \big)
\end{aligned}
$$

Box 12.

$$
\begin{aligned}
\sum_{i=0}^{\infty} ta\big(s_i\big) &= ta\big(s_0\big) + ta\Big(\delta_{int}\big(s_0\big)\Big) + ta\Big(\delta_{int}\big(\delta_{int}\big(s_0\big)\big)\Big) + \cdots \\
&= ta\big(s_0\big) + ta\big((signal_1, \top)\big) + ta\big((signal_2, \top)\big) + \cdots \\
&= ta\big(s_0\big) + \infty + \infty + \cdots \\
&= \infty
\end{aligned}
$$

enter into a never-ending cycle of states despite the absence of inputs. The cycle itself is not a problem, but we must ensure that time advances at each repetition.

We have yet to give the complete specification of the Worker model (see Box 13).

Recall that when the office worker is at their workstation (i.e., after an input phase of "Present" is received), they alternate between "Typing" and "Reading". When they are reading it is possible for the lights to turn off (i.e., an input level of "Dark" may be received). This causes the Worker to start "Waving" until the light returns. The transition functions in previously mentioned provide a formal description of this behavior.

We encourage the reader to further study how this specification fulfills the informal requirements presented near the beginning of the chapter. But our task at the moment is to determine mathematically whether the specification is legitimate. It will simplify things greatly if we notice that δ_{int} always assigns the state variable *sent* the value $\top$.

Box 13.

$$Worker\left(\Delta t_{Typing}, \Delta t_{Reading}\right) = \left\langle X, Y, S, \ \delta_{ext}, \ \delta_{int}, \lambda, \ ta\right\rangle$$

$$X = X_{phase} \bigcup X_{level}$$

$$X_{phase} = \left\{\left("phase_{in}", phase\right) \mid phase \in Phases\right\}$$

$$X_{level} = \left\{\left("level_{in}", level\right) \mid level \in Levels\right\}$$

$$Y = \left\{\left("action_{out}", action\right) \mid action \in action\right\}$$

$$S = \left\{\left(action, \Delta t_r, sent\right) \middle| \begin{array}{c} action \in Actions \\ 0 \le \Delta t_r \le \infty \\ sent \in \left\{\top, \bot\right\} \\ \left(action = "Gone"\right) \Rightarrow \left(\Delta t_r = \infty\right) \end{array} \right\}$$

$$\delta_{ext}\left(\left(\left(action, \Delta t_r, sent\right), \Delta t_e\right), x\right) = \left(action', \Delta t_r', sent'\right)$$

$$\left(\begin{array}{c} x = \left("phase_{in}", "Present"\right) \\ action = "Gone" \end{array}\right) \Rightarrow \left(\begin{array}{c} action' = "Typing" \\ \Delta t_r' = \Delta t_{Typing} \\ sent' = \bot \end{array}\right)$$

$$\left(\begin{array}{c} x = \left("phase_{in}", "Absent"\right) \\ action \ne "Gone" \end{array}\right) \Rightarrow \left(\begin{array}{c} action' = "Gone" \\ \Delta t_r' = \infty \\ sent' = \bot \end{array}\right)$$

$$\left(\begin{array}{c} x = \left("level_{in}", "Dark"\right) \\ action = "Reading" \end{array}\right) \Rightarrow \left(\begin{array}{c} action' = "Waving" \\ \Delta t_r' = \Delta t_r - \Delta t_e \\ sent' = \bot \end{array}\right)$$

$$\left(\begin{array}{c} x = \left("level_{in}", "Light"\right) \\ action = "Waving" \end{array}\right) \Rightarrow \left(\begin{array}{c} action' = "Reading" \\ \Delta t_r' = \Delta t_r - \Delta t_e \\ sent' = \bot \end{array}\right)$$

$$\left[\begin{array}{c} \text{above conditions} \\ \text{are all false} \end{array}\right] \Rightarrow \left(\begin{array}{c} action' = action \\ \Delta t_r' = \Delta t_r - \Delta t_e \\ sent' = sent \end{array}\right)$$

$$\delta_{int}\left(\left(action, \Delta t_r, sent\right)\right) = \left(action', \Delta t_r', \top\right)$$

continued on following page

Box 13. Continued

$$\neg sent \Rightarrow \begin{pmatrix} action' = action \\ \Delta t_r' = \Delta t_r \end{pmatrix}$$

$$\begin{pmatrix} action = "Typing" \\ sent \end{pmatrix} \Rightarrow \begin{pmatrix} action' = "Reading" \\ \Delta t_r' = \Delta t_{Reading} \end{pmatrix}$$

$$\begin{pmatrix} action \in \{"Reading", "Waving"\} \\ sent \end{pmatrix} \Rightarrow \begin{pmatrix} action' = "Typing" \\ \Delta t_r' = \Delta t_{Typing} \end{pmatrix}$$

$$\lambda\big((action, \Delta t_r, sent)\big) = \big("action_{out}", action'\big)$$

$$\neg sent \Rightarrow \big(action' = action\big)$$

$$\begin{pmatrix} action = "Typing" \\ sent \end{pmatrix} \Rightarrow \big(action' = "Reading"\big)$$

$$\begin{pmatrix} action \in \{"Reading", "Waving"\} \\ sent \end{pmatrix} \Rightarrow \big(action' = "Typing"\big)$$

$$ta\big((action, \Delta t_r, sent)\big) = \Delta t_{int}$$

$$\neg sent \Rightarrow \big(\Delta t_{int} = 0\big)$$

$$sent \Rightarrow \big(\Delta t_{int} = \Delta t_r\big)$$

$$\delta_{int}\big((action, \Delta t_r, sent)\big) = \big(action', \Delta t_r', \top\big)$$

With *sent* being $\top$, time is always advanced by the value of the state variable Δt_r.

$$ta\big((action, \Delta t_r, \top)\big) = \Delta t_r$$

According to S, it is a possibility that Δt_r is 0. This concerns us because it leaves open the possibility that the key term affecting legitimacy, $ta(\delta_{int}(s))$, is also 0 (see Box 14).

Note that S also tells us that if *action* = "Gone", $\Delta t_r = \infty$. If Δt_r is guaranteed to be ∞ at any point, the specification is legitimate. We can therefore focus on the remaining three actions, "Typing", "Reading", and "Waving". These actions are addressed by the conditions in δ_{int} (see Box 15).

Box 14.

$$S = \left\{ \left(action, \Delta t_r, sent \right) \; \middle| \; \begin{array}{c} action \in Actions \\ 0 \leq \Delta t_r \leq \infty \\ sent \in \left\{ \top, \perp \right\} \\ \left(action = "Gone" \right) \Rightarrow \left(\Delta t_r = \infty \right) \end{array} \right\}$$

Box 15.

$$\left(\begin{array}{c} action = "Typing" \\ sent \end{array} \right) \Rightarrow \left(\begin{array}{c} action' = "Reading" \\ \Delta t_r' = \Delta t_{Reading} \end{array} \right)$$

$$\left(\begin{array}{c} action \in \left\{ "Reading", "Waving" \right\} \\ sent \end{array} \right) \Rightarrow \left(\begin{array}{c} action' = "Typing" \\ \Delta t_r' = \Delta t_{Typing} \end{array} \right)$$

Box 16.

$$\sum_{i=0}^{\infty} ta\left(s_i \right) = ta\left(s_0 \right) + ta\left(\delta_{int}\left(s_0 \right) \right) + ta\left(\delta_{int}\left(\delta_{int}\left(s_0 \right) \right) \right) + \cdots$$

$$= \left(\begin{array}{c} ta\left(s_0 \right) + \Delta t_{Typing} + \Delta t_{Reading} + \Delta t_{Typing} + \Delta t_{Reading} + \cdots \\ or \\ ta\left(s_0 \right) + \Delta t_{Reading} + \Delta t_{Typing} + \Delta t_{Reading} + \Delta t_{Typing} + \cdots \end{array} \right)$$

$$= ta\left(s_0 \right) + \lim_{n \to \infty} n \cdot \left(\Delta t_{Reading} + \Delta t_{Typing} \right)$$

We see that Δt_r must be one of two values, Δt_{Typing} or $\Delta t_{Reading}$. And because the state variable *action* will alternate between "Typing" and "Reading" after at most one event, Δt_r will alternate between Δt_{Typing} and $\Delta t_{Reading}$. With this observation, we can derive an expression for the total accumulated time (see Box 16).

We do not know the value of $ta(s_0)$. However, we can assure ourselves that it is not necessarily ∞, so we should focus on the second term. To guarantee legitimacy, the second term must be ∞. We can see that this will be the case as long as $(\Delta t_{Typing} + \Delta t_{Reading}) > 0$.

As an aside, note that regardless of legitimacy we should know that $\Delta t_{Typing} \geq 0$ and $\Delta t_{Reading} \geq 0$. Why? For one thing, it makes no sense for the Worker to type or read for a negative duration. But mathematically, a negative Δt_{Typing} or $\Delta t_{Reading}$ would render the Worker model inconsistent. To see this inconsistency, review the DEVS formalism's conventions for the time advance function.

Having assessed the legitimacy of the Worker model, we now realize that a nonnegative Δt_{Typing} and $\Delta t_{Reading}$ is not enough. We now know that their sum must be positive, which means that one of the parameters must be positive. Combined, we have the following constraints.

$$\Delta t_{Typing} \geq 0$$

$$\Delta t_{Reading} \geq 0$$

$$\left(\Delta t_{Reading} > 0\right) \vee \left(\Delta t_{Typing} > 0\right)$$

Whereas the Detector and Fixture specifications were unconditionally legitimate, the Worker specification is legitimate only if we restrict the model parameters. This result makes sense. If Δt_{Typing} and $\Delta t_{Reading}$ are both 0, the Worker will alternative between typing and reading an infinite number of times at a single instant of simulated time. Assessing legitimacy is useful, as dangers like $\Delta t_{Typing} = \Delta t_{Reading} = 0$ can go undiscovered until after simulation software is deployed. Another useful discovery from the above analysis is the fact that if exactly one of the two parameters is 0, the specification is legitimate. Our model can represent an office worker who only spends time typing, or only spends time reading.

If a time advance function always yields a positive value, may we assume that the specification is legitimate? The intuitive answer is yes, but the correct answer is no. Consider the following partial specification of the model Pitfall:

$$Pitfall = \left\langle X, Y, S, \delta_{ext}, \delta_{int}, \lambda, ta \right\rangle$$

$$S = \left\{ \Delta t \mid 0 < \Delta t \leq \infty \right\}$$

$$\delta_{int}\left(\Delta t\right) = \frac{\Delta t}{2}$$

$$ta\left(\Delta t\right) = \Delta t$$

In Box 17 is the result of *ta* is the value of the one and only state variable Δt. According to S, Δt may never be 0, so we know that time will advance between every internal event. The guaranteed advancement of time suggests legitimacy, unless it turns out that the sum of the time intervals converges. Here δ_{int} scales down Δt by a factor of 2 at each event. Decreasing at this rate, the intervals will in fact converge. If the initial value of the state variable is Δt_0, and if there are no intervening inputs, the simulation will progress no further than twice Δt_0.

The set of states permits $\Delta t_0 < \infty$, in which case $2 \cdot \Delta t_0 < \infty$; therefore, the Pitfall specification is not legitimate.

Because the Worker model has only discrete state variables and none of them are unbounded, the model has a finite number of possible states. For such a model, legitimacy requires that every possible cycle of states contains at least one state s for which $ta(s) > 0$. The relevant cycle in the Worker model was the "Typing"/"Reading" cycle, and indeed we found that a positive duration is required for at least one of these two states.

Box 17.

$$
\begin{aligned}
\sum_{i=0}^{\infty} ta\left(s_i\right) &= ta\left(\Delta t_0\right) + ta\left(\delta_{int}\left(\Delta t_0\right)\right) + ta\left(\delta_{int}\left(\delta_{int}\left(\Delta t_0\right)\right)\right) + \cdots \\
&= \Delta t_0 + \delta_{int}\left(\Delta t_0\right) + \delta_{int}\left(\delta_{int}\left(\Delta t_0\right)\right) + \cdots \\
&= \Delta t_0 + \frac{\Delta t_0}{2} + \delta_{int}\left(\frac{\Delta t_0}{2}\right) + \cdots \\
&= \Delta t_0 + \frac{\Delta t_0}{2} + \frac{\Delta t_0}{4} + \cdots \\
&= \sum_{i=0}^{\infty}\left(\frac{1}{2}\right)^i \cdot \Delta t_0 \\
&= 2 \cdot \Delta t_0
\end{aligned}
$$

Note that this "cycle of states" rule is insufficient for models like Pitfall that have an infinite number of possible states. For these types of models, even if $ta(s) > 0$ for all s, the specification may still not be legitimate. In such cases, one technique for ensuring legitimacy is to require $ta(\delta_{int}(s)) > \Delta t_\varepsilon$ for all $s \in S$, where Δt_ε is some small but positive constant duration.

DEVS COUPLED MODELS

At this point we have an atomic model specification for the Detector, the Fixture, and the Worker. To complete a specification of the Automatic Lighting Environment, we need only link the atomic models together as submodels of a DEVS coupled model. The conventions for doing this are in Box 18.

We can see that, like an atomic model, a coupled model has a set of inputs X and a set of outputs Y. Coupled models also have ports associated with their inputs and outputs. We will give our Environment model an input port for the two possible phases in the office worker's schedule, "Present" and "Absent". We will also define two output ports, one for the office worker's actions and one for the lighting level. These outputs contain information relevant to the performance of the automatic lighting system. An occurrence of the "Waving" action indicates inconvenience for an office worker left momentarily in the dark, and any time elapsed while the lights are on and the office worker is "Gone" could be viewed as a waste of electricity.

The input and output ports of the Environment model are shown in Figure 6, along with the relationships between these ports and the ports of the three submodels.

Box 19 contains the specification of the Environment model, with the exception of the tie-breaking function. We will look at *Select* later.

Box 18.

$\langle X, Y, D, M, EIC, EOC, IC, Select \rangle$ *is the structure of a DEVS coupled model*
     X *is the set of input values*
     Y *is the set of output values*
     D *is the set of submodel IDs*
     $M : D \rightarrow \mathcal{M}$ *is the ID – to – submodel mapping function*
      $\mathcal{M}$ *is the set of possible DEVS models*
     EIC *is the set of external input couplings*
     EOC *is the set of external output couplings*
     IC *is the set of internal couplings*
     $Select : 2^D \rightarrow D$ *is the tie – breaking function*

Figure 6. Coupled model of an automatic lighting environment

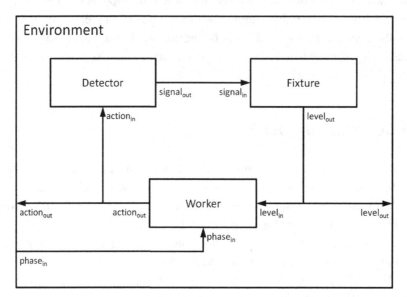

Note that a large part of this specification is merely a formal representation of the information in Figure 6. The set *D* contains a unique ID for each submodel, and here we have used the same labels as in the diagram. The empty string "" serves as the ID of the coupled model itself (sometimes "Self" or other symbols are used).

Each coupling between ports takes the form ((([source ID], [output port]), ([destination ID], [input port])). The diagram shows that the Environment's one input port, "phase$_{in}$", is connected to the "phase$_{in}$" input port of the "Worker" submodel. The port names match in this case, but they need not. The relationship is represented by (("","phase$_{in}$"), ("Worker", "phase$_{in}$")) in the set *EIC*. Similarly, the links in the diagram between the submodels and the Environment's output ports can be found in *EOC*, and the links from submodel to submodel are in *IC*.

The variable *M* specifies the DEVS model associated with each submodel ID. Observe that we have used its definition to distribute the parameters of the Environment model to the individual submodels. Here we are treating *M* as a function that maps an ID *d* to the corresponding DEVS submodel $M(d) = \langle X_d, Y_d, \ldots \rangle$. Note that *M* is often defined instead as a set of submodels M_d. Either way, consistency requires that for every coupling, the possible values for the source's output port constitute a subset of the possible values for the destination's input port.

Earlier we presented the simulation procedure associated with DEVS atomic models. Now that we are missing the transition functions, the output function, and the time advance function, what is the simulation procedure for coupled models? It turns out that the procedure is the same. DEVS has a property known as closure

Box 19.

$$
\begin{aligned}
&Environment\left(\Delta t_{Saving}, \Delta t_{Typing}, \Delta t_{Reading}\right) = \left\langle X, Y, D, M, EIC, EOC, IC, Select\right\rangle \\
&X = \left\{\left(" phase_{in} ", phase\right) \middle| phase \in Phases\right\} \\
&Y = Y_{action} \bigcup Y_{level} \\
&\quad Y_{action} = \left\{\left(" action_{out} ", action\right) \middle| action \in Actions\right\} \\
&\quad Y_{level} = \left\{\left(" level_{out} ", level\right) \middle| level \in Levels\right\} \\
&D = \left\{" Detector ", " Fixture ", " Worker "\right\} \\
&M\left(d\right) = m \\
&\quad \left(d = " Detector "\right) \Rightarrow \left(m = Detector\right) \\
&\quad \left(d = " Fixture "\right) \Rightarrow \left(m = Fixture\left(" t_{Saving}\right)\right) \\
&\quad \left(d = " Worker "\right) \Rightarrow \left(m = Worker\left(\Delta t_{Typing}, \Delta t_{Reading}\right)\right) \\
&EIC = \left\{\left(\left("", " phase_{in} "\right), \left(" Worker ", " phase_{in} "\right)\right)\right\} \\
&EOC = \left\{\begin{array}{l} \left(\left(" Fixture ", " level_{out} "\right), \left("", " level_{out} "\right)\right), \\ \left(\left(" Worker ", " action_{out} "\right), \left("", " action_{out} "\right)\right) \end{array}\right\} \\
&IC = \left\{\begin{array}{l} \left(\left(" Worker ", " action_{out} "\right), \left(" Detector ", " action_{in} "\right)\right), \\ \left(\left(" Detector ", " signal_{out} "\right), \left(" Fixture ", " signal_{in} "\right)\right), \\ \left(\left(" Fixture ", " level_{out} "\right), \left(" Worker ", " level_{in} "\right)\right) \end{array}\right\}
\end{aligned}
$$

Box 20.

$$
\begin{aligned}
&\left\langle X, Y, D, M, EIC, EOC, IC, Select\right\rangle \quad is\,the\,structure\,of\,a\,DEVS\,coupled\,model \\
&\left\langle X, Y, S, \delta_{ext}, \delta_{int}, \lambda, ta\right\rangle \quad is\,the\,structure\,of\,a\,DEVS\,atomic\,model
\end{aligned}
$$

under coupling, which guarantees that the behavior of any coupled model can be represented using the conventions associated with atomic models. In Box 20 are both sets of conventions.

The 8 variables that compose a coupled model can be mapped into the 7 variables of an atomic model, yielding what is referred to as the resultant. We will review this mapping informally to highlight the sequences of events that occur in coupled models. First, the input and output sets X and Y are the same in both a coupled model and its resultant. The state of the resultant includes the total state of every model in M. Therefore, the set of states S includes all possible combinations of all possible total states for every submodel.

A coupled model experiences an external event when it receives an input. In that case, the resultant's δ_{ext} redirects the input to all receiving submodels as specified by *EIC*. Each receiving submodel then experiences its own external event; their δ_{ext} functions are invoked. For example, a "phase$_{in}$" input received by the Environment model will get redirected to the "phase$_{in}$" port of the Worker model. The Worker model will then receive the same input and experience an external transition.

The resultant's *ta* yields the time before any one submodel experiences an internal event. If this time elapses, the coupled model experiences an internal event as well. The resultant's λ and δ_{int} invoke the λ and δ_{int} functions associated with the one submodel that triggered the event. The triggering submodel's output is redirected to receiving submodels according to *IC*, and those receiving submodels experience external events. For example, if the Detector model triggers an internal event, a "signal$_{out}$" output will be sent to the Fixture model. The Fixture model will then experience an external event.

If, according to *EOC*, the triggering submodel's output is linked to the output of the entire coupled model, then the resultant's λ reflects that output. Otherwise, the resultant's λ yields $\varnothing$. So if the Fixture model sends an output, the Environment model sends the same output as well. But if the Detector model sends an output, the Environment model outputs $\varnothing$.

Note that when an event of any kind occurs in a coupled model, the elapsed time associated with every submodel is updated.

That mostly describes the behavior of a coupled model, though there is one remaining complication: multiple submodels may try to trigger internal events at the same time. In such cases, the select function is used to break the tie. The function takes the argument D_{imm}, the set of IDs of all imminent submodels. A submodel is imminent if it is scheduled to experience an internal event at least as soon as any other. The result of *Select* is d_s, the ID of the submodel selected to trigger the internal event ($d_s \in D_{imm}$). Here is the select function for the Environment model:

$$Select\left(D_{imm}\right) = d_s$$

$$\left("Fixture" \in D_{imm}\right) \Rightarrow \left(d_s = "Fixture"\right)$$

$$\left(\begin{array}{c} "Detector" \in D_{imm} \\ "Fixture" \notin D_{imm} \end{array}\right) \Rightarrow \left(d_s = "Detector"\right)$$

$$\begin{pmatrix} "Worker" \in D_{imm} \\ "Detector" \notin D_{imm} \\ "Fixture" \notin D_{imm} \end{pmatrix} \Rightarrow \left(d_s = "Worker" \right)$$

When we first specified DEVS atomic models for the Detector and the Fixture, we assumed that neither model would ever have an input coincide with the elapsing of $ta(s)$. In other words, we would never have to choose between an external event and an internal event for these models. This select function validates that assumption, at least in the context of the Environment model. For example, suppose the Detector and Fixture submodels are both imminent. According to *Select*, the Fixture model experiences the internal event first. By the time the Detector model triggers an internal event and signals the Fixture model, the Fixture model is in a new state and is no longer imminent. In a similar fashion, *Select* prevents the Worker model from sending actions to an imminent Detector model.

One cannot always rely on *Select* to prevent collisions between external and internal events. The Worker model in the "Reading" state may well receive a "Dark" input at the same time that it is scheduled to transition to "Typing". Will the Worker start "Waving" in response to the loss of light, or will it simply start "Typing"? According to the simulation procedure we presented for DEVS models, external events take priority. So the Worker will enter the "Waving" state immediately, revert to "Reading" in response to another input when the lights come back on, and only then enter the "Typing" state. We will assume this behavior is acceptable, but otherwise we would modify the Worker model specification.

It is common practice to define the select function with a list of submodel IDs; for example, ("Fixture", "Detector", "Worker"). Whenever there is a tie, the submodel closest to the front of the list is selected. A list offers less flexibility than a function. But in many cases, including our Environment model, it would suffice.

LEGITIMACY OF COUPLED MODELS

When we say a coupled model is legitimate, we mean that its resultant is legitimate based on the definition presented earlier for atomic models. As one would expect, for a coupled model to be legitimate, all of its submodels must be legitimate. The question is, if all of its submodels are legitimate, may we assume that the coupled model is legitimate? It turns out that if there are no feedback loops in the coupled model, the answer is yes. But if there are feedback loops, we have more work to do.

A feedback loop in a coupled model is any circular path formed by traversing couplings from their source submodels to their destination submodels. There is one feedback loop in the Environment model, as the Worker sends outputs to the Detector which outputs to the Fixture which outputs to the Worker. The problem is not the existence of a feedback loop, but rather the possibility that a sequence of self-perpetuating events propagates around the loop an infinite number of times in a finite duration of time.

Recall that when assessing the legitimacy of an atomic model, one generally studies the value of $ta(\delta_{int}(s))$. Here we are considerably more interested in $ta(\delta_{ext}((s, \Delta t_e), x))$, the delay between receiving an input and sending an output. Why? The time required for a sequence of events to propagate around a feedback loop is the sum of these delays. Suppose the circular propagation of events repeats itself indefinitely. If all of these $ta(\delta_{ext}((s, \Delta t_e), x))$ delay values either equal 0 or their sum converges on 0, the model is not legitimate.

In the case of the Environment model, all submodels have a finite number of states. With this type of model, the only concern is the possibility that all $ta(\delta_{ext}((s, \Delta t_e), x))$ values equal 0. Let us start with the Worker model, and determine all cases in which there is no delay. Because we are worried about cycles of events with no time advancement whatsoever, we may simplify matters by assuming the elapsed time Δt_e is 0. Also, although the Worker model has two input ports, the "phase$_{in}$" is not part of the feedback loop and can be ignored. In Box 21, the Worker model's external transition function can be found with these simplifications.

Box 21.

$$\delta_{ext}\left(\left(\left(action, \Delta t_r, sent\right), 0\right), \left("level_{in}", level\right)\right) = \left(action', \Delta t_r', sent'\right)$$

$$\left(\begin{array}{c} level = "Dark" \\ action = "Reading" \end{array}\right) \Rightarrow \left(\begin{array}{c} action' = "Waving" \\ \Delta t_r' = \Delta t_r \\ sent' = \perp \end{array}\right)$$

$$\left(\begin{array}{c} level = "Light" \\ action = "Waving" \end{array}\right) \Rightarrow \left(\begin{array}{c} action' = "Reading" \\ \Delta t_r' = \Delta t_r \\ sent' = \perp \end{array}\right)$$

$$\left[\begin{array}{c} above\ conditions \\ are\ all\ false \end{array}\right] \Rightarrow \left(\begin{array}{c} action' = action \\ \Delta t_r' = \Delta t_r \\ sent' = sent \end{array}\right)$$

We must also look at the Worker model's time advance function.

$$ta\left(\left(action, \Delta t_r, sent\right)\right) = \Delta t_{int}$$

$$\neg sent \Rightarrow \left(\Delta t_{int} = 0\right)$$

$$sent \Rightarrow \left(\Delta t_{int} = \Delta t_r\right)$$

Substituting the result of the external transition function into the time advance function, we get a formula for the delay Δt_{int} between the Worker model's inputs and outputs (see Box 22).

There are 3 conditions in total, but the third one is uninteresting since the state of the model has been left unchanged. So effectively there are 2 cases to consider in which $\Delta t_{int} = 0$.

If we perform the same exercise for the Detector model, the delay is given by that shown in Box 23.

Again there are 3 conditions, but we may ignore the third one because the resulting delay can never be 0. So effectively we have another 2 cases.

In Box 24 is the delay for the Fixture model.

Now there are 4 conditions, but again only 2 of them are relevant. For the third condition, the state is unchanged. For the fourth, the delay is never 0. Although the delay in the second condition is not necessarily 0, we have yet to rule out $\Delta t_{Saving} = 0$.

Box 22.

$$ta\left(\delta_{ext}\left(\left(\left(action, \Delta t_r, sent\right), 0\right), \left("level_{in}", level\right)\right)\right) = \Delta t_{int}$$

$$\begin{pmatrix} level = "Dark" \\ action = "Reading" \end{pmatrix} \Rightarrow \left(\Delta t_{int} = 0\right)$$

$$\begin{pmatrix} level = "Light" \\ action = "Waving" \end{pmatrix} \Rightarrow \left(\Delta t_{int} = 0\right)$$

$$\begin{bmatrix} \text{above conditions} \\ \text{are all false} \end{bmatrix} \Rightarrow \left(\Delta t_{int} = ta\left(\left(action, \Delta t_r, sent\right)\right)\right)$$

Box 23.

$$ta\left(\delta_{ext}\left(\left(\left(signal,sent\right),0\right),\left("action_{in}",\ action\right)\right)\right)=\Delta t_{int}$$

$$\left(\begin{array}{c}action \in \left\{"Typing","Waving"\right\}\\ s = "Still"\end{array}\right) \Rightarrow \left(\Delta t_{int} = 0\right)$$

$$\left(\begin{array}{c}action \in \left\{"Gone","Reading"\right\}\\ s = "Moving"\end{array}\right) \Rightarrow \left(\Delta t_{int} = 0\right)$$

$$\left[\begin{array}{c}above\ conditions\\ are\ all\ false\end{array}\right] \Rightarrow \left(\Delta t_{int} = \infty\right)$$

Box 24.

$$ta\left(\delta_{ext}\left(\left(\left(level,\Delta t_{int}\right),0\right),\left("signal_{in}",signal\right)\right)\right)=\Delta t_{int}$$

$$\left(\begin{array}{c}signal = "Moving"\\ level = "Dark"\end{array}\right) \Rightarrow \left(\Delta t_{int} = 0\right)$$

$$\left(\begin{array}{c}signal = "Still"\\ level = "Light"\\ \Delta t_{int} = \infty\end{array}\right) \Rightarrow \left(\Delta t_{int} = \Delta t_{Saving}\right)$$

$$\left(\begin{array}{c}signal = "Still"\\ level = "Light"\\ \Delta t_{int} \neq \infty\end{array}\right) \Rightarrow \left(\Delta t_{int} = ta\left(\left(level,\Delta t_{int}\right)\right)\right)$$

$$\left[\begin{array}{c}above\ conditions\\ are\ all\ false\end{array}\right] \Rightarrow \left(\Delta t_{int} = \infty\right)$$

Now we must consider all combinations of states that may lead to a perpetual cycle of events with no delay. The task seems daunting, but fortunately we can neglect all combinations of states that fail to satisfy any of the 6 conditions previously mentioned for which $\Delta t_{int} = 0$ is a possibility. The first condition in the Worker's Δt_{int} formula suggests a potential problem if the Fixture has become "Dark" while the Worker is "Reading." In that case, the Worker will start "Waving." Looking at the Detector model's Δt_{int}, a "Waving" input is only dangerous if the state is "Still."

Figure 7. Cycle of states in the environment model's feedback loop

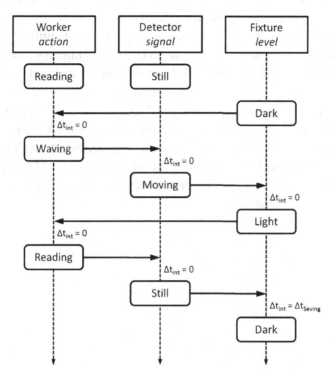

So we consider the initial combination of states in which the Worker's *action* is "Reading," the Detector's *signal* is "Still," and the Fixture's *level* has just become "Dark." Figure 7 shows the sequence of states resulting from these initial conditions.

The "Reading," "Still," "Dark" combination of states does indeed lead to a self-perpetuating cycle of events. The office worker waves to trigger the lighting system, the lights turn on, the office worker resumes reading, the lights eventually turn off, and the cycles repeats. Figure 7 shows the state of each submodel at each stage in the cycle. The key thing to note is that the submodels end up in the original combination of states, which produces the repetition.

It so happens that this cycle involves all 6 of the relevant cases in the delay formulas mentioned above. Furthermore, if we consider each case one by one like we did for the first condition in the Worker's Δt_{int} formula, we will end up with the same sequence of states. The initial combination of states may differ, but the cycle will be the same. Therefore, the legitimacy of the Environment model depends only on whether time advances at all during this cycle.

Notice for each step in the cycle, Figure 7 shows the delay between receiving an input and sending the resulting output. The delay values came directly from the

6 cases in the formulas for Δt_{int}. According to these values, it takes a time of Δt_{Saving} for events to propagate twice around the feedback loop, or for one repetition of the cycle of states. Therefore, the Environment model is only legitimate if $\Delta t_{Saving} > 0$.

This result is not particularly intuitive, as there is nothing fundamentally wrong with modeling a lighting fixture that turns off immediately when no motion is detected. In fact, if we modify the Worker model to include a positive delay before transitioning from "Reading" to "Waving," $\Delta t_{Saving} = 0$ would yield a legitimate Environment model. This might be a worthwhile exercise for the reader. The important point is that DEVS provides techniques to assess the legitimacy of both atomic and coupled model specifications. Had we not analyzed the specifications in our example, we may not have become aware of the necessary constraints on the Environment model's parameters:

$$\Delta t_{Saving} > 0$$

$$\Delta t_{Typing} \geq 0$$

$$\Delta t_{Reading} \geq 0$$

$$\left(\Delta t_{Reading} > 0\right) \vee \left(\Delta t_{Typing} > 0\right)$$

HIERARCHICAL MODELS

Closure under coupling tells us that we could have described the Automatic Lighting Environment as an atomic model instead of a coupled model. However, the modular design approach we adopted allowed us to avoid this potentially difficult task. Instead of attempting to produce one complex atomic model for the Environment system, we specified and combined 3 simpler atomic models.

For extremely complicated systems, even the task of coupling submodels can be problematic. Imagine, for example, the complexity of a coupled model composed of several dozen distinct atomic models. In these situations one should consider a hierarchical approach to model design. Because every coupled model has a resultant, which is essentially an atomic model, one coupled model can be a submodel of another. This nesting of coupled models produces a hierarchy. Note that when replacing the flat structure of a single coupled model with the multi-leveled structure

Figure 8. Cycle of states in the environment model's feedback loop

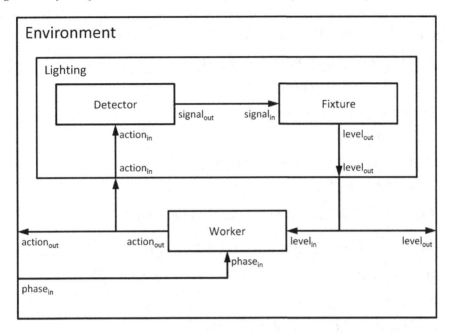

of a hierarchical model, the total number of atomic models remains unchanged. We are simply trading one complex coupled model for several simpler coupled models.

Let us return once again to our Environment model specification. Previously we used a single coupled model composed of 3 atomic models. Here we provide an alternative specification featuring a hierarchical structure. The Environment model will now consist of only 2 submodels, the Worker model and a new Lighting model that represents the Automatic Lighting System. The Lighting model is also specified as a coupled model, and it consists of the Detector model and the Fixture model. The new model structure, with additional ports and slightly different relationships, is shown in Figure 8.

The conventions for specifying hierarchical models are exactly the same as those for specifying coupled models; we need only apply these conventions multiple times. For our example, we first produce the specification of the Lighting model (see Box 25).

Now we provide an alternative specification of the Environment model. Note that the set of input values X and the set of output values Y are the same as in the previous version, the one coupling all 3 atomic models directly. The fact that the Lighting submodel now replaces the Detector and Fixture submodels does not change the behavior represented by the specification (see Box 26).

Box 25.

$$Lighting\left(\Delta t_{Saving}\right) = \left\langle X, Y, D, M, EIC, EOC, IC, Select\right\rangle$$

$$X = \left\{\left("action_{in}", action\right) | action \in Actions\right\}$$

$$Y = \left\{\left("level_{out}", level\right) | level \in Levels\right\}$$

$$D = \left\{"Detector", "Fixture"\right\}$$

$$M\left(d\right) = m$$

$$\left(d = "Detector"\right) \Rightarrow \left(m = Detector\right)$$

$$\left(d = "Fixture"\right) \Rightarrow \left(m = Fixture\left(\Delta t_{Saving}\right)\right)$$

$$EIC = \left\{\left(("", "action_{in}"), ("Detector", "action_{in}")\right)\right\}$$

$$EOC = \left\{\left(("Fixture", "level_{out}"), ("", "level_{out}")\right)\right\}$$

$$IC = \left\{\left(("Detector", "signal_{out}"), ("Fixture", "signal_{in}")\right)\right\}$$

$$Select\left(D_{imm}\right) = d_s$$

$$\left("Fixture" \in D_{imm}\right) \Rightarrow \left(d_s = "Fixture"\right)$$

$$\left(\begin{array}{c}"Detector" \in D_{imm} \\ "Fixture" \notin D_{imm}\end{array}\right) \Rightarrow \left(d_s = "Detector"\right)$$

In summary, a simple system can be effectively specified using a single atomic model. Given a more complex system, one may benefit from a modular approach in which the single atomic model is replaced with a single coupled model containing several atomic models. For an even more complex system, one may couple models in a hierarchical fashion. The single coupled model is then replaced with several coupled models nested within one another.

DEVS AND OBJECT-ORIENTED PROGRAMMING

Support for modular and hierarchical model design is one of the DEVS formalism's most compelling attributes. It is often remarked, however, that widely adopted object-oriented programming practices provide the same benefits. Technically, object-orientation and DEVS are not alternatives to one another. Many simulations have been implemented using object-oriented programming features in conjunction

Box 26.

$$Environment\left(\Delta t_{Saving}, \Delta t_{Typing}, \Delta t_{Reading}\right) = \langle X, Y, D, M, EIC, EOC, IC, Select\rangle$$

$$X = \left\{\left("phase_{in}", phase\right) | phase \in Phases\right\}$$

$$Y = Y_{action} \bigcup Y_{level}$$

$$Y_{action} = \left\{\left("action_{out}", action\right) | action \in Actions\right\}$$

$$Y_{level} = \left\{\left("level_{out}", level\right) | level \in Levels\right\}$$

$$D = \left\{"Lighting", "Worker"\right\}$$

$$M\left(d\right) = m$$

$$\left(d = "Lighting"\right) \Rightarrow \left(m = Lighting\left(\Delta t_{Saving}\right)\right)$$

$$\left(d = "Worker"\right) \Rightarrow \left(m = Worker\left(\Delta t_{Typing}, \Delta t_{Reading}\right)\right)$$

$$EIC = \left\{\left(("", "phase_{in}"), ("Worker", "phase_{in}")\right)\right\}$$

$$EOC = \left[\begin{array}{l}\left(("Lighting", "level_{out}"), ("", "level_{out}")\right), \\ \left(("Worker", "action_{out}"), ("", "action_{out}")\right)\end{array}\right]$$

$$IC = \left[\begin{array}{l}\left(("Worker", "action_{out}"), ("Lighting", "action_{in}")\right), \\ \left(("Lighting", "level_{out}"), ("Worker", "level_{in}")\right)\end{array}\right]$$

$$Select\left(D_{imm}\right) = d_s$$

$$\left("Lighting" \in D_{imm}\right) \Rightarrow \left(d_s = "Lighting"\right)$$

$$\left(\begin{array}{l}"Worker" \in D_{imm} \\ "Lighting" \notin D_{imm}\end{array}\right) \Rightarrow \left(d_s = "Worker"\right)$$

with DEVS conventions. That said, the analogy between object-oriented classes and DEVS models deserves some discussion.

In an objected-oriented language, classes include methods that take arguments, deliver return values, and reassign member variables. Similarly, DEVS models include transition functions that take inputs, deliver outputs, and reassign state variables. The difference is that these transition functions also depend on the simulated time elapsed since the previous event. It is possible to include this temporal information in object-oriented code, but it is not the norm.

The other major difference between object-orientation and DEVS is that, with the former, it is common practice to design classes that reference one another explicitly.

For example, one might implement a Detector class that invokes a receive_signal method on a reference to a Fixture object. With DEVS, models almost never reference the other models with which they interact. In our Detector specification, there is no mention of the Fixture it was designed to influence. The Detector model simply outputs a signal with no particular destination, and it is up to the encompassing coupled model to direct the signal to the Fixture model. Some pairs of interacting object-oriented classes exhibit a similar degree of independence. But typically, at least one of these classes will depend on the other.

The pseudocode below illustrates an object-oriented but DEVS-unaware implementation of the Detector model. Note that there is no representation of time in the receive_action method, the main function responsible for state transitions. Also note that the lighting fixture is explicitly referenced.

```
class Detector_OO:
    private variable signal
    private variable fixture
    public method set_fixture(f):
        fixture:= f
    public method receive_action(action):
        new_signal:= [...]
        if not signal = new_signal:
            signal:= new_signal
            fixture.receive_signal(signal)
```

Compare the implementation above to the following Detector implementation which combines DEVS with object-oriented programming. Time is now represented. In the external_transition function, the time elapsed since the previous event is given by the argument elapsed. If the elapsed time were needed in the internal_transition function, it could be obtained by invoking time_advance. Note that there is no longer an explicit reference to the lighting fixture. It is up to the coupled model, which would be implemented in a separate class, to ensure that the result of the output method is delivered to a lighting fixture object.

```
class Detector_DEVS inherits from AtomicModel:
    private variable signal
    private variable sent

    public method external_transition(elapsed, action):
        signal, sent:= [...]
```

```
public method internal_transition():
    sent:= true

public method output():
    return ["signal_out", signal]

public method time_advance():
    if not sent:
        dt:= 0
    else:
        dt:= infinity
    return dt
```

Our DEVS-aware Detector class inherits from a base class named AtomicModel. The idea is that a generic simulation procedure can be implemented once for Atom-icModel, and applied to any application-specific derived class like Detector_DEVS. Admittedly, this use of inheritance does not require a well-established modeling formalism. However, by following DEVS conventions, an object-oriented program-mer ensures that his or her simulation code is sufficiently generic to accommodate any discrete-event simulation.

DEVS AND PARALLEL COMPUTING

In what ways can one exploit multi-core processors, multi-process computers, and multi-computer networks to accelerate computer simulations developed with DEVS? One option is to parallelize only the few most time-consuming functions. The drawback to this approach is that, given a large coupled model, it requires the execution time to be dominated by only a few of the many atomic models. Further-more, the parallelization effort is invested in certain models while others will show no improvement. Another option is to run multiple simulations simultaneously with different sets of parameters, as is frequently done for Monte Carlo or cost minimiza-tion problems. Unfortunately, this technique is of little use if one must accelerate a single simulation run. A third option is to exploit the modularity of DEVS to automate the parallelization of a coupled model. For this approach, DEVS practitioners often adopt a variant of the formalism called Parallel DEVS (Chow & Zeigler, 1994).

Recall that the select function orders the internal events of imminent submodels. In our example, if the Detector and the Fixture were scheduled to experience internal events at the same time, we ensured that the Fixture's transition would occur first. Parallel DEVS eliminates the select function. The order of simultaneous events is deliberately left ambiguous to allow the functions of multiple imminent submodels to be executed concurrently.

With Parallel DEVS, all imminent models send outputs simultaneously. This raises two issues which the variant addresses. First note that the outputs of multiple imminent submodels may be directed to a single receiving model. This receiving model must recognize that the order in which its inputs arrive is essentially arbitrary and best ignored. For that reason, the external transition function of a Parallel DEVS atomic model takes a bag of inputs instead of a single input. A bag is like a set in that its items are unordered, but different in that it can contain duplicate items.

The other issue raised by simultaneous outputs is the possibility that one submodel sends an output to a second submodel at the same time that the second submodel sends its own output. Clearly the output functions get evaluated for both models. But since the second model is both receiving an input and sending an output, which transition function should be called? In many cases it makes sense to call δ_{int} first, since the output function has already been evaluated, and then to call δ_{ext} to process the input. But that raises the question of what elapsed time value to pass into δ_{ext}: should it be 0 or the previous $ta(s)$? Parallel DEVS addresses the issue by requiring atomic models to have a confluent transition function δ_{con}. It is invoked in place of δ_{ext} or δ_{int} whenever external and internal events collide.

Earlier in the chapter when we specified atomic models for the Detector and Fixture, we assumed that external and internal events would never collide. We later used *Select* to guarantee that internal events would be fully processed before inputs were received. Had we used Parallel DEVS, we would have defined both confluent transition functions as follows to achieve the same effect.

$$\delta_{con}\left(\left(s, ta(s)\right), x_{bag}\right) = \delta_{ext}\left(\left(\delta_{int}\left(s\right), 0\right), x_{bag}\right)$$

SUMMARY AND FURTHER READING

With state transitions that depend in part on the time elapsed since the previous event, a DEVS model can represent practically any real-world system that varies in time. The DEVS formalism provides first and foremost a set of conventions for specifying atomic models, along with a procedure for performing simulations with these models. If one specifies a coupled model, then due to closure under coupling one has implicitly defined an equivalent atomic model. This modular approach can be used to avoid a complex atomic model in favor of multiple simpler atomic models. Similarly, by combining models in a hierarchical fashion, one avoids a complex coupled model in favor of multiple simpler coupled models.

It is important to ensure that every DEVS model has a legitimate specification, one that always allows a simulation to properly advance time. For atomic models, this requires an examination of the delay between events in an infinite sequence of internal events. For coupled models, one must look at the delay between inputs and outputs for every submodel in a feedback loop.

We have applied these core DEVS concepts by developing and analyzing specifications representing an office lighting system and its various components. As mentioned at the outset, more information on the DEVS formalism and related theory can be found in Zeigler et al. (2000).

It is helpful to understand the similarities and differences between the DEVS formalism and the conventions used by modern software developers. We have already compared DEVS with object-orientation, but another noteworthy set of conventions is the Unified Modeling Language (UML). Traditional UML is somewhat limited in its ability to represent the timing of events. This shortcoming is partially addressed by an extension of UML designed for real-time software systems (UML-RT). Huang & Sarjoughian (2004) provide a detailed comparison of UML-RT with DEVS, and explain how the DEVS formalism's treatment of time is better suited to simulation studies.

DEVS users should familiarize themselves with several variants of the formalism. One of these variants is Parallel DEVS, which we have already discussed. Another notable variant is Cell-DEVS, which applies DEVS to models composed of an array of cells (Wainer & Giambiasi, 2001). Among other things, Cell-DEVS has been used to model the spread of forest fires, the diffusion of heat, and urban traffic. Stochastic DEVS (STDEVS) is one of several ways one can introduce randomness into a DEVS model (Castro et al, 2008). It replaces the deterministic results of the transition functions with probability spaces. There is also a variant called Dynamic Structure DEVS (DSDEVS), which allows a coupled model's submodels and connections to be added and deleted during a simulation (Barros, 1995).

Several noteworthy books cover DEVS from different perspectives. Written for simulation practitioners, Wainer (2009) demonstrates the application of DEVS and the Cell-DEVS variant to physical, biological, environmental, communication, and urban systems. Nutaro (2011) focuses on the implementation of simulation software using object-oriented techniques and Parallel DEVS. A chapter on hybrid systems shows how DEVS can be integrated with various differential equation solving techniques. For those interested in the latest developments in the field, Wainer & Mosterman (2011) provide a collection of recent DEVS research.

REFERENCES

Barros, F. J. (1995). Dynamic structure discrete event system specification: A new formalism for dynamic structure modeling and simulation. In Proceedings of the 27th conference on Winter simulation (pp. 781-785). Miami, FL: WSC.

Castro, R., Kofman, E., & Wainer, G. A. (2008). A formal framework for stochastic DEVS modeling and simulation. In Proceedings of the 2008 Spring Simulation Multiconference (pp. 421-428). Ottawa, Canada: ACM.

Chow, A. C. H., & Zeigler, B. P. (1994). Parallel DEVS: a parallel, hierarchical, modular, modeling formalism. In Proceedings of the 26th conference on Winter Simulation (pp. 716–722). Orlando, FL: Society for Computer Simulation International.

Huang, D., & Sarjoughian, H. (2004). Software and Simulation Modeling for Real-Time Software-Intensive Systems. In Proceedings of the 8th IEEE International Symposium on Distributed Simulation and Real-Time Applications (pp. 196-203). Budapes, Hungary: IEEE.

Nutaro, J. J. (2011). *Building Software for Simulation: Theory and Algorithms with Applications in C*. Hoboken, NJ: John Wiley & Sons.

United Nations Environment Programme (2009). Buildings and Climate Change: Summary for Decision Makers.

Vangheluwe, H. (2000). DEVS as a common denominator for multi-formalism hybrid systems modelling. In Proceedings of IEEE International Symposium on Computer-Aided Control System Design (pp. 129–134). Anchorage, AK: IEEE.

Wainer, G. A. (2009). *Discrete-Event Modeling and Simulation: A Practitioner's Approach*. Boca Raton, FL: CRC Press. doi:10.1201/9781420053371.

Wainer, G. A., & Giambiasi, N. (2001). Timed Cell-DEVS: Modelling and simulation of cell spaces. In *Discrete Event Modeling & Simulation: Enabling Future Technologies*. Berlin, Germany: Springer-Verlag. doi:10.1007/978-1-4757-3554-3_10.

Wainer, G. A., & Mosterman, P. J. (2011). *Discrete-Event Modeling and Simulation: Theory and Applications*. Boca Raton, FL: CRC Press.

Zeigler, B. P. (1976). *Theory of Modeling and Simulation*. New York: Wiley-Interscience.

Zeigler, B. P., Praehofer, H., & Kim, T. G. (2000). *Theory of Modeling and Simulation* (2nd ed.). San Diego, CA: Academic Press.

KEY TERMS AND DEFINITIONS

Atomic Model: An indivisible DEVS model specified with state transition functions, an output function, a time advance function, and sets of input values, output values, and states.

Closure under Coupling: A property of the DEVS formalism which guarantees that the behavior of any coupled model can be captured by an atomic model specification.

Confluent Transition Function: A state transition function used in the Parallel DEVS variant to handle collisions between external and internal events.

Consistent: Describes a model specification that contradicts neither itself nor the conventions of the modeling formalism.

Coupled Model: A DEVS model composed of other DEVS models; a hierarchy is produced when coupled models are composed of other coupled models.

Discrete Event Simulation: A simulation in which time is repeatedly advanced by a variable, non-negative duration to the time of the next event.

Discrete Time Simulation: A simulation in which time is repeatedly advanced by a fixed time step.

External Transition Function: The state transition function invoked whenever an input is received.

Feedback Loop: A circular path in a coupled model formed by traversing couplings from their source submodels to their destination submodels.

Imminent: Describes a submodel that is scheduled to experience an internal event at least as soon as any other in the same coupled model.

Internal Transition Function: The state transition function invoked immediately after the output function.

Legitimate: Describes a model that, in the absence of inputs, is guaranteed to allow simulated time to advance towards infinity without stopping or converging.

Memoryless: Describes a model which has no state, and can therefore produce an output value that depends only on present information such as a just-received input.

Model Parameter: Represents a value that can be supplied to a model, but remains constant throughout a simulation.

Output Function: A function invoked to obtain an output value whenever the duration given by the time advance function elapses.

Port: A label assigned to a model to distinguish a particular type of input or output from other types of inputs or outputs.

Resultant: An atomic model that represents the behavior of a coupled model; closure under coupling guarantees that for every coupled model, a resultant exists.

Select Function: A function used to order the internal events of multiple imminent submodels; in the Parallel DEVS variant, the function is excluded to allow all imminent submodels to produce outputs simultaneously.

State: A set of conditions associated with a system at a particular point in time; the system's history influences its current state, which in turn influences the system's future behavior.

State Variable: A variable used to represent part of a system's state.

Time Advance Function: A function invoked at the beginning of a simulation and after any state transition to give the duration that must elapse before the next internal event occurs.

Total State: A representation of a system's state which includes both state variables that remain constant between events, and the continuously changing time that has elapsed since the previous event.

Chapter 4

Thermal Analysis of the MIPS Processor Formulated within DEVS Conventions

Alejandro Moreno Astorga
Universidad Nacional de Educación a Distancia, Spain

Eva Besada-Portas
Universidad Complutense de Madrid, Spain

José L. Risco-Martín
Universidad Complutense de Madrid, Spain

Luís de la Torre
Universidad Nacional de Educación a Distancia, Spain

Joaquín Aranda
Universidad Nacional de Educación a Distancia, Spain

ABSTRACT

The MIPS processor is used in computer architecture courses in order to explain matters such as performance analysis, energy consumption, and reliability. Currently, due to the desire for more powerful computers, it is interesting to learn how to reallocate certain components in order to achieve heat reduction with low cooling costs. DEVS is a general formalism for modeling and analysis of discrete event systems based on set theory and represents a basis for discrete event abstractions by formalizing the concept of activity which relates to the specification and heterogeneous distribution of events in space and time. The MIPS simulator is built upon known techniques for discrete event simulation and its definition within a formal language such as DEVS provides completeness, verifiability, extensibility, and maintainability. In this chapter, the authors carry out a thermal analysis of the MIPS processor using a DEVS simulator and show a register reallocation policy based on evolutionary algorithms that notably decreases the resulting register bank temperature.

DOI: 10.4018/978-1-4666-4369-7.ch004

INTRODUCTION

The MIPS processor is used in computer architecture courses in order to explain matters such as performance analysis, energy consumption, or reliability. The current integration scales introduce new phenomena's that significantly degrade the consistency of the chips. Electro migration, power consumption, performance, and temperature are some of the parameters to take into account.

Nowadays, due to the desire for more powerful computers, it is interesting to learn how to reallocate certain components in order to achieve heat reduction, with low cooling costs.

DEVS is a general formalism for modeling and analysis of discrete event systems based on set theory. This is a standard term in the field of simulation referring to a modular and hierarchical formalism that is commonly used to model and analyze different systems. DEVS was originally introduced by Zeigler (Zeigler, 1984a; 1984b) in 1976 to provide a computational basis to express behavior of widespread discrete event formalisms (event-scheduling, activity-scanning, process-interaction, and more) alongside with other basic systems formalisms (continuous state systems and hybrid continuous state and discrete event systems). DEVS can reproduce *Discrete Time System Specifications* (DTSS) and approximate continuous modeling paradigms (*Differential Equation System Specification* (DESS)). DEVS approaches continuous systems using numerical integration methods. Hence, simulation tools based on DEVS are potentially more general than others including continuous simulation tools (Kofman, 2004).

DEVS represents a basis for discrete event abstractions by formalizing the concept of activity which relates to the specification and heterogeneous distribution of events in space and time. This arrangement offers a new way to unify the computational representation of both continuous and discrete phenomena and to simulate them with the greater efficiency and flexibility afforded by object-oriented discrete event environments.

In this chapter, the MIPS simulator is built upon known techniques for discrete event simulation (DEVS). The definition of the MIPS processor within a formal language such as DEVS provides completeness, verifiability, extensibility, and maintainability. Moreover, DEVS conceptually separates models from the simulator, making possible to simulate the MIPS processor and its experimental frame using different simulators working in centralized, parallel or distributed execution modes. Also, models can be simulated with a simple ad-hoc program written in any language.

The simulation of the MIPS processor lets us generate a profile that stores the operations performed on each register. This profile allows the extraction of information such as the power consumed by each register.

The high employment of resources and power consumption is therefore the source of the problems facing microprocessor designers. High power densities lead to high temperatures consequently damages the reliability of components and increases the power drain. The temperature acquired by the register bank of a processor, at a larger scale a chip surface, is linked to the use of registers. Hence, the optimization of the usage of certain registers by efficient allocation policies will minimize the energy dissipated. It avoids the negative impact brought about by the warming of these storage elements, such as increased power consumption, deterioration of the processor. Otherwise, it would require a cooling of the chip which would increase costs.

The optimization phase of the MIPS register bank allocation is carried out by a *Multi-Objective Evolutionary Algorithm* (MOEA). Hottest elements must me placed as far as possible in the chip to minimize maximum temperature.

In this chapter, we start with the MIPS architecture, followed by a brief overview of DEVS explained alongside with the models of the MIPS processor. We continue with a thermal analysis of the MIPS processor using a DEVS simulator. Next, we describe a register reallocation policy based on evolutionary algorithms that notably decreases the resulting register bank temperature. Finally, some conclusions and future views are drawn.

MIPS

MIPS (acronym for Microprocessor without Interlocked Pipeline Stages) is a reduced instruction set computer (RISC) instruction set architecture (ISA) developed by MIPS Technologies. The current revisions are MIPS32 (for 32-bit implementations) and MIPS64 (for 64-bit implementations). MIPS32 and MIPS64 define a control register set as well as the instruction set. From now on we will refer to MIPS architecture as the MIPS32 revision.

The MIPS processor, designed in 1984 by researchers at Stanford University, is a RISC processor. Compared with their CISC (Complex Instruction Set Computer) counterparts (such as the Intel Pentium processors), RISC processors typically support fewer and much simpler instructions.

The premise is, however, that a RISC processor can be made much faster than a CISC processor because of its simpler design. Currently, it is generally accepted that RISC processors are more efficient than CISC processors and even the only prevalent CISC processor that is still in use, internally translates the CISC instructions into RISC instructions before they are executed (Hennessy, 2007).

The basic concept was to increase performance through the use of deep instruction pipelines. Pipelining as a basic technique was well known before but not developed into its full potential. CPUs are built up from a number of dedicated sub-units such as instruction decoders, ALUs (integer arithmetic's and logic), load and store units (memory handling), and more. In a traditional design, a particular instruction in a program sequence must be completed before the next can be issued for execution, but in a pipelined architecture, successive instructions can instead overlap in execution. Pipelining allows overlapping execution of multiple instructions with the same circuit. The circuit is usually divided up into stages, including instruction decoding, arithmetic, and registers fetching stages, where each stage processes one instruction at a time. For instance, at the same time a math instruction is fed into the floating point unit, the load/store unit can fetch the next instruction.

One major barrier to pipelining was that some instructions, like division, take longer to complete and consequently the CPU has to wait before passing the next instruction into the pipeline. One solution to this problem is to use a series of interlocks that allows stages to indicate that they are busy, pausing the other stages upstream. However, these interlocks were a major performance drawback since they had to communicate to all the modules in the CPU which takes time, and appeared to limit the clock speed. A major aspect of the MIPS design was to fit every sub-phase of all instructions into one cycle, thus removing any needs for interlocking, and permitting a single cycle output.

Even though this design eliminated a number of useful instructions such as multiplication and division, the overall performance of the system was increased. This growth of the speed would be difficult with interlocking involved, as the time needed to set up locks is as much a function of die size as clock rate. The elimination of these instructions became a contentious point.

The goal of designing machines with MIPS architecture is to enable parallelism in instruction execution and reduce memory access to increase performance and speed of execution. Moreover, given the clear and simple set of instructions, the MIPS design is often used to teach computers architecture in schools and universities.

OPERATION MODE

An instruction set architecture is an interface that defines the hardware operations which are available to software. Any instruction set can be implemented in many different ways.

- In a basic single-cycle implementation all operations take the same amount of time—a single cycle.

- A multi-cycle implementation allows faster operations to take less time than slower ones, so overall performance can be increased.
- Finally, pipelining lets a processor overlap the execution of several instructions, potentially leading to big performance gains.

In this chapter, we will describe the implementation of a single-cycle MIPS-based instruction set supporting arithmetic, data transfer and control operations. All instructions take one clock cycle, therefore, the cycle time must be equal to or greater than the more complex instruction. This makes the implementation cycle time-consuming, because otherwise you would get unexpected results due to errors in the internal modules. Consequently, execution is quite slow, thus complex instructions such as division and multiplication or operations with intricate addressing modes cannot be implemented.

On the other hand, each functional unit can only be used once per cycle, which forces to adapt hardware using multiplexers to reuse the blocks or, for example, to divide memory into two modules: data storage and instructions, otherwise it would be impossible to complete necessary reads and writes in one cycle. Unfortunately, this solution increases the cost of hardware.

TIMING

The fundamental idea underlying the data path single-cycle is the existence of two sequential barriers between which runs the entire combinational workload and constitute a cycle (and therefore, a statement), as shown in Figure 1. The only sequential modules that appear in the path are the register that acts as a program counter (PC), the register bank and data memory.

In a typical instruction execution all registers should be loaded simultaneously, although in selectively mode, values spread through combinational networks until

Figure 1. Single-cycle timing

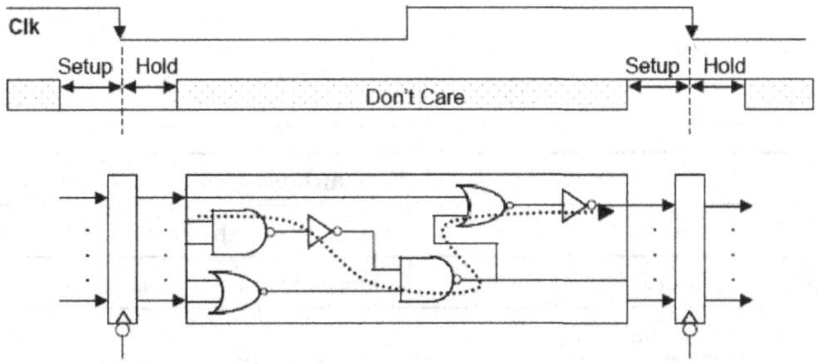

they stabilize in the registries entries. This process is repeated indefinitely and continuously being adjusted by signals produced by the control unit.

In short, the typical execution of an instruction on a single-cycle processor consists of the following phases:

- Registers are loaded simultaneously and selectively.
- The values are propagated through the combinational networks until they are stable at the entrance of the registers.
- Repeat the process indefinitely.

We'll explain the instruction format, instruction set, then the datapath first and the control unit.

INSTRUCTION FORMAT

MIPS instructions are encoded as 32-bit values and divided into three types: (R-Type) arithmetic instructions, which, as its name suggests, are responsible for performing arithmetic, (I-Type) memory reference instructions, which serve to store data in memory or extract data from it, and (J-Type) jump instructions, which are used for branching in the program.

Table 1 shows the formats of the instructions described above, showing how many bits correspond to each field. The fields for the core instruction set are:

- **op:** Instruction operation code.
- **rs, rt and rd:** Source and destination registers.
- **shamt:** Amount to shift (shift operations).
- **funct:** Specifies a particular arithmetic operation.
- **address:** Jump destination address.
- **immediate:** Immediate operand or jump to base-register address.

Table 1.

Type	-31- Format(bits) -0-					
R	op (6)	rs (5)	rt (5)	rd (5)	shamt (5)	funct (6)
I	op (6)	rs (5)	rt (5)	immediate (16)		
J	op (6)	address (26)				

INSTRUCTION SET

Now we describe several MIPS-based instructions supported by the MIPS processor described throughout this chapter. PC stands for program counter, stores the memory address that contains the instruction to execute.

Type I Format

- lw rt, inmed(rs)
  - $rt \leftarrow Memory(rs + SignExt(inmed)), PC \leftarrow PC + 4.$
  - A word is loaded into a register from the specified address.
    - Box 1
- sw rt, inmed(rs)
  - $Memory\ (rs + SignExt(inmed)) \leftarrow rt, PC \leftarrow PC + 4$
  - The contents of **rt** is stored at the specified address.
    - Box 2
- beq rs, rt, inmed
  - $if\ (rs = rt)\ then\ (PC \leftarrow PC + 4 + 4 \cdot SignExt(inmed))\ else\ PC \leftarrow PC + 4$
  - Branches if the two registers are equal.
    - Box 3

Type R Format

- add rd, rs, rt
  - $rd \leftarrow rs + rt, PC \leftarrow PC + 4$

Box 1.

0x23: 6	rs: 5	rt: 5	inmed: 16

Box 2.

0x28: 6	rs: 5	rt: 5	inmed: 16

Box 3.

4: 6	rs:5	rt: 5	rd: 5	Inmed: 16

- ◦ Adds two registers and stores the result in a register.
  - ▪ Box 4
- sub rd, rs, rt
  - ◦ *rd ← rs - rt, PC ← PC + 4*
  - ◦ Subtracts two registers and stores the result in a register.
    - ▪ Box 5
- and rd, rs, rt
  - ◦ *rd ← rs and rt, PC ← PC + 4*
  - ◦ Bitwise "ands" two registers and stores the result in a register.
    - ▪ Box 6
- or rd, rs, rt
  - ◦ *rd ← rs or rt, PC ← PC + 4*
  - ◦ Bitwise logical "ors" two registers and stores the result in a register.
    - ▪ Box 7
- slt rd, rs, rt
  - ◦ *if (rs < rt) then (rd ← 1) else (rd ← 0), PC ← PC+4*
  - ◦ If rs is less than rt, rd is set to one. It gets zero otherwise.

Box 4.

0: 6	rs:5	rt: 5	rd: 5	0:5	0x20:6

Box 5.

0: 6	rs:5	rt: 5	rd: 5	0:5	0x22:6

Box 6.

0: 6	rs:5	rt: 5	rd: 5	0:5	0x24: 6

Box 7.

0: 6	rs:5	rt: 5	rd: 5	0:5	0x25: 6

Type J Format

- j inmed
  - $PC \leftarrow inmed$
  - Jumps to the calculated address.
    - Box 8

Example: Bubble Sort

The following example shows the resultant MIPS instructions after compiling the C code of bubble sort algorithm (see Figure 2). Bubble sort is a simple sorting algorithm that works by repeatedly stepping through the list to be sorted, comparing each pair of adjacent items and swapping them if they are in the wrong order. The pass through the list is repeated until no swaps are needed, which indicates that the list is sorted. The algorithm gets its name from the way smaller elements "bubble" to the top of the list. Because it only uses comparisons to operate on elements, it is a comparison sort.

After compiling the code above, we get through a cross compiler the binary MIPS processor archive. In the MIPS version, memory addresses of each instruction in hexadecimal are shown (see Figure 3).

Box 8.

2: 6	Inmed:26

Figure 2. C code for bubble sort

```
#define N 10000

int main() {
        int i, j, Tmp, Flipped;

        int ListInt[N];
        for(i=0; i<N; i++)
                ListInt[i] = N-i;

        for(i=N;--i>=0;) {

                Flipped = 0;
                for(j=0; j<i; j++){
                        if (ListInt[j] > ListInt[j+1]){
                                Tmp = ListInt[j];
                                ListInt[j] = ListInt[j+1];
                                ListInt[j+1] = Tmp;
                                Flipped = 1;
                        }
                }

                if(Flipped==0) return;

        }

        return 0;
}
```

As we can observe in the code, new pseudoinstrucciones appear: li, move or beqz. These "macros" are translated by the processor to the instruction set on running the program. They serve to maintain compatibility between different processor families, and arise due to the limited set of instructions that has a RISC processor.

There are other special instructions such as nop (no operation of English), translated into sll $ 0, $ 0.0, break to break the normal sequence of execution, and syscall, for calls to the operating system.

MIPS Datapath and Controller

Processors consist of two main components: a controller and a datapath. The datapath handles all required arithmetic computations. The controller is responsible for telling the datapath what to do according to the instructions in the executing program. Datapaths typically contain a register file in order to store data, whose outputs are connected to the inputs of an ALU (arithmetic logic unit). Therefore, a controller can achieve a specific computation by reading values from the register file and telling the ALU to perform a specific operation. The result of the ALU can then be stored back into the register file. Generally, actual datapaths are more complicated in order to implement all operations needed by an instruction set. Figure 4 illustrates a datapath and controller of a MIPS-based processor able to support the aforementioned instructions.

During the following sections we will describe how the MIPS processor is formulated within DEVS conventions.

DEVS

The DEVS *Modeling & Simulation* (M&S) formalism (Zeigler, Kim, & Praehofer, 2000) provides several advantages to analyze and design complex systems: completeness, verifiability, extensibility, and maintainability. DEVS conceptually separates models from the simulator, making possible to simulate the same model using different simulators working in centralized, parallel or distributed execution modes. Due to the modular and hierarchical modeling views, as well as its simulation-based analysis capability, the DEVS formalism and its variations have been used in many application of engineering and science.

DEVS was created for modeling and simulation of discrete event dynamic systems. As a result, it defines a formal way to define systems whose states change either upon the reception of an input event or due to the expiration of a time delay. In order to deal with the system under study, the model can be organized hierarchically in such a way that higher-level components in a system are decomposed

Figure 3. MIPS instructions for bubble sort

0:	34039c40	li	v1,0x9c40
4:	03a3e823	subu	sp,sp,v1
8:	00002021	move	a0,zero
c:	24052710	li	a1,10000
10:	00041080	sll	v0,a0,0x2
14:	005d1021	addu	v0,v0,sp
18:	00a41823	subu	v1,a1,a0
1c:	ac430000	sw	v1,0(v0)
20:	24840001	addiu	a0,a0,1
24:	28822710	slti	v0,a0,10000
28:	1440fff9	bnez	v0,10 <main+0x10>
2c:	00000000	nop	
30:	2404270f	li	a0,9999
34:	00003821	move	a3,zero
38:	00004021	move	t0,zero
3c:	1880000f	blez	a0,7c <main+0x7c>
40:	00000000	nop	
44:	00071080	sll	v0,a3,0x2
48:	005d1821	addu	v1,v0,sp
4c:	8c660000	lw	a2,0(v1)
50:	8c650004	lw	a1,4(v1)
54:	00a6102a	slt	v0,a1,a2
58:	10400004	beqz	v0,6c <main+0x6c>
5c:	00000000	nop	
60:	ac650000	sw	a1,0(v1)
64:	ac660004	sw	a2,4(v1)
68:	24080001	li	t0,1
6c:	24e70001	addiu	a3,a3,1
70:	00e4102a	slt	v0,a3,a0
74:	1440fff3	bnez	v0,44 <main+0x44>
78:	00000000	nop	
7c:	15000003	bnez	t0,8c <main+0x8c>
80:	00000000	nop	
84:	08000027	j	9c <main+0x9c>
88:	00000000	nop	
8c:	2484ffff	addiu	a0,a0,-1
90:	0481ffe8	bgez	a0,34 <main+0x34>
94:	00000000	nop	
98:	00001021	move	v0,zero
9c:	34089c40	li	t0,0x9c40
a0:	03a8e821	addu	sp,sp,t0
a4:	03e00008	jr	ra
a8:	00000000	nop	

Figure 4. Datapath and controller

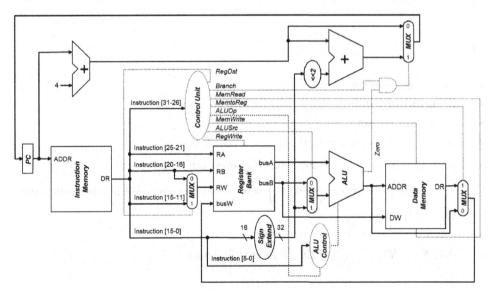

into simpler elements. DEVS defines system behavior as well as system structure. System behavior in DEVS is described using the input and output events and states. To this end, DEVS has two kinds of models to represent systems: atomic model and coupled model. The atomic model is the irreducible model definition that specifies the behavior for any modeled entity. The coupled model is the aggregation/composition of two or more atomic and coupled models connected by explicit couplings between ports. The coupled model itself can be a component in a larger coupled model system giving rise to a hierarchical DEVS model construction. The top-level coupled model is usually called the root coupled model.

The Classic DEVS Formalism

Classic DEVS is an intrinsically sequential formalism that allows for the description of system behavior at two levels: at the lowest level, an atomic DEVS describes the autonomous behavior of a discrete event system as a sequence of deterministic transitions between states and its reaction to external inputs. At the higher level, a coupled DEVS describes a discrete event system in terms of a network of coupled components. Each component may be an atomic DEVS model or a coupled DEVS model in its own right, as we will see in the following sections.

The Atomic DEVS

An atomic DEVS model is specified by a 7-tuple

$$M = \langle X, Y, S, \delta_{int}, \delta_{ext}, \lambda, ta \rangle$$

where

- X is the *input* set.
- Y is the *output* set.
- S is the *state* set.
- $\delta_{int} : S \to S$ is the *internal transition function*.
- $\delta_{ext} : Q \times X \to S$ is the *external transition function*,
  $Q = \left\{ (s, e) : s \in S, e \in [0, ta(s)] \right\}$ is total state set and is the elapsed time since the last transition.
- $\lambda : S \to Y$ is the *output* function.
- $ta : S \to R_0^+ \bigcup \infty$ is the *time advance function*.

There are no restrictions on the sizes of the sets, which typically are product sets, i.e., $S = S_1 \times S_2 \times \cdots S_n$. In the case of the state set S, this formalizes multiple concurrent parts of a system, while it formalizes multiple input and output ports in the case of sets X and Y. The time base is not mentioned explicitly and is continuous. For a discrete event model described by an atomic-DEVS model, the behavior is uniquely determined by the initial total state $\left(s_0, e_0\right) \in Q$ and is obtained by means of the iterative simulation procedure described below (refer to Figure 5).

At any given moment, an atomic DEVS model is in state $s \in S$. In the absence of external events, it remains in that state for a period of time defined by $ta(s)$. When $ta(s)$ expires, the model outputs the value $\lambda(s)$ through a port, and it then changes to a new state s_1 given by $\delta_{int}(s)$. This transition is called an internal transition. Then, the process starts again (see bottom gray arrow). On the contrary, an external transition may occur due to the reception of external events through input ports. In this case, the external transition function determines the new state s_2 given by $\delta_{ext}(s,e,x)$, where s is the current state, e is the time elapsed since the last transition (external or internal), and x is the external event received. After an external transition, the model is re-scheduled and the process starts again (see left grey arrow), setting the elapsed time e to 0.

The CPU Clock

The CPU clock of the MIPS processor is formulated as a DEVS atomic model. The state set is composed of a time variable σ that holds the time remaining to the next internal transition and a variable clk that takes two values; rising and falling clock edges. The input set is empty since it doesn't receive any external stimulus and consequently never launches the external transition. While the output set consist of a clock signal in order to output its current value. It only triggers its internal transi-

Figure 5. State transitions of an atomic DEVS model (1/2)

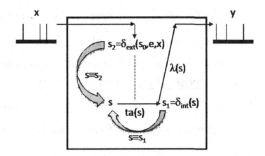

tion every time half of the time period T expires. Hence, it signals the rest of the components with the clock edge.

$$CLK = \langle X, S, Y, \delta_{int}, \delta_{ext}, \lambda, ta \rangle$$

$$X = \{\varnothing\}.$$

$$S = \sigma \in R_0^+ \times clk \in \{\downarrow, \uparrow\} \times T \in R_0^+$$

$$Y = \left\{ \left(out,\ clk \in \{\downarrow, \uparrow\} \right) \right\}$$

$$\lambda \left(o, clk, T \right) = (clk)$$

$$ta(\sigma, clk, T) = \sigma$$

$$\delta_{int} \left(\sigma, clk, T \right) = \begin{cases} \left(\dfrac{T}{2}, \uparrow, T \right) & if\ clk = \downarrow \\ \left(\dfrac{T}{2}, \downarrow, T \right) & if\ clk = \uparrow \end{cases}$$

Following the previous definition, an atomic model has structure and behavior. Regarding the structure, as seen on the previous example, we can make modeling easier by introducing input and output ports and the state variable:

- The *set of input ports* through which external events are received. The set of input events X is composed by a set of pairs input port and valid data: $X = \left\{ (p,v) \mid p \in InPorts, v \in X_p \right\}$, where $InPorts$ represents the set of input ports and X_p represents the set of values for the input port p.
- The *set of output ports* through which external events are sent. The set of output events Y is composed by a set of pairs output port and valid data: $Y = \left\{ (p,v) \mid p \in OutPorts, v \in Y_p \right\}$, where $OutPorts$ represents the set of output ports and Y_p represents the set of values for the output port p.

- The set of *state variables* and parameters: one state variables is always present, *sigma* (in the absence of external events the system stays in the current state for the time given by *sigma*: σ).

With respect to the behavior, we can find:

- The *time advance function* which controls the timing of internal transitions – usually, this function just returns the value of σ.
- The *internal transition function* which specifies to which next state the system will transit after the time given by the time advance function (sigma) has elapsed.
- The *external transition function* which specifies how the system changes state when an input is received – the effect is to place the system in a new state and σ thus scheduling it for a next internal transition; the next state is computed on the basis of the present state, the input port and value of the external event, and the time that has elapsed in the current state.
- The *output function* which generates an external output just before an internal transition takes place.

In summary, σ holds the time remaining to the next internal transition. This is precisely the time-advance value to be produced by the time-advance function. In the absence of external events the system stays in the current state for the time given by σ.

The Program Counter

The Program Counter (PC) of the MIPS datapath is a register structure that contains the address pointer value of the current instruction (see Figure 6). Each cycle, the value at the pointer is read into the instruction decoder and the program counter is

Figure 6. Program counter

updated to point to the next instruction. For RISC computers updating the PC register is as simple as adding the machine word length (in bytes) to the PC.

Next, we define the PC in terms of DEVS specifications (see Box 9). In contrast with the CPU clock defined above the PC only sends an output whenever it receives an input. The state set is composed by σ, a "word" of 32 concatenated binary values w and a time delay t. The input set comprehends a word w, a clock edge clk and a binary value $pcwrite$. The output set only consists of w. When the δ_{ext} triggers due to an external input it checks whether the $pcwrite$ input port is enabled with 1 and the clk input is on a falling edge in order to override the current state w value with the incoming w'. Then σ is set to t so as to launch λ and next δ_{int} within the given time delay. Finally, λ outputs the w value and δ_{int} sets σ to ∞.

As shown in the PC, the time advance function can take any real number between 0 and ∞. A state for which $ta(s) = 0$ is called *transitory* state. In contrast, if $ta(s) = \infty$, then s is said to be a *passive* state, in which the system will remain perpetually unless an external event is received.

Box 9.

$$PC = \langle X, S, Y, \delta_{int}, \delta_{ext}, \lambda, ta \rangle$$

$$X = \left\{ \left[in, \ w \in \left\{ \left(0 \cup 1 \right)^{32} \right\} \right], \left(CLK, clk \in \{\downarrow, \uparrow\} \right), \left(PCWrite, \ pcwrite \in \{0,1\} \right) \right\}.$$

$$S = \sigma \in R_0^+ \times w \in \{ \left(0 \cup 1 \right)^{32} \} \times t \in R_0^+, t \ is \ the \ delay \ time$$

$$Y = \left\{ \left[out, \ w \in \left\{ \left(0 \cup 1 \right)^{32} \right\} \right] \right\}$$

$$\lambda \left(\sigma, w, t \right) = (w)$$

$$\delta_{int} \left(\sigma, w, t \right) = \left(\infty, w \right)$$

$$\delta_{ext} \left(\sigma, w, t, e, \left(in, w' \right), \left(CLK, clk \right), \left(PCWrite, pcwrite \right) \right)$$

$$= \begin{cases} \left(t, w' \right) & if(clk = \downarrow \ and \ pcwrite = 1) \\ \left(t, w \right) & if(clk \neq \downarrow) \end{cases}$$

MIPS Atomic Models

Next, we describe the remaining modules of the datapath of the MIPS processor.

Adder

The adder module is responsible for summing the values of its two inputs and signaling its output (see Figure 7). The datapath has two adders. One takes care of adding 4 to the program counter; the other adds the immediate value of the jump to the program counter. It has basically the same DEVS structure as the program counter except for that it lacks of a clock signal and an input to enable the sum of the two input values. When the δ_{ext} is triggered it sums the two input values and stores the result into the state set. Next, sends the sum through its output port and passivates in order to wait for new inputs (see Box 10).

Multiplexer

The multiplexer selects one of several input signals and forwards the selected input into a single line. A multiplexer of 2^n inputs has n select lines, which are used to select which input line to send to the output. Multiplexers are mainly used to increase the amount of data that can be sent over the network within a certain amount of time and bandwidth. When the δ_{ext} is triggered it selects one of the two input values depending on the control input value and stores its value into the state set. Then, it sends the value through its output port and passivates in order to wait for new inputs (see Box 11).

Arithmetic Logic Unit (ALU)

An ALU is a circuit that performs arithmetic and logical operations (see Figure 8). The ALU is a fundamental building block of the central processing unit of a computer, and even the simplest microprocessors contain one for purposes such as maintaining timers. In contrast with the Multiplexer and the Adder, the ALU ac-

Figure 7. Adder

Box 10.

$$SUM = \left\langle X, S, Y, \delta_{int}, \delta_{ext}, \delta_{con}, \lambda, ta \right\rangle$$

$$X = \left\{ \left(in0, w_0 \in \left\{ \left(0 \cup 1\right)^{32} \right\} \right), \left(in1, w_1 \in \left\{ \left(0 \cup 1\right)^{32} \right\} \right) \right\}.$$

$$S = \sigma \in R_0^+ \times w \in \left\{ \left(0 \cup 1\right)^{32} \right\} \times t \in R_0^+, t \, is \, the \, delay \, time$$

$$Y = \left\{ \left(out, w \in \left\{ \left(0 \cup 1\right)^{32} \right\} \right) \right\}$$

$$\lambda \left(\sigma, w, t \right) = (w)$$

$$\delta_{int} \left(\sigma, w, t \right) = \left(\infty, w, t \right)$$

$$\delta_{ext} \left(\sigma, w, t, e, \left(in0, w_0 \right), \left(in1, w_1 \right) \right) = \left(t, \left(w_0 + w_1 \right), t \right)$$

Box 11.

$$MUX(2 \, to \, 1) = \left\langle X, S, Y, \delta_{int}, \delta_{ext}, \lambda, ta \right\rangle$$

$$X = \left\{ \left(in0, w_0 \in \left\{ \left(0 \cup 1\right)^{32} \right\} \right), \left(in1, w_1 \in \left\{ \left(0 \cup 1\right)^{32} \right\} \right), \left(control, ctl \in \left\{ 0, 1 \right\} \right) \right\}.$$

$$S = \sigma \in R_0^+ \times w \in \left\{ \left(0 \cup 1\right)^{32} \right\} \times t \in R_0^+, t \, is \, the \, delay \, time$$

$$Y = \left\{ \left(out, w \in \left\{ \left(0 \cup 1\right)^{32} \right\} \right) \right\}$$

$$\lambda \left(\sigma, w, t \right) = (w)$$

$$\delta_{int} \left(\sigma, w, t \right) = \left(\infty, w, t \right)$$

$$\delta_{ext} \left(\sigma, w, t, e, \left(in0, w_0 \right), \left(in1, w_1 \right) \left(control, ctl \right) \right) = \begin{cases} \left(t, w_0, t \right) & if \, ctl = 0 \\ \left(t, w_1, t \right) & if \, ctl = 1 \end{cases}$$

cepts all the input values but performs an operation selected by the control input and stores the result in the state set (see Box 12). If the result of the operation is 0, also sends and output through its output Zero.

Figure 8. Arithmetic logic unit (ALU)

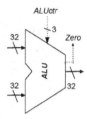

Box 12.

$$ALU = \langle X, S, Y, \delta_{int}, \delta_{ext}, \lambda, ta \rangle$$

$$X = \left\{ \left[in0, w_0 \in \left\{ \left(0 \cup 1\right)^{32} \right\} \right], \left[in1, w_1 \in \left\{ \left(0 \cup 1\right)^{32} \right\} \right], \left[ALUctr, ctl \in \left\{ \left(0 \cup 1\right)^{3} \right\} \right] \right\}.$$

$$S = \sigma \in R_0^+ \times w \in \left\{ \left(0 \cup 1\right)^{32} \right\} \times t \in R_0^+, t\, is\, the\, delay\, time$$

$$Y = \left\{ \left[out, w \in \left\{ \left(0 \cup 1\right)^{32} \right\} \right], \left(Zero, z \in \left\{0,1\right\} \right) \right\}$$

$$\lambda(\sigma, w, t) = \begin{cases} (w, 0) \, if\, w = 0^{32} \\ (w, \varnothing) \, if\, w \neq 0^{32} \end{cases}$$

$$\delta_{int}(\sigma, w, t) = (\infty, w, t)$$

$$\delta_{ext}\left(\sigma, w, t, e, (in0, w_0), (in1, w_1)(ALUctr, ctl)\right) = \begin{cases} \left(t, w_0\, \textbf{and}\, w_1, t\right) if\, ALUctr = 000 \\ \left(t, w_0\, \textbf{or}\, w_1, t\right)\quad if\, ALUctr = 001 \\ \left(t, w_0\, \textbf{add}\, w_1, t\right) if\, ALUctr = 010 \\ \left(t, w_0\, \textbf{sub}\, w_1, t\right) if\, ALUctr = 110 \\ \left(t, w_0\, \textbf{slt}\, w_1, t\right)\quad if\, ALUctr = 111 \end{cases}$$

Sign Extend

The sign extension module adapts the 16-bit immediate operand to a word size of 32 bits (see Figure 9). The value of the left-most bit of the immediate operand (bit 15) is copied to all bits to the left (into the high-order bits). So if the 16-bit immediate operand is a 16-bit two's complement negative integer, the 32-bit ALU operand is a 32-bit version of the same negative integer. The left-most bit of a two's complement integer is sometimes called the "sign bit" (see Box 13).

Shift Left

Shifting by two positions is the same as performing a one-position shift two times. Shifting by zero positions leaves the pattern unchanged. Shifting an N-bit pattern left

Figure 9. Sign extend

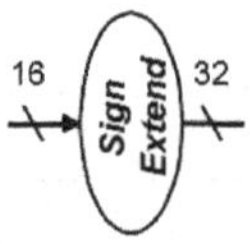

Box 13.

$$SE = \langle X, S, Y, \delta_{int}, \delta_{ext}, \lambda, ta \rangle$$

$$X = \left\{ \left[in, \mathrm{w} \in \left\{ \left(0 \bigcup 1\right)^{16} \right\} \right] \right\}.$$

$$S = \sigma \in R_0^+ \times w \in \left\{ \left(0 \bigcup 1\right)^{32} \right\} \times t \in R_0^+, t\, is\, the\, delay\, time$$

$$Y = \left\{ \left[out, w \in \left\{ \left(0 \bigcup 1\right)^{32} \right\} \right] \right\}$$

$$\lambda\left(\sigma, w, t\right) = (w)$$

$$\delta_{int}\left(\sigma, w, t\right) = \left(\infty, w, t\right)$$

$$\delta_{ext}\left(\sigma, w, t, e, \left(in, w'\right)\right) = \begin{cases} \left(t, (1^{16} + \mathrm{w'}), t\right) & if\, w[0] = 1 \\ \left(t, (0^{16} + \mathrm{w'}), t\right) & if\, w[0] = 0 \end{cases}$$

Figure 10. Shift left

Box 14.

$$SHIFT = \left\langle X, S, Y, \delta_{int}, \delta_{ext}, \lambda, ta \right\rangle$$

$$X = \left\{ \left(in, w \in \{(0 \cup 1)^{32}\} \right) \right\}.$$

$$S = \sigma \in R_0^+ \times w \in \{(0 \cup 1)^{32}\} \times t \in R_0^+, t \, is \, the \, delay \, time$$

$$Y = \left\{ \left(out, w \in \left\{ (0 \cup 1)^{32} \right\} \right) \right\}$$

$$\lambda(\sigma, w, t) = (w)$$

$$\delta_{int}(\sigma, w, t) = (\infty, w)$$

$$\delta_{ext}\left(\sigma, w, t, e, (in, w') \right) = \{(t, w \ll 2)$$

by N or more positions changes all of the bits to zero (see Figure 10). This module shifts two positions to implement the multiplication by 4 (see Box 14).

Registers

The register file stores thirty-two 32-bit values (see Figure 11 and Box 15).

- Each register specifier is 5 bits long.
- You can read from two registers at a time (2 ports).
- RegWrite is 1 if a register should be written.

Memory

The memory must have an idealized behavior, therefore integrated into the CPU, and with the following characteristics:

Figure 11. Registers

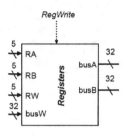

Box 15.

$$REG = \langle X, S, Y, \delta_{int}, \delta_{ext}, \lambda, ta \rangle$$

$$X = \left\{ \left[busW, bw \in \left\{ \left(0 \bigcup 1\right)^{32} \right\} \right], \left[RA, ra \in \left\{ \left(0 \bigcup 1\right)^{5} \right\} \right], \left[RB, rb \in \left\{ \left(0 \bigcup 1\right)^{5} \right\} \right], \right.$$

$$\left. \left(RegWrite, regwrite \in \{0,1\} \right), \left[RW, rw \in \left\{ \left(0 \bigcup 1\right)^{5} \right\} \right], \left(CLK, clk \in \{\downarrow, \uparrow\} \right) \right\}.$$

$$S = \sigma \in R_0^+ \times data \in \left\{ \left(0 \bigcup 1\right)^{32} \right\}^{32} \times va \in \left\{ \left(0 \bigcup 1\right)^{32} \right\} \times vb \in \left\{ \left(0 \bigcup 1\right)^{32} \right\} \times t \in R_0^+$$

$$Y = \left\{ \left[busA, ba \in \left\{ \left(0 \bigcup 1\right)^{32} \right\} \right], \left[busB, bb \in \left\{ \left(0 \bigcup 1\right)^{32} \right\} \right] \right\}$$

$$\lambda\left(\sigma, data, va, vb, t\right) = \left(va, vb\right)$$

$$\delta_{int}\left(\sigma, data, va, vb, t\right) = \left(\infty, data, va, vb, t\right)$$

$$\delta_{ext}\left(\sigma, data, va, vb, t, e, \left(busW, bw\right), \left(RA, ra\right), \left(RB, rb\right), \left(RW, rw\right), \left(RegWrite, regwrite\right), \left(CLK, clk\right)\right)$$

$$= \begin{cases} \left(t, data, data\left[ra\right], \varnothing, t\right) & if\left(ra \neq \varnothing \, and \, rb = \varnothing \, and \, regwrite = 0\right) \\ \left(t, data, \varnothing, data\left[rb\right], t\right) & if\left(ra = \varnothing \, and \, rb \neq \varnothing \, and \, regwrite = 0\right) \\ \left(t, data, data\left[ra\right], data\left[rb\right], t\right) & if\left(ra \neq \varnothing \, and \, rb \neq \varnothing \, and \, regwrite = 0\right) \\ data\left[rw\right] = bw; \left(\infty, data, \varnothing, \varnothing, t\right) & if\left(regwrite = 1 \, and \, clk = \downarrow\right) \end{cases}$$

- Byte-addressable, but able to accept and provide 4 bytes per access.
  ○ Address entry.
  ○ 1 output of 32 bits.
  ○ 1 input 32-bit data (only data).
- Assuming that behaves temporarily as the register file (synchronously) and has an access time less than the cycle time.

- Splits into two to make two memory accesses in the same cycle:
  - Instructions or memory, shown in Figure 12.
  - Data memory, shown in Figure 13.
- Data memory is responsible for storing program data. The instruction memory is equivalent, but does not require writing.
- Box 16

The Coupled DEVS

Coupled DEVS models are specified by a 7-tuple:

$$N = \left\langle X, Y, D, \{M_i\}, \{I_j\}, \{Z_{j,k}\}, \gamma \right\rangle$$

where:

- X is the *input* set.
- Y is the *output* set.
- D is the set of *component indexes*.
- $\{M_i \mid i \in D\}$ is the set of *components*, each M_i being an atomic-DEVS:

Figure 12. Instruction memory

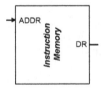

Figure 13. Data memory

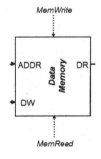

Box 16.

$$MEM = \left\langle X, S, Y, \delta_{int}, \delta_{ext}, \lambda, ta \right\rangle$$

$$X = \left\{ \left[ADDR, a \in \left\{ \left(0 \bigcup 1\right)^{32} \right\} \right], \left[DW, w \in \left\{ \left(0 \bigcup 1\right)^{32} \right\} \right], \left(CLK, clk \in \{\downarrow, \uparrow\} \right), \right.$$

$$\left. \left(MemWrite, memwrite \in \{0, 1\} \right), \left(MemRead, memread \in \{0, 1\} \right) \right\}.$$

$$S = \sigma \in R_0^+ \times data \in \left\{ \left(0 \bigcup 1\right)^{32} \right\}^N \times vr \in \left\{ \left(0 \bigcup 1\right)^{32} \right\} \times t \in R_0^+$$

$$Y = \left\{ \left[DR, dr \in \left\{ \left(0 \bigcup 1\right)^{32} \right\} \right] \right\}$$

$$\lambda \left(\sigma, data, vr, t \right) = \left(vr \right)$$

$$\delta_{int} \left(\sigma, data, vr, t \right) = \left(\infty, data, vr, t \right)$$

$$\delta_{ext} \left(\sigma, data, vr, t, e, \left(ADDR, a \right), \left(DW, w \right), \left(CLK, clk \right), \left(MemWrite, memwrite \right), \left(MemRead, memread \right) \right)$$

$$= \begin{cases} \left(t, data, data[a], t \right) & if \ (memread = 1) \\ data\left[a \right] = w; \left(\infty, data, \varnothing, t \right) & if \ (memwrite = 1 \ and \ clk = \downarrow) \end{cases}$$

$$M = \left\langle X_i, Y_i, S_i, \delta_{int,i}, \delta_{ext,i}, \lambda_i, ta_i \right\rangle$$

$$\left\{ I_j \mid j \in D \bigcup \{self\} \right\}$$

is the set of all influencer sets, where

$$I_j \subseteq D \bigcup \{self\}, j \notin D$$

is the influencer set of j.

$$\left\{ Z_{j,k} \mid j \in D \bigcup \{self\}, k \in I_j \right\}$$

is the set of output-to-input translation functions, where:

$$Z_{j,k} : X \rightarrow X_k, \ if \ j = self$$

$$Z_{j,k} : Y_j \to Y, \ if \ k = self$$

$$Z_{j,k} : Y_j \to X_k, \ otherwise$$

$$\gamma : 2^D \to D$$

is the *select function*.

The sets X and Y typically are product sets, which formalizes multiple input and output ports. To each atomic-DEVS in the network is assigned a unique identifier in the set *D*. This corresponds to model names or references in a modeling language. The coupled DEVS *N* itself is referred to by means of *self* $\notin$ *D*. This provides a natural way of indexing the components in the set $\{M_i\}$, and to describe the sets $\{I_j\}$, which explicitly describes the network structure, and $\{Z_{j,k}\}$.

Figure 14 shows an example of a coupled DEVS. In this case, $I_A = \{self\}$, $I_B = \{self, A\}$ and $I_{self} = \{B\}$. For modularity reasons, a component may not be influenced by components outside its enclosing scope, defined as $D \bigcup \{self\}$. The condition $j \notin I_j$ forbids a component to directly influence itself, to prevent instantaneous dependency cycles. The functions $Z_{j,k}$ describe how an influencer's output is mapped onto an influencer's input. The set of output-to-input transition functions implicitly describes the coupling network structure, which is sometimes divided into External Input Couplings (EIC, from the coupled-DEVS' input to a component's input), External Output Couplings (EOC, from a component's output to the coupled-

Figure 14. A coupled DEVS

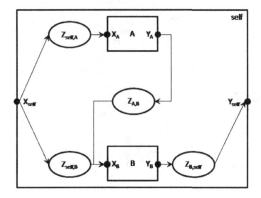

DEVS' output), and Internal Couplings (IC, from a component's output to a component's input).

As a result of coupling concurrent components, multiple internal transitions may occur at the same simulation time t. Since in sequential simulation systems only one component can be activated at a given time, a tie-breaking mechanism to select which of the components should be handled first is required. The classic coupled-DEVS formalism uses the select function γ to choose a unique component from the set of imminent components, which are defined as:

$$\Pi_t = \left\{ i \mid i \in D, \sigma_i = 0 \right\}$$

That is, Π_t includes those components that have an internal transition scheduled at time *t*. The component returned by $\gamma\left(\Pi_t\right)$ will thus be activated first. For the other components in the imminent set, we are left with the following ambiguity [2]: when an external event is received by a model at the same time as its scheduled internal transition, which elapsed time should be used by the external transition: e=0 of the new state, or e=ta(s) of the old state? These collisions are resolved by letting e=0 for the unique activated component, and e=ta(s) for all the others.

The MIPS Controller

The controller of the MIPS processor consists of a control unit and an ALU control (see Figures 15 and 16). Hence, the controller of the MIPS processor is a coupled

Figure 15. Control unit

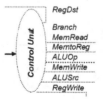

Figure 16. ALU control

model with two atomic models. The controller, shown in Figure 4, is responsible for everything to work properly. Its tasks are:

- Select the operations to be performed by the multifunction modules.
- Control the flow of data, enabling the selection input signal multiplexers and registers load.

All instructions share the same arithmetic operation code and during execution all the general signs of the data path are equal. Therefore, single-cycle MIPS controller uses:

- A primary control for decoding the operation code field (op) and set the overall data path.
- A local control to the ALU to decode the field arithmetic (funct) and select the operation to be performed by the ALU.
- Additionally, no arithmetic operations (lw, sw and beq) the main control may order an operation to the ALU to compute the SD or make comparisons.

ALUop uses the intermediate signal whose value is:

- 00 in memory access operations.
- 01 in diving operations.
- 10 in arithmetic.

In order to control what direction you should load the PC is to be an intermediate signal Branch (activated during beq instruction) that will be the y-Zero logic signal generated by the ALU (see Box 17).

For example, the following schedule of Figure 17 represents the execution of load instruction: lw.

Now, we formally describe the MIPS controller coupled model with an analogous definition for better understanding. A different definition of coupled models is:

$$N = \left\langle X, Y, D, \left\{ M_d \mid d \in D \right\}, EIC, EOC, IC, \gamma \right\rangle$$

where:

- EIC is the set of the external input couplings.
- EOC is the set of the external output couplings.
- IC is the set of the internal couplings.

Figure 17. Complete schedule of instruction lw

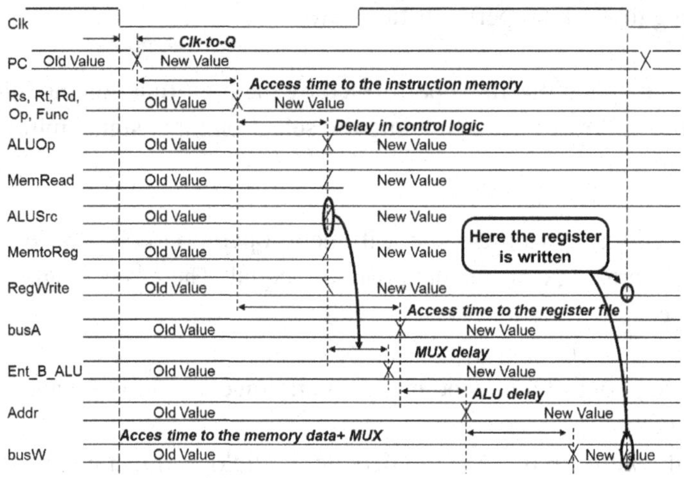

Succeeding the previous coupled model definition, the MIPS controller is as follows in Box 18.

The input set consists of two input ports and several output ports that connect the inputs and outputs of the coupled model to the inputs and outputs of the internal atomic models. The set of models comprehends the control unit and the ALU control. The external internal couplings consist of the inputs of the coupled model linked to the ALU control, *func* and the control unit, *INSTR*. While the external output couplings connect all the outputs of the control unit except for the one coupled with the ALU control *ALUop* to the coupled model outputs, and the output of the ALU Control to the remaining output *ALUCtrl*. Finally, the internal couplings consist of the connection among the output of the control unit *ALUop* to the ALU control input.

EXPERIMENTAL FRAME-MIPS

An experimental frame is a specification of the conditions under which a system is observed or experimented with (Zeigler et al., 2000). The experimental frame is the operational formulation of the objectives encourages a modeling and simulation project. There might be different objectives in modeling a system or different systems can be modeled with the same objectives. Thus, multiple experimental frames may be designed for the same system and in turn, the same experimental frame may suit different systems (see Figure 18).

Box 17.

$$ALUControl = \langle X, S, Y, \delta_{int}, \delta_{ext}, \lambda, ta \rangle$$

$$X = \left\{ \left[ALUop, op \in \left\{ \left(0 \bigcup 1 \right)^2 \right\} \right], \left[funct, f \in \left\{ \left(0 \bigcup 1 \right)^6 \right\} \right] \right\}.$$

$$S = \sigma \in R_0^+ \times ALUCtrl \in \left\{ \left(0 \bigcup 1 \right)^3 \right\} \times t \in R_0^+$$

$$Y = \left\{ \left[ALUCtrl, ctrl \in \left\{ \left(0 \bigcup 1 \right)^3 \right\} \right] \right\}$$

$$\lambda \left(\sigma, ALUCtrl, t \right) = (ALUCtrl)$$

$$\delta_{int} \left(\sigma, ALUCtrl, t \right) = \left(\infty, ALUCtrl, t \right)$$

$$\delta_{ext} \left(\sigma, ALUCtrl, t, e, \left(ALUop, op \right), \left(funct, f \right) \right)$$

$$= \begin{cases} \left(t, 010, t \right) if \left(ALUop = 00 \right) lw \ \& sw \\ \left(t, 110, t \right) if \left(ALUop = 01 \right) beq \\ \left(t, 010, t \right) if \left(f = 100000 \, and \, ALUop = 10 \right) add \\ \left(t, 110, t \right) if \left(f = 100010 \, and \, ALUop = 10 \right) sub \\ \left(t, 000, t \right) if \left(f = 100100 \, and \, ALUop = 10 \right) and \\ \left(t, 001, t \right) if \left(f = 100101 \, and \, ALUop = 10 \right) or \\ \left(t, 111, t \right) if \left(f = 101010 \, and \, ALUop = 10 \right) slt \end{cases}$$

$$ControlUnit = \langle X, S, Y, \delta_{int}, \delta_{ext}, \delta_{con}, \lambda, ta \rangle$$

$$X = \left\{ \left(INSTR, i \in \left\{ I \right\} \right), where \, I \, is \, a \, set \, of \, type \, I, R \, or \, J \, Intructions \right\}.$$

$$S = \sigma \in R_0^+ \times regDest \in \left\{ 0, 1 \right\} \times ALUSrc \in \left\{ 0, 1 \right\} \times MemToReg \in \left\{ 0, 1 \right\}$$

$$\times RegWrite \in \left\{ 0, 1 \right\} \times MemRead \in \left\{ 0, 1 \right\} \times MemWrite \in \left\{ 0, 1 \right\}$$

$$\times Branch \in \left\{ 0, 1 \right\} \times ALUop \in \left\{ \left(0 \bigcup 1 \right)^2 \right\} \times t \in R_0^+$$

$$Y = \left\{ \begin{matrix} regDest \in \left\{ 0, 1 \right\}, ALUSrc \in \left\{ 0, 1 \right\}, MemToReg \in \left\{ 0, 1 \right\}, RegWrite \in \left\{ 0, 1 \right\}, MemRead \\ \in \left\{ 0, 1 \right\}, MemWrite \in \left\{ 0, 1 \right\}, Branch \in \left\{ 0, 1 \right\}, ALUop \in \left\{ \left(0 \bigcup 1 \right)^2 \right\} \end{matrix} \right\}$$

$$\lambda \left(\sigma, regDest, ALUSrc, MemtoReg, RegWrite, MemRead, MemWrite, Branch, ALUop, t \right)$$

$$= (regDest, ALUSrc, MemtoReg, RegWrite, MemRead, MemWrite, Branch, ALUop)$$

$$\delta_{int} \left(\sigma, regDest, ALUSrc, MemtoReg, RegWrite, MemRead, MemWrite, Branch, ALUop, t \right)$$

$$= \left(\infty, regDest, ALUSrc, MemtoReg, RegWrite, MemRead, MemWrite, Branch, ALUop, t \right)$$

$$\delta_{ext} \left(\sigma, regDest, ALUSrc, MemtoReg, RegWrite, MemRead, MemWrite, Branch, ALUop, t, e, \left(INSTR, i \right) \right)$$

$$= \begin{cases} \left(t, 0, 1, 1, 1, 1, 0, 0, 00, t \right) if \left(i = lw \right) \\ \left(t, X, 1, X, 0, 0, 1, 0, 00, t \right) if \left(i = sw \right) \\ \left(t, X, 0, X, 0, 0, 0, 1, 01, t \right) if \left(i = beq \right) \\ \left(t, 1, 0, 0, 1, 0, 0, 0, 10, t \right) if \ (type(i) = R) \end{cases}$$

Box 18.

$Controller = \langle X, Y, D, \{M_d \mid d \in D\}, EIC, EOC, IC \rangle$

where:

$X = \left\{ \left(funct, f \in \left\{ \left(0 \bigcup 1\right)^6 \right\} \right), \left(INSTR, i \in \{I\} \right) \right\}$

$Y = \{ regDest \in \{0,1\}, ALUSrc \in \{0,1\}, MemToReg \in \{0,1\}, RegWrite \in$

$\{0,1\}, MemRead \in \{0,1\}, MemWrite \in \{0,1\}, Branch \in \{0,1\}, \left(ALUCtrl, ctrl \in \left\{ \left(0 \bigcup 1\right)^3 \right\} \right) \}$

$D = \{ControlUnit, ALUControl\}$

$\{M_{ControlUnit} = ControlUnit; M_{ALUControl} = ALUControl\}$

$EIC = \left\{ \begin{array}{l} \left((Controller, func), (ALUControl, func) \right), \\ \left((Controller, INSTR), (ControlUnit, INSTR) \right) \end{array} \right\}$

$EOC = \left\{ \begin{array}{l} \left((ALUControl, ALUCtrl), (Controller, ALUCtrl) \right), \\ \left((ControlUnit, regDest), (Controller, regDest) \right), \\ \left((ControlUnit, ALUSrc), (Controller, ALUSrc) \right), \\ \left((ControlUnit, MemToReg), (Controller, MemToReg) \right), \\ \left((ControlUnit, RegWrite), (Controller, RegWrite) \right), \\ \left((ControlUnit, MemRead), (Controller, MemRead) \right), \\ \left((ControlUnit, MemWrite), (Controller, MemWrite) \right), \\ \left((ControlUnit, Branch), (Controller, Branch) \right) \end{array} \right\}$

$IC = \left\{ \left((ControlUnit, ALUop), (ALUControl, ALUop) \right) \right\}$

For this example the experimental frame is a system that interacts with the system of interest (MIPS) to obtain the data of interest under certain conditions. The frame is a measurement system or observer.

We assume a single-cycle MIPS simulator fully implemented using DEVS as seen on previous sections. We added one DEVS model (Transducer) that allows us to obtain a trace of registers. Connections are made so that the inputs to the register bank are also entries for the transducer.

As output, we obtain a log that stores the reads and writes that are performed on each register so that we get a profile of the registers. This profile will allow the

Figure 18. DEVS MIPS registers EF

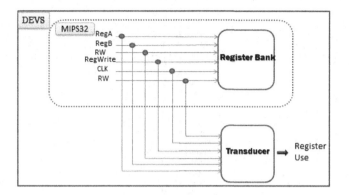

extraction of information such as the power consumed by each register. According to the operation performed, adding the energy value of reading or writing respectively to the affected register.

Each profile provides a benchmark for the use of registers with which we calculate the power density of each other and proceed to the thermal study.

Example: Bubble Sort

Now, we show the transducer output of the DEVS simulation of a MIPS single-cycle processor at 1 GHz of the bubble sort algorithm described in previous sections. Figure 19 depicts the total number of registers accesses (reads and writes) of the simulation for 10^6 cycles.

As shown in Figure 19 for the bubble sort algorithm, only a selected group of registers are used (0 to 8 and 29).

Thermal Analysis

The high employment of resources and power consumption is therefore the source of the problems facing microprocessor designers. In the initial stage of design, understanding the characteristics of power and its ramifications is essential since the architectural decisions can have a major impact on overall efficiency. In addition, weaknesses at the architectural level are too difficult to correct in later design stages.

High power densities lead to high temperatures consequently damages the reliability of components and increases the power drain. Optimize the power dissipation depends on effective and efficient modeling covering different disciplines and levels, from device physics to architectural design.

Figure 19. Accesses per register

```
Register #0 = 673870
Register #1 = 14
Register #2 = 743801
Register #3 = 326138
Register #4 = 131574
Register #5 = 439205
Register #6 = 429202
Register #7 = 357682
Register #8 = 214622
Register #9 = 0
Register #10 = 0
Register #11 = 0
Register #12 = 0
Register #13 = 0
Register #14 = 0
Register #15 = 0
Register #16 = 0
Register #17 = 0
Register #18 = 0
Register #19 = 0
Register #20 = 0
Register #21 = 0
Register #22 = 0
Register #23 = 0
Register #24 = 0
Register #25 = 0
Register #26 = 0
Register #27 = 0
Register #28 = 0
Register #29 = 81537
Register #30 = 0
Register #31 = 0
```

The temperature acquired by the register bank of a processor, at a larger scale a chip surface, is linked to the use of registers. If we can optimize the use of certain registers by efficient allocation policies, we will minimize the energy dissipated. In this way we avoid the negative impact brought about by the warming of these storage elements, such as increased power consumption, deterioration of the processor, otherwise it would require a cooling of the chip, which would increase costs.

Thermal Impact

The register allocation phase of a compiler also has an impact on the system temperature. It may cause the following errors:

- **Concurrent access to the same register:** It occurs when the compiler assigns distinct logical registers repeatedly to the same physical register, and therefore this register will suffer a further warming.
- **Access to registers located in the same area:** It happens when registers are assigned close to each other in physical space of the chip and this causes heat to concentrate in a particular area. Moreover, the heat flow is associated with

a temperature difference and in this case there is a heat conduction temperature gradient, so that heat adjacent to that used registers.

For all this, finding a relocation of the register bank means an increase in the consistency of components.

Finally, using benchmarks, we turn to the verification step of temperature reduction achieved with the new reassignment.

Profiles

Thermal profiles depend on temporal distribution and spatial potency. Next we need to quantify the thermal impact under study. We study the energy consumed by the register bank for a set of 3 different benchmarks that follow patterns of access. Some originate a prolonged use of a reduced set of registers, and others in a more dispersed use of the 32 registers available.

For this study the register bank is a matrix of 32 x 1, 16 x 2 and 8 x 4, but other configurations are allowed. Each basic cell corresponds to a register and its dimensions are:

$$Width = 2, Length = 6$$

$$Dimensions : 50\mu m \times 50\mu m$$

Temperature

Thermal analysis in an integrated circuit is the simulation of heat transfer through heterogeneous material among heat producers and heat consumers.

We decompose the discrete chip heating elements, which may be of varying shapes and sizes. Adjacent heating elements interact via heat diffusion. Each element has power dissipation, temperature, thermal capacitance and thermal resistance to the adjacent elements.

The following equation governs the heat conduction in chips:

$$C\frac{dT(t)}{dt} + AT\left(t\right) = Pu(t)$$

where the thermal capacitance matrix, C is a diagonal matrix of $N \times N$. Heat conduction matrix, A is a sparse matrix $N \times N$ cells, $T\left(t\right)$ and $P(t)$ are temperature and power vectors $N \times 1$, $u(t)$ is the step function of time.

Thermal analysis at steady state is characterized by the temperature distribution when heat flow does not vary with time. Therefore, for steady-state analysis left the term that expresses temperature variation with time is zero. Thus:

$$A T\left(t\right) = P \rightarrow T = A^{-1} P$$

Thus, given the thermal resistance matrix and the power vector P, the main task of the thermal analysis is to invert A. The computational complexity of this analysis is therefore determined by the size of A.

Energy

Prior to the calculation of the power we need to find the energy consumed by each register. This energy is a factor that depends on the number of accesses to the registry. This calculation is done on all registers obtaining the total read and write accesses on each one.

We use a model (McDonald-Maier, 2009) that describes the energy consumed as follows:

Where Er and Ew is the energy consumed by read and write accesses respectively. In this study we focused on the energy consumed by operations on the register file, only considering the energy that involve reads and writes.

The values of Er and Ew (Yeager, 1996) defines:

$$Er = Nr{\cdot}Edr$$

$$Ew = Nw{\cdot}Edw$$

Nr, Nw : Number of reads and writes.

Edr, Ewr : *Energy consumed for each operation.*

$$Edw = 0.1408576^{-9} J$$

$$Edr = 0.25455^{-9} J$$

The number of reads and writes are obtained by running the MIPS simulator for DEVS.

Example: Bubble Sort

Figure 20, Figure 21, and Figure 22 depict a temperature map of the register bank after computing the thermal impact of the reads and writes of the execution of bubble sort algorithm within the MIPS DEVS simulator. Each figure represents a different physical distribution of the registers:

- 32x1: 32 registers in one column.
- 16x2: 2 columns of 16 registers each.

Figure 20. Bubble sort 32x1

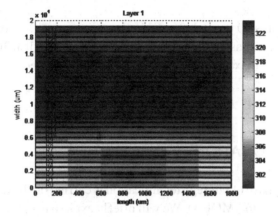

Figure 21. Bubble sort 16x2

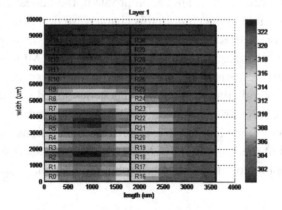

Figure 22. Bubble sort 8x4

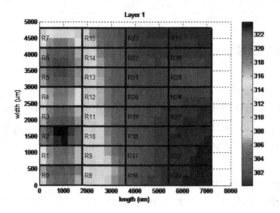

- 8x4: 4 columns of 8 registers each.

As seen in Figures 20 through 26 and in the previous section, only the first registers are used, so it is reasonable to think that if they were redistributed throughout the register bank the maximum temperature would be reduced.

$$AT(t) = P \rightarrow T = A^{-1}P$$

REGISTER ALLOCATION

The optimization phase of our register allocation is carried out by a Multi-Objective Evolutionary Algorithm (MOEA). We will briefly explain in the following the main characteristics of a MOEA algorithm and why it is the best strategy to solve the register allocation optimization.

In the thermal aware register allocation problem, the hottest elements must be placed as far as possible in the chip. In this chapter, we describe a straightforward MOEA based on NSGA-II (Kalyanmoy Deb 2002), which tries to minimize maximum temperature while fulfilling all the topological constraints. MOEAs are stochastic optimization heuristics where the exploration of the solution space of a certain problem is carried out by imitating the population genetics stated in Darwin's theory of evolution. Selection, crossover and mutation operators, derived directly from natural evolution mechanisms, are applied to a population of solutions, thus favoring the birth and survival of the best solutions. MOEAs have been successfully applied to many NP-hard combinatorial optimization problems and work by encoding potential solutions (individuals) to a problem by strings (chromosomes), and by combining their codes and, hence, their properties. In order to apply MOEAs to a problem, a genetic representation of each individual has first to be found.

Furthermore, an initial population has to be created, as well as defining a cost function to measure the fitness of each solution. As a second step, we need to design the genetic operators that will allow us to produce a new population of thermal-aware register assignment solutions from a previous one, by capturing the interdependencies of the different topological constraints working concurrently. Then, by iteratively applying the genetic operators to the current population, the fitness of the best individuals in the population converges to targeted solutions, according to the metric/s to be optimized and the weight of each of these metrics. For an overview of MOEAs the reader is referred to (Carlos A. Coello Coello, 2002).

Genetic Representation and Operators

The chip is split into small blocks as we will see now. The design space has a maximum width W, and maximum length L. We define the vector (x_i, y_i) as the geometrical location of block B_i, where $0 \leq x_i \leq L - l_i, 0 \leq y_i \leq W - w_i$. We use (x_i, y_i) to denote the left-bottom coordinate of block B_i while we assume that the coordinate of left-bottom corner of the resultant chip is $(0, 0, 0)$.

In order to apply a MOEA correctly we need to define a genetic representation of the design space of all possible register alternatives. Moreover, to be able to apply the NSGA-II optimization process and cover all possible interdependencies of the topological constraints, we must guarantee that all the chromosomes represent real and feasible solutions to the problem and ensure that the search space is covered in a continuous and optimal way. To this end, we use a permutation encoding (Carlos A. Coello Coello, 2002), where every chromosome is a string of labels, which represents a position in a sequence. Figure 23 depicts the three genetic operators used in our MOEA on a register problem. A chromosome in Figure 23 is formed by 8 registers R_i. In every cycle of the optimization process (called generation) two chromosomes are selected by tournament. To this end, we select two random chromosomes from the whole population and we select the best of these. This task is repeated twice in order to obtain two chromosomes (called parents, see Figure 23). Next, as Figure 23 depicts, we apply the cycle crossover: starting with the first allele of chromosome A (R_4), we look at the allele at the same position in chromosome B. Next, we go to the position with the same allele in A, and add this allele to the cycle. Then, we repeat the previous step until we arrive at the first allele of A. Finally, we put the alleles of the cycle in the first child on the positions they have in the first parent, and take next cycle from second parent. Finally, in the mutation step some blocks are chosen with a certain probability, and swapped.

Fitness Function

Each chromosome represents the order in which blocks are being placed in the design area. Every block B_i is placed taking into account all the topological constraints and the maximum temperature in the chip with respect to all the previously placed blocks $B_j : j < i$. In order to place a block i, we take the best point (x_i, y_i) in the remaining free positions. To select the best point we establish a dominance relation taking into account the following objectives in our multi-objective evaluation.

The first objective is determined by the topological relations among placed blocks. It represents the number of topological constraints violated (no overlapping between placed blocks and current area less or equal than maximum area).

The second objective is a measure of the thermal impact, based on the power consumption. To compute the thermal impact for every power-consumption we cannot use an accurate thermal model, which includes non-linear and differential equations. In a classical thermal model, the temperature of a unitary cell of the chip depends not only on the power density dissipated by the cell, but also on the power density of its neighbors. The first factor refers to the increase of the thermal energy due to the activity of the element, while the second one is related to the diffusion

Figure 23. MOEA operators

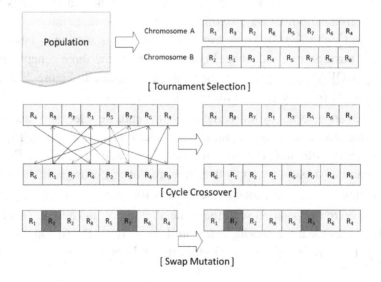

process of heat (Paci, 2007). Taking this into account, we use the power density of each block as an approximation of its temperature in the steady state.

This is a valid approximation because the main term of the temperature of a cell is given by the power dissipated in the cell; the contribution of its neighbors does not change significantly the thermal behavior. Thus, our remaining objectives can be formulated as:

$$\sum_{i<j \in 1..32} \frac{\left(dp_i * dp_j\right)}{d_{ij}}$$

Figure 24. Optimized bubble sort 32x1

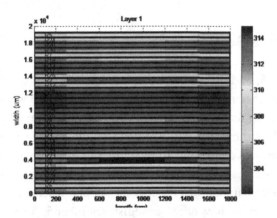

Figure 25. Optimized bubble sort 16x2

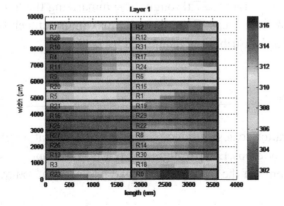

Figure 26. Optimized bubble sort 8x4

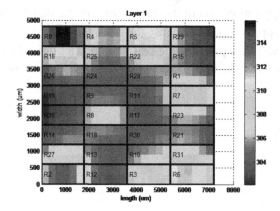

where dp_i is the power density of block i, and d_{ij} is the Euclidean distance between blocks i and j.

Example: Bubble Sort

Figure 24, Figure 25, and Figure 26 depict a temperature map of the register bank after computing the thermal impact of the registers reads and writes. But this time, the registers have been reallocated. This new register assignment is the outcome of the MOEA described above; an optimized register allocation according to the thermal impact and physical constraints of the chip. For example, in Figure 24 register number 5 is at the old position of register number 31 (see Figure 20). The compiler reassigns the register number 5 to number 31. Hence whenever the processor accessed register number 31, now accesses register number 5. As expected in all three cases the warmest registers have been redistributed throughout the register bank and consequently the maximum temperature has been reduced.

Finally, we obtain Figures 27 through 29 summarizing the temperature values obtained in the previous steps. Regarding the maximum temperature, the highest decline is in the 32x1 distribution, quantified by 2.2%.

CONCLUSION

The current integration scales introduce new phenomena's that significantly degrade the consistency of the chips. Electro migration, power consumption, performance and temperature are some of the parameters to take into account today. In this chapter

Figure 27. Bubble sort 8x4 comparisons

Configuration	Tmax	Tmean	Tgrad
Original	320.7114 K	305.5141 K	323.0247 K
Optimized	313.6823 K	305.6045 K	314.8381 K

Figure 28. Bubble sort 32x1 comparisons

Configuration	Tmax	Tmean	Tgrad
Original	320.7542 K	307.4562 K	323.1206 K
Optimized	314.9498 K	306.6345 K	316.2305 K

Figure 29. Bubble sort 16x2 comparisons

Configuration	Tmax	Tmean	Tgrad
Original	320.7542 K	306.9405 K	323.4912 K
Optimized	314.4087 K	306.4656 K	315.6918 K

we have addressed the heat problem, and particularly its impact on the register bank of a processor. To reduce this impact, we have shown a methodology that, through reallocation of registers, reduces the overall temperature.

This methodology first analyzes the register accesses of original applications compiled with a standard compiler. With this analysis we can determine the power consumption of each of the registers and, therefore, the thermal impact of the application. Finally, through an optimization, we obtain a policy of reallocation of registers that has as main objective to evenly distribute the temperature, decreasing hot spots.

Although the proposed methodology is applicable to any target architecture, the examples given in this paper have been implemented on a MIPS processor simulator. The simulator is built upon known techniques for discrete event simulation (DEVS). The definition of the MIPS processor within a formal language such as DEVS provides completeness, verifiability, extensibility, and maintainability. Moreover, DEVS conceptually separates models from the simulator, making possible to simulate the MIPS processor and its experimental frame using different simulators working in centralized, parallel, or distributed execution modes. Also, models can be simulated with a simple ad-hoc program written in any language.

The simulator allows obtaining the power consumption profile aforementioned. Later, we developed a thermal model in several configurations MIPS register bank.

The analysis of the different configurations reveals that the proposed methodology is applicable to any physical arrangement of the register bank, which again validates the independence of the process followed with regard to the target architecture.

The register reallocation algorithm is based on evolutionary computation. This algorithm uses the thermal model to evaluate the goodness of the different policies of reallocation, which naturally evolve by classical operators of bio-inspired systems such as selection, crossover or mutation.

The analysis of the results reveals that a good policy can reduce the temperature reallocation of the register bank to about 10° K, which represents 3.2% of the maximum temperature in the original allocation policy.

REFERENCES

Coello, C. C., van Veldhuizen, D.A., & Lamont, G. B. (2002). Evolutionary Algorithms for Solving Multi-Objective Problems. *Genetic Algorithms and Evolutionary Computation, 5.*

Hennessy, J. L., Patterson, D. A., & Arpaci-Dusseau, A. C. (2007). *Computer Architecture: A Quantitative Approach.* Burlington, MA: Morgan Kaufmann.

KDeb, K., Pratap, A., Agarwal, S., & Meyarivan, T. (2002). A Fast and Elitist Multi-Objective Genetic Algorithm: NSGA-II. *Evolutionary Computation, 6.*

Kofman, E. (2004). Discrete Event Simulation of Hybrid Systems. *SIAM Journal on Scientific Computing, 25*(5), 1771–1797. doi:10.1137/S1064827502418379.

McDonald-Maier, K., & MuhammadYasir, Q. (2009). Data Cache-Energy and Throughput Models: Design Exploration for Embedded Processors. *EURASIP Journal on Embedded Systems, 2009,* 7.

Paci, G., F. P., Benini, L., & Marchal, P. (2007). Exploring temperature-aware design in low-power MPSoCs. *International Journal of Embedded Systems, 3.*

Yeager, K. C. (1996). The MIPS R10000 Superscalar Microprocessor. *IEEE Micro,* 16.

Zeigler, B. P. (1984a). *Multifacetted Modelling and Discrete Event Simulation.* London: Academic Press.

Zeigler, B. P. (1984b). *Theory of Modelling and Simulation.* Malabar, FL: Krieger Publishing Company.

Zeigler, B. P., Kim, T. G., & Praehofer, H. (2000). *Theory of Modeling and Simulation.* New York: Academic Press.

Chapter 5
Specification and Description Language for Discrete Simulation

Pau Fonseca i Casas
Universitat Politècnica de Catalunya - Barcelona Tech, Spain

ABSTRACT

Designing a new simulation model usually involves the participation of personnel with different knowledge of the system and with diverse formations. These personnel often use different languages, making more difficult the task to define the existing relations between the key model elements. These relations represent the hypotheses that constrain the model and the global behavior of the system, and this information must be obtained from the system experts. A formalism can be a powerful tool to understand the model complexity and helps in the communication between the different actors that participate in the definition of the model. In this chapter we review the use of the "Specification and Description Language," a standard and graphical language that simplifies the model understanding thanks to its modular nature. To do this we present a complete example, representing a simple queuing model that helps the reader to understand the structure and the nature of the language.

INTRODUCTION

The principal motivation of Operations Research (OR) is to understand the behavior of systems through representative models. Alternatives can be evaluated without interacting with or disturbing reality to choose the most appropriate system modification. Models can be used not only to compare alternatives but also to predict the

DOI: 10.4018/978-1-4666-4369-7.ch005

behavior of a known system when variables are modified within a specific range. Hence, operations research simulation models can yield solutions for possible future situations. The simulation field contains a variety of different paradigms to model a real system; this study uses a specification and description language to represent discrete-event simulation models. Based on (Law & Kelton, 2000) Law & Kelton (2000), Guasch, Piera, Casanovas, & Figueras (2002)(Guasch, Piera, Casanovas, & Figueras, 2002), and (Fishman, 2001) Fishman (2001), discrete-event simulation consists of three major methodologies: process interaction, activity scanning, and event scheduling.

The event-scheduling methodology is based on an initial description of events. Events are the elements of the model that cause modifications in the state variables of the model. A function is defined for each event. The functions are executed when the time associated with an event is the same as or very close to that shown on the model clock1. The events are sorted in an event list by their time and priority. The time between two events is irregular. The simulation clock therefore jumps from one time to the next without following any set pattern (Law & Kelton, 2000).

To model a system that is composed of a server that receives elements over time according to a specific distribution, different events can be generated that represent the elements entering the system if the intervals between the events are known. Similarly, if the distribution that defines the time that the server requires to process an element is known, an event that defines the service time for a specific element can be generated. This information is illustrated in Table 1.

From Table 1, the diagram (time chart) shown in Figure 1 can be generated.

This figure shows an M|M|1, following Kendall's notation (Kendall, 1953), is a representation of a system composed by one machine proceeded by a queue (FIFO)2. The initial state of the server is free, and the events shown in Table 1 define the behavior of the model. In the event-scheduling paradigm, one event is processed in each simulation loop and the procedure related to this event is executed. The pro-

Table 1. Events

Time between Arrivals		Service Time	
a1	35	b1	40
a2	12	b2	30
a3	29	b3	30
a4	47	b4	20
a5	12	b5	30

Figure 1. Event-scheduling time chart

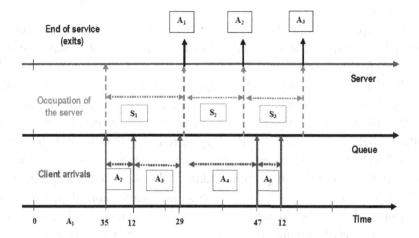

cedure definition and the event-selection procedure determine the behavior of the model. The specification and description language (SDL) is based on the description of the process that defines the action after the different simulation elements receive a specific event (SIGNAL in the realm of SDL). Therefore, this model is a discrete simulation paradigm, which is similar to an event scheduling approach.

DESCRIPTION OF SDL

History of SDL

The motivation behind presenting the history of SDL is to understand its evolution and to understand that it is an evolving language that attempts to meet the needs of the professionals that work with it. A good review on the history of SDL can be found in (Reed, SDL-2000 new presentation, 2000)Reed (2000), which is an online PowerPoint presentation that includes comments and is an excellent review of SDL-2000.

SDL is an object-oriented, formal language that is standardized by the International Telecommunication Union, Telecommunication Standardization Sector (ITU–T) (formerly Comité Consultatif International Télégraphique et Téléphonique [CCITT]) as Recommendation Z.100 (ITU-T, 1999). The language is designed to specify complex, event-driven, real-time, interactive applications that involve many concurrent activities using discrete signals to enable communication (Doldi, 2003;

ITU-T, 1999) (Doldi L., 2003). Additionally, SDL can be easily used in combination with UML.

The development of SDL began with an ITU study in 1968. The main concern of that study was to find a way to handle stored program control switching systems. The primary finding in that study (in 1972) was that it is necessary to develop languages for the specification of complex systems. In 1976, the first SDL standard, the Orange Book, which contains a simple graphical language, was produced.

In 1980, the Yellow Book, which contained the semantics for the processes, was published. Then, in 1984, the Red Book appeared, defining the structure and the data. The Red Book also included a more rigorous definition of the tools that were necessary to support the language. Some additional tools were developed that same year. The development of the first SDL tools significantly changed the evolution of SDL because the tools forced both the users and the designers to be more formal. Increasing the level of formalism implies an increased level of work that is required to define the language. However, some benefits arise from the formalism, such as the identification of errors in the syntax of the model and the capability to vary parameters to perform effective model simulations. In the early 1980s, computer graphics were just starting to be commonplace, and the prices of computers were becoming reasonable. Therefore, the tools to incorporate a graphical facility to simplify interactions with the user were developing.

Another interesting aspect is that because the users want to evaluate "what-if" scenarios, it is necessary to develop a program from the SDL representation of the model that can provide the different alternatives. In that sense, it is common that some SDL tools, such as Cinderella (CINDERELLA SOFTWARE, 2007) or PragmaDev (PragmaDev SARL, 2012), among others, allow for the automatic generation of code, usually C or C++ code, from the SDL representation of the model3.

In 1988, the Blue Book was published (SDL-88), with well-defined syntax and a formal definition of the language. Additionally, effective tools were developed.

The next version, SDL-92, included object-oriented types; in other words, blocks and processes could be assigned types, with associated inheritance and parameterization of the object instances. In 1996, an addendum was published, which added minor modifications to the language.

With the creation of tools that understand SDL, increased formalism is required to make the models capable of solving "what-if" questions. Solving "what-if" problems is an example of how validation and verification processes come together to achieve a common objective, that the tool and the model represent exactly what we want them to represent.

The message sequence chart (MSC) is an interaction diagram from the SDL family (see Figure 2). In concept, the MSC is similar to UML's sequence diagram, and it is standardized by the International Telecommunication Union. The definition of SDL lacks information describing how the signals travel through the system; MSC defines the communication behavior in real-time systems; specifically, telecommunication electronic switching systems.

In 1992, MSC appeared as a separate standard. MSC had been proposed as a standard in 1989, and then, in 1996, major additions to the standard were published. Some studies have explained how to harmonize UML sequence diagrams and MSC (Rudolph, Grabowski, & Graubmann, 1999). The 1996 version introduced high-level message sequence charts (HMSC) (ITU-TS, 1997), the MSC system for expressing state diagrams. In the latest version of MSC (2000) (ITU-TS, 2004), object orientation was included, the use of data and time in the diagrams was refined, and the concept of a remote method call was added. SDL-2000 was designed to address two important issues. One requirement was the ability to link with object modeling, specifically UML, and the other was to improve the implementation ability of SDL or, more specifically, to simplify the automatic generation of an implementation through code generation. The changes implemented to meet those requirements

Figure 2. MSC obtained from PragmaDev MSC Tracer © [2013 [PragmaDev]. Used with permission.

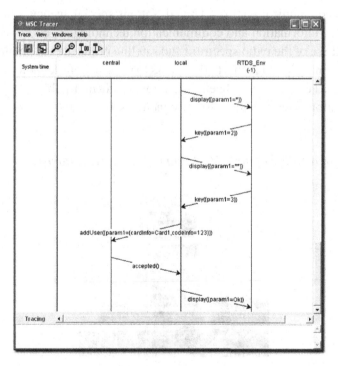

include exception handling and the introduction of textual algorithms to be used on diagrams. More details on SDL-2000 can be found in (Reed, SDL-2000 form New Millenium Systems, 2000) Reed (2000).

The upcoming version of SDL (SDL-2010) improves the language in many ways; specifically, for the scope of discrete simulation, it allows the definition of delays and priorities implicit in the signals, thus simplifying the representation of the dynamic behavior of the model.

One of the main attributes of SDL is that it can be considered to be a bridge between specification and implementation because it supports modeling at an abstract level but also details a complete unambiguous description of the implementation. One of the strengths of SDL is that the users have the power of a clear and formal textual syntax, and another strength is the ease-of-use that is provided by having a clear graphical representation.

SDL is also related to other ITU-T standards and, with MSC, provides a complete solution for the specification and design of systems. SDL can also be integrated with ASN.1 for protocol definition and with TTCN for validation and testing.

ITU Standards

The International Telecommunication Union (ITU, from French: Union Internationale des Télécommunications) is a United Nations special agency. This agency is responsible for information and communication technologies, coordination of the shared global use of the radio spectrum and satellite orbits, development of technical standards, and improvements to the access to information technologies by world communities. ITU has always been an intergovernmental public/private partnership organization. Membership currently includes 191 countries (member states)

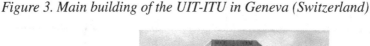

Figure 3. Main building of the UIT-ITU in Geneva (Switzerland)

and more than 700 public and private sector companies. International and regional telecommunication entities (sector members and associates) are also represented.

The standardization work of ITU started with the birth of the International Telegraph Union, which became a United Nations special agency in 1947. The International Telegraph and Telephone Consultative Committee (CCITT, from French: Comité Consultatif International Téléphonique et Télégraphique) was created in 1956. This agency was renamed ITU-T in 1993.

The ITU Telecommunication Standardization Sector (ITU-T) is one of the three divisions of the International Telecommunication Union (ITU). The main mission of ITU-T is the coordination of standards for telecommunications.

The Telecommunication Standardization Bureau (TSB) is the permanent secretariat of the ITU-T. It is located at the ITU headquarters in Geneva, Switzerland (see Figure 3).

ITU is one of the most universally well-recognized information and telecommunications standards disseminators. As an example, in 2007, ITU-T produced over 160 new and revised standards (named ITU-T Recommendations).

All of the ITU standards are called "recommendations" because they recommend standards to national bodies. The generation of these standards is the result of collaborative work. These standards are unambiguous, clear, precise, easy to use, easy to communicate, and easy to learn. The standards also support analysis, modeling, abstraction, and, importantly, product development, such that several tools currently understand the language. SDL and MSC have become international standards that are well-supported by many commercially available tools (as of 2000: Cinderella from Cinderella [CINDERELLA SOFTWARE, 2007], SDL, IBM SDL Suite [IBM, 2009], and PragmaDev RTDS[PragmaDev SARL, 2012]). A UML profile based on SDL has been standardized by ITU-T: Z.109.

Figure 4. SDL levels

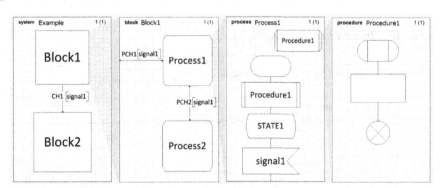

Specification and Description Language

To define a simulation model, its structure and its behavior must be defined. SDL allows the user to define the structure, behavior, and other aspects, as follows:

- **Structure:** System, blocks, processes and hierarchy of the processes.
- **Behavior:** Defined through the different processes.
- **Data:** Based on abstract data types (ADT).
- **Communication:** Signals, and the parameters and channels that the signals use to travel.
- **Inheritances:** Used to describe the relationships between, and specialization of, the model elements.

Figure 5. System diagram (Doldi L., 2003). Three BLOCKS compose this model, block1, block2 and block3. The communication mechanism between them is represented by the channels. In this case, delaying channels are used, which are called DLCaSU, DLCbSU and DLCaDL.

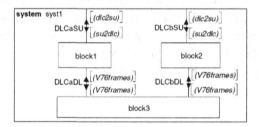

Figure 6. SDL block diagram (Doldi, 2003)

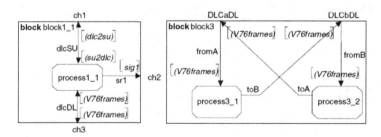

Table 2. Some important SDL blocks used in PROCESS diagrams

	Start. Defines the first operation to be executed at the initial state of a process. This operation can be used to define the initial conditions of a simulation model.
	State. A state element contains the name of a state. This element defines the states of behavioral diagrams (such as PROCESS diagrams).
	Input. Input elements describe the types of events that can be received by a process. All of the branches of a specific state start with an Input element because an object changes its state only when a new event is received.
	Create. This element allows the creation of an SDL AGENT.c
	Task. This element allows the interpretation of informal text, semi-formal actions (C code), or formal actions (SDL action language). In this chapter, following SDL-RT (PragmaDev SARL, 2006), we use C code here.
	Procedure call. These elements perform a procedure call. A PROCEDURE can be defined in the last level of the SDL language. It can be used to encapsulate pieces of the model for its reuse.
	Output. These elements describe the type of SIGNAL to be sent, the parameters that the signal carries and the destination or the CHANNEL the SIGNAL must follow. Other attributes of the event can also be detailed (e.g., priority, delay).
	Decision. These elements describe bifurcations. Their behavior depends on how a related question is answered.

The language is modular, allowing either top-down or bottom-up modeling and simplifying the validation of complex systems. The language has 4 levels: (i) SYSTEM, (ii) BLOCKS, (iii) PROCESSES and (iv) PROCEDURES, as shown in Figure 4. SYSTEMS, BLOCKS and PROCESSES are called AGENTS.

SDL System Diagrams

System diagrams represent all of the objects that make up a model and the communication channels between them. A SYSTEM is the outermost agent that communicates with the environment. Figure 5 shows a system that contains three blocks [12].

SDL Block Diagrams

The next stage in SDL specification is the construction of a block diagram for each of the different BLOCKS defined in the system diagram. Figure 6 represents the block diagram for the block1 and block3 elements defined above (Doldi, 2003(Doldi L., 2003)).

Each rectangle represents a BLOCK. The lines that join the BLOCKS are the communication channels (bidirectional or unidirectional communication elements). The channels are joined to the objects through ports. Ports are important elements for implementing and reusing objects because they ensure the independence of the different objects. An AGENT only knows its own ports, which are the doors through which it communicates with its environment.

Each BLOCK has a name specified by the block keyword. The block diagram contains a number of PROCESSES and can also contain other BLOCKS (also mixed with PROCESSES in SDL-2000). PROCESSES communicate via channels (in versions previous to SDL-2000, signal routes can be used), which connect to other PROCESSES or channels external to the BLOCK.

SDL Processes

The PROCESSES is an AGENT that describes the behavior. Each of the PROCESSES of an AGENT has one or more states. For each of the states of a PROCESS, SDL describes how the state behaves depending on the different SIGNALS that can be received (events from the point of view of a discrete simulation). An AGENT can

Figure 7. SDL process diagram (Doldi, 2003)

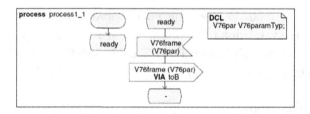

Figure 8. SDL PROCEDURE and PROCEDURECALL. C is used to represent the code of the SDL model following SDL-RT (PragmaDev SARL, 2006).

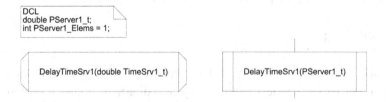

also react differently to a SIGNAL, depending on the port that sends the SIGNAL. The PROCESS is defined using graphical elements that describe operations or decisions. Table 2 shows some of the elements used in the SDL PROCESS diagrams to represent the model behavior. Figure 7 shows an example of an SDL PROCESS.

SDL Procedures

The last level of the specification and description language is the definition of the different procedures that appear in the SDL diagrams.

PROCEDURES allow parts of the PROCESS to be encapsulated to increase the readability. As an example, Figure 8 shows a PROCEDURE called DelayTimeSrv1 that calculates the time needed to perform an operation. The procedure is declared in the PROCEDURE element and can be used throughout the PROCESS with the PROCEDURECALL block.

Often, from the point of view of model understanding, it is not necessary to define what occurs inside PROCEDURES. However, to obtain the code or to perform

Figure 9. Relation between the non-graphical SDL and the graphical SDL

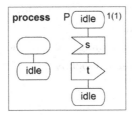

Figure 10. Non-delaying channels

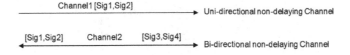

Figure 11. Delaying channels

an execution from the SDL specification, PROCEDURES must be completely defined.

The diagrams assist in the description and the specification of the model, detailing the most important aspects at the necessary level, depending on the target requirements.

To learn more about SDL, recommendation Z.100 (ITU-T, 1999) can be consulted, or information can be reviewed online at www.sdl-forum.org or in (SDL Tutorial) SDS Tutorial (Reed, Re: SDL-News: Request for Help: Initialisation of Pids, 2000) or (Doldi L., 2003)Doldi (2003), among other sources.

SDLP/PR

A textual SDL exists (see an example in Figure 9). This non-graphical SDL is not used in this study. The representation capabilities of the two SDL forms are equivalent (ITU-T, 1999).

SDL Channels

An SDL CHANNEL is the path that the SIGNALS follow to reach their final destination. They connect AGENTS between them or AGENTS with the environment. They can be uni- or bi-directional, they can have identifiers, and they can retain lists of all of the signals that they carry.

From the point of view of the management of the SIGNALS that a CHANNEL receives, a CHANNEL is a path that, depending on its nature, might introduce a delay.

Figure 12. SIGNAL declaration

```
SIGNAL
Sig1, Sig2(INTEGER), Sig3;
```

Figure 13. Explicit signal routing using TO

```
SIG TO PServer1
```

Two main types of channels exist, which are the delaying and non-delaying channels. Non-delaying channels do not introduce any delay in the transmission of the SIGNALS. Thus, the SIGNALS reach their destinations immediately (at least from the point of view of the model's logic).

The representation of non-delaying channels is shown in Figure 10.

The delaying channels, as shown in Figure 11, introduce a delay in the transmission of the SIGNAL. The delay cannot be defined in SDL because, from the point of view of a discrete simulation, delaying channels cannot be used. It is necessary to completely control the model representation of the delays, as shown in Table 1.

In the following section, the representation of time in SDL discrete simulation models will be described.

SDL Signals

SIGNALS in SDL represent the events that trigger the behavior of the simulation model. Each of the SIGNALS must be defined in a text area, as shown in Figure 12.

The declaration of a signal includes the type of signal and identifies whether the signal carries a parameter. Once the SIGNALS are defined, they are assigned to different CHANNELS in the model. It is easy to define the paths that the events must follow in the diagrams; however, sometimes a SIGNAL that must be sent from one PROCESS to another PROCESS can use different channels to reach its destination. Additionally, it is possible that different CHANNELS share the SIGNALS that

Figure 14. All of the SDL PROCESSES have a FIFO queue to process the SIGNALS that arrive at the AGENT.

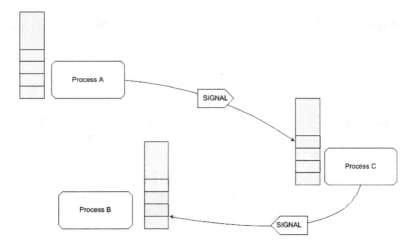

can travel through them; hence, an addressing mechanism is needed to avoid sending a SIGNAL to a different PROCESS than the target.

To accomplish the foregoing steps, SDL allows the user to define the destination of an OUTPUT in several ways. If nothing is specified, then the destination is implicit. Usually, the use of an implicit destination occurs when only one destination is possible. If more than one destination is possible, then one of the PROCESSES receives the SIGNAL; however, it is not certain which of the possible destinations actually receives the SIGNAL. To avoid this ambiguity, it is preferable to use explicit addressing.

With explicit addressing, we can specify a PId (process identifier) that unequivocally identifies a PROCESS in the model (i.e., the PROCESS that must receive the SIGNAL). In other words, the keyword to can be used to identify the PROCESS that must receive the SIGNAL (see Figure 13).

With respect to the PId, no rules exist to define this identifier; SDL requires only that all of the PROCESSES in the model have a unique PId.

Four keywords obtain specific PIss from the model, as follows:

- **SELF:** Returns the PIs of the PROCESS itself.
- **SENDER:** Returns the PIs of the PROCESS from which the last SIGNAL came.

Figure 15. Passing parameters in the SIGNALS. In the figure, two PROCESSES are sharing information through the parameters of the SIGNALS.

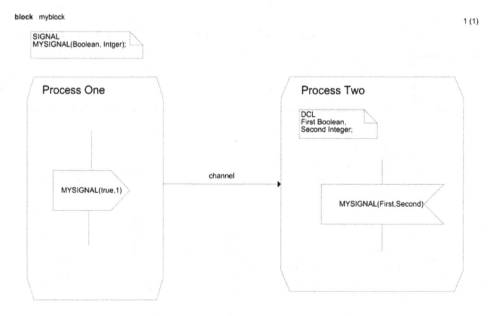

- **OFFSPRING:** Returns the PIs of the last PROCESS that was created by the CREATE element in the current PROCESS.
- **PARENT:** Returns the PIs of the PROCESS that created the current PROCESS.

SDL can also route the SIGNALS using the VIA method. In this case, we can specify the channel that we want to use to send the SIGNAL to its final destination. Thus, it is possible to broadcast a SIGNAL with VIA ALL.

Each SIGNAL is processed and discarded following the arrival order. All of the SIGNALS are queued in a FIFO queue that belongs to the PROCESS, as shown in Figure 14. In SDL-2010, the order can be modified by using the delay parameter, as discussed in section 2.3.8.

The SIGNALS in SDL can also include passing parameters. As an example (see Figure 15), a SIGNAL A sends two parameters (True, 5). The PROCESS that receives the signal P2 contains a declaration of two variables, V1 of type Boolean and V2 of type Integer. When the SIGNAL A is received, the INPUT elements of these two variables are filled with the values sent by PROCESS P1.

If no variables are defined in the INPUT element of the P2 process, then the values are discarded; it is important to be certain that the types are compatible with the values that are received. It is also possible to ignore some values by simply not including them. As an example, we can define "INPUT A(,V2)." In this case, the first value, the Boolean, is discarded.

Because the management of the delays in the simulation model is a key aspect of the model, the manner in which SDL manages delays will be reviewed in the following section.

Working with Time in SDL

In a discrete simulator, to completely define the behavior of a model, it is necessary to describe the time connected to the execution of each of the different events involved in its functions. Usually, each type of event has a specific probability distribution

Figure 16. A delayable SDL signal. Note that this signal needs 2 units of time to reach its destination. Furthermore, the priority is defined to avoid ambiguity that exists if two signals with the same execution time reach the destination at the same time.

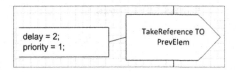

that decides when the event must be executed. In an event-scheduling simulator, the engine manages the timing of all of the events and decides where and when all of the events must be sent to other simulation elements, or AGENTS, in an SDL model.

SDL has two main structures for managing time, timers and delaying channels (ITU-T, 1999).

Delaying channels cannot be used as a mechanism for representing the delays in a simulation model because no mechanism exists in SDL to define the time that is required to reach the destination using the channels. The delaying channel represents a delay in the transmission of the signal, but we cannot define the probability distribution that rules the delay. Timers and the other mechanisms that are available in SDL to manage time cannot handle simulation delays because for each different instance of a signal that can travel in parallel, a new timer must be defined. For example, if a signal must be sent to represent the arrival of new entities at a machine, then each time that a new arrival is sent to this machine, the timer is reprogrammed, implying that if the signal has not arrived to its final destination, it can be lost. Only one instance of the signal represented by the timer can travel through the system at a time. Additionally, an important feature of discrete simulation models is that priorities cannot be set using timers.

Figure 17. This diagram shows the main representation of the system. The interaction of the system and the environment is defined at this level. The events that are being sent from the main elements (SDL agents) of the model can also be observed. In this case, the events are FinishService1, FinishService2, NewService1 and NewService2.

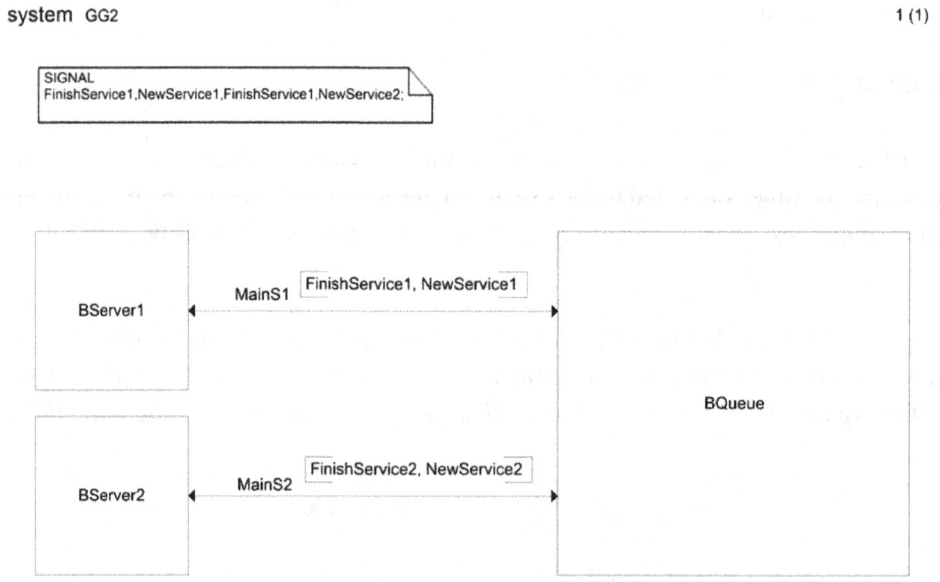

160

The problem of how to manage delays in SDL has been studied by several authors (Bozga, Graf, Mounier, Kerbrat, Ober, & Vincent, 2000;(Bozga M., Graf, Mounier, Kerbrat, Ober, & Vincent, 2000) (Bozga M., Graf, Mounier, Ober, Roux, & Vincent, 2001) Bozga, Graf, Mounier, Ober, Roux, & Vincent, 2001). In (Bozga M., Graf, Mounier, Ober, Roux, & Vincent, 2001)Bozga, Graf, Mounier, Ober, Roux, & Vincent (2001), an extension that defines three types of transitions, (i) eager (i.e., consumed without delay), (ii) lazy (i.e., not urgent) and (iii) delayable (has an enabling condition depending on time), are presented. In that study, the authors note that an eager transition is equivalent to a delayable transition with the temporal condition set to now=x (Bozga M., Graf, Mounier, Ober, Roux, & Vincent, 2001) (Bozga, Graf, Mounier, Ober, Roux, & Vincent, 2001). In general, an event in an event-scheduling simulation engine can carry the following as parameters: (i) ExecutionTime, or delay representing the time when the event must be executed; (ii) Priority, the priority of the event, which is used to avoid a possible simultane-

Figure 18. Decomposition of BlockServer1. In this case, inside the structure of the element, only one PROCESS is defined. The PServer1 PROCESS must contain the description of the behavior of BlockServer1 of the model.

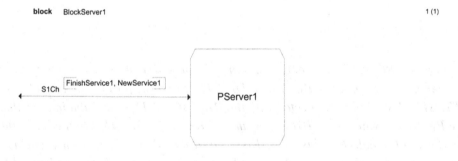

Figure 19. Decomposition of the BQueue. A single PROCESS defines its behavior. Two channels allow communication with both servers of the model.

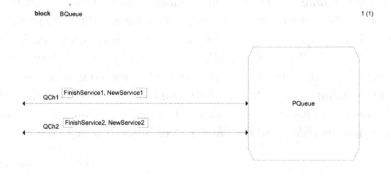

ity of events; (iii) CreationTime, representing the time when the event is created; (iv) Id, an identifier of the event; and (v) Time, the clock of the process (represents the time related to the last event processed by the process). From the point of view of a discrete simulator, all of the transitions can be considered delayable because all of the events have a time that defines when they can be executed. With these considerations in mind, some extensions were proposed (Fonseca i Casas, Colls, & Casanovas, Towards a representation of environmenal models using specification and description language, 2010)(Fonseca i Casas, Colls, & Casanovas, 2010; Fonseca i Casas, Colls, Casanovas, & Josep, 2010; (Fonseca i Casas P., Colls, Casanovas, & Josep, 2010) (Casas & Pau, 2010) Casas & Pau, 2010)and finally incorporated into the latest version of SDL (SDL-2010) to simplify the representation of time delays, as follows:

1.   All of the signals can have a delay time. In other words, each signal instance output has a parameter that defines the time that is required to travel to its final destination (i.e., a delay or the value of the ExecutionTime value minus the current time) and a parameter that defines the priority with respect to other signal instances in the destination input queue scheduled for the same time (i.e., the same ExecutionTime value). A signal instance is, therefore, only available

Figure 20. PROCESS PServer1, describing the behavior of the server. Two states are defined in this process, BUSY and IDLE. The first state for the process is IDLE. (The START symbol is connected with the IDLE state.) This situation implies that the PROCESS waits in the IDLE state until it receives a SIGNAL, in this case, the NewService1 signal. Once this SIGNAL is received, the PROCEDURE DelayTimeSrv1 is executed, obtaining a value for the PServer1_1 variable. This value is used to represent the delay of the EndService SIGNAL that is sent from the PROCESS to itself. As seen in the diagram, once the EndService SIGNAL is sent, the PROCESS waits in the BUSY state, representing in the model that the system machine is performing some action with the entity. In the BUSY state, the PROCESS receives the EndService SIGNAL (previously sent by itself with a delay calculated by the DelayTimeSrv1 PROCEDURE). This SIGNAL causes the PROCESS to increment the value of the number of elements served (PServer1_Elems) and generates a report with this information (report PROCEDURE that is not defined in this example). To inform the queue that the server is again IDLE, a SIGNAL (FinishService1) is sent to the queue with no delay, and the PROCESS changes its state to IDLE.

continued on following page

Figure 20. Continued

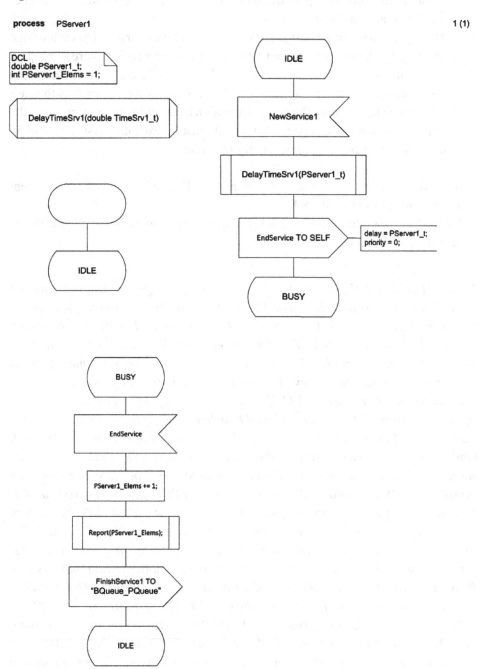

in the destination input port when the current time is greater than or equal to the ExecutionTime value.

2. The signals in the input port are scanned in a set order (first by ExecutionTime and then by the order of arrival time) to determine whether there is a signal that is enabled. For inputs with the same ExecutionTime and the same arrival time, the signal priority determines which signal is processed first. In the case when two signals have the same ExecutionTime and the same priority, the implementation must define what signal must be executed first (because, in that case, the model does not specify the order).

In this chapter, the convenient solution shown in Figure 16 is adopted to represent time and priorities in the SIGNALS.

With all of the system parts defined, a simple system composed by a FIFO queue with two identical servers can now be modeled.

Figure 21. This PROCESS defines the behavior of the Queue. The behavior for the EMPTY state is described. The PROCESS starts by defining the time of the first arrival (in the ArrivalTime PROCEDURE, using the PQUEUE_t variable). A SIGNAL (NewArrival) is sent to itself to represent the arrival of the first client to the system. In the initialization step, two variables, S1_available and S2_available (which represent the states of the servers), are initialized to 1, showing that both servers are IDLE. On an EMPTY state, the queue can receive three different signals, NewArrival, FinishService1 and FinishService2. If the PROCESS receives FinishService1 (signifying that the server has finished its operation), the QUEUE modifies the value that represents the state of the server S1_available to 1 (the server is now free) and remains in the EMPTY state (this procedure is the same for FinishService2). If NewArrival is received by the PROCESS, a NewArrival SIGNAL must be generated (this is usual in every event scheduling entity generation process). Once this procedure is finished, an available server must be found. The first server is inspected first (which shows an inherent prioritization for the first server). If Server1 is available, then we modify the variable showing that it is now BUSY, and we send an immediate SIGNAL to server1. Because the QUEUE does not have elements waiting, it remains in the EMPTY state. If the first server is BUSY, but the second is IDLE (S2_available DECISION), then the process is equivalent (now both servers are working. If both servers are BUSY, then the QUEUE must increment the number of elements waiting (PQueue_Elems +=1;), send or write a report, and change its state to NOEMPTY.

continued on following page

Figure 21. Continued

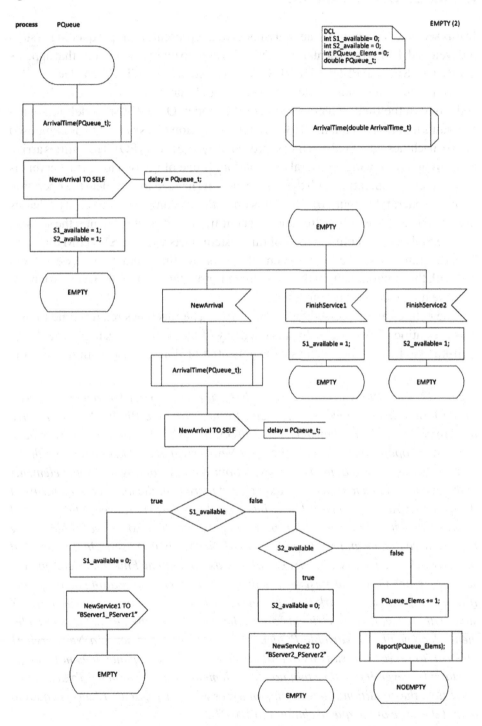

165

A SIMPLE GG2 EXAMPLE

In this section, an example of an SDL model that represents a simple queuing system is developed. In this representation, ANSI C is used to represent the code that appears in PROCESSES and PROCEDURES, as suggested in SDL-RT (PragmaDev SARL, 2006), because this choice often creates a model that more closely resembles the code used in the final implementation of the model. Our G|G|24 model, following Kendall's notation (Kendall, 1953), is a representation of a system that is composed of two machines (identical machines) preceded by a queue (FIFO). The entities arrive at the system following a general distribution. If one of the two identical servers is free, it starts its operation with the entity (the time needed to complete the operation is also a general distribution). Once this operation is completed, the entity releases the server (the server is now free and other entities in the queue can enter the server).

The SDL model representation of this system starts with the SYSTEM diagram. This diagram shows the main system elements and the interaction between them and with the environment. In this case, there is no interaction with the environment because the model is self-contained.

The entities are processed by the machines. The machines require time to process the entities. This time, which is the delay of the operation, is represented by a well-known distribution, such as an exponential or Poisson distribution. Once the

Figure 22. This PROCESS defines the behavior of the QUEUE agent. The NO-EMPTY state is described in this agent. In this state, the PROCESS can receive the FinishService1 and FinishService2 SIGNALS (showing that the servers have finished the operation with the entity) or a NewArrival SIGNAL, announcing that a new entity has arrived at the system (with both servers working and some elements in the queue). In this last case, the queue must increment the number of elements in the queue (PQueue_Elems+=1;), write or send a report (if desired) and, as usual in an event scheduling generation process, generate the next arrival (calculating the next arrival time and sending the SIGNAL NewArrival to itself). In the case that the SIGNAL received is FinishService1 (or its equivalent FinishService2 for the second server), the queue must see whether some elements are waiting in the queue. If not, the queue must mark that the server is IDLE and return it to the EMPTY state. Otherwise, if some elements are in the queue, then the queue takes one element (decrements the variable PQueue_Elems by one) and sends a NewService1 SIGNAL to server 1 to start its operation. In that case, the queue does not change its state; however, it could be that no other elements are in the queue. To detect this condition, the condition is added that analyzes whether PQueue_Elems is equal to 0, and the state of the queue changes to EMPTY.

continued on following page

Figure 22. Continued

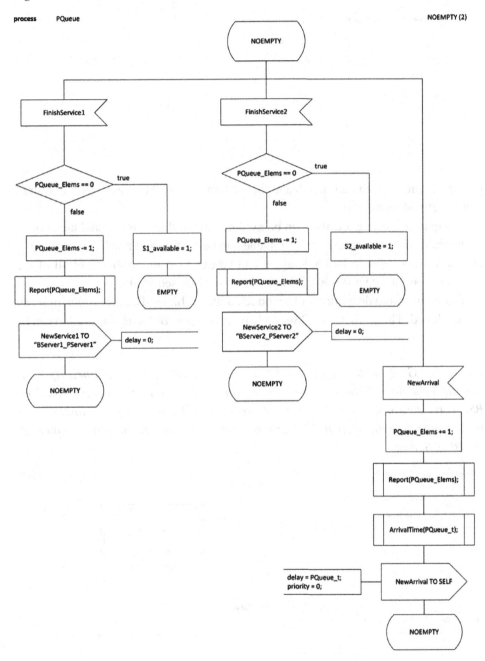

Figure 23. BlockServer type defining the generic behavior of the server

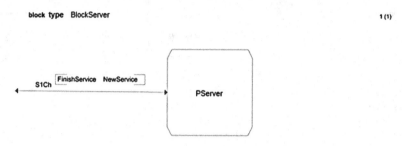

process is finished, the entities leave the system. Figure 17 represents the system that is defined using SDL.

In Figure 17, the agents that can be executed in parallel in the model are shown. In this case, the two servers and the queue can be in different machines. All of the events that are inside a BLOCK agent can be executed in parallel, and all of the events that are inside a PROCESS agent are executed sequentially.

From this initial definition of the model, a hierarchical SDL decomposition can be developed. The elements of BServer1, BServer2 and BQueue (Figure 19) can be

Figure 24. GG2 model using instantiation. The model can be defined by writing the behavior of the different servers once. Both servers are described on BServer(2,2):BlockServer. The first "2" represents the number of instances at the beginning, while the second "2" represents the maximum number of instances of the BlockServer.

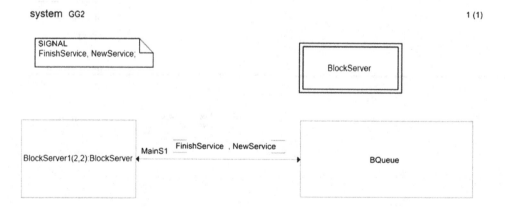

Figure 25. PServer PROCESS now can be used by all of the servers in the model. The main difference is that the FinishService SIGNAL now represents the end of the service for all of the servers in the model.

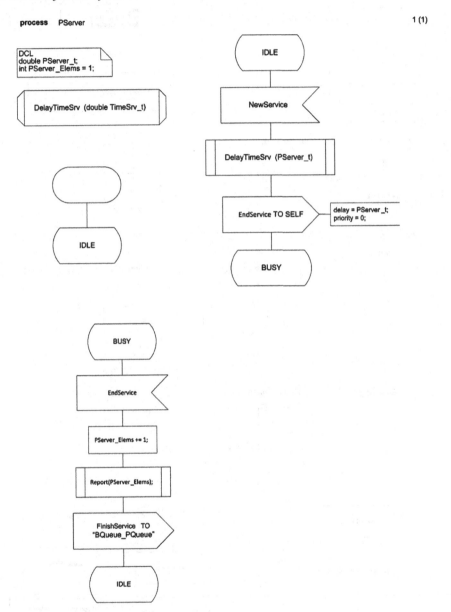

Figure 26. Definition of the PQueue PROCESS for the EMPTY state

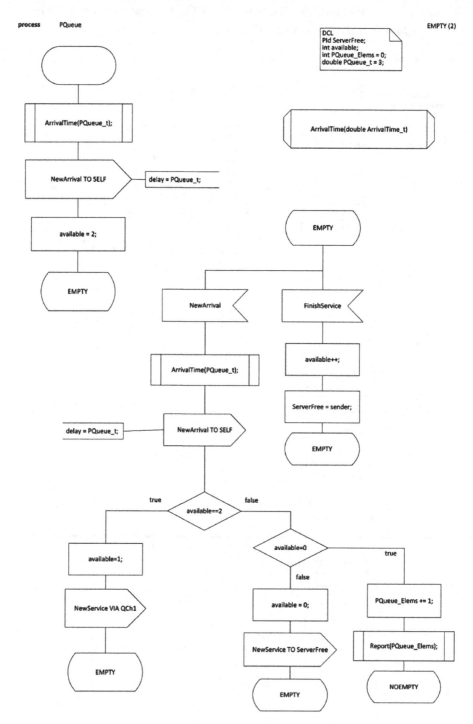

Figure 27. Definition of the PQueue PROCESS for the NOEMPTY state

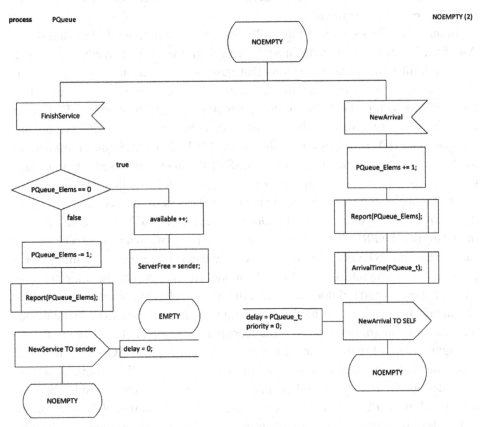

defined. For each one of these blocks, its complete behavior can be defined based on the definition of new BLOCKS. Finally, some PROCESSES must be defined that detail the specific behavior of the model.

Figure 18 shows the structure of the server. In this case, only one PROCESS is defined.

The channel describes how the SIGNALS (which represent the events in the simulation model) travel through the model. Until this point, the model contained only the description of the structure of the model. The diagrams that define the behavior of the model begin with the PROCESS diagrams. Figure 20 shows the process that defines the behavior of the first server (PServer1). Both of the servers are equivalent. SDL allows the definition of objects and, through inheritance, the definition of instances; in section 3.1, the method SDL uses to manage inheritance is described. Using inheritance, one definition of a server can be used for all of the identical servers in the model.

In the PROCESS shown in Figure 20, two states are defined, BUSY and IDLE. All of the PROCESS diagrams in SDL begin with the START symbol, "Ò." This symbol defines the initial transitions that must be executed in each of the model PROCESSES and, hence, the initial conditions for each one of the different PRO-CESSES. As seen in the diagram, the server starts its execution in the IDLE state. From the point of view of the discrete simulation, between the START symbol and the first state (IDLE in this case), the events (SDL SIGNALS) that initialize the model are sent. As shown in the PROCESS of the queue, the events that are sent represent the generation of the first model elements (clients that are going to be served by one of the two servers). Once the process is in one STATE, it remains there until it receives a SIGNAL. Once it receives a SIGNAL (representing a model event), the PROCESS starts its execution, finishing in a new STATE (which can be the same STATE). The report PROCEDURE represents something that is performed with the information from the model (such as record the information in a file or show a chart); it does not affect the model behavior, but it is necessary to obtain information from the model. Depending on the tool used to code the model, this procedure might not be used if the reports can be obtained from the tool.

Figure 21 and Figure 22 detail the behavior of the queue AGENT. The initial conditions of the model are defined in Figure 21. A PROCEDURE named Arrival-Time defines the time required between two arrivals. Once this value is obtained, it is stored in the PQueue_t variable (see the declaration in the DCL block on the right side of the figure). This variable is used to delay the reception of the SIGNAL (representing the time needed for the first customer to arrive at the system). The SDL-2010 DELAY SIGNAL parameter is used to accomplish this step. During initialization, the state of the servers is stored in the two variables, S1_available and S2_available; thus, the location to send the new customers is known. This step is required because SDL is a modular language (i.e., the state of the other PROCESSES cannot be accessed), and there is no assurance that the implementation of the model will include a shared memory mechanism that allows direct access to the variables of other AGENTS. The only way to know the state of the other AGENTS is to store this information locally or to send a SIGNAL. In addition, each SDL PROCESS can be executed on a different computer.

This simple example illustrates the use of SDL to model a well-known system. In this example, two identical elements are modeled twice; however, with SDL, a class of AGENTS was defined, allowing the reuse of model components. In the next section, this model is reviewed and defined in a simpler way.

SDL Instantiation and Inheritance

SDL is an object-oriented language, accepting instantiation and inheritance as a standard way of defining common behavior for different elements of the model.

Instantiation allows defining from an AGENT TYPE specific instances that can be used inside the simulation model. Each one of the new instances has a different PId.

Inheritance is a general mechanism that applies to interaction diagrams, to behavior diagrams and to data types (Reed, SDL-2000 form New Millenium Systems, 2000)(Reed, 2000). In data types, it is allowed to add new operations. In PROCESS diagrams, we can add new transitions that can lead to new states. For example, if it is desired for Server 2 to define server breakdown, then the diagram can be extended to show what happens, specifically for Server 2, when the SIGNAL NewBreakdown is received. To represent what parts can be rewritten, SDL uses the word redefined. None of the other parts can be changed. Because an AGENT can inherit from an AGENT that inherits from another AGENT (and so on), the system must determine when no more modifications can be performed. To express this criterion, SDL uses the word finalized, which signifies that the new subclasses cannot be modified. On the header of the AGENT that implements a new instance, it must clearly be indicated that the definition is a type with the keyword inherits.

Similar to in an instantiation, the AGENT that inherits from an agent type obtains a new PId.

With these considerations, it is easy to rewrite the model with a single BLOCK defining both servers and with the same name for the SIGNALS that travel from one AGENT to the other (using the TO parameter, as shown in the example).

First, it is necessary to define a BLOCK class that defines the generic behavior of the server (see Figure 23).

Then, it is easy to rewrite the main diagram showing the similar behavior of both servers (see Figure 24).

If needed, extra functionality can be added to the definition of the BLOCKS BServer1 and BServer2.

The diagrams show that PQueue prioritizes the use of Server 1; thus, if both servers are free, the SIGNAL is always sent to the first server (see Figures 26 and 27). This process is conducted using the VIA parameter (it is not necessary to know the PId of the PROCESS).

When one of the two servers is free, the destination of the SIGNAL must be known. In that case, a PId variable, ServerFree, is used to store the PId of the PROCESS that represents the Server that is currently available. (If both servers are free, then this variable is unnecessary because the elements are sent to the first server).

With the above considerations, the model is rewritten as follows. Both PServer1 and PServer2 are now represented by a single PROCESS named PServer, which is defined inside the BServer BLOCK that inherits from BlockServer (see Figure 25).

Several other alternatives exist to handle different instances of an AGENT type; the most common alternative is to save the different PIds for the elements where the SIGNALS are to be sent. A common procedure to initialize the values is reviewed in (Reed, Re: SDL-News: Request for Help: Initialisation of Pids, 2000)Reed (2000).

TO LEARN MORE

SDL is a modern language that is under continuous evolution. However, it has standard, clear and concise documentation generated by the ITU-T, which helps in the understanding of the language elements and also helps to implement tools based on this language.

The main documentation of the language can be obtained from the ITU-T website, and other documentation sources exist, such as (Doldi L., 2003) Doldi (2001; 2003), (Doldi L., 2001)ITU-T (1999), (ITU-T, 1999)ITU-TS (2004) or (SDL Tutorial) SDL Tutorial. The best source of current information is located on the Website of the SDL Forum Society at http://sdl-forum.org/.

In this section, the SDL language is introduced, and its use in the field of operations research is discussed using an interactive example that represents a simple queuing model. However, SDL is a powerful language that can be used to describe the behavior and the structure of more than interactive models. Some examples of further research can be found in Fischer, Kühnlenz, Ahrens, & Eveslage (2009) (Fischer, Kühnlenz, Ahrens, & Eveslage, 2009), Fonseca i Casas, Colls, Casanovas, & Josep (2010(Fonseca i Casas P., Colls, Casanovas, & Josep, 2010)), (Fonseca, Colls, & Casanovas, 2011)Fonseca, Colls, & Casanovas (2011), Rodríguez-Cayetano (2011)(Rodríguez-Cayetano, 2011), (Braun, Gotzhein, & Wiebel, 2011)Braun, Gotzhein, & Wiebel (2011), (Kraemer, Slåtten, & Herrmann, 2009) Kraemer, Slåtten, & Herrmann (2009), or (Weigert, et al., 2007)Weigert et al., 2007.

REFERENCES

Bozga, M., Graf, S., Mounier, L., Kerbrat, A., Ober, I., & Vincent, D. (2000). SDL for Real-Time: What Is Missing? SAM'2000. Grenoble, France.

Bozga, M., Graf, S., Mounier, L., Ober, I., Roux, J.-L., & Vincent, D. (2001). Timed Extensions for SDL. In Proceedings of SDL-Forum'01. Copenhagen, Denmark: SDL.

Braun, T., Gotzhein, R., & Wiebel, M. (2011). Integration of FlexRay into the SDL-Model-Driven Development Approach. In Kraemer, F., & Herrmann, P. (Eds.), *System Analysis and Modeling: About Models* (pp. 56–71). Berlin, Germany: Springer. doi:10.1007/978-3-642-21652-7_4.

Casas, F. I. (2010). Using Specification and Description Language to define and implement discrete simulation models. In Proceedings of the 2010 Summer Simulation Multiconference. Ottawa, Canada: SCS.

CINDERELLA SOFTWARE. (2007). Cinderella SDL. Retrieved March 31, 2009, from http://www.cinderella.dk

Doldi, L. (2001). *Sdl illustrated - Visually design executable models.* TRANSMETH SUD OUEST.

Doldi, L. (2003). *Validation of Communications Systems with SDL: The Art of SDL Simulation and Reachability Analysis.* New York: John Wiley & Sons, Inc. doi:10.1002/0470014156.

Fischer, J., Kühnlenz, F., Ahrens, K., & Eveslage, I. (2009). Model-based Development of Self-organizing Earthquake Early Warning Systems. In I. Troch, & F. Breitenecker (Eds.), Proceedings of MATHMOD 2009. Vienna, Austria: ARGESIM.

Fishman, G. S. (2001). *Discrete-Event Simulation: Modeling, Programming and Analysis.* Berlin, Germany: Springer-Verlag. doi:10.1007/978-1-4757-3552-9.

Fonseca, P., Colls, M., & Casanovas, J. (2011). A novel model to predict a slab avalanche configuration using m:n-CAk cellular automata. *Computers, Environment and Urban Systems, 35*(1), 12–24. doi:10.1016/j.compenvurbsys.2010.07.002.

Fonseca i Casas, P., Colls, M., & Casanovas, J. (2010). Towards a representation of environmenal models using specification and description language. In Proceedings on the International Joint Conference on Knowledge Discovery, Knowledge Engineering and Knowledge Management. Valencia, Spain: Springer.

Fonseca i Casas, P., Colls, M., Casanovas, J., & Josep, C. G. (2010). *Representing Fibonacci function through cellular automata using specification and description language.* Ottawa, Canada.

Guasch, A., Piera, M. À., Casanovas, J., & Figueras, J. (2002). *Modelado y simulación.* Barcelona, Spain: Edicions UPC.

IBM. (2009). Retrieved from http://publib.boulder.ibm.com/infocenter/rsdp/v1r0m0/index.jsp?topic=/com.ibm.help.download.sdlttcn.doc/topics/sdlttcn_download63.html

IBM. (2009). TELELOGIC. Retrieved March 31, 2009, from http://www.telelogic. com/

ITU-T. (1999). Specification and Description Language (SDL). Retrieved April 2008, from http://www.itu.int/ITU-T/studygroups/com17/languages/index.html

ITU-TS. (1997). *ITU-TS Recommendation Z.120: Message Sequence Chart (MSC)*. Geneva, Switzerland: ITU-TS.

ITU-TS. (2004). *ITU-TS Recommendation Z.120: Message Sequence Chart (MSC)*. Geneva, Switzerland: ITU-T.

Kendall, D. (1953). Stochastic Processes Occurring in the Theory of Queues and their Analysis by the Method of the Imbedded Markov Chain. *Annals of Mathematical Statistics*, *24*(3), 338–354. doi:10.1214/aoms/1177728975.

Kraemer, F., Slåtten, V., & Herrmann, P. (2009). Model-Driven Construction of Embedded Applications Based on Reusable Building Blocks – An Example. In Reed, R., Bilgic, A., & Gotzhein, R. (Eds.), *SDL 2009: Design for Motes and Mobiles (Vol. 5719*, pp. 1–18). Berlin, Germany: Springer. doi:10.1007/978-3-642-04554-7_1.

Law, A. M., & Kelton, W. D. (2000). *Simulation Modeling and Analysis*. New York: McGraw-Hill.

PragmaDev SARL. (2006). *SDL-RT standard V2.2*. Paris: Standard, PragmaDev SARL.

PragmaDev SARL. (2012). Retrieved from http://www.pragmadev.com/product/ codeGeneration.html

Reed, R. (2000). Re: SDL-News: Request for Help: Initialisation of Pids. Retrieved April 2009, from http://www.sdl-forum.org/Archives/SDL/0032.html

Reed, R. (2000). SDL-2000 form New Millenium Systems. Telektronikk 4.2000, 20-35.

Reed, R. (2000). SDL-2000 new presentation. Retrieved June 18, 2012, from http:// www.sdl-forum.org/sdl2000present/index.htm

Rodríguez-Cayetano, M. (2011). Design and Development of a CPU Scheduler Simulator for Educational Purposes Using SDL. In *System Analysis and Modeling: About Models (Vol. 6598*, pp. 72–90). Oslo, Norway: Springer. doi:10.1007/978-3-642-21652-7_5.

Rudolph, E., Grabowski, J., & Graubmann, P. (1999). Towards a Harmonization of UML-Sequence Diagrams and MSC. In Dssouli, R., Bochmann, G. V., & Lahav, Y. (Eds.), *SDL'99 - The Next Millenium*. Bochum, Germany: Elsevier. doi:10.1016/ B978-044450228-5/50014-X.

Tutorial, S. D. L. (n.d.). IEC International Engineering Consortium. Retrieved January 2009, from http://www.iec.org/online/tutorials/sdl/

Weigert, T., Weil, F., Marth, K., Baker, P., Jervis, C., & Dietz, P. ... Mastenbrook, B. (2007). Experiences in Deploying Model-Driven Engineering. In E. Gaudin, E. Najm, & R. Reed (Eds.), SDL 2007: Design for Dependable Systems (Vol. 4745, pp. 35-53). Berlin, Germany: Springer. doi: doi:10.1007/978-3-540-74984-4_3.

KEY WORDS AND DEFINITIONS

AGENT: The term agent is used to denote a system, block or process that contains one or more extended finite state machines.

BLOCK: A block is an agent that contains one or more concurrent blocks or processes and can also contain an extended finite state machine that owns and handles data within the block.

BODY: A body is a state machine graph of an agent, procedure, composite state, or operation.

CHANNEL: A channel is a communication path between agents.

ENVIRONMENT: The environment of the system is everything in the surroundings that communicates with the system in an SDL-like manner.

GATE: A gate represents a connection point for communication with an agent type. When the type is instantiated, it determines the connection of the agent instance with other instances.

INSTANCE: An instance is an object created when a type is instantiated.

OBJECT: The term object is used for data items that are references to values. ITU-T Rec. Z.100 (11/2007) 5.

PId: The term PId is used for data items that are references to agents.

PROCEDURE: A procedure is an encapsulation of part of the behavior of an agent, which is defined in one place but can be called from several places within the agent. Other agents can call a remote procedure.

PROCESS: A process is an agent that contains an extended finite state machine and can contain other processes.

SIGNAL: The primary means of communication is by signals that are output by the sending agent and input by the receiving agent.

SORT: A sort is a set of data items that have common properties.

STATE: An extended finite state machine of an agent is in a state if it is waiting for a stimulus.

STIMULUS: A stimulus is an event that can cause an agent that is in a state to enter a transition.

SYSTEM: A system is the outermost agent that communicates with the environment.

TIMER: A timer is an object owned by an agent that causes a timer signal stimulus to occur at a specified time.

TRANSITION: A transition is a sequence of actions an agent performs until it enters a state.

TYPE: A type is a definition that can be used for the creation of instances and can also be inherited and specialized to form other types. A parameterized type is a type that has parameters. When these parameters are given different actual parameters, different un-parameterized types are defined that, when instantiated, give instances with different properties.

VALUE: The term value is used for the class of data that is accessed directly. Values can be freely passed between agents.

ENDNOTES

[1.] The model clock is a real number that represents the time in the model. In a continuous paradigm, this number is continuously modified. In a discrete paradigm, the number is modified based on the time between the events that are processed by the simulation loop (Guasch, Piera, Casanovas, & Figueras, 2002).

[2.] This diagram is used to represent the behavior of a global system to analyze the evolution of events over time. It is usually used to represent the event evolution in an event-scheduling paradigm.

[3.] Some well-known SDL modeling tools are Telelogic Tau, PragmaDev RTDS, Cinderella, Safire-SDL, and ObjectGeode (now off the market). PragmaDev RTDS supports both SDL and SDL-RT. Some interesting additional projects are JADE, which is a Java-based specification environment, and SDLPS, which is a C++ simulation environment.

[4.] We are following here Kendall's notation for queuing models, A/B/C/K/N/D, where A represents the arrival process, B the service time distribution, C the number of servers, K the number of places in the system, N the population and D the queue's discipline.

Chapter 6
Modeling a Chilean Hospital Using Specification and Description Language

Jorge Leiva Olmos
Universitat Politècnica de Catalunya - Barcelona Tech, Spain

Pau Fonseca i Casas
Universitat Politècnica de Catalunya - Barcelona Tech, Spain

Jordi Ocaña Rebull
University of Barcelona, Spain

ABSTRACT

In this chapter, the authors present a formal model of the Anesthesia Unit and Surgical Wards (UAPQ) of a Chilean hospital. The objective was to document and to understand its operation, to assist hospital management and to facilitate its simulation. The model was built with Specification and Description Language (SDL). This methodology was used because it allows the design of a model that represents the system in a graphical, modular, and standard way. Our design contains the following agents: the system, 11 blocks, and 52 processes. The blocks and the processes describe the clinical and administrative activities. The environment of the UAPQ model contains 3 components: clinical services, emergency units, and support units.

DOI: 10.4018/978-1-4666-4369-7.ch006

INTRODUCTION

The anesthesia unit and surgical wards (UAPQ, in Spanish, "Unidad de Anestesia y Pabellones Quirúrgicos") play a strategic role in the quality of patient care and in the health objectives in a hospital. Their complexity and high cost of operation, combined with scarce resources and high demand, pose a constant optimization challenge. This optimization challenge requires the specification and documentation of all processes involved.

Documentation of the processes is difficult for many reasons. Often, there is no procedures manual, or the existing manual cannot be updated with the required frequency. Functions and tasks do not always follow protocols and are transmitted by informal channels instead. Clinical and administrative processes are not all measured or quantified; there are limited available resources (economic, human, material and time) to perform such tasks (often prioritizing short-term needs and urgent health activities). In addition, the lack of knowledge of new tools for institutional administrative management and logistics presents difficulties when specifying processes of this complexity in a hospital.

Models are increasingly used to solve real life problems and to assist in decision-making. They can describe processes, facilitating understanding of the system. A simplified version of the model development process is presented in Figure 1. The problem is the system (actual or proposed), the conceptual model is the logical-mathematical representation of the system and the computerized model is the conceptual model implemented using a computer application (Sargent, 2007).

Figure 1. Simplified version of the modeling process (Sargent, 2007)

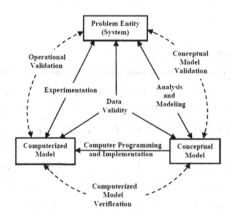

The conceptual model is developed through different phases of analysis and modeling involving the behavior, structure, and data available in the system. The computerized model is developed by means of a programming or software application, using the conceptual model as the specification. At the conclusion of the modeling phase, the model is used for experiments (simulations), to perform model operational validation and implementation verification (Sargent, 2007).

Validation of the conceptual model is defined as the determination that the theories and the assumptions that support the conceptual model are correct and the representation of the problem is reasonable for its intended purpose. Verification of the computerized model is defined as ensuring that the programming or computer application that represents the conceptual model is correct. Operational validation is defined as the determination that the computational model outputs are sufficiently accurate for the purpose envisaged and in the domain of applicability of the model. Data validity (regarding its quality and quantity) ensures availability of the information required for the construction of the models.

In this chapter, we focus mainly on the definition of the conceptual model (formal definition), which helps to solve some of the aforementioned problems, reinforcing the idea that a model by itself is a product (Brade, 2000).

There are many types of models (physical, mental, symbolic, etc.) that may be used to represent a system. If one of the main goals is digital simulation, the model should formalize the knowledge of the system in a concise, unambiguous way that can be processed by a computer.

In this chapter, we present a formal model of the UAPQ of a Chilean hospital. The model was built with the above-mentioned goals in mind. The following results are expected: a) to obtain a graphic model using a formal language to facilitate the description and understanding of the system, b) to facilitate the transcription of the model to an application, and c) to study the processes in a modular fashion. Additionally, to test the capabilities stated in b, a short-term objective was also d) to simulate a phase of the process. The end goal was to increase collaboration in the design and management of the hospital.

LITERATURE REVIEW

Many investigations have been performed on the use and improvement of surgical wards. Most of these focused on literature review (Cardoen, Demeulemeester, & Beliën, 2010), system description (Baumgart, et al., 2007) (Baumgart et al., 2007), occupation time quantification (Dexter, Macario, & Traub, 2003), capacity or evaluation of optimal use (Ballard & Kuhl 2006; Dexter, Macario, Lubarsky, & Burns, 1999; etc.). Different techniques for modeling, simulation and optimization, individually or combined, have been used. The most widely used description technique has been the flowchart (Baumgart, et al., 2007)(Baumgart et al., 2007). The most widely used simulation techniques have been the following: queuing theory (Lucas, et al., 2001)(Lucas, et al., 2001), discrete simulation (Dexter, Macario, & Traub, 2003) and Monte Carlo methods (Dexter, Macario, Lubarsky, & Burns, 1999). With respect to the simulation tools used to implement the models, we have found (i) programming languages such as Matlab (Shaw & Marshall, 2007), C (Denton, Rahman, Nelson, & Bailey, 2006), VB and Java (Persson & Persson, 2009) and (ii) applications, such as Microsoft Excel (Dexter, Macario, & Traub, 2003), Arena ® from Rockwell (Ballard Sarah M & Kuhl, 2006)(Ballard & Kuhl, 2006), Simio® (Zheng et al., 2010)(Zheng, et al., 2010), Extend® (Fei, Meskenst, & Chu, 2006), MedModel® (Lowery & Davis, 2009), Witness® (Niu et al., 2007)(Niu, et al., 2007) and Network® (Su & Shen, 2010), among many others. The most-used optimization tools have been linear programming (Dexter et al., 2002(Dexter, et al., 2002)), integer programming (Cardoen, Demeulemeester, & Bel, 2006), nonlinear integer programming (Jeang & Chiang, 2010), mixed integer programming (Jebali, Hadj Alouaneb, & Ladeta, 2006), stochastic programming (Denton, Rahman, Nelson, & Bailey, 2006) and heuristics methods (Fei, Meskenst, & Chu, 2006).

Finally, other techniques that have been used are data analysis (Cerda, De pablos, & Rodríguez, 2001), structural equation models (Dexter, Macario, Lubarsky, & Burns, 1999), minimal cost analysis (Dexter, Macario, & O'Neill, 2000), data mining (Steins & Persson, 2010) and decision support systems (DSS) models (Kusters & Groot, 1996).

Many studies have characterized the UAPQ as a resource rather than a system (with processes and clinical and administrative threads), with permanent availability. These studies make no distinction between surgery rooms. They also establish that the entities are related, describing relational behavior (channels of communication, signals, data, directionality, temporality, hierarchy, etc.). This presents a number of difficulties in properly describing the system; estimating the demand, occupation and waiting times; and incorporating elements to represent uncertainty and human behavior (Sibbel & Urban, 2001). To overcome some of these difficulties, the following features were incorporated into the UAPQ analysis:

- Administrative processes and clinical threads.
- Channels, signals, directionality, temporality and hierarchy that are related to or define a process.
- Categorization of surgical wards. Given the increased complexity of pathologies, the technological advances and the new surgical techniques, some of the surgery rooms are designed, equipped and/or intended for certain purposes (by specialty, such as cardiovascular, ophthalmology or traumatology, among

others, or by complexity, such as emergency, minor surgery, major ambulatory surgery, etc.). Other rooms remain undifferentiated (i.e., any type of surgery can be performed in them).

- A graphic language that allows participation and understanding within a multidisciplinary group (doctors, clinical staff, administrators, etc.).
- The choice of a specification language and software that enables modular simulation, thus facilitating the study by stages.

These elements gave rise to a better understanding and description of the behavior of the system.

THE HOSPITAL AND THE UAPQ

The model was developed for the Dr. Gustavo Fricke Hospital (Chile), a very complex organization (Ministerio de Salud de Chile, 2009) (see Figure 2). The hospital user population is nearly a half million people. It has 496 beds and has an occupational index of nearly 90%. It annually performs more than 1,300 surgeries, 250,000 specialist consultations and 24,000 hospitalizations. With a wide gap between availability and demand, the hospital has waiting lists that are among the largest in the country. In December, 2009, 23,579 specialists' consultations and 9,820 surgical interventions were pending (Ministerio de Salud de Chile, 2009).

In the hospital, health care (consultations, examinations and surgical procedures) are divided into two types:

1. Emergency treatment, and
2. Elective treatment.

Figure 2. Hospital Dr. Gustavo Fricke (Chile)

An emergency treatment is not programmable and cannot be postponed. An elective treatment is scheduled and placed on the waiting list. The treatments are also divided into inpatient (those not requiring hospitalization) and outpatient (those requiring hospitalization). Once treated, patients can be discharged and/or can be put onto the waiting list, should they require further attention.

The origin of the patient can be home or another health care institution (primary care, emergency vehicle, other hospitals, etc.), and patients can access one of the two routes of admission (emergency or elective care).

The structure of health care is shown graphically in Figure 3.

The UAPQ is a strategic unit in the hospital. Its activity directly influences emergency surgical care and the reduction of waiting lists. It delivers services to internal users (i.e., surgical services), and to external users (i.e., patients). Its supply is limited and is conditioned by high demand, scarcity of resources (financial and human), and complexity of operation. These factors can cause an increase in the percentage of surgeries suspended, complex programming, underutilization of resources, slow progress on the waiting lists, increased purchases and costs of services, breach of health targets, and increased user dissatisfaction.

The UAPQ infrastructure consists of 11 surgical wards (7 with medium and high complexity, 1 with low complexity, 2 for emergency operations, and 1 maternity unit) (see Figure 4).

Operations are performed under three types of schedules: urgent, normal, and extended time. Surgery types are classified as (i) maternal (gynecological and obstetric), (ii) major non-ambulatory surgery, (iii) major ambulatory surgery, and (iv)

Figure 3. Structure of health care

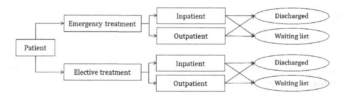

Figure 4. Surgical ward

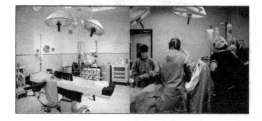

minor surgery. The UAPQ interacts with clinical services, the emergency units, and the support units (administrative, logistical and diagnostic and therapeutic). Support units help to implement the services. Clinical services manage the waiting lists. Emergency units allocate patients according to demand.

A summary of the path of a patient through the UAPQ processes is as follows:

The patient is hospitalized in a clinical service (access to the service is provided by an elective hospitalization or, in an emergency, a non-elective hospitalization) or is in an emergency unit. When a surgical ward is available, the patient is referred to a reception room, where the patient's background (personal data, clinical service, type of surgery, etc.) is reviewed. Then, the patient is sent to another room, where the process of preanesthesia is performed. Preanesthesia includes a review of the patient's medical history, review of the patient's condition, cleanliness, and patient preparation. Once the assigned operating room is ready to be occupied, the patient is admitted to the room, and the process of anesthesia and patient monitoring is started. Once the patient is anesthetized, surgery is performed (which may include one or more surgeries and one or more surgeons). Finally, after the surgery, the patient is carried to a recovery room where he or she is monitored, discharged, and referred to a clinical service. Figure 5 shows this summary.

One difficulty in these processes is that the UAPQ of the Hospital Dr. Gustavo Fricke unit does not have an adequate description of the operation model. There is information transmitted through informal channels, as well as tasks and functions that are not documented. This work focuses first on defining the problem, developing the conceptual model and validating the data. To a lesser extent, it also focuses on the computational implementation and verification of the model.

Figure 5. Summary of the path of a patient through the UAPQ

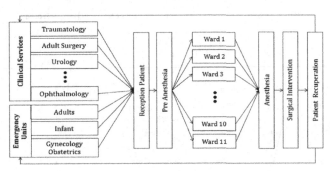

METHODS

With the participation and supervision of UAPQ hospital staff, tasks, functions, resources, needs, messages, and relations between the various components of the system were studied. The study was both qualitative (bibliographic) and quantitative (performed in the field and laboratory). It began in January 2010 and continued for 15 months. Data collection and validation was performed from the institutional database. Modeling was performed using SDL.

SDL was originally created to model telecommunications systems, but it can be used also in industrial, organizational, and social behavior systems, among others. Standardized by the International Telecommunication Union (ITU), is unambiguous, and can easily be used in combination with other standard languages such as Unified Modeling Language (UML). The standard lets you choose between two different ways to represent systems. The first one is graphical representation using SDL/GR, a graphical language that defines the structure and flow control of the system. The second is phrase representation using SDL/PR, which is a textual representation. There have been several editions of the language since 1976, the latest of which is known as SDL-2010. The language defines four levels (with a type of diagram for each level) to describe the structure and behavior of the model: system, blocks, processes, and procedures. Blocks and processes are called agents; the outer block is called a system and is an agent itself (that can communicate with the environment). Figure 6 illustrates this hierarchy.

The communication is based on the exchange of signals (asynchronous messages) traveling through channels by communicating agents. Each agent has a port of entry where the signal remains in a queue following a FIFO discipline (first in - first out). Data can be received by the input of signals, stored in variables, manipulated, and used on expressions, allowing decisions that determine how the agent behaves and the signals it sends to its outputs.

Figure 6. Sketch of the structure of a system in the SDL/GR notation (Doldi, 2003)

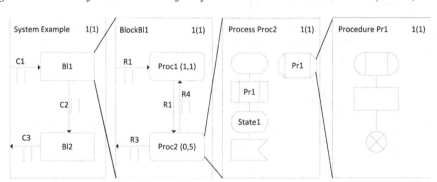

To fully describe the behavior of a system and its structural properties, the language is based on the following three main semantic models:

1. **Model architecture:** This defines the interconnection of functional entities (such as the system, blocks, sub-blocks, processes, procedures, and channels) and a hierarchical organization following the design from top to bottom.
2. **Behavior:** A model is described by a set of processes that communicate through the exchange of signals and variables. The behavior of each process is described by an extended finite state machine (EFSM).
3. **Data items used within the model:** These correspond to the structures of data handled by the processes and the abstract data types.

The main advantages of describing a system using SDL are the following:

- Simplification of documentation, understanding and modeling of a wide variety of systems using a graphical language.
- Adequate representation of detail, structure, behavior, and relations between the different elements of the system processes.
- Use of a standard language (ITU-T), compatible with several tools that can automate the implementation of the model, maintaining independence between the model and the tool selected to implement the simulation.
- Easy model verification and validation. Its full semantics allows quick system description checking, and debugging.
- Modular representation of the system.
- Formalization of communication channels and messages between the various entities that interact within the system.
- Graphical representation, which allows communication and learning about the system within interdisciplinary teams.

The main symbols used to represent a process or procedures in a system in SDL are shown in Table 1.

Some of the guiding concepts and principles that must be followed when using SDL are the following:

- A description must contain exactly one system.
- The system must contain at least one block.
- A block contains processes.
- Each process contains a set of states that describes its behavior.
- The structure consists of a system, blocks, and processes that are hierarchically related.

Table 1. Main symbols used to represent a process in SDL (Esteban Sastre, 2010)

Symbol	Name	Use
	Include	Is used to include SDL libraries in the system.
	Text	Contains declarations of the structures, variables, timers, and signals. To declare variables, the DCL keyword is used followed by the name and type of the variable to be declared. To declare constants, the SIGNAL keyword is used followed by the name of the signal and the parameters contained in parentheses. The block and system levels are used to declare channels and signals.
	Start	Indicates the beginning of a process.
	State	Indicates the state of the system.
	Input	Indicates waiting for an input signal, i.e., it is a symbol blocker. Is always found immediately after a state symbol. If the signal is received, it receives the signal and produces a state transition, making the information carried by the signal available. If the information carried by the signal, i.e., parameters, must be copied into local variables of the process, there must be a local variable in the process with the same name that indicates the parameter of the signal. Otherwise the value is discarded and not stored.
	Output	Sends a signal, usually at the end of a transition.
	Task	Is used to perform general tasks, such as variable assignments or operations on timers. It may contain a list of assignments separated by commas.
	Decision	Is used to choose between two alternative routes as the result of a condition.
	Stop	Indicates the termination of a process.
	Procedure call	Executes the call to a procedure previously declared.
	Procedure reference	Declares a procedure that is called in the current process.
	Procedure start	Begins the definition of a procedure.
	Procedure return	Ends a procedure and returns to where it was called.
	Text extension	Is used to include comments.

- Communication occurs through signals, although roads of communication (channels), and signals optionally contain parameters that can also convey data.

- The behavior is defined by different processes.
- Inheritance is useful to describe the relations between objects and their specialization.
- Blocks and processes are called agents. Each agent has a set of states (as an EFSM) to describe its behavior and the system behavior is defined by the agents acting together.
- The essential difference between a block (or system) agent, and a process agent is that instances of agents within a block (or system) agent behave simultaneously and asynchronously with each other (i.e., concurrently), while the instances within a process are scheduled to run one at a time (i.e., interleaved).
- In addition to containing other agents, agents can contain a set of states, data variables, and procedures.
- A diagram of an SDL agent is the definition of a set of instances of the agent. Each agent instance of this set is created either when the instance that contains the set has been created or when a create action takes place in another agent instance. The agent system is created when the system is initialized.

MODELING THE UAPQ

Model Description

We defined and documented the relevant processes in a graphical model, creating a standard description of the system to create a modular representation. The model thus designed contains the following agents: the system, 11 blocks, and 52 processes. The environment of the UAPQ contains 3 components: (i) the clinical services, (ii) the emergency units, and (iii) the support units. The blocks describe the following activities:

1. **Surgical committee:** This block evaluates and distributes the available hours for surgeries on a weekly basis.
2. **Surgical table:** This determines the type of surgery, the patients on whom to operate, the schedule, and the clinical team (surgeons, nurses, anesthesiologists, etc.).
3. **Materials request:** This determines the stock and the required materials to perform the surgeries.
4. **Patient reception:** This is the reception point prior to patient surgery.
5. **Preanesthesia:** This is the preparation of the patient before surgery.

6. **Anesthesia:** This is the administration of the anesthesia and checking the patient health conditions.
7. **Surgical intervention:** This is the operation on the patient.
8. **Patient recovery:** This is the patient post-operative and health checkup.
9. **Maintenance requirement:** This determines infrastructure needs and requested repairs or improvements.
10. **Equipment medical requirement:** This determines the equipment needed by the team of doctors and requests repairs or improvements.
11. **Secretariat:** This is the administrative and secretarial work.

The processes occur according to the hierarchical model shown in Figure 7.

The entities communicate through 135 channels using 137 different signals. The model was developed using SDL/GR and is shown in Figure 8 and Figure 9.

By means of Microsoft Visio (Sandrila Pluig-in) we performed a syntax check of the model, detecting, and correcting several syntax errors.

Figure 8 contains the blocks oriented to clinical activities. "Block_04_Patient" performs patient reception and checking of clinical, and administrative documentation (in one room set aside for this procedure). First, a request for sending the patient (signal "Patient_request" on "Channel_4b") is performed. When the patient is sent from the clinical service to UAPQ, the patient's clinical information (signal "Surgical_table_daily" on "Channel_11a") is received. After the checkup, the patient is sent to preanesthesia (signals "Shipping_patient" and "Documentation" on "Channel_4c").

"Block_05_Preanesthesia" represents the activity of patient preparation before anesthesia and surgery. At this stage, the patient is received (in the preanesthesia room), evaluated, and prepared. If the patient has a condition that impedes surgery, the patient is returned to the clinical service (signal "Shipping_patient" on "Channel_5b"). Alternatively, if the patient meets the conditions for operation, the patient is delivered to the ward (the signals "Shipping_patient," "Documentation," and "Num_surgical_ward" are generated on "Channel_5a").

In the surgical ward, the patient is monitored and anesthetized ("Block_06_Anesthesia"). In the "Block_07_Surgical_intervention," the activities related to surgeries are represented. When surgery is completed, the operating room is prepared to receive a new patient. After this task, the surgical ward is available for the next patient to enter (signal "State_surgical_ward" on "Channel_7c"). Clinical information is sent to the secretary for registration (signal "Clinical_information2" on "Channel_7a"). Surgical instruments are also checked and sent for sterilization in this block (signal "Shipping_instrument" on "Channel_7b"). Finally, the patient is sent to the recovery room (signal "Shipping_patient" on "Channel_7d").

Figure 7. The UAPQ hierarchical model

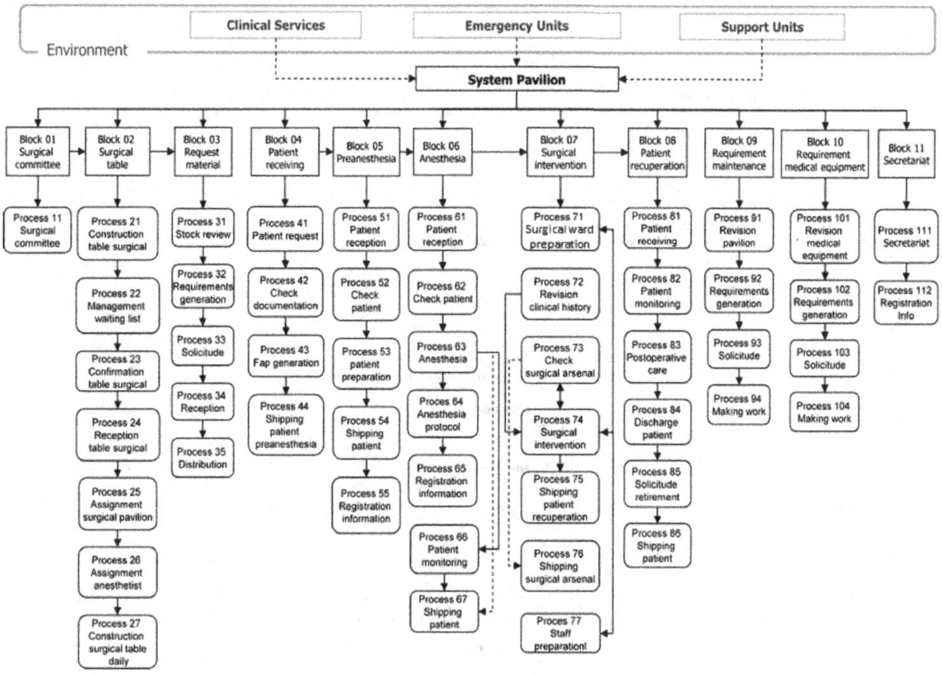

In "Block_08_Patient_recuperation," the patient recovers after surgery. When the patient is recovered, the clinical services are informed that the patient can be retired (signal "Retirement_patient" on "Channel_8a" and "Shipping_patient" on "Channel_8b").

Figure 9 shows the blocks for administrative activities. In "Block_01_Surgical_committee," the use of the surgical wards is revised and distributed. The clinical services submit the hours the surgeons are available (signal "Hours_offer_surgeons" on "Channel_1a"). The surgeons' hours, combined with the available resources (human resources, inputs, infrastructure, etc.), hospital management (health goals, financial resources, etc.), and other events (trade union activities, catastrophes or other), allow the weekly use of the surgical wards to be distributed and a schedule to be generated and transmitted (signal "Weekly_programming" on "Channel_1b" and on "Channel_1c").

In "Block_02_Surgical_table," the surgical tables (daily list of patients undergoing operations) are constructed, collected, and consolidated. The block receives the weekly schedule from the surgical wards (signal "Weekly_programming" from above), the tentative surgical tables (signal "Surgical_table_tentative" on "Channel_2a") from clinical services, the emergency surgeries (signal "Emergency_surgery" on

Figure 8. The UAPQ theoretical model (1 of 2)

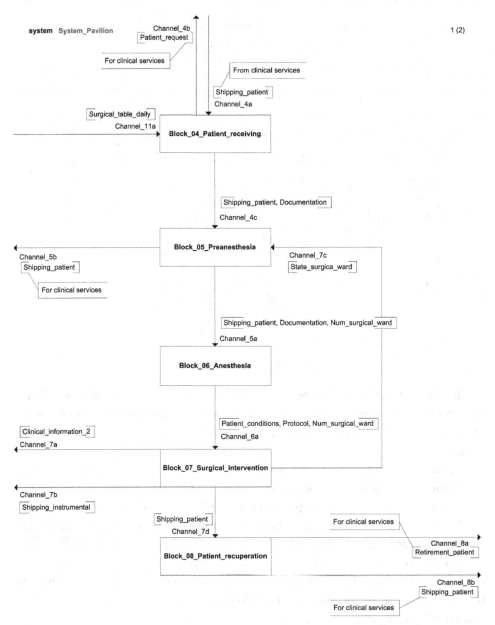

"Channel_2d") from the emergency units, the material availability (signal "Availability_material" on "Channel_2f") from "Block_03_Request_material", the availability of maintenance or repair of the surgical wards (signals "Availability_maintenance",

Figure 9. The UAPQ theoretical model (2 of 2)

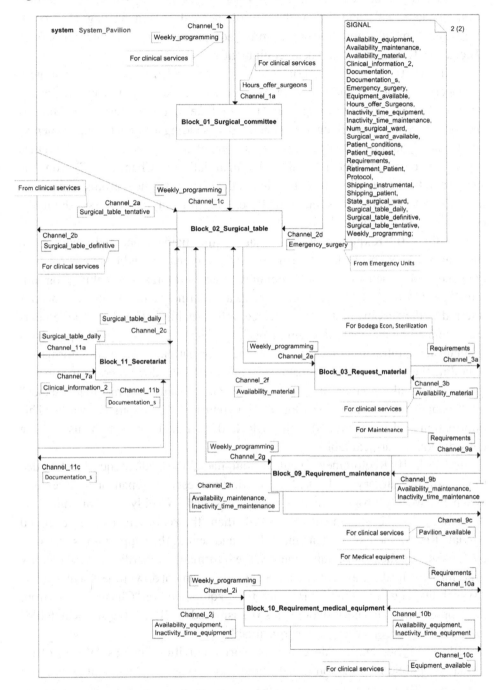

and "Inactivity_time_maintenance" on "Channel_2h") from "Block_09_Requirement_maintenance", and the availability of medical equipment (signals "Availability_equipment", and "Inactivity_time_equipment" on "Channel_2j") from "Block_10_Requirement_medical_equipment").

In "Block_03_Request_material," the supplies needed to perform the surgery are checked, requested and delivered. When use of the surgical wards is requested (signal "Weekly_programming" on "Channel_2e"), the material stockpile is checked; then, the requirements are generated by sending a signal ("Requirements" on "Channel_3a") to the support units (supply, pharmacy, etc.). After the return signals are received (signal "Availability_material" on "Channel_3b") from the support units, the supplies are distributed to the various surgical rooms. This information (signal) is also transmitted to "Block_02_surgical_table" to be used in the construction of the surgical tables.

In "Block_09_Requirement_maintenance," the maintenance and repair of the surgical wards is checked, and, if necessary, maintenance and/or repair requests are generated. When weekly programming is received (signal "Weekly_programming" on "Channel_2g"), the surgical wards are routinely checked, and any need is referred to the support units (maintenance, infrastructure, etc.). The requirements are generated by a signal ("Requirements" on "Channel_9a") to the support units (maintenance, infrastructure, etc.). After the information is received, information regarding the availability to perform the maintenance and downtime for the operating room (signals "Availability_maintenance" and "Inactivity_time_maintenance" on "Channel_9b") from the support units is returned to the surgical wards. This information is also transmitted to the "Block_02_surgical_table" to be used in the construction of surgical tables.

In "Block_10_Requirement_medical_equipment," the medical equipment needed to perform the surgery is checked, generating requests for repair or replacement. When the weekly programming is received (signal "Weekly_programming" on "Channel_2i"), the equipment is checked; then, the requirements are generated (signal "Requirements" by "Channel_10a") and sent to the support units (medical equipment, supplies, etc.). Subsequently, the information regarding the availability to perform medical equipment maintenance and equipment downtime is sent (signals "Availability_equipment" and "Inactivity_time_equipment" on "Channel_10b") from the support units. This information is also transmitted to "Block_02_surgical_table" to be used in the construction of surgical tables.

"Block_11_Secretariat" develops secretarial activities, such as delivery of information, public information and documentation (signal "Documentation_s" on "Channel_11b") received from any other unit of the hospital or external agencies. The coordination between clinical services and the UAPQ is also performed in this block (signal "Surgical_table_daily" on "Channel_11a" and "Clinical_information_2" on "Channel_7a").

SDL creates a modular specification of the system. We will describe only blocks and processes related to the surgical interventions.

"Block_07_Surgical_intervention" (Figure 10): In this block, the activities associated with the surgery are developed. To perform a surgery, a number of activities are developed simultaneously, prior to the surgery. These processes include the following:

- **Process_71_Surgical_ward_preparation:** The preparation of the ward consists in cleaning, checking medical equipment and collecting the supplies needed to perform the surgery. When these tasks are completed, it is reported that the operating room is ready for occupancy (signal "Preparated_surgical_ward" on "Channel_71a").
- **Process_72_Revision_clinical_history:** This process reviews the patient's history. The background is received from the signals "Patient_conditions," "Protocol" and "Num_surgical_ward" on "Channel_6a." When this task is completed, the process reports completion (signal "Clinical_information_1" on "Channel_72b").
- **Process_73_Check_surgical_arsenal:** This process checks and ships the surgical instruments prior to surgery (signal "Checked_surgical_arsenal" on "Channel_73a"). When surgery is completed, the surgical instruments are received back (signal "Surgical_arsenal" on "Channel_74b"). Then, it checks the instruments and sends them for washing (signal "Surgical_arsenal" on "Channel_73b").
- **Process_74_Surgical_intervention:** This is the process of the surgery on the patient. When the processes 71, 72, 73, and 77 are complete, surgery begins.
- **Process_75_Shipping_patient_recuperation:** This process refers the patient to the recovery room (signal "Shipping_patient" on "Channel_7d").
- **Process_76_Shipping_surgical_arsenal:** This process sends the surgical instruments to be sterilized (signal "Shipping_instrumental" on "Channel_7b").
- **Process_77_Staff_preparation:** This process prepares the personnel performing the surgery, and then reports when the staff is ready (signal "Preparated_staff" on "Channel_77a").

When the surgery is completed, the status of the operating room is reported (empty in this case) to call the next patient (signal "State_surgical_ward" on "Channel_7c") and the surgical information is sent to the registry (signal "Clinical_information_2" on "Channel_7a").

Figure 10. Block_07_Surgical_intervention

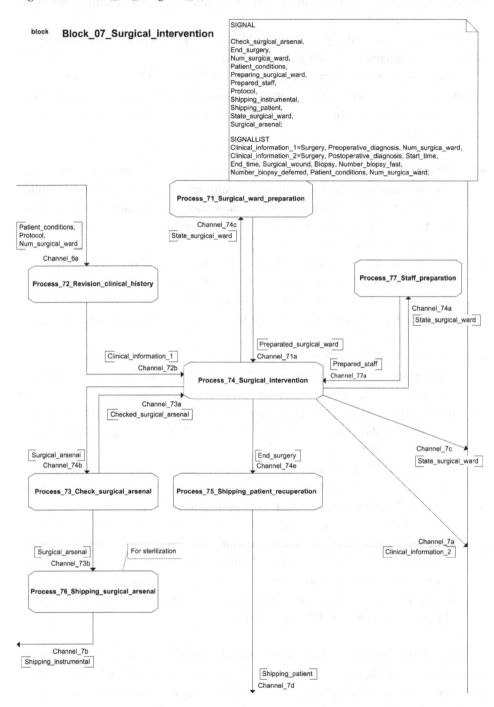

In the following, we will describe the process of the surgery. The code used to model the process is written in C, using a similar approach to that proposed in SDL-RT (PragmaDev SARL, 2006).

Process_74_ Surgical_intervention (Figure 11): The symbol ⊂⎯⎯⊃ indicates the start of the process, which begins in the state "Empty," waiting to receive signals[1].

The signals that can be received[2] are the following: The preparation of the surgical ward ("Preparing_surgical_ward"), the checking of the surgical instruments ("Check_surgical_arsenal"), the review of the patient's medical history ("Clinical_information_1") and the preparation of the surgical staff ("Preparing_staff").

When all signals have been received[3], a procedure that calculates the time of each surgery is run, depending on the surgical ward. Then, the process generates an internal output signal ("Time_surgery TO SELF") with a delay surgery time that remains in state "Operating." After the surgery[4], the process generates a series of signals,[5] and the pavilion state is reset to "Empty."

As an example of the procedure, "Procedure74_surg_pv1" that calculates the time of surgery[6] will be described in detail.

Procedure74_surg_pv1 (Figure 12): The symbol ⊂⎯⎯⊃ indicates the start of the procedure[7]. The number of surgeries is calculated using the function "Num_surg_pv1" and the length of the surgery is calculated using the function "Time_surg_pv1." Then, the counter is incremented by one and the total time of the surgeries is increased by "Time_aleat = Time_op + Time_aleat." The question, "Counter == Num_op," allows the cycle of the procedure to be repeated the same number of times as the estimated number of operations, "Num_op." When the counter equals the number of surgeries, the procedure ends, and the total time of the surgeries is calculated. The variable "Time_aleat" is used by "Process_74_Surgical_intervention."

DISCUSSION

This study enabled the creation of unambiguous documentation and a full understanding of the UAPQ processes by clinical and administrative staff at the hospital. This in turn led to the collaboration of the hospital management teams through the evaluation of the different processes. The information channels (to allow the signal transmission), signals, directionality, and hierarchy between different processes have been defined. This complete definition of the system features, combined with the modular structure of the language, enables a clear identification of the relations between different system elements.

Figure 11. Process_74_ Surgical_intervention

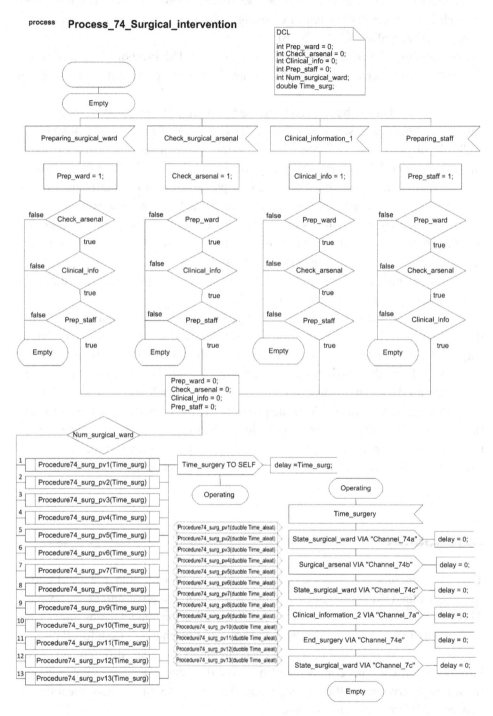

The design includes protocols for administrative activities, such as those associated with support units, including those tasks and knowledge (often tacit) transmitted through informal channels.

This complete model representation facilitates the selection of a tool to perform the simulation. Because the model definition is modular, different research lines can be simultaneously pursued, such as continuing to simulate the UAPQ processes or optimizing some of the individual processes. In addition, the collaborative validation of the model is simplified using this modular structure.

For the continuation of this work, we simulated parts of the model ("Block_06_Anesthesia" and "Block_07_Surgical_intervention") and are currently assessing the conceptual model validity, verifying the computational implementation for the simulated process, evaluating records for the past 5 years of UAPQ activity and constructing a written manual to complement the SDL code.

Figure 12. Procedure74_surg_pv1

procedure **Procedure74_surg_pv1(duoble Time_aleat)**

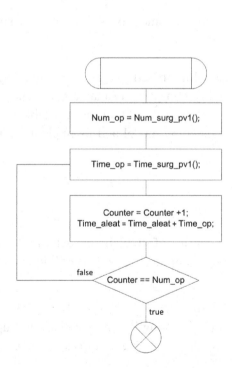

DCL

```
int Num_op = 0;
double Time_op = 0;
int Counter = 0;
```

Num_op = Num_surg_pv1();

Time_op = Time_surg_pv1();

Counter = Counter +1;
Time_aleat = Time_aleat + Time_op;

false

Counter == Num_op

true

Some of the difficulties we found include the following:

- The inherent complexity of the system, based on specifying a large number of processes.
- Institutional changes, which produced delays in the work.

Future goals for the project include the following:

- Expand use of the simulation for other processes, according to the system priorities, availability of information and available resources.
- Complete the evaluation of data quality.
- Quantify the demand, availability, cost, and occupation times for the simulated processes.
- Assess amendments and proposals for improving the system and determine the sensitivity of the model.
- Establish requirements and characteristics for measuring data and the needed instruments for the non-evaluated processes.
- Perform an equivalence test, based on distances, to study the goodness of adjusting the current simulation models to the real data, as a complementary validation test.
- Assess the modification or deletion of some processes to obtain a simplified version of the model.

In conclusion, the proposed methodology, based on SDL, provides many advantages in the representation of a hospital system, using an unambiguous and graphical language. Because SDL is an ITU standard, several tools are available to perform the simulation, differentiating the simulation model and its implementation, and simplifying the verification process.

REFERENCES

Ballard, S. M., & Kuhl, M. E. (2006). The use of simulation to determine maximum capacity in the surgical suite operating room. In *Proceedings of Winter Simulation Conference*. Monterey, CA: WSC.

Baumgart, A., Zoeller, A., Denz, C., Bender, H.-J., Heinzl, A., & Badreddin, E. (2007). Using Computer Simulation in Operating Room Management: Impacts on Process Engineering and Performance. In *Proceedings of International Conference on System Sciences*. Waikoloa, HI: IEEE.

Brade, D. (2000). Enhancing modeling and simulation accreditation by structuring verification and validation results. In J. A. Joines, R. R. Barton, K. Kang, & P. A. Fishwick (Eds.), In *Proceedings of Winter Simulation Conference*. Orlando, FL: ACM.

Cardoen, B., Demeulemeester, E., & Bel, J. (2006). *Optimizing a multiple objective surgical case scheduling problem*. Katholieke Universiteit Leuven, Leuven-Belgium.

Cardoen, B., Demeulemeester, E., & Beliën, J. (2010). Operating room planning and scheduling: A literature review. *European Journal of Operational Research*, *201*(1), 921–932. doi:10.1016/j.ejor.2009.04.011.

Cerda, E. De pablos, L., & Rodríguez, M. (2001). La gestión de las listas de espera quirúrgica en España. Ministry of Economy and Finance Institute of Fiscal Studies, Spain.

CINDERELLA SOFTWARE. (2007). *Cinderella SDL*. Retrieved March 31, 2009, from http://www.cinderella.dk

De la Fuente, P. (n.d.). *Universidad de Valladolid*. Retrieved, fromhttp://jair.lab. fi.uva.es/~pablfue/leng_simulacion/materiales/v_v_0405.pdf

Denton, B., Rahman, A., Nelson, H., & Bailey, A. (2006). Simulation of a multiple operating room surgical suite. In *Proceedings of Winter Simulation Conference*. Monterey, CA: WSC.

Dexter, F., Blake, J., Penning, D., Sloan, B., Chung, P., & Lubarsky, D. (2002). Use of linear programming to estimate impact of changes in a hospital's operating room time allocation on perioperative variable costs. *Anesthesiology*, *96*(3), 718–724. doi:10.1097/00000542-200203000-00031 PMID:11873050.

Dexter, F., Macario, A., Lubarsky, D., & Burns, D. (1999). Statistical method to evaluate management strategies to decrease variability in operating room utilization: Application of linear statistical modeling and Monte Carlo simulation to operating room management. *Anesthesiology*, *91*(1), 262–274. doi:10.1097/00000542-199907000-00035 PMID:10422952.

Dexter, F., Macario, A., & O'Neill, L. (2000). Scheduling surgical cases into overflow block time - Computer simulation of the effects of scheduling strategies on operating room labor costs. *Anesthesia and Analgesia*, *90*, 980–988. doi:10.1213/00000539-200004000-00038 PMID:10735811.

Dexter, F., Macario, A., & Traub, R. (2003). Operating room utilization alone is not an accurate metric for the allocation of operating room block time to individual surgeons with low caseloads. *Anesthesiology, 98*(5), 1243–1249. doi:10.1097/00000542-200305000-00029 PMID:12717148.

Doldi, L. (2003). *Validation of Communications Systems with SDL: The Art of SDL Simulation and Reachability Analysis*. New York: John Wiley & Sons, Inc. doi:10.1002/0470014156.

Esteban Sastre, D. (2010). *Introducción a SDL*. Retrieved December 2010, from http://pegaso.ls.fi.upm.es/~lmengual/telelogic/INTRODUCCION_SDL.pdf

Fei, H., Meskenst, N., & Chu, C. (2006). An operating theatre planning and scheduling problem in the case of a block scheduling strategy. In *Proceedings of International Conference on Service Systems and Service Management*. Shanghai, China: IEEE.

Fonseca i Casas, P. (2008). SDL distributed simulator. In *Proceedings of Winter Simulation Conference*. Miami, FL: INFORMS.

IBM. (2009). *TELELOGIC*. Retrieved March 31, 2009, from http://www.telelogic.com/

Jeang, A., & Chiang, A.-J. (2010). Economic and Quality Scheduling for Effective Utilization of Operating Rooms. *Journal of Medical Systems, 34*. PMID:20814721.

Jebali, A., Hadj Alouaneb, A., & Ladeta, P. (2006). Operating rooms scheduling. *International Journal of Production Economics, 99*, 52–62. doi:10.1016/j.ijpe.2004.12.006.

Kusters, R., & Groot, P. (1996). Modelling resource availability in general hospitals – Design and implementation of a decision support model. *European Journal of Operational Research, 88*, 428–445. doi:10.1016/0377-2217(95)00201-4.

Lowery, J., & Davis, J. (2009). Determination of operating room requirements using simulation. In *Proceedings of Winter Simulation Conference*. Austin, TX: IEEE.

Lucas, C., Buechter, K., Coscia, R., Hurst, J., Meredith, J., & Middlcton, J. et al. (2001). Mathematical modeling to define optimum operating room staffing needs for trauma centers. *Journal of the American College of Surgeons, 192*(5), 559–565. doi:10.1016/S1072-7515(01)00829-8 PMID:11333091.

Ministerio de Salud de Chile. (2009). *Compromisos de Gestión*. Viña del Mar.

Ministerio de Salud de Chile. (2009). *Producción Anual.* Hospital Dr. Gustavo Fricke, Viña del Mar.

Niu, Q., Peng, Q., ElMekkawy, T., Tan, Y. Y., Bryant, H., & Bernaerdt, L. (2007). Performance analysis of the operating room using simulation. *The Canadian Design Engineering Network (CDEN) and the Canadian Congress on Engineering Education (CCEE), 38.* Winnipeg, Canada.

Persson, M., & Persson, J. (2009). Health economic modelling to support surgery management at a Swedish hospital. *Omega, 37*(4). doi:10.1016/j.omega.2008.05.007 PMID:20161166.

PragmaDev SARL. (2006). *SDL-RT standard V2.2.* Standard, PragmaDev SARL. Paris, France. Retrieved April 5, 2012, from http://www.sdl-rt.org/standard/V2.2/pdf/SDL-RT.pdf

Rico, R., & Martínez, S. (2008). *Gestiopolis.com.* Retrieved July 1, 2010, from http://www.gestiopolis.com/administracion-estrategia/lenguaje-de-modelacion-en-sistemas.htm#mas-autor

Sargent, R. G. (2007). Verification and validation of simulation models. In S. G. Henderson, B. Biller, M.-H. Hsieh, J. Shortle, J. D. Tew, & R. R. Barton (Eds.), *Proceedings of the 2007 Winter Simulation Conference.* Washinton, DC: IEEE.

Saucier, R. (2000). *Computer Generation of Statistical Distributions.* Retrieved from http://ftp.arl.mil/random/

Shaw, B., & Marshall, A. (2007). Modelling the flow of congestive heart failure patients through a hospital system. *The Journal of the Operational Research Society, 58,* 212–218.

Sibbel, R., & Urban, C. (2001). *Agent-Based Modeling and Simulation for Hospital Management.* Dordrecht, The Netherlands: Kluwer Academic Publishers.

Steins, K., & Persson, F. (2010). Increasing Utilization in a Hospital Operating Department Using Simulation Modeling. *Simulation, 86*(8-9), 463–480. doi:10.1177/0037549709359355.

Su, Y., & Shen, N. (2010). Modeling the Effects of Information Quality on Process Performance in Operating Room. In *Proceedings of 12th International Conference on Computer Modelling and Simulation.* Cambridge, UK: IEEE.

Telecommunication standardization sector of ITU. (1999). *Specification and Description Language (SDL).* Retrieved April 2010, from http://www.itu.int/ITU-T/studygroups/com17/languages/index.html

Zheng, Q., Chen, S., Shen, J., Liu, Z., Fang, K., & Xiang, W. (2010). Simulation Modeling of the Operating Room Based on SIMIO. *Applied Mechanics and Materials*, *37-38*, 1162–1166. doi:10.4028/www.scientific.net/AMM.37-38.1162.

ENDNOTES

1. A number of variables are declared and initialized to zero, indicating that signals have not yet been received.

2. Listed in random order; the arrival time depends on the probability distribution of each signal.

3. Each time a signal arrives, the associated variable is assigned the value 1 and then verifies that other signals have arrived. The verification is performed by serially questioning the variables. If a signal has arrived, the answer is "true"; otherwise, it is "false." If any of the answers is "false," the process remains in the "Empty" state. After receiving all the signals, the variables "Prep_ward," "Check_arsenal," "Clinical_info" and "Prep_staff" are assigned the value 0.

4. Time it takes to generate the signal "Time_surgery TO SELF".

5. "State_surgical_ward" to "Process_71_Surgical_ward_preparation," "Process_77_Staff_preparation" and "Blok_04_Patient_receiving," "Surgical_arsenal" to "Process_73_Check_surgical_arsenal," "Clinical_information_2" to "Block_11_Secretariat" and "End_surgery" to "Process_75_Shipping_patient_recuperation."

6. All procedures associated with "Process_74_Surgical_intervention" are similar, differentiated by the associated probability distributions obtained by external code programmed in C.

7. This procedure contains a number of variables initialized to zero ("Num_op" is the number of operations, "Time_op" is the length of the surgery and "Counter" is a counter) and a variable equal to the total time of the surgeries ("Time_aleat").

Chapter 7
Formal Consistency Verification of UML Requirement and Analysis Models

Mouez Ali
University of Sfax, Tunisia

Hanene Ben-Abdallah
University of Sfax, Tunisia

Faïez Gargouri
University of Sfax, Tunisia

ABSTRACT

To capture and analyze the functional requirements of an information system, UML and the Unified Process (UP) propose the use case and sequence diagrams. However, one of the main difficulties behind the use of UML is how to ensure the consistency of the various diagrams used to model different views of the same system. In this chapter, the authors propose an enriched format for documenting UML2.0 use cases. This format facilitates consistency verification of the functional requirements with respect to the sequence diagrams included in the analysis model. The consistency verification relies on a set of rules to check the correspondence among the elements of the documented use cases and those of the sequence diagrams; the correspondence exploits the implicit semantic relationship between these diagrams as defined in UP. Furthermore, to provide for a rigorous verification, the authors formalize both types of diagrams and their correspondence rules in the formal notation Z. The formal version of the analysis model is then verified through the theorem prover Z/EVES to ensure its consistency.

DOI: 10.4018/978-1-4666-4369-7.ch007

INTRODUCTION

Requirement engineering (RE) is the front-end activity in software development. It includes requirement elicitation/capturing followed by requirement analysis. Being a *de facto* standard, several development processes have been proposed to derive requirement models using UML (e.g., Rational Unified Process [RUP] [Kruchten, 1999] and the Unified Process [UP] [Jacobson et al., 1999]). According to UP, the functional requirements can be modeled with a use case diagram in three phases. In the first phase, the designer identifies all the *actors* or organizations related to the system under development. In the second phase, he/she identifies the set of functions pertinent to each actor; these functions are represented by *use cases*. Finally, in the third phase, the designer must document the use cases using a natural language.

Once captured, the requirements are then analyzed by the designer through a set of analysis models. With UP, the designer analyzes the use case diagram by specifying UML sequence and/or collaboration diagrams. In this UP step, the designer identifies a set of *objects* and *messages* to illustrate the interactions among the actors and the system's components.

Evidently, both the requirement and analysis models are semantically related and complementary in presenting various details about the system. Thus, a basic hypothesis is the consistency of the analysis models with respect to the captured requirements. In addition, any consistency verification approach must explicitly take into account both the syntactic and semantic dependences between the two models. The syntactic relationships between the requirements and analysis models can be derived through the UML meta-model (OMG, 2003). On the other hand, UP informally specifies the semantic relationships between these two models: UP considers that the use case diagram is *specified by* the sequence diagrams and that these latter are *equivalent* to the collaboration diagrams. However, being informally specified through derivation "good-practice" guidelines, these two semantic relationships do not confidently ensure the consistency of these models.

This UP limitation motivated several works (*cf.* (Engels et al., 2001; Reggio et al., 2001; Yang et al., 2004; Liu & Araki, 2005) to propose consistency verification approaches for UML models. The efficiency of the proposed approaches is limited by the high level of abstraction of the use cases. Furthermore, the use case documentation does not resolve this difficulty since the documentation formats so far used are unstructured and are expressed in natural language.

The first contribution of this chapter is the proposition of a new format for use case documentation that facilitates the specification of the set of interactions between the actors and the system. Its second contribution is the exploitation of this documentation to *formally* verify the consistency of the requirements and analysis models. For this, we formalize in Z (Spivey, 1992) the meta-models of the use case and sequence diagrams, we then define a set of dependency rules to ensure the consistency of both models. The formalization of the meta-model is the used to prove in the theorem prover Z/EVES (Saaltink, 1997) the consistency of particular requirement and analysis models.

The remainder of this chapter is organized as follows: In Section 2, we give an overview of works related to functional requirements modeling and analysis. In Section 3, we propose a structured format to document, at the use case level, the interactions between the actors and the system. In Section 4, we formalize the requirements and analysis meta-models; this formalization provides for the analysis of any instance of these models and the verification of their mutual consistency. It is based on a set of constraints and rules expressed in the formal language Z and verified through its Z\eves theorem prover. In section 5, we illustrate our consistency verification approach through an example. Finally, the conclusion summarizes the presented work and outlines ongoing work.

RELATED WORKS

In this section, we first give an overview of requirement modeling in UML according to the UP process. Secondly, we present current proposals for formal analysis of UML models.

Requirement Modeling in UML

In the case of the UP process, requirements can be modeled in three phases with a use case model (as a set of use case diagrams). In the first phase, the designer identifies all the *actors/organizations* interacting with the system by answering the following questions: which users will use the system? Which other systems must interact with it? Thus, an actor represents any external entity using the system. It communicates with the system by exchanging (sending and receiving) messages to perform functionality.

In the second phase, the designer identifies for each actor the set of functions it initiates or participates in by looking at how the actor communicates/interacts with the system. These functions are represented by use cases. For example, Figure 1 shows parts of the use case diagram of an ATM system. In this model, the designer focused on two actors (*customer* and *Bank Host*) and three use cases (*withdraw money, identify user, check amount*).

Each identified use case describes a coherent unit of work, task or activity provided by the system and that is carried by one (or more) actor(s). It identifies each actor's sequence of events used to complete the task. For example, the *withdraw*

Figure 1. Use case diagram of an ATM system

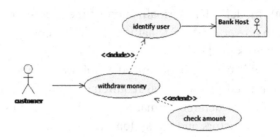

money use case describes the withdraw process in which a customer enters a PIN code and requests an amount of money that should not exceed his/her account balance. To describe the interaction details, UP recommends that the designer (in the third step) documents each use case using a natural language. Thus, each use case will be described through a sequence of sentences each of which represents an interaction between the system and an actor.

After capturing the functional requirements, the next UP step analyzes them. To do so, the designer must specify UML sequence and/or collaboration diagrams. Here, the designer identifies a set of *objects* and *messages* to illustrate the interactions between the actors and the system. To assist the designer in this step, UP only proposes informal guidelines or good-practices. For our ATM example, Figure 2 shows a sequence diagram that analyzes the *withdraw money* use case.

The first two phases of UP produce two models: the requirement model (composed of the use case diagrams) and its analysis model (composed of a set of sequence diagrams). The syntactic and semantic consistency of these two models is evi-

Figure 2. A sequence diagram analyzing the «withdraw money» use case

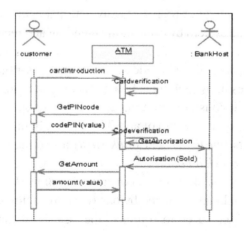

dently vital for the remaining development phases. To ensure such consistency, the designer must overcome two main problems: how to analyze the captured requirement and analysis models, and how to verify the absence of contradicting or missing information between these two models.

Requirement Analysis and Verification

There is an important number of works giving a description of the UML core concepts and providing rules for analyzing their properties (Engels et al., 2001; Litvak et al., 2003; Reggio et al., 2001). However, the majority of these works focuses only on one diagram, namely: the class (Yang et al., 2004; Liu & Araki, 2005) and state-transition diagrams (Martin & Rogardt, 2004).

For the analysis of requirements, other researches use formal techniques. For example, in (Bézivin, 1999), the authors present the semantics of the use cases with message sequence charts; because of the level of details needed, this approach appears more suitable for the specification of human-computer or computer-computer interfaces. In addition, in (Grieskamp & Lepper, 2000), the authors use the Z language (Spivey, 1992) to formalize use cases and analyze them using the ZETA environment (ZETA, 1999); this work treats use cases as executable code. On the other hand, in Dong & Woodcock (2003), the authors give an approach to represent use cases based on goals; each use case represents a goal and an informal guideline is given to analyze these identified goals. Furthermore, Martin & Rogardt (2004) formalizes in first order logic the pre- and post-conditions of the use cases; hence, the analysis is limited to these conditions. Overall, these works focus only on the requirements model and do not provide for consistency verification of the requirements with respect to their analysis model.

On the other hand, Pons et al. (2003) formalizes the use cases through mathematical contracts (Meyer, 1992). In this formalization, a contract represents an interaction between an actor and the system. Such a contract must be respected in any model derived through UP. However, the authors neither show how the contracts are respected by all derived models, nor do they provide for a means to verify that the contracts are respected. In Paige et al. (2002), the authors propose an approach to check the consistency constraints between two views of object-oriented systems described in BON (Walden & Nerson, 1995); the proposed constraints are implemented in PVS (Owre et al., 2001). Recently, the OMG (OMG, 2003) proposed OCL (OCL, 2003) to express some constraints of an UML model; however, a few tools exist (e.g., USE [Gogolla et al., 2007]), for the edition and the verification of OCL constraints. In addition, no attempt has been made to express in OCL all necessary consistency constraints between the requirement and analysis models.

As noted in the introduction, the main difficulty behind consistency verification between the requirement and the analysis models is the high level of abstraction of the use case model. To overcome this difficulty, we propose in the next section a format for use case documentation that facilitates both requirements capturing and consistency verification.

ENRICHED USE CASES

Recall that a use case describes a coherent work unit or task carried out by one or more actors. An actor represents an entity interacting with the system by using its functionalities. Actors characterize the roles played by external objects that inter-act with the system within a use case. We next present a documentation format to capture the interactions within a use case. We illustrate this documentation format through the ATM example.

Use Case Documentation Format

As illustrated in Figure 3, each *documented* use case indicates:

- The set of actors involved in the use case;

Figure 3. The format of the use case documentation

```
Use case < name >
Actors: < Actor1, ::: >
PreConditions: < condition1, ...>
ExtensionPoint: < condition; Usecase uj >
/* Basic flow */
BF:
Begin
< Num > [< preCondition >] < Actor | System >< name >
< Num > [< preCondition >] < Actor | System >< name >
End
/*Alternative flows */
AF1:
Begin < Event, begin at Num >
< Num > [< preCondition >] < Actor | System >< name >
< Num > [< preCondition >] < Actor |System >< name >
theBasic flow resume at Num
End
...
/*Error flows */
EF1:
Begin < Event, begin at Num k >
< Num > [< preCondition >] < Actor j System >< name >
< Num > [< preCondition >] < Actor j System >< name >
End
...
PostConditions :< condition1, ... >
End Use case
```

- The pre-conditions (as Boolean expressions) specify the conditions to be checked before the beginning of the use case;
- The post-conditions which must satisfied at the end of the use case;
- The use case that, under a given condition, extends the documented use case; and
- The set *scenarios* each of which enumerates a flow of interactions between the system and the involved actors. In addition, to account for compulsory, alternative and exceptional interactions, the set of scenarios are partitioned, respectively, into: a single basic flow, a (possibly empty) set of alternative flows, and a set of (possibly empty) error flows.

The basic flow (*BF* in Figure 3) describes the sequence of actions done by an actor and its corresponding reactions offered by the system. Each alternative flow (*AF$_i$* in Figure 3) describes a sequence of actions-reactions that is trigged when a particular event occurs (e.g., a pre-condition is not satisfied, a particular message is sent, etc). Once an alternative flow is executed, execution is resumed at a specified return point in the basic flow. On the other hand, each error flow (*EF$_j$* in Figure 3) describes the sequence of actions-reactions that must be executed when an irrecoverable error occurs in the basic flow, for example the system shuts down when an intrusion is detected.

ATM Withdraw Example

We illustrate our proposed documentation format using the Automatic Teller Machine (ATM) example whose functional requirements are captured in the use case diagram of Figure 1. We will focus on the *withdraw money* use case and its included *identification process*. The documentation of the *withdraw money* use case with its possible scenarios is the following:

```
Use case < withdraw money>
Actors: <customer, Bank Host>
Preconditions: < ATM is ready>
ExtensionPoint: <? Verify Sold, Use Case check amount>

/* Basic flow*/
BF: Begin
    1: <Customer>, <inserts card >
    2: <ATM>, <check card validity>
    3: <ATM>, <displays prompt>
    4: <Include> use case "identify user" <include>
```

```
    5: <ATM>, <displays options>
    6: <Customer>, <chooses option>
    7: <ATM>, <displays list accounts>
    8: <ATM>, <displays prompt>
    9: <Customer>, < chooses account>
   10: <ATM>, <displays prompt>
   11: <Customer>, <enters amount>
   12: <ATM>, <checks the account balance>
   13: <ATM>, <delivers the money>
   14: <ATM>, <registers the transaction>
   15: <BankHost>, <updates the account>
   16: <ATM>, <prints a receipt>
   17: <ATM>, <ejects card>
End
```

/*Alternative flows (AF)*/
AF1: Begin
<*Desired_amount* > *balance_amount*, AF2 **begin at** 12 >
   13: <ATM>,<indicates("Requested *amount is bigger than*
     account balance")>
End, The Basic flow resume at **5**

AF2: Begin
<Refused ticket, AF3 **begin at** 16 >
   17: <Customer>, <refuses the ticket>
End, The Basic flow resume at **5**

/*Errors Flow EF*/
EF1: Begin
<Card not valid, **begin at** 2>
   3: <ATM>, <indicates ("*an invalid card*")>
   4: <ATM>, <confiscates card >
The end of use case "withdraw money"

EF2: Begin
<unauthorized withdraw, **begin at** 12>
   13: <BankHost>, <interdicts all withdraw>
   14: <ATM>, <ejects the card>
The end of use case "withdraw money"

```
EF3: Begin
<Card not takes, begin at 17>
    18: <After 15 seconds>, <ATM>, <confiscates card>
    19: <ATM>, <informs the Bank Host>
The end of use case "withdraw money"

EF4: Begin
<Ticket money not takes, begin at 17>
    18: <After 30 seconds>, <ATM>, <confiscates ticket money>
    19: <ATM>, <informs bankHost>
The end of use case "withdraw money"
Post-conditions: <Customer gets his money, Customer gets his
card>
End Use case
```

As this example illustrates, the documentation format is intuitive to use and can be of a great assistance to the designer in the second phase of requirements capturing through any UML editor. In our work, we added a plug-in to the open source, UML editor ArgoUML (ArgoUML, 2006) to assist the designer in the documentation process. The developed plug-in saves use case documentations as XML documents according to a grammar formalized as a DTD (Document Type Definition). The detailed structure of our use case documentation is described by the DTD of Table 1.

Table 1. The DTD of a use case documentation

```
<?xml version="1.0" encoding="iso-8859-1" ?>          <!ELEMENT NameN(#PCDATA)>
<!ELEMENT UseCase (title,Resume,ListofActors,          <!ELEMENT SAlternative (NameScenarioA, EventA,
Version,DateCreation,DateMAJ,Precondition,Postcondi    StartActionA, ActionA+, Resume)>
tion,ListOfRelationShip,NbreSA,NbreSE,SBasic,          <!ATTLIST SAlternatif num CDATA #REQUIRED>
SAlternative* . SError*)>                              <!ELEMENT NameScenarioA(#PCDATA)>
<!ELEMENT title (#PCDATA)>                             <!ELEMENT EventA (#PCDATA)>
<!ELEMENT Resume (#PCDATA)>                            <!ELEMENT StartActionA(#PCDATA)>
<!ELEMENT ListeOfActors (Acteur+)>                     <!ELEMENT ActionA (NumA,
<!ELEMENT Actor (#PCDATA)>                             PreconditionA?,ActorA|SystemA, NameA)>
<!ELEMENT Version (#PCDATA)>                           <!ELEMENT NumA(#PCDATA)>
<!ELEMENT DateCreation (#PCDATA)>                      <!ELEMENT PreconditionA (#PCDATA)>
<!ELEMENT DateMAJ (#PCDATA)>                           <!ELEMENT ActorA (#PCDATA)>
<!ELEMENT Precondition (#PCDATA)>                      <!ELEMENT systemA(#PCDATA)>
<!ELEMENT Postcondition (#PCDATA)>                     <!ELEMENT NameA (#PCDATA)>
<!ELEMENT ListofRelationShip                           <!ELEMENT Resume(#PCDATA)>
(Include*,Extend*,Generalize*)>                        <!ELEMENT SError (NameScenarioE,
<!ELEMENT Include (#PCDATA)>                           EvenementE,StartActionE, ActionE+)>
<!ELEMENT Extend (#PCDATA)>                            <!ATTLIST SError num CDATA #REQUIRED>
<!ELEMENT Generalize (#PCDATA)>                        <!ELEMENT NameScenarioE (#PCDATA)>
<!ELEMENT NbreSA(#PCDATA)>                             <!ELEMENT EventE (#PCDATA)>
<!ELEMENT NbreSE (#PCDATA)>                            <!ELEMENT StartActionE (#PCDATA)>
<!ELEMENT SBasic(ActionN+)>                            <!ELEMENT ActionE (NumE,PreconditionE?,
<!ELEMENT ActionN(NumN, PreconditionN?,                ActorE|SystemE, Name)>
ActorN|SystemN, NameN )>                               <!ELEMENT NumE( #PCDATA)>
<!ELEMENT NumN(#PCDATA)>                               <!ELEMENT PreconditionE (#PCDATA)>
<!ELEMENT PreconditionN (#PCDATA)>                     <!ELEMENT ActorE (#PCDATA)>
<!ELEMENT ActorN (#PCDATA)>                            <!ELEMENT systemE(#PCDATA)>
<!ELEMENT systemN(#PCDATA)>                            <!ELEMENT NameE (#PCDATA)>
                                                       <?xml version="1.0" encoding="UTF-8"?>
```

A DTD defines the legal building blocks of an XML document. It defines the document structure with a list of legal *elements* (ELEMENT) and list of *attributes* (ATTLIST). For example, our DTD defines the following documentation elements (see Figure 3):

- `<!ELEMENT title (#CDATA)>`: Indicates the name of use case,
- `<!ELEMENT ListOfActors(Actor+)>`: Represents the list of the actors,
- `<!ELEMENT Actor(#PCDATA)>`: Represents the name of an actor,
- `<!ELEMENT SBasic (ActionN+)>`: Indicates that a basic scenario is composed of at least one ActionA which represents an interaction element as: `<!ELEMENT ActionN (NumN, PreconditionN?, ActorN|SystemN,)>` The interaction element specifies: the number of the action (NumN), its optional pre-condition (PreconditionN), who is doing the action (either the actor or the system), and the name of the action (NameN).

Besides the structures of the elements contained in the documentation, the DTD describes the attributes each element might have (Table 1).

Besides the integration of the documentation format into an UML editor, in the next section, we show how this documentation format can be also used to verify the consistency of the use case and sequence diagrams.

REQUIREMENT-ANALYSIS CONSISTENCY VERIFICATION

UP highlights several implicit, semantic relationships among the various system models such as "specified by," "realized by," "implemented by," and so forth. The UP model dependencies implicitly imply dependencies among the UML2.0 diagrams used (Ali et al., 2005). These implicit relationships are the basis of our approach to verify the consistency between the requirements model and the analysis model.

Before, presenting UML inter-diagram dependencies, we next present an overview of our consistency verification approach. Afterwards, we present an outline of the Z notation and the Z/EVES tool. Next, we give the UML diagram formalization. Finally, we give the formalization of the inter-diagram consistency.

An Overview of Our Approach of Consistency Verification

In general, the consistency of a model is defined as follows: "the models of various views need to be syntactically and semantically compatible with each other (i.e. horizontal/vertical consistency)" (Engels et al., 2002). To ensure the consistency of a UML model (as a set of diagrams), first, we explicitly define the relationships between all diagrams as proposed in UP. Secondly, based on these relationships, we define a set of rules whose satisfaction ensures the consistency between any two related diagrams (Ali, 2010).

Furthermore, to provide for a rigorous verification of the consistency of two diagrams, we rely on their formalization along with their consistency rules in the formal notation Z (Spivey, 1992) and its verification tool Z/EVES (Saaltink, 1997). More specifically, as illustrated in Figure 4, the verification of the satisfaction of the consistency of a UML model is conducted in two steps (Figure 4):

Step 1: *Instantiation*❶: This step consolidates and instantiates the formal specifications of the UML meta-model (Section 4.4) with the given UML model. The result of this step is a complete formal specification (UML meta-model + UML model). It is represented as a Z specification.

Step 2: *Proof*❷*:* This step involves the analysis of the satisfaction of the set of consistency rules pertinent to the diagrams in the given UML model. It consists of demonstrating a set of Z theorems describing the consistency rules.

Figure 4. An overview of our consistency verification approach

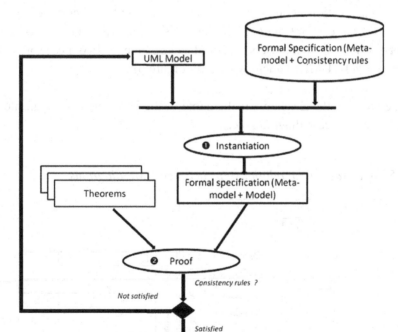

Inter-Diagram Relationships

As mentioned in the introduction, our approach to validate the consistency of the requirement model with respect to the analysis model relies on the inter-diagram dependencies as derived from the UP process. Figure 5 shows the implicit dependencies among the UML diagrams used in these two models [2]. In this chapter, we focus on the relationship denoted "Spec" representing the specification relationship between the use case and the sequence diagrams. Its satisfaction implies that the use case and the sequence diagrams are consistent.

To verify its satisfaction, we have identified and formalized a set of rules that characterize the specification relationship. These rules will be presented along with the formalization of the diagrams in Section 4.4.3.

Overview of the Z Notation and the Z/EVES Tool

In our work, we formalized the UML diagrams and their relationships with the formal notation Z (Spivey, 1992). The choice of Z is justified by three essential facts: i) its expressive power sufficient to model both diagrams; ii) its relatively simple notation; and iii) its freeware theorem *Z\EVES prover* (Saaltink, 1997). In this section, we give an overview of the Z notation through the Z/EVES interfaces.

The formal notation Z combines predicate calculus with set theory. A Z specification consists of a set of *schemas*. Each schema is composed of a name, its elements and a set of invariants that must be satisfied by its elements. In our case, a Z schema is used to model a UML element where (*cf.* Figure 6):

- The name of the Z schema is the name of the UML element (e.g., message, use case, use case diagram, etc.),

Figure 5. An extract of the relationships between UML diagrams

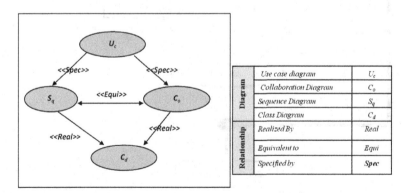

Figure 6. Verification of a Z schema with Z/EVES

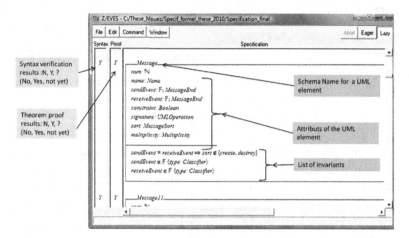

- The Z schema elements specify the UML element constituents (e.g., a message is composed of a name, a sender, a receiver, a Boolean constraint, etc.), and
- The Z schema invariants specify the syntactic and semantic constraints that the UML element constituents must always satisfy.

In Z/EVES (Figure 6), Z schemas can be entered and checked one paragraph at a time; checked paragraphs can be revised and rechecked. Each paragraph is checked for two aspects: its syntax and the validity of its invariants. The syntactic status and proof status (in terms of typing and satisfaction of the invariants) of each paragraph is shown in the two columns to the left of the paragraph.

Besides the edition of Z specifications and their syntactic and type checking, Z/EVES allows the specification of theorems that can be proven either automatically or interactively. In our work, among the useful examples of theorems are initialization theorems: these theorems are used to demonstrate that the set of Z schemas that formalize a UML diagram are correct; that is, they do not contain any contradiction. For examples, we use following theorems:

- *verifInitUMLUseCaseDiagram: verify that use case diagram is correct,*
- *verifInitUMLSequenceDiagram: verify that use case diagram is correct.*

In Z/EVES, after specifying a theorem to be proven, often the theorem prover is incapable of producing a complete proof automatically; instead, it requires the assistance of the designer to elaborate the proof. For this, Z/EVES offers an inter-

Figure 7. Z/EVES proof GUI: Interactive proof elaboration (left); result of applying prove by reduce (right)

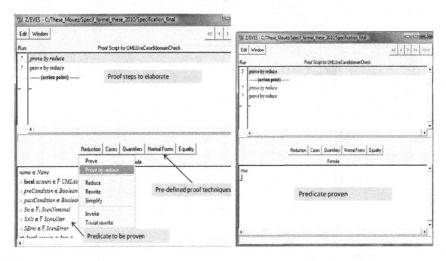

face through which the designer can either apply a pre-defined proof technique, or define and use *axioms* that advances the proof.

As illustrated in Figure 7, Z/EVES offers a set of proof techniques to reduce (*e.g., prove by reduce, rewrite …*), to elaborate the different cases to be proven, to normalize the predicate to be proven (*e.g., with normalize reduce*), etc. In addition,

Figure 8. Z/EVES interface: theorem and axiom definition

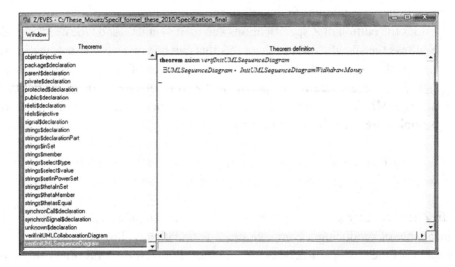

Z/EVES allows the designer to define his/her own theorem and axioms to use in the elaboration of a proof (Figure 8). The next section shows the use of Z and Z/EVES for the specification and consistency verification of the use case and sequence diagrams along with their relationships.

UML Diagram Formalization

In our formalization, we will use the following generic types:

- **[Name]:** Name of an UML element.
- **[Classifier]:** An UML classifier.
- **Visibility:**= *private | public | protected*
- **UMLParameter:** Parameters of an operation or action:

> ⌐*UMLParameter*—
> *name: Name*
> *type: Classifier*

- **UMLAttribute:** A schema specifying an UML attribute in a given diagram:

> ⌐*UMLAttribute*—
> *name: Name*
> *type: Classifier*
> *visibility: VisibilityKind*
> *multiplicity: Multiplicity*

- **UMLOperation:** A schema specifying the details of an UML operation in a given diagram:

> ⌐*UMLOperation*——
> *name: Name*
> *returntype: Classifier*
> *paramlist:* $\mathbb{F}$ *UMLParameter*
> *visibility: VisibilityKind*
> *isAbstract: Boolean*
>
> [1] Ap_1, p_2: *parameters* ∞ p_1 . *name* = p_2 . *name* ſ p_1 . *type* = p_2 . *type* $\Rightarrow$ p_1= p_2

Within an operation, the parameter names are unique (1).

Formalization of the Use Case Diagram

To formalize the use case diagram, we first start by formalizing its concepts: actors, actions, and so forth. Each actor is defined by the following *UMLActor* schema:

> ┌*UMLActor*─
> │ *name: Name*
> │ *IsActif: Boolean*
> └_____

where the declarative part defines the name of the actor and its activity status. This declaration reflects the UML meta-model definitions (OMG, 2003).

As the documentation format of Table 1 indicates, each use case is described by a set of flows (basic, alternative and error). Each flow is defined by a Z schema (Figure 5) named *basicFlow:*

> ┌*BasicFlow*─
> │ *sequences:* seq *Action*
> │_____
> │ **[1]** ¬ *sequences* = ⟨⟩ ∧ # *sequences* ⩾ 2
> │ **[2]** ∀*a1, a2: Action*
> │ · *sequences* 1 = *a1* ∧ *sequences* 2 = *a2*
> │ ⇒ *a1 . agentType* = *Acteur* ∧ *a2 . agentType* = *System*
> └_____

The invariant (1) ensures that there are at least 2 actions in the basic flow. In addition, the second invariant (2) ensures that the first action is realized by an actor: It is evident that a use case (*i.e.,* a task) should be initiated by an actor, after which the system reacts.

In addition, a flow represents a sequence of actions each of which is formalized through the following Z schema:

> ┌*Action*─
> │ *preCondition: Boolean*
> │ *agentType: agent*
> │ *name: Name*
> │ *parameters:* seq *UMLParameter*
> │_____
> │ **[1]** ∀p_1, p_2: ran *parameters*

$$\cdot\, p_1 \cdot name = p_2 \cdot name \wedge p_1 \cdot type = p_2 \cdot type \Rightarrow p_1 = p_2$$

An action is conducted by an agent (actor/system), it is subject to a pre-condition and it can manipulate a set of parameters. Within an operation, parameter names are unique (1).

Each alternative flow is described by the following schema:

ScenAlter—
  event: Event
  numStart: ℕ
  sequences: seq *Action*
  numResume: ℕ

  [1] *# sequences* > 0 ∧ *numStart* > 0
  numStart < *numResume* ∧ *numResume* > 0
  [2] ∀*a: Action*
       · *sequences* 1 = *a* ∧ *event . preCondition = True*
       ⇒ *a . preCondition = True* ∧ *a . agentType = Acteur*

Each alternative flow defines a triggering event, the number of the first action in the nominal scenario *(numStart)*, a sequence of actions and the number of action taken at the basic scenario *(numResume)*. In addition, the schema *AlterFlow* has two invariants: the invariant (1) ensures that there is at least one action in the alternative flow; and invariant (2) checks that event pre-condition is true to start a given alternative flow. The error flows in a use case is formalized in a similar way without the *NumResume* element since the error scenario terminates the interactions.

Finally, each use case can now be defined as follows:

UMLUseCase—
  name: Name
  acteurs: 𝔽 *UMLActeur*
  preCondition: Boolean
  postCondition: Boolean
  Sn: 𝔽$_1$*BasicFlow*
  SAls: 𝔽 *AlterFlow*
  SErrs: 𝔽 *ErrorFlow*

  [1] *# acteurs* > 0 ∧ *# SAls* > 0 ∧ *# SErrs* > 0
  [2] ∀*a: acteurs · a . type* ∈ *Classifier*

[3] $\forall u, v:$ seq *Action*
  $\cdot \forall sn: Sn \mid \# u > 1 \wedge u = sn$. *sequences*
    $\cdot \exists sa: SAls$
      $\mid v = sa$. *sequences* $\wedge 1 \leqslant \# v$
      $\wedge sa$. *numStart* $+ 1 \leqslant \# uf\ 1 \leqslant sa$. *numStart*
      $\cdot \exists a, b: Action \mid a = u\ sa$. *numStart* $\wedge b = v\ 1$
      $\cdot \neg u = \langle \rangle \wedge \neg v = \langle \rangle \wedge a$. *preCondition* =
        False $\wedge b$. *preCondition* = *True*
  $\cdot \forall se: SErrs$
  $\cdot \forall n3: \mathbb{N} \infty\ \forall a: Action$
    $\cdot \forall sqn, sqe:$ seq *Action*
    $\cdot sqn = sn$. *sequences*
      $\wedge n3 = se$. *numStart* $\wedge 1 \leqslant n3$
      $\wedge n3 \leqslant \# sn$. *sequences* $\Rightarrow n3 \leqslant \# sqn$
        $\wedge n3 \geqslant 1 \wedge sqe = se$. *sequences*
        $\wedge a = sqn\ n3 \wedge a$. *preCondition* = *False*

The complete use case schema includes three invariants. The invariant (1) imposes the existence of at least one actor involved in the use case. The invariant (2) specify that each actor has its own classifier. The invariant (3) ensures that a given flow (alternative or errors) can be started only if its starting action exists in the basic flow actions and it has failed.

Finally, the use case diagram is composed of a set of actors, a set of use cases that can be related through generalization, inclusion, extension and communication associations. The complete Z schema of a use case diagram contains seven invariants. They are of two types: invariants to define the domains and co-domains of the elements (*e.g.*, invariant (1)), and invariants for the syntactic consistency (*e.g.*, invariants (2 and 3)) and semantic consistency of the diagram (*e.g.*, invariant (4), (5), (6) and 7)).

UMLUseCaseDiagram—
actors: $\mathbb{F}$ *UMLActor*
usecases: $\mathbb{F}$ *UMLUseCase*
GenActeur: UMLActeur → *UMLActeur*
GenUseCase: UMLUseCase → *UMLUseCase*
Include: UMLUseCase → *UMLUseCase*
Extend: UMLUseCase → *UMLUseCase*
Communicate: UMLActeur → *UMLUseCase*

[1] dom *GenActeur* $\subseteq$ *acteurs*

ran *GenActeur* $\subseteq$ *acteurs*

dom *GenUseCase* $\subseteq$ *usecases*

ran *GenUseCase* $\subseteq$ *usecases*

dom *Include* $\subseteq$ *usecases*

ran *Include* $\subseteq$ *usecases*

dom *Extend* $\subseteq$ *usecases*

ran *Extend* $\subseteq$ *usecases*

dom *Communicate* $\subseteq$ *acteurs*

ran *Communicate* $\subseteq$ *usecases*

[2] $\forall a_1, a_2$: *acteurs* $\cdot$ a_1 . *name* = a_2 . *name* $\Rightarrow a_1 = a_2$

$\forall u_1, u_2$: *usecases* $\cdot$ u_1 . *name* = u_2 . *name* $\Rightarrow u_1 = u_2$

$\forall u$: *usecases* $\cdot$ $\forall a$: *acteurs* $\cdot$ u . *name* $\neq a$. *name*

[3] *#actors* > 0 $\wedge$ *#usecases* > 0

[4] $\forall a_1, a_2, a_3$: *actors* $\cdot$ *GenActor*(a_1) = a_2 $\wedge$ *GenActor*(a_2) = a_3 $\Rightarrow$
GenActor(a_1) $\neq a_3$

$\forall u_1, u_2, u_3$: *usecases* $\cdot$ *GenUseCase*(u_1) = u_2 $\wedge$ *GenUseCase*(u_2) = u_3
$\Rightarrow$ | *GenUseCase*(u_1) $\neq u_3$

[5] $\forall u_1, u_2$: *usecases*

$\cdot$ $\forall sa_1$: u_1 . *SAls* ∞ $\forall sa_2$: u_2 . *SAls*

$\cdot$ $\forall se_1$: u_1 . *SErrs* ∞ $\forall se_2$: u_2 . *SErrs*

$\cdot$ $\forall sq_1 sq_2, sq_3$, sq_4: seq *Action* $\cdot$ sq_1 = sa_1 . *sequences*

$\wedge$ sq_2 = sa_2 . *sequences* $\wedge$ sq_3 = se_1 . *sequences*

$\wedge$ sq_3 = se_2 . *sequences* $\wedge$ *Include* (u_1) = u_2

$\Rightarrow u_1$. *acteurs* = u_2 . *acteurs* $\wedge$ sq_1 $\subseteq sq_2$ $\wedge$ sq_3 $\subseteq sq_4$

[6] $\forall u_1, u_2$: *usecases*

$\cdot$ $\forall sa_1$: u_1 . *Sals* $\cdot$ Asa_2: u_2 . *SAls*

$\cdot$ $\forall se_1$: u_1 . *SErrs* ∞ Ase_2: u_2 . *SErrs*

$\cdot$ $\forall sq_1$: seq *Action* $\cdot$ $\forall sq_2$: seq *Action*

$\cdot$ $\forall sq_3$: seq *Action* $\cdot$ $\forall sq_4$: seq *Action*

$\cdot$ $\exists p$: *Boolean* $\cdot$ sq_1 = sa_1 . *sequences*

$\wedge$ sq_2 = sa_2 . *sequences* $\wedge$ sq_3 = se_1 . *sequences*

$\wedge$ sq_3 = se_2 . *sequences* $\wedge$ *Extend* u_1 = u_2

$\Rightarrow sa_1$. *event* . *preCondition* = *True*

$\vee se_1$. *event*. *preCondition* = *True*

[7] $\forall u_1, u_2$: *usecases*

$\cdot$ $\forall sa_1$: u_1 . *SAls* $\cdot$ $\forall sa_2$: u_2 . *SAls*

$\cdot$ $\forall se_1$: u_1 . *SErrs* $\cdot$ $\forall se_2$: u_2 . *SErrs*

$\cdot$ $\forall sq_1$: seq *Action* $\cdot$ $\forall sq_2$: seq *Action*

$\cdot$ $\forall sq_3$: seq *Action* $\cdot$ $\forall sq_4$: seq *Action*

$\cdot$ sq_1 = sa_1 . *sequences* $\wedge$ sq_2 = sa_2 . *sequences*

$\wedge$ sq_3 = se_1 . *sequences* $\wedge$ sq_3 = se_2 . *sequences*

$\wedge$ *GenUseCase* u_1 = u_2 $\Rightarrow sa_1$. *event* = sa_2 . *event* $\wedge$ se_1

$$. event = se_2 . event$$

Formalization of the Sequence Diagram

A sequence diagram presents either a collection of object symbols and arrows mapping to instances and stimulus, or a collection of classifier-role symbols and arrows mapping to classifiers and message (OMG, 2003).

Thus, an object can be formalized in Z as follows:

> ┌─ *Object* ─
> *value: oid*
> *type: Classifier*
> *attributelinks: UMLAttribute $\twoheadrightarrow$ $\mathbb{F}$ AttributeLink*
> *stimuli: UMLOperation $\twoheadrightarrow$ Stimulus*
> *isActive: Boolean*

As defined in the UML meta-model (OMG, 2003), this schema includes the object value, the classifier, the set of attribute links, etc. Such an object can send and/or receive messages.

Similar to the UML meta-model, the message schema describes the *sender* and the *receiver* as message ends indicating their corresponding object roles. *Sort* is a free Z type specifying that the message is a *creation*, a *deletion*, a *procedure call* or a *signal*. The schema box of a message is described as follows:

> ┌─ *Message* ─
> *num:* $\mathbb{N}$
> *name: Name*
> *sender:* $\mathbb{F}_1 MessageEnd$
> *receiver:* $\mathbb{F}_1 MessageEnd$
> *constraint: Boolean*
> *signature: UMLOperation*
> *sort: MessageSort*
> *multiplicity: Multiplicity*
> ───────
> *sender = receiver $\Rightarrow$ sort $\notin$ {create, destroy}*
> *sender $\in$ $\mathbb{F}\langle$type: Classifier$\rangle$*
> *receiver $\in$ $\mathbb{F}\langle$type: Classifier$\rangle$*

Now, the sequence diagram, as a set of objects and messages, is specified through the *UMLSequenceDiagram* schema which includes five invariants:

UMLSequenceDiagram—
objects: $\mathbb{F}$ *Object*
messages: $\mathbb{F}$ *Message*

---

[1] # *objects* $\geqslant$ 2 $\wedge$ # *messages* $\geqslant$ 1
[2]$\forall o_1, o_2$: *objects* $\cdot$ o_1 . *value* = o_2 . *value* $\wedge$ o_1 . *type* = o_2 . *type*
   $\Rightarrow o_1 = o_2$

[3] $\forall o$: *objects*
   $\cdot$ $\forall m$: *messages*
      $\cdot$ $\forall s$: *ConnectableElement*
         $\cdot$ *m* . *sort* = *create*
         $\Rightarrow o$. *isActive* = *True*
[4]$\forall o1, o2$: *objects*
   $\cdot$ $\forall m$: *messages*
      $\cdot$ *m* . *sort* = *destroy*
      $\Rightarrow o1$. *isActive* = *True* $\wedge$ *o2* . *isActive* = *False*
[5]$\forall m$: *messages*
   $\cdot$ *m* . *sender* $\in$ $\mathbb{F}$ $\langle type: Classifier \rangle$
   $\wedge$ *m* . *receiver* $\in$ $\mathbb{F}$ $\langle type: Classifier \rangle$

As mentioned above, the invariants in a Z schema ensure the consistency within each model. However, a designer is also interested in verifying the consistency of the requirements model with respect to the analysis model. In the next section, we show how the above schemas must be augmented with a set of formal rules to ensure this second type of model consistency.

Formal Inter-Diagram Consistency Verification

We focus on the specification relationship, denoted by "Spec," in which a use case diagram is specified by at least one sequence diagram. To verify the consistency between a use case diagram and its corresponding sequence diagrams, we suppose that: *Each use case* u *is specified by at least one sequence diagram Sq.*

To ensure this relationship, we augment our above formalized models with seven invariants to establish the correspondence between the use case concepts and those of its sequence diagram(s); each invariant reflects a consistency rule:

┌*Spec*─
  Uc: 𝔽 *UMLUseCaseDiagram*
  Sq: 𝔽 *UMLSequenceDiagram*
  ────────────
  [Rule 1]
  [Rule 2]
  [Rule 3]
  [Rule 4]
  [Rule 5]
  [Rule 6]
  [Rule 7]
└

In the remainder of this section, we describe these seven rules to ensure the consistency between the two diagrams *Uc* and *Sq*.

Rule 1: Each basic flow *BF is specified by* a sequence diagram *Sq* such that *rule 1* is satisfied:

┌*[Rule 1]*
  ────────────
  [1] ∀*ui: Uc.usecases*
  · ∀*actj: ui.BF.sequences*
  · *mk: Sq.messages*
  · *ui.BF.actj.name =Sq.mk.signature.name*
  · *ui.BF.actj. preCondition = Sq.mk. signature.preCondition*
  [2] ∀ *actj: Action*
  ·∃ *o1, o2: Sq.objects*
  ∃ *k1, k2:* ℕ
  · *actj* ∈ *seqOfActions(ui.BF)* ∧ *mk* ∈ *sentMsg (o1)* ∪ *receiveMsg (o2)*
  ∧ *sentEvent (o1, k1)* ∈ *{procedureCall, create, destroy }*
  ∧ *receiveEvent(o2, k2)* ∈ *{signal}*
  ∧ *k2 > k1*
└

In this rule, the invariant (1) ensures that each action has a corresponding message (same signature, same guard condition). On the other hand, the invariant (2) ensures that the order of actions (in a basic flow) is similar to the order of emission and receiving messages (in *Sq*).

Rule 2: For each actor, there exists an object where the object is an instance of an existing classifier such that:

> **[Rule 2]**
>
> ---
>
> $\forall a:$ *Uc.actors*
> $\cdot \exists\, o:Sq.objects$
> $\cdot$ *instanceOf(a)* $=o \lor$ *classifierRole (a)* $=o$

In some systems, a use case can have alternative and/or error flows. We have identified the correspondence, depending on the flow type, through Rule 3 or 4.

Rule 3: A use case documented by an alternative flow *(AFk)* is specified by a sequence diagram respecting [Rule 3]:

> **[Rule 3]**
>
> ---
>
> $\forall$ *ui: Uc.usecases*
> $\cdot \exists\, j, h:\, \mathbb{N}^+$
> $\cdot \exists$ *actj, acth: Action*
> $\cdot \exists$ *mk: Sq.messages*
> $\cdot\, j =$ *startPoint (ui.AFk.Event)* $\land$
> $h=$ *resumePoint (ui.AFk)* $\land$
> *actj* $\in$ *seqOfActions (ui.BF)* $\land$
> *acth* $\in$ *seqOfActions (ui.BF)* $\land$
> *Sq.mk.signature.preCondition = getCondtion (ui.SAk.Event)*

Rule 4: A use case documented by an error flow *(EFh)* is specified by a sequence diagram satisfying *[Rule 4]:*

> **[Rule 4]**
>
> ---
>
> $\forall ui:$ *Uc.usecases*
> $\cdot \exists$ *mk: Sq.messages*
> $\cdot \forall\, j, k, h:\, \mathbb{N}^+$
> $\cdot$ *startPoint(ui.EFh.Event)* $=j \land$ *actj* $\in$ *seqOfActions (ui.BF)*
> $\land$ *getCondition (ui.EFh.event) = Sq.mk. signature. precondition*

In addition to the above four correspondence rules, consistency must account for the relations among the use cases: "use cases may be related to other use cases by extend, include, and generalize relationships" (OMG, 2003). We next illustrate the rule for the *inclusion* and *extension* relationships; the remaining is expressed in a similar way.

Consistency of Use Case Inclusion

The "include" relationship between two use cases implies that the first will also have the behavior of the second. To check the consistency of this relationship Rule 5 will be used.

Rule 5: Each action in *u1* is specified by a message in the corresponding sequence diagram. When arriving to the inclusion point in *u1*, the actions of *u2* are specified by messages of the second part of the sequence diagram:

> *[Rule5]*
> _____
>
> $\cdot \forall u1, u2$: *Uc.usecases| Uc.Include(u1)=u2*
> $\cdot \forall m$: *Sq.messages*
> $\cdot \exists ah$: *Action* $\cdot$ $\exists mk$: *Sq.messages*
> $\cdot$ *ah* $\in$ *seqOfActions (u1.BF)* $\in$ *{mk.sender, mk.receiver}*
> $\subseteq$ *Sq.objects*
> $\cdot$ *sentEvent (mk.sender)* $\in$ *{ procedureCall, signal}* $\wedge$
> *receeiveEvent (mk.receiver)* $\in$ *{return, ack}*
> $\cdot$ $\exists$ *aj: Action*
> $\cdot$ *u1.aj.name = mk.signature.name* $\wedge$ u_1.*BF.postCondition =*
> *Sq.mk.signature.preCondition*

where *BF*1 and *BF*2 are respectively the basic flows of the use cases *u1* and *u2*.

Consistency of Use Case Extension

The "*extend*" relationship from use case *u1* to use case *u2* implies that the behavior of *u1* will be extended by the behavior of the second *u2* after the satisfaction of the guard condition in *u1*.

Rule 6: Each action in *u1* is specified by a message in the corresponding sequence diagram. When arriving to the extension point in *u1*, the actions of *u2* specified by messages of the second part of the sequence diagram and the guard condition must be satisfied.

> **[Rule6]**
>
> · $\forall u1, u2$: *Uc.usecases| Uc.Extend(u1)=u2*
> · $\forall m$: *Sq.messages*
> · $\exists ah$: *Action* · $\exists mk$: *Sq.messages*
> · *ah* ∈ *seqOfActions (u1.BF)* ∈ *{mk.sender, mk.receiver}* ⊆ *Sq.objects*
> · *sentEvent (mk.sender)* ∈ *{ procedureCall, signal}* ∧
> *receeiveEvent (mk.receiver)* ∈ *{return, ack}*
> · $\exists aj$: *Action*
> · *u1.aj.name = mk.signature.name* ∧ u_1*.BF.postCondition =*
> *Sq.mk.signature.preCondition*

where *BF*1 and *BF*2 are respectively the basic flows of the use cases *u1* and *u2*.

Figure 9. Documentation and sequence diagram of the "identify user" use case

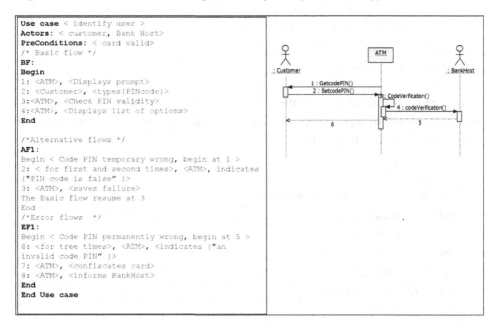

ATM EXAMPLE

In this section, we apply our consistency rules and verification approach on the ATM example introduced in Section 2.1.

For this example, our consistency verification approach (Figure 4) receives the following input and produces the consistency analysis results:

- **Input:** The three diagrams: a use case diagram (Figure 1) and two sequence diagrams: *withdraw money* (Figure 2) and *identify user* (Figure 9). In addition, we have the documentation of the "withdraw money" use case (Section 3.2) and the "identify user" use case (Figure 9).
- **Analysis results:** When we applied the above rules on our ATM example, we found out that the documented use case diagram and its sequence diagrams were inconsistent due to the violation of rules 1, 2 and 5.

Result Explanation 1: According to the Rule 1 (each action must have an equivalent message in the corresponding sequence diagram), we found out that the following actions have no equivalent messages:

```
5:  <ATM>, <displays options>
9:  <Costumer>, < chooses account>
10: <ATM>, <displays prompt>
12: <ATM>, <checks the account balance>
13: <ATM>, <delivers the money>
14: <ATM>, <registers the transaction>
16: <ATM>, <prints a receipt>
17: <ATM>, <ejects card>
```

To correct this inconsistency, the following messages must be added to the sequence diagram in order to represent their counterpart actions in the documentation of the "withdraw money" use case:

- *display_options ()*
- *choose_ option (withdraw money)*
- *get_ authorisation()*
- *display_ prompt()*
- *check_ balance()*
- *deliver_ money()*
- *registers_ transaction()*
- *print_ recipient()*

- *eject_Card()*

Result Explanation 2: According to Rule 2 (for each actor, there exists an object where the object is an instance of an existing classifier), we found out that the actor "BankHost" in the basic flow of the "withdraw money" use case needs a corresponding object in the sequence diagram. Indeed, going back to the documentation, we find that:

```
15: <BankHost>, <updates the account>
```

To resolve the inconsistency, a new object "Bankhost" must be added to the sequence diagram specifying the "withdraw money" use case. In addition, this object must receive a message indicating updating the customer account.

Result Explanation 3: Rule 5 verifies the consistency of use case inclusion between the "withdraw money" and "identify user" use cases. When verifying this rule, the prover detects that the message *codeverification(value)* is missing in the sequence diagram specifying the *withdraw money* use case (see Figure

Figure 10. Rectified sequence diagram specifying withdraw money and including the identification of the customer

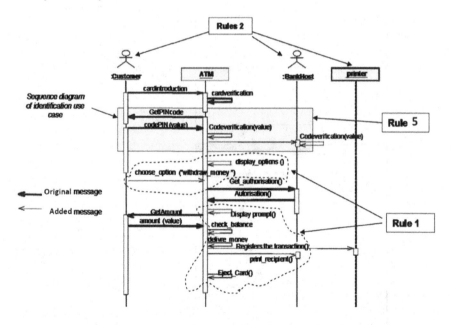

Figure 11. A part of the formal specification of "Spec" relationship between "withdraw money" use case diagam, "withdraw money" and "identify user" sequence diagrams

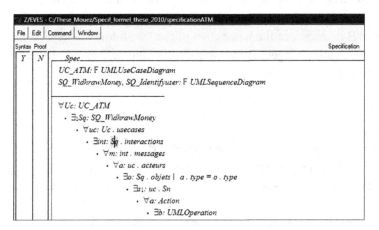

Figure 12. ATM consistency verification through ΖEVES

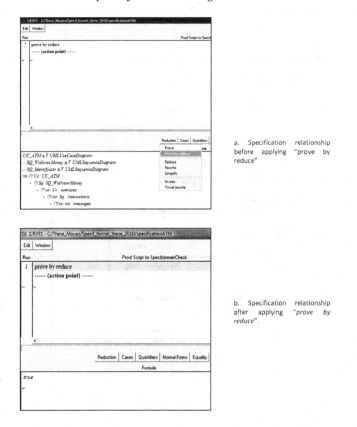

a. Specification relationship before applying "prove by reduce"

b. Specification relationship after applying *"prove by reduce"*.

2). This message must be added to account for the inclusion relationship from *withdraw money* to *identify user*.

Once we fixed the above detected inconsistencies, we obtained the sequence diagram shown in Figure 10; the added elements (objects and messages) are represented in bold. When resubmitted to the Z/EVES theorem prover, these corrected models were proven through Z\EVES to be consistent as shown in Figure 11 (also see Figure 12).

CONCLUSION AND FUTURE WORKS

UP and UML propose respectively a process and notations for capturing and analyzing requirements. More specifically, in UP, use cases capture the requirements of the system and guide their development process. A use case can be analyzed using sequence diagram in the UP analysis model. In this chapter, we presented an augmented format of use case.

In this chapter, our first contribution consists in proposing a documentation format for use cases. This format has a twofold objective. First, it is used to detail out to some extend the set of interactions between the actors and the system; being simple, this format can assist in the requirements capturing phase. Secondly, it is used to analyze the requirements and to verify their consistency with respect to the analysis model (i.e., the sequence diagrams).

The second contribution of this chapter consists in a formal definition for the use case diagram and sequence diagram. In this formalization with Z, we established a set of rules that ensure the syntactic and semantic consistencies between both models. We are currently extending our work to cover the consistency between the remaining models derived through UP.

REFERENCES

Ali, M. (2010). *Verification and validation of UML models: approaches and tools*. Editions Universitaires Europeennes.

Ali, M., Ben-Abdallah, H., & Gargouri, F. (2005). Towards a Validation Approach of UP Conceptual Models. In *Proceedings of the Workshop Consistency in Model Driven Engineering in European Conference on Model Driven Architecture-Foundations and Applications* (pp. 143–154).

ArgoUML tool. (2006). Retrieved from www.argouml.org.

Bézivin, J., & Muller, P. A. (1999). *A Formal Approach to Use Cases and Their Relationships* (Vol. 618). New York: Springer. Retrieved from http://citeseer.ist. psu.edu/overgaard99formal.html

(2003). InDong, J. S., & Woodcock, J. (Eds.). Lecture Notes in Computer Science: *Vol. 2885. A Relational Model for Formal Object-Oriented Requirement Analysis in UML*. New York: Springer.

Engels, G., Kuester, J., & Groenewegen, L. (2002). Consistent interaction of software components. *Journal of Integrated Design & Process Science*, 6(4), 2–22.

Engels, G., Küster, J. M., Heckel, R., & Groenewegen, L. (2001). *A methodology for specifying and analyzing consistency of object-oriented behavioral models* (Vol. 26). New York: ACM. DOI http://doi.acm.org/10.1145/503271.503235

Gogolla, M., Büttner, F., & Richters, M. (2007). USE: A UML-Based Specification Environment for Validating UML and OCL. *Science of Computer Programming*, 69(1-3), 27–34. doi:10.1016/j.scico.2007.01.013.

Grieskamp, W., & Lepper, M. (2000). *Using Use Cases in Executable Z*. Washington, DC: IEEE Computer Society.

Jacobson, I., Booch, G., & Rumbaugh, J. (1999). *The unified software development process*. Boston, MA: Addison-Wesley.

Kruchten, P. (1999). *The Rational Unified Process: An introduction*. Boston, MA: Addison-Wesley.

Litvak, B., Tyszberowicz, S., & Yehudai, A. (2003). *Behavioral Consistency Validation of UML Diagrams* (Vol. 00). Los Alamitos, CA: IEEE. DOI http://doi. ieeecomputersociety.org/10.1109/SEFM.2003.1236213

Liu, Z., & Araki, K. (2005). *Theoretical Aspects of Computing - ICTAC 2004, First International Colloquium*. Guiyang, China: Springer.

Martin, G., & Rogardt, H. (2004). Lecture Notes in Computer Science: *Vol. 3273. From Informal to Formal Specifications in UML*. New York: Springer.

Meyer, B. (1992). *Applying Design by Contract (Vol. 25)*. Washington, DC: IEEE.

OCL language. (2003). http://www.omg.org

OMG. (2003). *UML specification*. Retrieved from http://www.omg.org

Owre, S., Shankar, N., Rushby, J. M., & Stringer-Calvert, D. W. J. (2001). *PVS System Guide 2.4*. Menlo Park, CA: SRI International.

Paige, R. F., Jonathan, S. O., & Phillip, J. B. (2002). *Checking the Consistency of Collaboration and Class Diagrams using "PVS.* London: British Computer Society.

Pons, C., Giandini, R., Baum, G., Garbi, J. L., & Mercado, P. (2003). *Specification and checking of dependence relations between UML models.* Hershey, PA: IGI Global.

Reggio, G., Cerioli, M., & Astesiano, E. (2001). *Towards a Rigorous Semantics of UML Supporting Its Multiview Approach.* London: Springer-Verlag. doi:10.1007/3-540-45314-8_13.

Saaltink, M. (1997). *The Z/EVES System* (pp. 72–85). Berlin, Germany: Springer-Verlag.

Soon-Kyeong, K., & David, C. (2004). A Formal Object-Oriented Approach to defining Consistency Constraints for UML Models. In *Proceedings of Australian Software Engineering Conference (ASWEC'2004).* Melbourne, Australia. IEEE.

Spivey, J. M. (1992). *The Z Notation: A Reference Manual.* Upper Saddle River, NJ: Prentice Hall.

Walden, K., & Nerson, J.-M. (1995). *Seamless Object-Oriented Software Architecture.* Upper Saddle River, NJ: Prentice Hall.

Yang, J., Long, Q., Liu, Z., & Li, X. (2004). *A Predicative Semantic Model for Integrating UML Models.* New York: Springer.

ZETA. (1999). *Zeta referential guide.* Technical report

Chapter 8
Model–Based System Design Using SysML:
The Role of the Evaluation Diagram

Anargyros Tsadimas
Harokopio University of Athens, Greece

Mara Nikolaidou
Harokopio University of Athens, Greece

Dimosthenis Anagnostopoulos
Harokopio University of Athens, Greece

ABSTRACT

Model-based system design is served by a single, multi-layered model supporting all design activities, in different levels of detail. SysML is a modeling language, endorsed by OMG, for system engineering, which aims at defining such models for system design. It provides discrete diagrams to describe system structure and components, to explore allocation policies crucial for system design, and to identify design requirements. In this chapter, SysML is used for the model-based design of enterprise information system architecture, supporting a systemic view of such systems, where software and hardware entities are treated as system components composed to create the system architecture. SysML extensions to facilitate the effective description of non-functional requirements, especially quantitative ones, and their verification are presented. The integration of evaluation parameters and results into a discrete SysML diagram enhances the requirement verification process,

DOI: 10.4018/978-1-4666-4369-7.ch008

while the visualization of evaluation data helps system engineers to explore design decisions and properly adjust system design. Based on the proposed extensions, a SysML profile is developed. The experience obtained when applying the profile for renovating the architecture of a large-scale enterprise information system is also briefly discussed to explore the potential of the proposed extensions.

INTRODUCTION

Model-based engineering (MBE) is about elevating models to a central and governing role in the engineering process for the specification, design, integration, validation, and operation of a system (Estefan, 2008). Model-based system design is supported by a number of methodologies (Estefan, 2008; Balmelli et al., 2006) and is effectively accommodated by Systems Modeling Language (SysML) (SysML, 2010). SysML, endorsed by OMG and INCOSE, facilitates the description of a broad range of systems and systems-of-systems in a hierarchical fashion, while it is fully supported by most UML modeling tools. It enables the description of allocation policies and provides a discrete diagram for requirements specification. To describe specific system domains, a SysML profile should be specified, using standard UML extension mechanisms, as stereotypes and constraints (OMG, 2007a).

Model-based design of information systems is explored by methodologies such as the ones presented in Nolan et al. (2008), ISO (2009), Izukura et al. (2011), and Nikolaidou et al. (2009). UML and recently SysML are adopted in all of them as the system modeling language. As indicated in most of them, when building large-scale information systems, software engineering is usually focused, while the combination of software and hardware and the way it might affect overall system performance is often neglected. Software architecture design decisions are influenced by network infrastructure design, while non-functional requirements, as performance requirements, can usually be satisfied by effective allocation of software components to hardware. In practice, both software and network infrastructure architecture should be designed in parallel to efficiently explore their interrelations and ensure non-functional requirement satisfaction.

In the following, a systemic view of enterprise information system (EIS) architecture design is explored, utilizing SysML as the system modeling language. Such an approach treats both software and hardware entities as system components interacting to achieve the desired functionality under specific performance and availability conditions.

SysML requirement diagram and corresponding entities should be severely extended to effectively support the description of non-functional design requirements, especially the quantitative ones, such as performance. Furthermore, their verification must be performed using quantitative methods, for example, simulation. While there is a wide number of efforts to simulate SysML models using external simulators, such as the ones described in Paredis et al. (2010), McGinnis & Ustun (2009), and Wang & Dagli (2008), one should consider the integration of evaluation results into SysML system models to enhance the verification of non-functional requirements by the system designer and the exploration of alternative design solutions.

To enable the analytical description and verification of non-functional requirements and the validation of related system design decisions, we propose to include a discrete diagram, called evaluation diagram, to serve system evaluation activity and manage evaluation results and requirement verification. Proposed architecture scenarios are evaluated (Kacem et al., 2006), as discrete evaluation scenarios are included in the evaluation diagram, and related design decisions may be properly adjusted by the system designer. Using the proposed extensions, a SysML profile for EIS architecture design was implemented as a plugin to the MagicDraw modeling tool (NoMagic, 2013) focusing performance requirement description and verification.

To explain the proposed concepts and discuss the benefits of applying them in model-based system design, a case study on renovating the architecture of a large-scale enterprise information system is also briefly presented as an example. Experience obtained may be applied in other domains as well.

BACKGROUND

Model-based system design using UML has been explored by a number of researchers in different domains (MARTE, 2009; ISO, 2009; Balmelli et al., 2006), resulting in corresponding profiles, such as the MARTE UML profile for the specification of real-time and embedded systems (MARTE, 2009). The adoption of UML for system modeling promotes the integration of system design with other activities especially when software development is involved (Balmelli et al., 2006). Since SysML was adopted as a standard, most of existing model-based system design efforts based on UML consider adopting SysML concepts (Espinoza et al., 2009; Balmelli et al., 2006). Furthermore, additional efforts are also adopting SysML for system design (Kerzhner & Paredis, 2010; Izukura et al., 2011). In either case, it is evident that SysML requirement diagram and corresponding entities should be severely extended to effectively support the description of non-functional design requirements, especially the quantitative ones, such as performance (Tsadimas et al., 2012). Non-functional requirement verification, based on quantitative methods, such as simulation, is not addressed in any of them.

MODEL-BASED METHODOLOGIES FOR ENTERPRISE INFORMATION SYSTEM DESIGN

UML4ODP is an ISO standard (ISO, 2009) promoting UML to describe Information System viewpoints according to RM-ODP framework. The Engineering Profile of UML4ODP expresses the concepts specified in the RM-ODP engineering view-point focusing system design. Based on the proposed concepts, the architecture of alternative system designs and software/hardware allocation policies are analytically described. Though, non-functional requirements or properties are not explicitly described. The system designer may only depict them as custom properties defined for specific model entities.

The Rational Unified Process for Systems Engineering (RUP-SE) (Nolan et al., 2008), targets information system engineering in Rational Unified Process and was based on UML. It also adopted SysML for model-based information system design (Balmelli et al., 2006). SysML block entities may be employed to describe software, hardware or workers within the system or systems under consideration, while SysML diagrams are used to describe different viewpoints. Non-functional requirements (NFRs) are defined during allocating software to hardware components. This is accomplished in the context of joint realization tables (JRTs) associating logical and distribution views, when NFRs are defined as properties (e.g., table columns) of each specific association. For example, response time requirements can be defined when allocating processes to localities. SysML requirement entity, while used to depict functional requirements, is not adopted for NFR description. The description of derived NFRs is also not emphasized. Furthermore, NFR verification is not addressed within the context of RUP-SE.

In Izukura et al. (2011), SysML extensions are proposed for information system design, which are implemented within the context of a custom tool called CASSI. CASSI targets information system integration, while three different design views are supported, depicted using SysML external and internal block diagrams. The allocation of system components between different views is also supported. SysML requirement entity is not used to associate requirements to system elements. Though, information system configurations defined using CASSI are evaluated using simulation to verify performance and availability requirements. This is accomplished using an external simulator. The behavior of system components is described within CASSI using sequence diagrams, transformed to simulation model by an external transformation tool. Although NFRs can be verified, this is performed by the system designer using external tools. Evaluation results are not integrated within the SysML system model and NFR verification is not performed using it.

In Nikolaidou et al. (2009), the authors proposed a methodology focusing on EIS architecture design, as depicted in Figure 1. In this case, EIS architecture design solution synthesis encompasses Functionality, Topology and Network Infrastructure definitions (Nikolaidou et al., 2009). *Functionality Definition* focuses on software architecture design, *Topology Definition* on software allocation process and *Network Infrastructure Definition* on hardware architecture design. For each of these concerns, a corresponding view is defined to explore functional requirements and corresponding design decisions. The *Software Architect*, concerned with software architecture design and software allocation, is served by Functional and Topology views to contribute in the construction of EIS Architecture. In a similar fashion, *Hardware Architect* is contributing to hardware configuration using Network Infrastructure View and the *Network Architect* builds the network architecture based on Topology and Network Infrastructure Viewpoint. In case more than one stakeholders involved in system design, are served by a specific view, this is an indication that their cooperation is needed.

Figure 1. EIS architecture design activities and corresponding system views

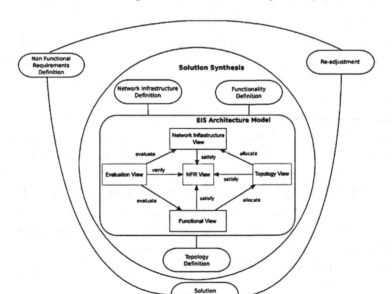

Non Functional Requirement (NFR) Definition should also be independently treated, since the conditions, under which the system should operate play a significant role in design decisions. For each of these definitions, a corresponding NFR view has been defined. In this manner, any of the system designers (for example software architect) is enabled to realize the affect of specific design decisions (e.g., the allocation of software to hardware resource) to non-functional requirements imposed to them (e.g., performance) and vice-versa. Using the corresponding NFR view, a system designer is enabled to explore non-functional requirements relationships, while, using other views, the relationship between non-functional requirements and design decisions is explored (Tsadimas et al., 2009). Such an approach allows for the progressive and independent execution of EIS architecture composition tasks in parallel, while the impact of design decisions adopted in each of them to the other ones is expressed in terms of non-functional requirements grouped in NFR view.

Furthermore, *EIS Architecture Evaluation* should be performed. In order to evaluate the designed solution, non-functional requirements definition is used, focusing on system performance and availability requirements essential for EIS architecture design. Then, solution evaluation is performed and evaluation results are used to check whether non-functional requirements are satisfied. If not, then EIS Architecture readjustment is performed until an acceptable EIS architecture synthesis is identified. To manage the evaluation process and maintain evaluation results a discrete *Evaluation View* is defined.

Simulation is a widely accepted model-based method to evaluate complex system behavior, especially when non-functional requirements should be verified (Estefan, 2008). Since non-functional requirements (e.g., performance requirements) are described using both qualitative and quantitative properties, simulation, as a quantitative method, is very effective to produce the necessary data for their verification. Thus, the system model, defined in the Evaluation View, should be simulated in an autonomous simulation environment with no additional effort by the system designer. Since EIS architecture design was addressed as a system composition problem, SysML was chosen as the modeling language.

SIMULATING SYSML MODELS

There are numerous efforts to simulate SysML system models to explore corresponding system performance (Paredis & Johnson, 2008; Peak et al., 2007; Topçu et al., 2008; Bocciarelli et al., 2012). Depending on the nature and specific characteristics of systems under study, different SysML diagrams are utilized. In Peak et al. (2007), the simulation of continuous systems using complex mathematical equations is presented, utilizing SysML parametric diagrams (Peak et al. (2007). In McGinnis & Ustun (2009), system models defined in SysML are translated to be simulated using Arena simulation software. In Wang & Dagli (2008), the utilization of Colored Petri Nets is proposed to simulate SysML models.

It should be noted that in any case SysML models should be defined in a way, which facilitates the simulation process (Tamburini, 2006), based on the specific characteristics of the simulation environment. In Kerzhner et al. (2011) and Paredis & Johnson (2008), simulation is performed using Modelica. To ensure that a complete and accurate Modelica model is constructed using SysML, a corresponding profile is proposed to enrich SysML models with simulation-specific capabilities (Paredis et al., 2010).

Besides simulating SysML models using external simulators, one should consider the integration of evaluation results into SysML system models to enhance the verification of non-functional requirements by the system designer and the exploration of alternative design solutions.

USING SYSML TO SUPPORT MODEL-BASED EIS ARCHITECTURE DESIGN

EIS architecture design views may be handled as discrete SysML block diagrams, emphasizing a different composition problem, such as software architecture design or hardware architecture design. Relations between design views are defined as SysML allocation between blocks that can be specialized based on a specific content (example.g., allocating software components to sites or software component replicas to hardware nodes). Since SysML can be extended or restricted to describe a specific system domain, it may be effectively serve solution synthesis and solution re-adjusted activities, enable the effective modeling and design of EIS architecture.

To enable the analytical description and verification of non-functional requirements in NFR view and the validation of related system designs in Evaluation View, we extended SysML to: a) include a discrete diagram to serve system evaluation activity and manage evaluation results and requirement verification and b) describe non-functional requirements in a quantitative fashion, focusing derived requirements (Tsadimas et al., 2012).

Based on the extensions, a SysML profile for EIS architecture design was implemented as a plugin for the MagicDraw modeling tool (NoMagic, 2013), focusing performance requirement description and verification. The basic concepts of the profile and the way they serve specific design activities are explained in the following.

SOLUTION SYNTHESIS AND REQUIREMENTS DEFINITION

As shown in Figure 1, system designers are provided with a common system model called *EIS Architecture Design model*, to perform architecture design tasks. Solution synthesis and requirement definition is performed using *Functional View*, *Topology View*, *Network Infrastructure View*, and *NFR View*. Design decisions and functional requirements are included in corresponding design view. All non functional requirements are aggregated in NFR view, while each of them is also included in the corresponding diagram that satisfies it, as depicted in Figure 1.

Functional view, represented as a block diagram, consists of the software architecture. Software tiers are represented as *Modules* (client & server) comprised of *services*. *Roles* depict the behavior of different user groups initiates services that belong to client Modules. Each service may invoke other services, depending on software functionality. Data Entities are used to represent portions of stored data.

Topology view, also represented as a block diagram, facilitates the description of system access points in terms of hierarchically related locations, called *sites* and the allocation of software, data and people resources in them. *Atomic sites* belong at the lowest level of hierarchy, whereas *composite sites* are comprised by others.

The allocation relation between Functional and Topology Views indicates that entities defined in Functional View and more specifically *application modules*, *data entities* and users modeled as *roles* are allocated to *sites*, defined in the Topology View. The allocation of modules, roles and data entities to sites corresponds to software architecture design.

Network architecture is defined in the Network Infrastructure view, also represented as a block diagram, where *networks*, either composite, consisting of others, or atomic ones, constituting of hardware elements (example.g., servers, workstations, or routers), are defined. Each atomic-network is further described by a block definition diagram which encompasses hardware elements, called *nodes*.

The allocation relation between Topology and Network Infrastructure View indicates that each site defined in the Topology Views is served by a network defined in Network Infrastructure View. When a site is allocated to a network, functional view entities allocated to each site must be specifically allocated to network nodes belonging to each network.

All these features could be easily described using existing SysML concepts. Since SysML supports a discrete requirement diagram, it was decided to use it for NFR view representation. To be accurately defined, non-functional requirements should be described using quantitative properties, while SysML requirements are defined in a qualitative fashion. Thus, SysML Requirement entity and corresponding relations should be extended to facilitate NFR description, as discussed in the following.

Extending SysML Requirement Diagram

Requirements in SysML are described in an abstract, qualitative manner, since they are specified by two properties, *id* and *text*, corresponding to a simple description. However, SysML specification suggests to use the stereotype mechanism to define additional properties for specific requirement categories. Requirements should by satisfied by entities belonging to other diagrams (*SysML satisfy* relation). Requirements are interrelated through a large relationship set, indicating the way they affect each other. The *derivedReqt* relation indicates a specific requirement is derived by others. In the case of NFRs, derived requirement quantitative properties should be automatically computed, by combining specific quantitative properties of requirements they derive from. The computation formulas may involve heuristics and become complicated. Constraints must be applied to derived requirements to enforce the automatic computation of derived properties, while computation algorithms must also be integrated in the SysML model.

SysML requirement entity must be extended to effectively represent:

1. The quantitative properties of requirements
2. The way derived requirements should be computed and
3. A requirement verification formula

The *containment* relationship, defined between requirements, indicates that the composite requirement is realized if and only if all the contained ones are realized. In this way, an abstract requirement may be composed of more specific ones, or a complex requirement may be described in a more detail fashion. In the case of system design, the notion of composite NFRs is essential to indicate the way a requirement defined for the system as whole may be described in terms of the detailed NFRs defined for system components.

As described in Figure 2, NFRs are defined as either *composite* or *extended*, both inheriting SysML requirement properties. Composite NFRs are abstract requirements (for example the EIS performance must be high) composed by extended NFRs, which describe specific requirements in a quantitative fashion. They obtain both qualitative and quantitative properties, while a *compareMethod* must also be defined for requirement verification based on information included in the Evaluation Diagram, as explained latter in this section. *Derived* NFRs, defined as a descendant of extended NFRs, must also include a *computationFormula* property.

NFR View consists of all NFRs that should be satisfied by entities belonging in the three aforementioned views. These requirements are progressively defined during model-based EIS Architecture design. Performance requirements are emphasized,

Figure 2. SysML NFRs entities

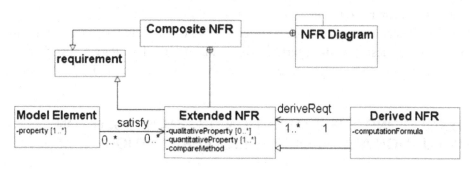

since they are essential in EIS architecture design. They can be defined as extended NFRs.

Regarding software performance, two NFRs are defined, namely *responseTime*, a *performance requirement* indicating the time interval within which a service should complete its execution, and *roleBehavior*, a *behavior requirement* indicating activation patterns for roles defined within Functional view. They are both satisfied by Services. Behavior requirements are used to indicate the conditions under which the EIS should be operating and don't need verification, as explained in the next section. Load requirements concerning the load imposed to network infrastructure resources are also defined for both services (*serviceQoS*) and modules (*moduleQoS*). While the first one is defined by the software architect, the second is a derived one based on the properties of the serviceQoS requirements of the services included in the corresponding module. Thus, it is described by *computational formula* additional property.

Derived load requirements are also satisfied by sites in Topology View (*traffic*) and Nodes and Networks in Network Infrastructure View (*load*). All four requirements are described by *maximum value*, *average value*, *deviation*, and *measurement unit* quantitative properties. There are three types of load requirement: *processing*, *storage*, and *traffic*. Load NFRs defined in the three design views are interrelated. For example, *Traffic-Load* requirement is related to *site-to-network* allocation decisions, and derived by corresponding *traffic* requirements, which in turn are derived by *traffic-Module-QoS* requirement of *Module-Replicas* allocated to *Sites*. *Module-Replicas* are instances of the Modules defined in Functional View.

Utilization and *Availability* requirements are associated with Network Infrastructure elements. Maximum and average values are defined for *Utilization* requirement and minimum and average values are defined for *Availability* requirement, while the accepted deviation of values is also defined. Availability and utilization requirements are defined by the network designer. An analytical description of all NFR view entities can be found in Tsadimas et al. (2009).

Defined performance and behavior requirements (indicated with red color) and corresponding design entities, participating in Functional, Topology, Network Infrastructure, satisfying them (indicated with yellow color) are summarized in Figure 3.

INTRODUCING THE EVALUATION DIAGRAM: SOLUTION EVALUATION AND REQUIREMENT VERIFICATION

SysML provides the means to describe a set of tests, which should be performed to verify whether a requirement is satisfied by system components. To depict such an activity, the *test case* entity, included in Requirement diagrams, is introduced. A test case is related to one or a set of requirements for their verification, while it is described through a behavior diagram (for example activity or state machine diagram) corresponding to the activity (as a set of tests) performed to verify related requirements. The way NFR requirements are handled in SysML is summarized in Figure 2.

Figure 3. Interrelating EIS performance requirements, design entities and evaluation entities

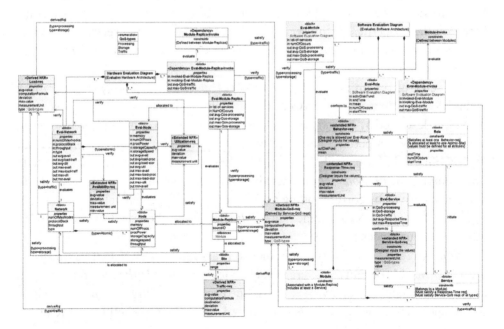

Since non-functional requirements (for example performance requirements) are described using both qualitative and quantitative properties, a quantitative method, such as simulation, should be employed to produce the necessary data for their verification. In such a case, the way system evaluation is performed, conforms to the corresponding simulation method. Thus, the definition of test cases is of less importance, since they could only be used to specify the conditions under which the system should be evaluated and not the evaluation method itself (Kerzhner et al., 2011).

In the case of EIS Architecture Design, Evaluation view should be described by a discrete SysML diagram, facilitating:

1.   Definition of the conditions under which the system will be evaluated,
2.   Depiction of the evaluation results, and
3.   Requirement verification, informing the system designers for any inconsistencies.

The *Evaluation Diagram* consists of *evaluation scenarios* defined, instead of SysML test cases, to verify composite NFRs. Evaluation Diagram is in fact a Block Definition diagram, where evaluation scenarios are depicted as independent Blocks further decomposed using discrete Block Definitions diagrams.

Evaluation scenarios comprise of *evaluation entities* used to evaluate design entities and verify corresponding requirements. NFR verification is usually performed via simulation. Regardless of the method used to perform system evaluation, evaluation entities have *input properties*, related to evaluated system entities, and *output properties*, depicting evaluation data. Based on the value of output properties, requirements are verified. In the case of quantitative requirements, the exact comparison between arithmetic values is not always appropriate. Thus, an appropriate comparison method (compareMethod attribute) should be defined for a specific requirement. Requirements may also be used to depict specific behavior forced to system components. In such case, there is no point in verifying them. Evaluation entity may conform to them, since they specify conditions under which the system architecture design should be evaluated.

In the case of EIS architecture design, each evaluation entity is created in order to evaluate a specific EIS Architecture entity and verify corresponding requirements. During system design, NFRs may also be used to depict specific behavior forced on system components (e.g., the way a traffic generator may behave under heavy traffic conditions). In this case, the corresponding evaluation entity may conform to them, providing input to the simulation environment. The relation between design and evaluation entities as well as corresponding requirements is depicted in Figure

4. In this case, a *design entity* satisfies two NFRs: *performance requirement*, depicting system performance restrictions, and *behavior requirement*, depicting system behavior. Only the first requirement must be verified by *eval-entity*, since the second provides input properties to the evaluation entity, indicating the conditions under which the evaluation should be done.

In the case of EIS architecture design, each evaluation scenario consists of two sub-views (diagrams), focusing on *Software* and *Hardware* design respectively (as shown in Figure 3). The entities participating in Software Evaluation diagram correspond to Functional View entities and are used a) to define the behavior of the software components during the evaluation of the proposed EIS architecture design, b) to evaluate the corresponding Functional View entity (for example *Eval-Module* evaluates a *Module* and c) to verify the requirements that should by satisfied by the Module. Hardware Evaluation diagram entities correspond to Topology (module replicas) and Network Infrastructure view entities, and are used a) to initialize a corresponding simulation model instance and b) to evaluate the design entity and verify the corresponding requirements.

For example, as depicted in Figure 3, the *Eval-Network* entity is introduced to evaluate Networks defined in Network Infrastructure view and verify *Traffic Load* requirements. Eval-Network input properties are the same with the corresponding Network properties, while output properties consist of the appropriate simulation results, facilitating the verification of requirements. Eval-Network entity verifies *Utilization, Availability* and *Load* requirements, so these attributes are defined as

Figure 4. The concepts of evaluation scenario and evaluation entity

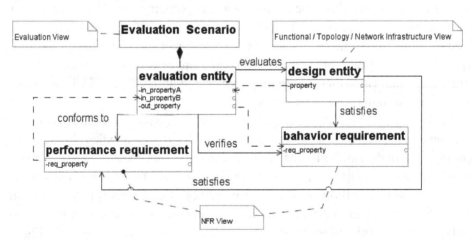

output attributes of the Eval-Network entity (*max-util, avg-util, min-avail, avg-avail, max-load-traf* and *avg-load-traf*). For example, the *max-load-traf* property of Eval-Network entity is compared to *max-value* property of traffic-Load requirement, to verify if the requirement is satisfied. The way this comparison is implemented is defined in the *compareMethod* property of Traffic Load requirement, as java code initialized whenever a corresponding constraint is initiated for all or a specific Eval-Network entity. More specifically, the following condition should be true: $Eval\text{-}Network.Max\text{-}load\text{-}traffic \in [max\text{-}value - deviation, max\text{-}value + deviation]$, where Eval-Network evaluates the Network satisfying the specific requirement.

Regarding software architecture, the *max and average ResponseTime* output properties of Eval-Service entity are compared to *ResponseTime* requirement properties, to verify if the requirement is satisfied. The value of derived requirements calculated for Module and Module-Invoke entities are also verified using *Eval-Module* entity. However, not all requirements related to a software component have to be verified. For example, the input properties of *Eval-Service* entity include the Service-QoS requirements that the corresponding service satisfies, and indicate the conditions under which the evaluation should be performed. In such case, the Eval-Service entity conforms to the Service-QoS requirement, defined for service component behavior in a quantitative fashion (Figure 3).

SOLUTION READJUSTMENT

System components participating in the 3 design views, failing to satisfy related performance measures, are visually identified in each Evaluation Scenario. Based on these observations, system engineers are responsible to properly adjust EIS architecture design (e.g., either to software or hardware architecture described in Functional, Topology or Network Infrastructure Views or even relax corresponding requirements). For example, if a service fails to satisfy the response time requirement that is associated with it, the system engineer has two options: either to adjust the response time or to lower the desired quality of service parameters that this service requires from the hardware and/or network resources. Based on the adjusted views, system designers may initiate another evaluation scenario. Since evaluation scenarios become part of the system model, system designers may refer to them to realize the effect of specific architecture decisions on the EIS architecture. Previous evaluation scenarios can help the designer to check alternative configurations and to decide which of them can help him to achieve the desired performance or satisfy all the defined requirements.

Simulating Evaluation Scenarios

Evaluation scenarios comprising Evaluation Diagram are parts of the EIS SysML profile. In order to be simulated, the corresponding simulation code should be automatically generated for a specific simulation environment and simulation results should be properly incorporated within the model as evaluation entity properties. As EIS SysML profile is formally defined, it can be exported from any ULM modeling tool, as Magic Draw, in an XMI format. The profile is defined as part of SysML, thus all the stereotypes included in it are described according to UML MOF 2.0 metamodel.

We argue that Evaluation Diagram entities may be transformed to executable simulation entities utilizing basic MDA concepts and corresponding transformation languages as QVT, provided that simulation is performed using a simulation framework/language that can be modeled according to MOF metamodel. In such case, bidirectional transformations may be easily defined between UML/SysML and any simulation language.

DEVS provides a conceptual framework for discrete event simulation and is supported by a wide variety of simulators built in numerous programming environments. DEVS models consists of DEVs coupled models, describing system structure, and DEVS atomic models, defining system behavior. Based on the similarities between system models defined using SysML and DEVS, Nikolaidou et al. (2008; 2010; 2012) proposed a methodology to automatically construct executable DEVS code for system models already defined in SysML and defined a DEVS MOF metamodel for this purpose.

Utilizing this metamodel, a QVT transformation was defined to map EIS profile evaluation entities, defined as SysML stereotypes, to a DEVS coupled model, used to simulate an evaluation scenario. The DEVS model corresponding to the evaluation scenario is consequently transformed into executable code for DEVS Java simulation environment, using existing tools (Nikolaidou et. al., 2012). EIS behavior is already defined as DEVS atomic models, incorporated in model libraries for DEVS Java. Simulation output is recorded in text files and, consequently, incorporated as output properties of evaluation entities, using a javascript plug-in, written especially for this purpose.

CASE STUDY

The proposed approach and corresponding SysML profile for EIS Architecture design was applied in a case study where the renovation of the legacy system of a public organization was explored (Tsadimas et al., 2012). One of the main objectives of legacy system architecture re-design was to enhance application performance without major rewriting the applications themselves. Alternative software architectures and their implications to hardware/network infrastructure were evaluated. Since performance plays a significant role, it was suggested to apply the EIS SysML profile, to explore related design decisions and evaluate them. Two different scenarios were explored: a) to support existing distributed database architecture and try to consolidate hardware and b) to establish a central database architecture resulting in minor applications code modifications. The organization constitutes of more than 350 interconnected regional offices technologically supported by a central IT Center responsible for IT diffusion and management. Regional offices are divided into three categories according to their size, structure, and personnel (large, medium, and small). Each category is treated differently in terms of network infrastructure requirements. To enhance the level of service provided by the organization, over the last decade an e-government portal was established. The main target of the portal is to provide easy access to citizens 24 hours per day, seven days per week and to minimize the need for citizen's presence in regional offices. The portal facilitates on-line transactional services and ensures on-line access to the databases of the legacy information system, serving almost one third of requests processed by the legacy system on a daily basis.

Software Architecture Design

Since application functionality is well-known, the identification of software architecture and related performance requirements was perceived as a trivial task. It was proved to be more complex than expected. To obtain this information the software architect had to communicate with application maintenance personnel in the corresponding department of the IT Center, playing the role of the software designer. RUP methodology (Kruchten, 1998; Cantor, 2003) was used for software development, thus application description models were developed within Rational Rose platform. Application description (e.g. applications, modules and services) as well as data structures were manually extracted from corresponding Rational Rose files. Unfortunately, the identification of service requirements was not a straightforward procedure, since non-functional requirements were not recorded, indicating the lack of Enterprise Architecture perception in the organization. Furthermore, neither software maintenance or administration personnel was able to accurate provide non-functional requirement information regarding response time or serviceQoS (Tsadimas et al., 2010). Response time requirements were finally defined by software designers, while serviceQoS requirements were obtained after monitoring application functionally during working hours by system administration personnel in the current version of the system. Service QoS requirement accurate definition was essential for the effective exploration of application performance based on alternative architecture scenarios.

Functional View

A snapshot of the Functional View corresponding to a distributed architecture scenario is depicted in Figure 6. All application logic is programmed within clients running on users' workstations, while data are distributed in local database servers located in each regional office. A central database is supported in the IT Center for data synchronization and lookup purposes. Client programs access the local database to store data, which are asynchronously replicated in the central database

Figure 5. Magic Draw, DEVS and simulator integration

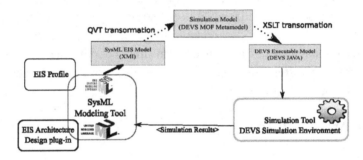

Figure 6. An excerpt of functional view

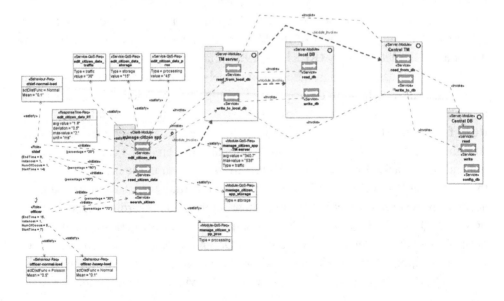

using a transaction management system (TMS). The IT Center and all regional offices participate in a private TCP/IP network to facilitate efficient data replication.

As an example, an excerpt of Functional View focusing on *manage citizens* application is depicted in Figure 6. This application is composed of three services, named *edit*, *search*, and *read* citizen data, called by two different user roles, the *officer* and the *chief*. Only *chief* role can edit citizen data, as indicated by the initiate relation between this role and the service. The *officer* role initiates the *read_citizen_data* service by 30% and the *search_citizen* service by 70%. The software designer may use a *Behavior* to model role behavior. In this example, the *officer* role may satisfy two different behavior requirements: one to describe normal workload and another to describe a heavy workload.

As an example, the invocation of *edit_citizen_data* service is presented in Figure 6. The service invokes the two services of the *TM server* module and these ones invoke two other services of *local DB* module. The *edit_citizen_data_RT* response-time requirement is defined for *edit_citizen_data* service.

After service-QoS requirements of all the services belonging to a specific module are defined by the software architect, an estimation of the Module-QoS requirements of this module is automatically computed. The corresponding processing and storage derived requirements are automatically computed based on a calculation formula (Tsadimas et al., 2012), implemented as a Java class of the EIS profile plugin. The third requirement, traffic Module-QoS requirement, cannot be assigned to a Module, but to a pair of modules, defining the amount of data transferred between them. In the Figure 6, the *manage_citizen_app-TM server* Traffic Module QoS requirement satisfied by the *Module_Invoke* relation between *manage_citizen_app* and

TM server modules) is automatically created.

Topology View

Topology view depicts the structure of the organization, consisting of regional offices and a central datacenter. According to regional office category (large, medium, and small) there is a difference in the number of officers employed in them. In large regional offices, each officer serves in a specific department and has access to the corresponding application. More than a hundred officers work in a large regional office. Small offices employ less than 15 officers having access to all applications. Medium regional offices employ around 60 officers, while the operation of specific department is merged into bigger ones. Thus, some officers have access to more than one application.

A fraction of the corresponding Topology view is depicted in Figure 7. The site hierarchy corresponding to a medium regional office is defined in this view. Regional Office is defined as a composite site named LocalOffice, where two atomic sites are included (defined with containment relationship): *LocalDataCenter* and *Registration Department*. The software architect allocates roles and software entities (module replicas) to atomic-sites. *Chief* and 5 *officers* are allocated to *Registration Department*. The Datacenter site has no allocated roles (no-one wants to work in a server room). Client module replicas are automatically allocated to sites in the Topology view. Since a role initiates client modules, it is reasonable to assume that for each module the role initiates, a module-replica should be allocated to the site where the role is allocated (see Figure 7). For each server module, a module-replica can be generated (using replica-of relation) by the software architect, right-clicking on the server module, and he/she is responsible to allocate it to a site.

To estimate of the traffic software entities are generating within a site and between sites, traffic requirements satisfied by sites are automatically created. Each site satisfies a traffic requirement, indicating data exchanged within the site and traffic requirements for sites that communicate with it. Traffic requirement attributes are derived and estimated based on a calculation formula. For example, *Registration Dept in* represents the traffic between modules that belong to *Registration Dept* site, while the *Registration Dept-LocalDataCenter* represents the traffic directed from *Registration Dept* to *LocalDataCenter* site. Traffic requirements may assist network designer to define the network architecture in Network Infrastructure View.

Hardware Architecture Design

The network architecture was mostly predefined. The software architect was enabled to explore the two different database architecture scenarios and the affect they had in the private network interconnecting regional offices and the IT Center. She modified software allocations in the Topology view and corresponding load requirements satisfied by the network infrastructure were automatically computed

Figure 7. Topology view excerpt for medium regional office

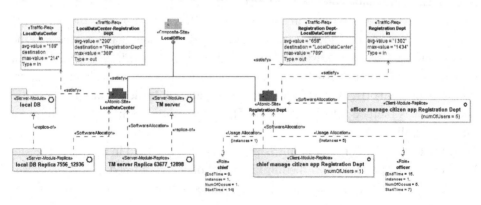

using the profile. Alternative hardware architecture designs were proposed for the Data Center taking into account restrictions imposed by hardware solution architects participating in the project. Restrictions were recorded in SysML as non-functional requirements associated to hardware components.

Network Infrastructure View

Network Infrastructure View represents existing network topology and is complementary to Topology View. To each network corresponding sites are allocated, indicating they are served by the specific network. Networks are either composite (which means that they consist of other networks) or atomic. Network Infrastructure view is described in two levels: at the first level network architecture and site allocations are presented and at the second level atomic networks are described by individual diagrams.

As seen in Figure 8, the two sites defined in Topology view (*Registration Dept* and *LocalDataCenter*) for a regional office are allocated to an atomic network, called *LocalOfficeLAN*. A composite network has been defined for the datacenter of the organization, composed by two atomic-networks: *DataCenter Admin Office* network and *DataCenter Server room*, which is interconnected with the *LocalOfficeLAN* through a Point-To-Point connection. To define the connection speed between two networks, load requirements of the networks and utilization of the network connection must be taken into account. Load requirements depend on the

Figure 8. Network infrastructure view excerpt atomic network diagram

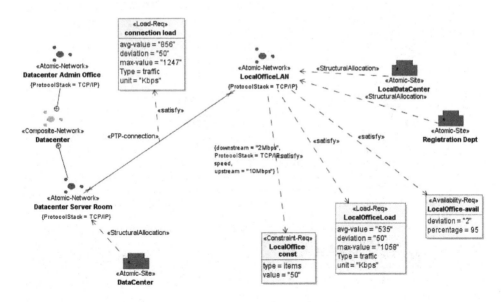

server distribution, meaning that if the servers are distributed across the local offices, the load will be higher whereas if the applications are Web-based, the load will be less. For a network of a higher hierarchy, load requirement is computed (is derived by) the load requirements of the lower lever networks. In order to calculate PTP connection utilization two parameters have to be defined: the network load and the network connection speed.

Atomic-network diagram, describing atomic networks, consist of network nodes and roles and module replicas allocated to them. As an example the *LocalOffice* atomic network diagram is presented in Figure 10. The reader can identify the roles and module replicas that were allocated to sites, consequently allocated to this network, to be included in this diagram. These entities are automatically added by a corresponding plug-in and the system engineer has only to define the hardware elements (workstations and servers), these elements are allocated to. A utilization requirement (*App & DB server util*) is defined as an example, for *App & DB server*, defining that the CPU utilization of the server should be between 60 and 90 percent.

Figure 9. Atomic network diagram excerpt: validation example

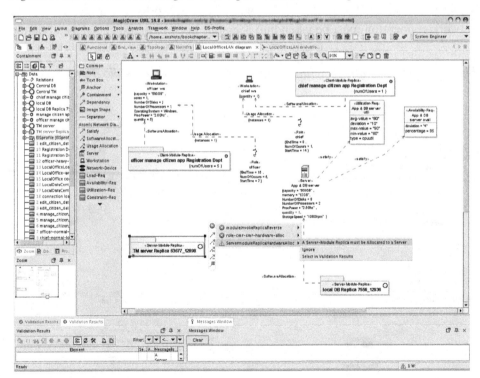

Figure 10. Atomic network diagram excerpt: derived load requirement addition

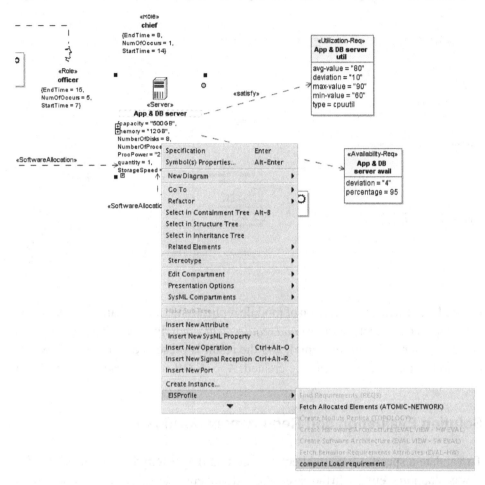

Validation rules are integrated within MagicDraw tool to assist the system designer to avoid errors, in the form of constraints. For example if a *module replica* is not allocated to a *hardware element*, the corresponding validation rule implemented in java is invoked, in order to inform the system designer to address this issue. Figure 9 indicates that the *TM server Replica 63677_12898* is not allocated to any node. This is one of the validation errors/warnings that is presented for this specific entity through the validation process (this example indicates that there are three validation errors). It should be noted that the validation process is supported by MagicDraw tool. Validation rules are implemented is java as part of the EIS profile plug-in.

Derived requirements, as the load requirement, are auto-created and auto-computed to enhance system designer knowledge of the system. For example in

Figure 11. Atomic network diagram excerpt: LocalOfficeLAN

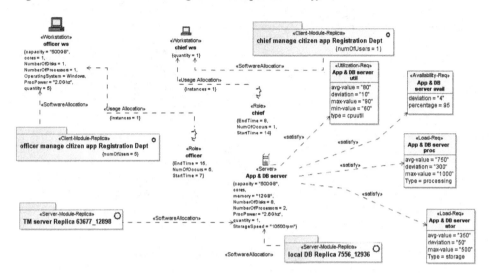

Figure 10 and after the allocation of module replicas and roles to hardware elements, the designer can select *compute Load requirement* when right-clicking to a hardware element (a server in our example), and the result is presented in Figure 11, where two kind of load requirements are created: *App & DB server proc* and *App & DB server stor*.

Solution Evaluation and Requirement Verification

To validate a specific EIS architecture solution, the system designer may create a new evaluation scenario. In the case of EIS Architecture design, evaluation scenarios are simulated using DEVS. The system model is extracted from Magic Draw in XMI format (OMG, 2007b) and consequently transformed according to DEVS MOF meta-model to be fed to DEVS Java simulator, as shown in Figure 5.

Evaluation entities corresponding to design entities belonging to the 3 design views (see Figure 3) are automatically added in the evaluation scenario diagram, both in software and hardware design diagram. The software design diagram has a similar structure to Functional View, focusing software performance, while hardware design diagram has a similar structure to Network Infrastructure View, focusing network and hardware performance. The evaluation entities' input properties are used to initialize the simulation model and the output properties are used to store simulation output.

To verify a performance requirement, the system engineer should be informed of any conflicts between evaluation entities output properties and corresponding

Figure 12. Evaluation diagram excerpt

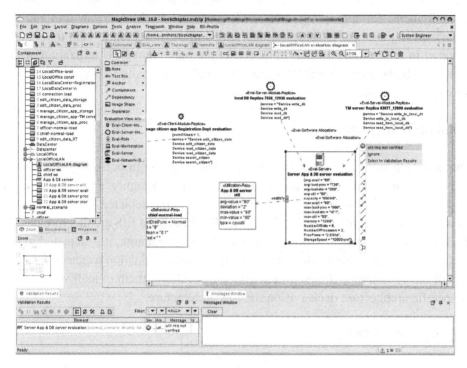

requirement properties, based on the compareMethod defined for this requirement (see Figure 2).

A portion of an evaluation scenario in the Evaluation Diagram corresponding to LocalOfficeLAN atomic network of Figure 8 is depicted in Figure 12.

Each evaluation entity, for example *Server App & DB server evaluation*, is described by input attributes (example.g., *memory, ProcPower, capacity*) computed from the attributes of the corresponding design entity (*App & DB server*) of *LocalOfficeLAN* atomic network diagram in Network Infrastructure View. Output properties (for example *max-load-proc, avg-load-proc, max-util, avg-avail*, etc) imported from the simulation environment, are used to verify corresponding requirements(as described in Figure 4).

After importing simulation results, the system designer may initialize the verification process, which is implemented as a set of validation rules. Each rule corresponds to the implementation of the *compareMethod* property of the NFR under verification. Evaluation entities output properties are automatically compared to the related requirement properties and a proper indication (color deviation) is provided to the system designer to indicate which NFRs are not verified.

In the example presented in Figure 12, the *Server App & DB server evaluation max-util* output property is 93%. After running requirement verification, requirement violation is found, as declared with a red color of the entity that fails to satisfy a requirement. An appropriate message is generated by MagicDraw tool and the unverified requirement is automatically added in the diagram, to help the system designer to realize the conflict. In this case, the maximum CPU utilization of the server can be between 88 and 92%, but the simulation results are showing that the max-util is 93%; thus, it is out of the bounds.

Solution Readjustment

Through performance evaluation scenarios, the conflicts in performance requirement verification are visually presented to the system designer. They are the ones responsible for adjusting architecture design decision depicted in the 3 design views or relax corresponding requirements. The history of EIS architecture design modifications is not depicted in the design diagrams. Though, it is depicted in the evaluation scenarios created for their validation. Since evaluation scenarios become part of the system model, system designers may refer to them to realize the effect of specific architecture decisions on the EIS architecture.

Experience Obtained

System designers that tested the tool in the case study appreciated the fact that all the information related to requirement verification was presented in a single view. They also found useful that all different experiment results were maintained, as evaluation scenarios, and could be used when making modification in architecture design. In fact, they ranked it as the most important feature of the proposed SysML extensions, since it enabled them to keep track of all redesign decisions and the reasons leading to them. Derived requirement computation was considered useful, but also a bit confusing for some of the experts using the tool. Furthermore, most of them also suggested that the tool could propose alternatives on system architecture modifications to satisfy imposed requirements.

FUTURE RESEARCH DIRECTIONS

The proposed EIS profile is currently tested using real-world case studies to identify limitations of the proposed approach. The way the exploration of complex models may affect the performance of EIS Architecture Design MagicDraw plugin, especially during derived requirement computation and evaluation scenario creation, is also under investigation.

Future work includes applying the proposed SysML extensions in other domains as well and integrating them with other UML and SysML profiles targeting non-functional requirements. In the case of EIS profile, DEVS model libraries were custom built to serve the needs of EIS simulation and simulation model initialization was performed by transforming an evaluation scenario to the initial DEVS coupled model to be simulated. Integrating the proposed profile with others, as DEVS SysML or SysML4Modelica (OpenModelica, 2013), enabling system simulation, would contribute to a generalized approach for NFR description and verification in SysML system models.

CONCLUSION

SysML provides distinct diagrams to describe system structure, explore allocation policies, and identify system requirements. However, during system design, non-functional requirements, such as performance requirements, should be effectively explored since they drastically affect efficient system operation. Proposed system designs should be validated and properly adjusted until an acceptable architecture is defined.

The integration of an Evaluation diagram consisting of evaluation scenarios facilitates system design validation and requirement verification, while evaluation results are included in the system model. As deduced from the experience obtained in the case study, the existence of the Evaluation diagram assists the system designer to better realize the affect of his/her redesign decisions.

REFERENCES

Balmelli, L., Brown, D., Cantor, M., & Mott, M. (2006). Model-driven systems development. *IBM Systems Journal, 45*(3), 569–585. doi:10.1147/sj.453.0569.

Bocciarelli, P., D'Ambrogio, A., & Fabiani, G. (2012). A model-driven approach to build hla-based distributed simulations from sysml models. [Rome, Italy: SciTe-Press.]. *Proceedings of SIMULTECH, 12,* 49–60.

Cantor, M. (2003, May). Rational Unified Process for Systems Engineering, RUP SE Version 2.0, IBM Rational Software white paper [Computer software manual].

Espinoza, H., Cancila, D., Selic, B., & Gérard, S. (2009). Challenges in combining SysML and MARTE for model-based design of embedded systems. In *ECMDA-FA* (*Vol. 5562*, pp. 98–113). New York: Springer. doi:10.1007/978-3-642-02674-4_8.

Estefan, J. A. (2008, June). Survey of model-based systems engineering (MBSE) methodologies - revision b [Computer software manual].

ISO. (2009, October). *Information technology –open distributed processing– use of UML for ODP system specifications*. Retrieved from ISO/IECCD19793.

Izukura, S., Yanoo, K., Osaki, T., Sakaki, H., Kimura, D., & Xiang, J. (2011). Applying a model-based approach to IT systems development using SysML extension. In *MoDELS* (*Vol. 6981*, pp. 563–577). New York: Springer. doi:10.1007/978-3-642-24485-8_41.

Kacem, M. H., Jmaiel, M., Kacem, A. H., & Drira, K. (2006). *A UML-based approach for validation of software architecture descriptions* (pp. 158–171). TEAA.

Kerzhner, A. A., Jobe, J. M., & Paredis, C. J. J. (2011). A formal framework for capturing knowledge to transform structural models into analysis models. *Journal Simulation, 5*(3), 202–216. doi:10.1057/jos.2011.17.

Kerzhner, A. A., & Paredis, C. J. J. (2010). Model-based system verification: A formal framework for relating analyses, requirements, and tests. In *Models in software engineering - Workshops and symposia at MODELS 2010* (pp. 279–292). Berlin, Germany: Springer-Verlag.

Kruchten, P. (1998). *Rational Unified Process: An Introduction*. Boston, MA: Addison-Wesley.

McGinnis, L. F., & Ustun, V. (2009). A simple example of SysML-driven simulation. In *Proceedings of Winter Simulation Conference* (pp. 1703–1710). Austin, TX: WSC.

Nikolaidou, M., Dalakas, V., & Anagnostopoulos, D. (2010). Integrating Simulation Capabilities in SysML using DEVS. In *IEEE International Systems Conference (SysCon 2010)*. San Diego, CA: IEEE Computer Society.

Nikolaidou, M., Dalakas, V., Mitsi, L., Kapos, G.-D., & Anagnostopoulos, D. (2008). A sysml profile for classical devs simulators. In *Proceedings of Software Engineering Advances, 2008. ICSEA '08. The Third International Conference* (p. 445 -450). Sliema, Malta: IEEE.

Nikolaidou, M., Kapos, G.-D., Dalakas, V., & Anagnostopoulos, D. (2012). Basic Guidelines for Simulating SysML Models: An Experience Report. In *Proceedings Of 7th International Conference on System of Systems Engineering*. Genova, Italy: IEEE.

Nikolaidou, M., Tsadimas, A., Alexopoulou, N., & Anagnostopoulos, D. (2009). Employing Zachman Enterprise Architecture Framework to systematically perform Model-Based System Engineering Activities. *Proceedings of, HICSS-42*, 1–10.

Nolan, B., Brown, B., Balmelli, L., Bohn, T., & Wahli, U. (2008). Model driven systems development with rational products [Computer software manual].

NoMagic. (2013). *MagicDraw UML*. Retrieved January 2013 from http://www.magicdraw.com

OMG. (2007a). *UML Superstructure Specification, Version 2.1.2.*

OMG. (2007b). *XML Metadata Interchange*. Retrieved January 2013 from http://www.omg.org/spec/XMI/2.1.1/PDF/index.htm.

OMG. (2009). *UML profile for MARTE: Modeling and analysis of real-time embedded systems specification, version 1.0.*

OMG. (2010). *Systems Modeling Language (SYSML) Specification, Version 1.2.*

OpenModelica. (2013). *OpenModelica*. Retrieved January 2013 from http://www.openmodelica.org/index.php/developer/tools/134

Paredis, C. J. J., Bernard, Y., Koning, R. M. B. H.-D., & Friedenthal, S. (2010). An overview of the SysML-Modelica transformation specification. *Jet Propulsion, 2*, 14.

Paredis, C. J. J., & Johnson, T. (2008). Using OMG'S SYSML to support simulation. In S. J. Mason, R. R. Hill, L. Mönch, O. Rose, T. Jefferson, & J. W. Fowler (Eds.), *Proceedings of Winter Simulation Conference* (pp. 2350–2352). Miami, FL: IEEE.

Peak, R., Burkhart, R., Friedenthal, S., Wilson, M., Bajaj, M., & Kim, I. (2007). Simulation-based design using sysml part 1: A parametrics primer. Paper presented at INCOSE International Symposium. San Diego, CA

Tamburini, D. (2006). *Defining executable design & simulation models using sysml.* Paper presented at Frontiers in Design & Simulation Research Workshop. Atlanta, GA.

Topçu, O., Adak, M., & Oguztüzün, H. (2008). A metamodel for federation architectures. *ACM Transactions on Modeling and Computer Simulation, 18*(3), 10:1–10:29.

Tsadimas, A., Nikolaidou, M., & Anagnostopoulos, D. (2009). Handling non-functional requirements in information system architecture design. In ICSEA '09 (p. 59-64).

Tsadimas, A., Nikolaidou, M., & Anagnostopoulos, D. (2010). Evaluating software architecture in a model- based approach for enterprise information system design. In *SHARK '10* (pp. 72–79). New York: ACM. doi:10.1145/1833335.1833346.

Tsadimas, A., Nikolaidou, M., & Anagnostopoulos, D. (2012). Extending SysML to explore non- functional requirements description and verification: The case of information system design. In *Requirements Engineering Track - 27th ACM Symposium on Applied Computing - SAC12*. Trento, Italy. ACM.

Wang, R., & Dagli, C. (2008). An executable system architecture approach to discrete events system modeling using SysML in conjunction with colored petri nets. In *IEEE Systems Conference 2008* (pp.1–8). Montreal, Canada: IEEE Computer Press.

KEY TERMS AND DEFINITIONS

DEVS: DEVS abbreviating Discrete Event System Specification is a modular and hierarchical formalism for modeling and analyzing general systems that can be discrete event systems which might be described by state transition tables, and continuous state systems which might be described by differential equations, and hybrid continuous state and discrete event systems. DEVS is a timed event system.

EIS Architecture Design: EIS architecture design is the process of defining and optimizing the architecture of the information system (both hardware and software) and exploring performance requirements, ensuring that all software components are identified and properly allocated and that hardware resources can provide the desired performance to software.

Evaluation Diagram: In order to effectively define EIS Architecture, the system architect should ensure that non-functional requirements are fulfilled. Evaluation Diagram is used to evaluate such requirements, as system performance, of different EIS Architecture configurations, as defined by the system architect in Functional and Network Infrastructure views. In practice, it is used to determine whether the proposed architecture meets specifications placed by non-functional requirements. Since EIS Architecture design process may require to evaluate and properly adjust the proposed architecture more than once, Evaluation diagram consists of multiple test cases used to evaluate alternative solutions.

Model-Based System Engineering: The INCOSE SE Vision 2020 (INCOSE-TP-2004-004-02 September, 2007) defines Model-based systems engineering (MBSE) as "the formalized application of modeling to support system requirements, design, analysis, verification and validation activities beginning in the conceptual design phase and continuing throughout development and later life cycle phases. MBSE is part of a long-term trend toward model-centric approaches adopted by other engineering disciplines, including mechanical, electrical and software. In particular, MBSE is expected to replace the document-centric approach that has been practiced by systems engineers in the past and to influence the future practice of systems engineering by being fully integrated into the definition of systems engineering processes." Applying MBSE is expected to provide significant benefits over the document centric approach by enhancing productivity and quality, reducing risk, and providing improved communications among the system development team.

NFR: In systems engineering and requirements engineering, a non-functional requirement is a requirement that specifies criteria that can be used to judge the operation of a system, rather than specific behaviors. This should be contrasted with functional requirements that define specific behavior or functions. The plan for implementing functional requirements is detailed in the system design. The plan for implementing non-functional requirements is detailed in the system architecture.

NFR Verification: All requirements should be verifiable. The most common method is by test. If this is not the case, another verification method should be used instead (e.g. analysis, demonstration or inspection or review of design). Non-functional requirements, which are unverifiable at the software level, must still be kept as a documentation of customer intent. However, they may be traced to process requirements that are determined to be a practical way of meeting them. For example, a non-functional requirement to be free from backdoors may be satisfied by replacing it with a process requirement to use pair programming. Other non-functional requirements will trace to other system components and be verified at that level. For example system reliability is often verified by analysis at the system level. Avionics software with its complicated safety requirements must follow the DO-178B development process.

Simulation: Simulation is the imitation of the operation of a real-world process or system over time. The act of simulating something first requires that a model be developed; this model represents the key characteristics or behaviors of the selected physical or abstract system or process. The model represents the system itself, whereas the simulation represents the operation of the system over time. In EIS Architecture design, where non-functional requirements are defined (for example performance requirements) are described using both qualitative and quantitative properties, a quantitative method, such as simulation, should be employed to produce the necessary data for their verification.

SysML: The Systems Modeling Language (SysML) is a general-purpose modeling language for systems engineering applications. It supports the specification, analysis, design, verification and validation of a broad range of systems and systems-of-systems.

SysML Profile: A profile in the Unified Modeling Language (UML) or the Systems Modeling Language (SysML) provides a generic extension mechanism for customizing UML models for particular domains and platforms. Extension mechanisms allow refining standard semantics in strictly additive manner, so that they can't contradict standard semantics. Profiles are defined using stereotypes, tag definitions, and constraints that are applied to specific model elements, such as Classes, Attributes, Operations, and Activities. A Profile is a collection of such extensions that collectively customize UML for a particular domain (e.g., aerospace, healthcare, financial) or platform (J2EE, .NET).

System View: A view model or viewpoints framework in systems engineering, software engineering, and enterprise engineering is a framework which defines a coherent set of views to be used in the construction of a system architecture, software architecture, or enterprise architecture. A view is a representation of a whole system from the perspective of a related set of concerns.

System Viewpoint: The purpose of views and viewpoints is to enable humans to comprehend very complex systems, to organize the elements of the problem and the solution around domains of expertise and to separate concerns. In the engineering of physically intensive systems, viewpoints often correspond to capabilities and responsibilities within the engineering organization. Each viewpoint satisfies an audience with interest in a particular set of aspects of the system. Each viewpoint may use a specific viewpoint language that optimizes the vocabulary and presentation for the audience of that viewpoint. Viewpoint modeling has become an effective approach for dealing with the inherent complexity of large distributed systems.

Chapter 9
Domain Specific Simulation Modeling with SysML and Model-to-Model Transformation for Discrete Processes

Oliver Schönherr
Universität der Bundeswehr München, Germany

Falk Stefan Pappert
Universität der Bundeswehr München, Germany

Oliver Rose
Universität der Bundeswehr München, Germany

ABSTRACT

In this chapter, the authors present an approach for developing a simulation-tool-independent description of manufacturing systems and how to convert such a general model into simulation-tool-specific models. They show why we need standards for these discrete processes, what the state of the art is, why SysML has the chance to become a standard in modeling discrete systems, and how to use it. The authors present SysML and explain how to model discrete systems with it. For that, they explain the concept of domain-specific modeling in detail. They furthermore have a look at model-to-model transformations and its validation and verification. Finally, the authors examine different SysML modeling tools and how to improve the usability of SysML tools for engineers.

DOI: 10.4018/978-1-4666-4369-7.ch009

INTRODUCTION

Production and logistic systems provide a diverse world of simulation applications with all kinds of systems and challenges to master. It ranges from small businesses employing only a few people over large manufacturing facilities with hundreds of workers to whole supply chains containing numerous businesses; from productions based on traditional craftsmanship to fully automated factories with robots doing most of the work. There are resources to be scheduled, assigned, and planned from groups of workers with different qualifications to machines capable of performing a number of completely different work steps; even the pure empty spaces in a manufacturing system sometimes need to be considered valuable resources, providing room to move or store large work pieces. On one hand, we see shipyards which sometimes build only a hand full of ships in a year; on the other hand, there are semiconductor facilities churning out thousands of chips every single day.

Simulation is used in a lot of these companies for numerous applications and purposes. Research to tap even more potentials with the help of simulation has been done for years and will continue for years to come. Fields of application range from asserting aerodynamic properties of new car designs to determining the course of etching processes on silicon wafers. Our interest focuses on simulation based optimization of the very production systems. We are analyzing the material flow within these highly dynamic discrete and sometimes continuous manufacturing environments, devising and testing strategies and approaches to improve them based on key performance indicators (e.g., work in progress, due date adherence, throughput, and cycle times). Furthermore, we work on optimizing resource assignments, maintenance schedules, and lot scheduling to improve the overall factory performance. Sometimes just providing a glimpse into the future is an invaluable advantage for decision makers.

Nowadays this work is mainly done by companies offering simulation consultants and universities; larger companies even have their own simulation departments utilizing the possibilities provided by discrete event simulation. Common to most of them is the use of simulation packages which are mostly bought off the shelf, and sometimes customized to a certain company or branch. Most of these tools base their modeling approach on their own proprietary languages. Files from one tool are not only incompatible with other tools; in some cases there are even major problems with loading files from different versions of the same simulation package. For companies using simulation as basis for their decision, these incompatibilities pose a significant economic thread.

Simulation based decision support systems rely on the manually created models or model generation systems. Creating these models and building infrastructures for automated model generation is an expensive and time consuming endeavor, one which sometimes takes years to reach a point where it pays off. These costs furthermore result in a dependency of companies on their current simulation packages. Moreover this dependency on simulation packages influences decisions for future simulation projects. The simulation package to be used is not only selected by assessing its fitness for the task at hand, but by considering compatibility and reusability of models and the cost of recreating existing models, even though there might be more appropriate tools available. In some cases this problem creates situations in which certain simulation packages have a very tight grip on a whole industry. Introducing newer and better simulators to this environment does not necessarily improve the situation as system compatibility needs some regard. The creation of new simulators will however not reduce the need to transfer models to other simulators. Furthermore there is usually a reason why simulator developers have their users create models in a certain way. This can be seen especially well with domain specific simulators, which excel in their field of application but are nearlyuseless for other challenges. To really change the current way of simulation modeling, we see the need for a general free modeling language, which is used as a standard to model production systems. In a next step these general models can be automatically transformed into the language of a simulator, which after consideration of all factors is the current simulation package of choice. Thereby can we not only use one common modeling language but furthermore utilize special properties of different simulation packages depending on the current goal. Using this standardized modeling language the need for model adaption and the need for model recreation is significantly reduced. There are four reasons which motivate such a development:

1. Modeling languages allow realizing projects with the principles of systems engineering. So the modeler obtains comprehensiveness even for large projects and reduces the discrepancy between model and reality.
2. A standard makes it possible to speak with one commonly accepted language. Thus, the exchange and understanding on various projects between different business units and stakeholders are simplified. This further reduces training times for new projects or personal.
3. Modeling languages are a core part of automatic code generation.
4. Standards are the first step for non-proprietary solutions.

In the field of software engineering automatic code generation from UML-Models by CASE-tools is very common and standardized (Fowler, 2003, p.23). The Model Driven Architecture from the OMG is here only one example. For modeling discrete processes there are many approaches called "Model Based Software Engineering" (MBSE) like *Stateflow Coder*, ASCET, or ADAGE, but none of them has yet been established as a standard. This could be due to the lack of an adequately powerful, non-proprietary or general modeling language. However, in particular for modeling discrete processes in production, automatic code generation is useful, because there are many different tools such as simulators, optimizers, or schedulers which cannot exchange their non-standardized models at the moment.

This work presents an approach for modeling and automated model transformation for discrete processes. We show how to develop discrete models by the means of SysML and how to convert from SysML models to a variety of (commercial) simulation tools. We based our work on our experience from past simulation projects, expert interviews, current literature and a market analysis of modeling and simulation tools. We created a general model for discrete processes in production systems, which was then adapted for other domains (e.g., civil engineering and health care). In addition we tested whether SysML is appropriate to support our general modeling approach.

In the first part of this chapter we show why formal languages are important for discrete processes. In a brief review we have a look at the standards and quasi-standards in the world of modeling and simulation. Here we consider Petri nets and project networks and why they are not suitable as standards for domain-specific models. We also discuss briefly modeling with commercial simulation tools, which is currently the common way in simulation modeling. Furthermore we have a look at Modelica, as it is established more and more as a standard in the world of continuous processes. Then we outline the requirements for a practicable standard of a formal language for simulation modeling. Subsequently we compare these requirements with the properties of SysML.

In the second part we present the SysML. We explain the structure and the concepts of SysML. SysML can be divided into two parts (behavioral and structural) and nine different types of diagrams. After that we explain the concept of domain-specific modeling in detail and how to use SysML for it (meta-models, stereotypes). In an example, we show the basic use of SysML and how to build domain-specific models using SysML. In this work we want to give the reader an introduction to SysML and show how to use SysML for modeling simulation problems. Therefore we do not describe all types of diagrams of SysML and the described diagrams not in every detail. In summary, the reader learns (1) the structure of SysML and how to model with SysML, (2) the domain-specific concept, (3) how to develop domain-specific models with SysML, and (4) how to describe different levels of model granularity.

In the third part of the chapter we have a look at model-to-model transformations. At first we explain the use of model-to-model transformation and what is model to model transformation. Then we explain various methods which are currently available. We show the OMG standard for model-to-model transformation QVT, transformation with graph grammars and an approach for imperative transformation. At the end of the third part we give a short overview on validation and verification.

In the fourth part of this chapter we examine different SysML modeling tools. We have a look at free, commercial, and our own tools. First, we define requirements which can be used to analyze the different tools, and then we show some tools. At the end we have a look at the usability of SysML tools for engineers and how an adequate modeling tool can support it.

BACKGROUND (STANDARDS FOR DISCRETE PROCESSES)

In many areas of science, like computer science or electrical engineering, modeling languages have been established; however, this is not the case in the field of discrete processes (Weilkiens, 2008). Also, for special domains of discrete processes--like production or logistic--there is no widely accepted standard. Usually models of these systems are developed with simulation tools. These tools are not standardized; they are proprietary and there is a large variety of tools available on the market (Noche & Wenzel, 2000). For modeling discrete processes there are many approaches like *Petri Nets*, project networks, or different simulation tools, but none of them has been established as a standard. This could be due to the lack of an adequate modeling language. Our criteria for an adequate modeling language are

1. Standardization
2. Non-proprietary
3. Sufficiently powerful to model
4. Scalability
5. Graphical representation
6. General but adaptable to domain specific problem space

In the field of modeling continuous processes Modelica has been established as a standard in recent years. Modelica is powerful enough to model scenarios from the fields of mechanical, electrical, thermodynamic, and process engineering. In Modelica there are libraries for a large variety of specific fields, some of which are free and some are proprietary. In order to work with the modeling standard Modelica there are (as for SysML) free and proprietary tools. In 1997 the Modelica Association published the first Modelica standard; the version of the recent standard is 3.2. Modelica is powerful, non-proprietary and useful for modeling very complex scenarios. Furthermore, by means of the modular concept of Modelica, it is easy to build models in domain specific problem spaces (Fritzson, 2011).

A good way to model sequential processes is to use graphs. With this representation it is easy to clearly show the logical structure of a task with all its operational and organizational, technological and temporal information (Seidel, 1998). Project

networks of structural relationships between the variables are close to human perception and thinking. In addition, there are many optimization methods based on
graphs. Network maps are particularly well suited to understand the dependencies
of project activities and related resources. So the user obtains quickly a rudimentary
understanding of sequence and function, without having detailed knowledge of the
processes (Pielok, 1995). Project networks have a long history and they are often
used in practical work. However, for very complex problems they are not powerful
enough. There are also some problems to model domain specific models (Neumann
& Schwidt, 1997; Major, 2008).

The first standard for modeling discrete processes were Petri nets (Petri, 1962).
After they received attention in the early 1980s in computer science, they were soon
used in many aspects for modeling discrete processes. For example, they have been
used for modeling asynchronous circuits, control systems, and business processes
(Reising, 2010). Even a part of the UML and SysML (activity diagrams) language
is based on Petri nets. Today they are available in various types with extensions
such as priorities, time and attributes; but these are not adequately standardized
(Klempien & Hinrichs, 2008; König, 2010). One of the strengths of Petri nets is
that in many applications properties of Petri nets have been proven, which help to
validate and verify Petri nets. However, this does not apply for most extended Petri
nets. A major issue with Petri nets is the modeling of realistic productions systems,
especially if there is the need to consider not only simple precedence constraints
but also resource schedules and further complex constraints. Creating these models
results in very large Petri nets, which are almost impossible to comprehend as a
human and often need unacceptable computing times.

Furthermore there are non-proprietary modeling languages especially designed
for the representation of discrete processes, such as MoogoNG, which is developed
at the Fraunhofer Institute for Production Systems and Design Technology, Germany.
Although simple scenarios can be represented easily, there are problems with large
numbers of components in more complex scenarios. Furthermore, domain-specific
adaptation options are missing. There are also many proprietary approaches to model
discrete processes for simulation. Especially in the field of production and logistics,
for instance, Plant Simulation, FlexSim or Simcron Modeler, Enterprise Dynamics
or AutoMod are very popular. Other products such as Arena and AnyLogic try to
cover a variety of domain-specific problem areas for discrete simulations (Noche
& Wenzel, 2000). Note that all of them are proprietary and own the point of view
of a particular tool developer.

In 2006, Huang, Ramamurthy, and McGinnis proposed an approach to describe
the structure of a production system with SysML. In their work they use the "block

definition diagram" and the "internal block diagram" to build a meta-model for flow shop problems (Huang & McGinnis, 2007, p. 798f). In our work, we try to create a general model for realistic models of all fields of production. Furthermore, for a large amount of other discrete processes we also work with SysML as modeling language. In 2008 Nikolaidou et al. proposed the use of SysML as a front end for DEVS (Nikolaidou et al., 2008, pp. 445-450). In the area of production systems current research mainly focuses on using SysML as a modeling language with further transformation into different simulation systems. In 2009 McGinnis and Ustun proposed the use of SysML for conceptual modeling and introduced automated transformation concepts of SysML models to simulations tools (McGinnis &Ustun, 2009, p. 1702ff).

Simulating SysML without prior transformation is currently still an open research goal, but there are approaches based on fUML (Weyprecht & Rose, 2011) and on MDSE technologies.

MAIN FOCUS OF THE CHAPTER

Modeling with SysML

SysML is a graphical modeling language for supporting specification, analysis, design, verification, and validation of systems. In June 2010, the OMG released SysML 1.2. There have been many controversies about SysML during the short period of time since its publication. SysML is spreading very fast. Today many of the most prominent developers of modeling tools like ARTiSAN, Telelogic, I-Logix, and Sparx Systems make use of SysML. In systems engineering, a significant amount of projects like the engineering of planes, helicopters, or ships are performed by using SysML. Pörnbacher describes how to model a software control of an automated manufacturing system with SysML and Modelica (Pörnbacher, 2010). Rosenberg and Mancerella develop embedded systems with SysML (Rosenberg & Mancerella, 2010). In November 2012 the OMG published a specification on how to transform SysML models into Modelica. We try to model a large variety of discrete problems from production, logistics, and civil engineering with SysML.

In accordance with UML, SysML distinguishes between model and diagram and divides the model into a structural and a behavior part. The model contains the complete description of the system and consists of diagrams that visualize particular aspects. The structural part describes the static structure, like the elements and their relationships, in a system. In the behavior part SysML describes the dynamic behavior at and between its elements (see Figure 1). SysML has been extended with some concepts. But, in contrast to UML important concepts such as time and the interaction diagram have been removed. SysML uses also a request and an assertion concept, which are extensions to basic UML (see Figure 1).

Domain Specific and Object Oriented Modeling

Anyone working with a commercial simulation program and the associated modeling language obtains a choice of given library elements, which can be connected and put into relation to each other. This is the concept that is closest to human intuition, but leads to two basic problems for the modeler. First the semantics and syntax are often not sufficiently well documented or clearly presented. Second, the user is strictly bound to the amount of provided elements and their given relationships and behavior.

The concept of meta-modeling remedies those two disadvantages, since models are extensible and semantics as well as syntax are well defined and applicable. First, the notions model and meta-model in terms of meta-modeling are discussed. A model is a description of a specific scenario with language elements (for example, elements and relations) of a well-defined language. A meta-model is the syntactic and semantic description of a modeling language. In a meta-model is thus clearly defined which language elements are available for the description of facts and what the concrete syntax and semantics look like. Specific issues that are defined within the meta-model options are presented in a model. It is furthermore possible to define meta-meta-models. A meta-meta-model defines language constructs for defining meta-models. The Meta-Object-Facility (MOF) of the OMG defines a meta-meta-model for the generation and specification of platform-independent meta-models. In the MOF the abstract syntax for describing abstract modeling languages is defined whereas in resulting meta-languages such as UML or SysML the abstract syntax and semantics are set. The meta-modeling approach of the OMG specifies a 4-layer

Figure 1. SysML structure

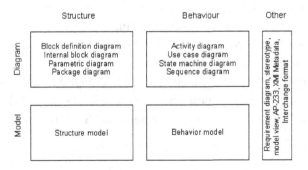

architecture which is suitable for object-oriented work with software. For the field of systems engineering, which uses stereotypes and domain-specific meta-models resulting from SysML, the approach is quite complex and therefore it is not elaborated here and we refer to common SysML literature.

SysML is an abstract language. In the structural part, blocks are available which can be named arbitrarily and any attributes can be provided. While SysML defines the syntax for the blocks, their attributes and relations contain no semantics. We can declare a block as a resource and give it appropriate attributes; we can also declare it as a chemical element or physical unit with the appropriate attributes. The only limit to declare various elements is the imagination of the user. Working with SysML in a particular domain is significantly improved by adapting an abstract SysML meta-model. SysML provides stereotypes, which enable the realization of domain specific modeling support. Stereotypes allow predefinition of names, attributes and semantics for a block, or even to expand relationships of attributes with corresponding attributes. To represent a particular domain, different stereotypes can be combined into a profile. The generated SysML profile now contributes to the meta-model, which can be used by the modeler, in a specific domain.

The Structural Model

The structural part describes the static structure, such as elements and their relationships, in a system. There are real objects, imaginary objects and auxiliary objects (see Figure 4). The imaginary objects like Arrival-/Departure-Processes, Queue and Processes are necessary for the simulation. The flow object is the central element. In the domain of production systems it represents the job/piece which moves through the facility and which is processed by the elements of the tool set.

In the following section, we explain how to model the structure with SysML. The capabilities of SysML are huge. In order to describe them completely, a great amount of literature is available that we recommend in the Appendix. In this work we want to give the reader an introduction to SysML and show how to use SysML for modeling simulation problems. Therefore we do not describe all types of diagrams of SysML and even the selected diagrams not in every detail.

As mentioned above the structural part of a SysML model can be found in the block definition diagram, internal block diagram, package diagram, and parametric diagram. The package diagram structures larger projects, which encapsulate various diagrams into packages. "The parametric diagram represents constraints on system property values such as performance, reliability, and mass properties, and serves as a means to integrate the specification and design models with engineering analysis models (OMG, 2012). The internal block diagram is similar to the UML composite structure diagram and describes internal structures of system elements and interac-

Figure 2. Structural example for SysML

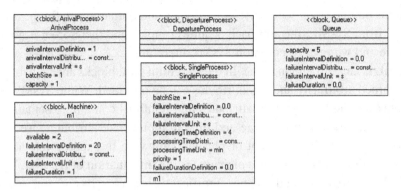

tions with their environment. More detailed information of the package diagram, internal block diagram, and parametric diagram can be found in Weilkiens (2006). Now we explain the block definition diagram which is the most important SysML diagram for describing structure. In our current work we found it sufficient to use only the block definition diagram to describe the structure of discrete problems.

The Block Definition Diagram

In UML the classes and their objects are the central elements. Classes are historically associated with software development, so they are deliberately not used in SysML. The static concepts and objects are herein referred to as system blocks. It is important to note that this concept is realized only as SysML blocks, in contrast to UML classes and objects. The user can define attributes for the SysML blocks as values and operations similarly to UML objects. An operation can be specified by a SysML behavior diagram. The user can additionally define constraints, parts, and references in SysML blocks. Constraints enable the user to define requirements for the block. The block can consist of different parts and refers to other blocks with references. For modeling discrete simulation models we use only attributes.

To create references between the various system components, SysML uses relationships which are designated as part properties or associations. Relations may have multiplicities and can be assigned by set relations.

In Figure 2 we show a small example of a scenario which is based on a meta-model for production systems. For example, "available = 2" at machine m1 means 2 pieces of machine m1 are available.

At the bottom of "Single Process" we can see machine m1 as property part. This means that single process needs one piece of machine type m1. If we want to increase the required number of machines for a single process we simply have to increase the multiplicity of the property part. This block definition diagram describes the structure of a specific scenario (machinery) from the field of production systems.

The Structural Concept

While every discrete system has the same imaginary objects, the domain is specified by the real and auxiliary objects. Real objects are flow objects which move through the system (entity, patient, etc.) and different kinds of resources (worker, room, machine, etc.). Auxiliary objects are not necessary but they simplify the modeling process. Relationships between the objects can be simply reservations of objects but they can also have very complex attributes or terms. An example is a process which needs a resource only half of its time or two processes which need the same resource in a sequence.

Meta-models based on this principle only vary in their domain specific properties (see Figure 4 and Figure 5).

Figure 4 shows a meta-model for production systems. Whereas in other areas workflows are determined by information flows, in production the entity flow controls the behavior of the model: the entity is the central element because it represents the job/piece which moves through the facility and is processed by the elements of the machinery. All events in a model, except for interruptions, are triggered by the entity. The entities enter the system through the arrival process and leave it through the departure process. While they move on specific routes, different processes execute actions on them; these may or may not require resources. Along their way, the entities can be stored in queues.

If a process can be performed differently with different resources, this is called a mode. It may be mapped to the class "modes" which is associated with the process (see Figure 4). In the following part the two attributes hold and release time

Figure 3. Structural modeling

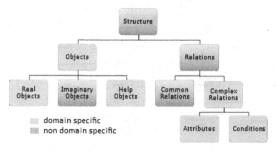

Figure 4. Meta-model for production systems

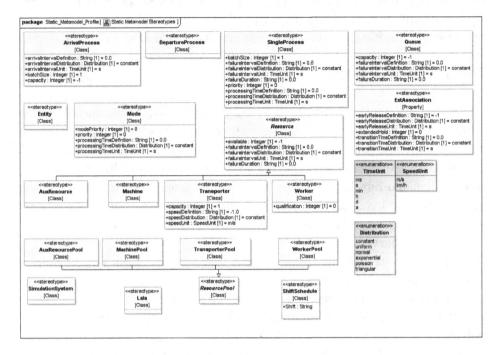

Figure 5. Meta-model for emergency rooms

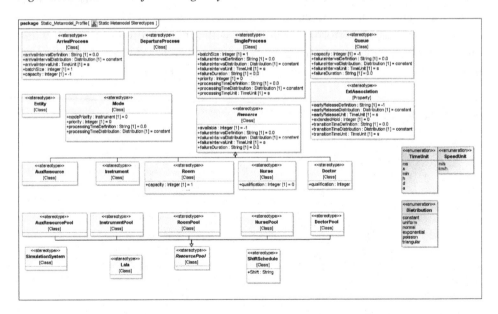

are described; they demonstrate how complex rules in relations (associations) of elements can be resolved by modeling.

In manufacturing processes, there is the possibility that resources must be held until the next process can be started. This occurs when there is no buffer between two processes. The holding of resources is only allowed if no early release of resources is possible. This "hold" is set with the attribute hold of the corresponding resource in a particular mode. Resources that are not required during the entire process time can be released early; this is only possible if holding a resource is not necessary. The attribute release time is set in a resource that is associated to this mode. Such special characteristics are modeled by advanced associations.

We can now construct specific scenarios using the meta-model described in Figure 4. The user has now the possibility to create any model that satisfies the meta-model. If the user requires elements or attributes of elements or relations that do not exist in the meta-model, the modeler may extend the meta-model and then generate the extended meta-model scenarios. The structural meta-model shown in Figure 4, was developed by us to represent a variety of optimization problems in the field of production. Other domains such as emergency rooms, logistics, or civil engineering can be modeled after simple adjustments.

Figure 5 shows a very simple adaptation of the meta-model to the emergency room domain and shall simply give the reader a better understanding of the functionality of SysML profiles and meta-models.

The Behavior Model

The behavioral part describes the dynamic behavior between model elements; for example, the movement of an entity through the production facility. We can describe the behavior in different levels of detail. In order to model the behavior of dynamical resources (agents) we can use state machines. For behavior related to an order or recipe we use activity diagrams (see Figure 6).

SysML provides four diagrams to describe behavior. Use-case diagrams trace back to the 1970s and were popularized by Ivar Jacobson (Störrle, 2005, p. 150). They are suitable to capture functional requirements (what task the system shall run) and non-functional requirements (all other conditions) (Störrle, 2005, p. 150). The semantics of the use case diagram is defined very vaguely and allows for many degrees of freedom (Weilkiens, 2008, p. 231). Due to the degrees of freedom in semantics they are not suitable for automatic code generation. But they are often rated as easy to understand and are therefore used for the communication between system engineers and stakeholders.

State diagrams are hierarchical, finite state machines and can be traced back to the object charts of Room (Störrle, 2005, p 170). They specify the behavior of indi-

Figure 6. Structure of modeling behavior

vidual objects (Seemann & Gudenberg, 2006, p. 105). They are suitable for object life cycles, use cases, device controllers, protocols, and dialogue processes (Störrle, 2005, p. 170). A state diagram consists of states and their state transitions. "A state is a time period in which an object waits for an event" (Balzert, 2005, p. 87). A state transition is invoked by an event. Events have no duration, but may be subject to conditions. An object may pass through several states. The next state depends on the current state and the event. States may have entry, exit, and do activities that are carried out at the entrance, execution and exit of a state. There is a state behavior and a protocol state machine. The state behavior machine can be used to model the dynamic behavior of classes and use cases. The protocol state machine expresses in which state and under what conditions the operations of a class can be accessed (Balzert, 2005, p. 197). Since processes are more important in production systems, in the following state behavior machines are considered.

Sequence diagrams as well as other interaction diagrams are derived from the block diagrams of electrical engineering (Störrle, 2005, p. 222). Communication diagrams are not suitable and sequence diagrams are only in theory suitable to define behavior precisely or completely (Oestereich, 2006, p. 325). "They describe the flow of communication in a group of objects" (Seemann & Gudenberg, 2006, p. 79). "The purpose of sequence diagrams is to represent one scenario rather than a lot of different processes. Therefore this possibility needs to be used with care. If you want to express the variety of sequence possibilities, you should rather use an activity diagram" (Oestereich, 2006, p. 331). In sequence diagrams the emphasis lies on the progression of the exchange of messages. Roles (classes) are shown as vertical lines. The messages are shown as horizontal arrows between the lines of the roles. There are synchronous and asynchronous messages, which can optionally have an answer as dashed arrows. The creation or removal of roles can also be displayed. Similarly, states are listed in which the object is found at a particular time. Sequence diagrams can be nested. Furthermore, there are several predefined operators for alternative processes, branching, and looping.

Activities have a long history and can be traced back to program schedules and Nassi-Shneiderman diagrams (Störle, 2005, p.194). However, there is a difference in the expressivness of the UML1 and UML2 activity diagrams. UML2 activity diagrams are based on the semantics of Petri nets (Oestereich, 2006, p. 307; Störle, 2005, p. 194). "Activity diagrams can be used to describe all kinds of processes. Activities have a powerful expressiability and can be used universally" (Störrle, 2005, p. 194). They are particularly suitable for the description of processes where the sequence of steps is important, such as the processing of a job (Seemann & Gudenberg, 2006, p. 27f.). "Using activity diagrams it is possible to display even very complex processes with many exceptions, variations, leaps and repetitions in a clear and comprehensive manner" (Oestereich, 2006, p. 303).

Use case diagrams and sequence diagrams are defined vaguely and are therefore less suitable for automatic code generation. State diagrams are suited to specify transitions of states of objects. This facilitates a clear description of agents–and also state changes of resources. For the description of processes, activity diagrams are particularly suitable. Since we mainly describe scenarios which describe a recipe as a process, activity diagrams are outlined in more detail hereafter. In order to become familiar with other SysML behavior diagrams, we refer to the literature.

The Activity Diagram

"This diagram represents a model that describes the sequence of elementary actions" (Weilkiens, 2006, p. 251) and, thus, is suitable for the description of discrete processes.

The SysML activity diagram is based on the activity diagram of UML 2.0, which differs to a large extent from that of the UML 1. Subsequently, only the activity diagram of UML 2 is described and only SysML compliant properties are dealt with. Afterwards the SysML extensions are addressed.

The activity describes processes and consists of several actions. Actions are elementary executable steps of an activity. Both activities and actions are depicted as a rectangle with rounded corners. While the name of an activity is placed in the upper right corner, the name of an action is written in the center. Within an activity the course of events is represented by nodes and edges. In addition, conditions of the execution can be placed in the top right corner using Boolean expressions. Activities can include input and output parameters; they are set as rectangles in the center of the frame. The name of the parameter is usually the parameter type. Activities are activated by the invocation of input parameters or the starting node and are terminated by the invocation of output parameters or end nodes.

The sequence of events of an activity is controlled by "tokens," and is similar to the semantics of a Petri net. This similarity went so far that Petri nets can be mapped to activity diagrams (Störrle, 2005). Furthermore, complex activity diagrams can be displayed as Petri nets (Störrle, 2005). When an activity starts, a control token is placed on each of its starting nodes and an object token on each input parameter. While control tokens describe information, object tokens represent moving objects. Object tokens can be consumed as input by activities via pins, whereas control tokens can be transferred without pins. Within an activity, control tokens can be converted to object tokens and vice versa. Then tokens move through various nodes that connect pins via edges.

In order to pass an edge a token needs to meet two requirements:

1. The requirements listed on an edge must be met. They may be in Boolean or in some numerical expression, which indicates how many tokens can pass through an edge simultaneously.
2. The target must be ready to receive a token. If a target receives tokens from two actions, these tokens are connected with an AND operation - in contrast to UML 1. Therefore tokens need to be provided on both edges in order to execute an action. In SysML this may be converted into an OR operation using the keyword <optional>, which needs to be listed on one of the edges.

Figure 7. Behavioral example for SysML

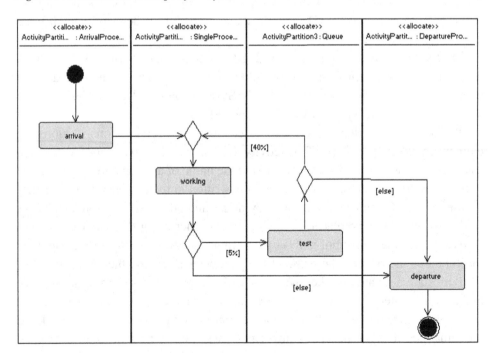

While the tokens move through the activity diagram, they may arrive at branches. Here an incoming edge meets a "branching node"; several optional procedures may leave such a branching node. The condition for selecting an edge follows the principle of "if A occurs, execute B, otherwise C." A branching node is shown as a diamond, which may have an arbitrary amount of outgoing edges. Its conditions are placed on the edges in square brackets (see Figure 7).

Its counterpart is the "consolidation" which is also depicted as a diamond; it brings together several optional procedures. The "splitting" converts a sequence into multiple sequences. The synchronization joins several concurrent processes. Both items are represented as a black bar (see Figure 1-5). If several nodes accumulate during splitting or synchronizing (for example, due to a blocked subsequent activity), the tokens are passed on according to the FIFO principle.

Based on their similarities the nodes and edges of activities can be assigned to *activity partitions*. This allows for allocating structures to the system. Each partition represents a structure; for example, a class. When modeling a production system, it is advantageous to assign elements of the system to the partitions. Figure 7 shows an example in which an entity passes through the elements of a workstation. The mentioned activity diagram is divided into partitions that are assigned to elements of the workstation and divide the graph vertically.

Through the action *arrival,* entities enter the system workstation in a distribution specified by the block arrival process from Figure 5. The entities are first sent to the single process and then served by the action "working" according to the distribution given by the block single process (see Figure 5). Subsequently their quality is checked in a decision node. While 95% of the entities are passed on to the final process and leave the system with the action "end," 5% need to be checked at the queue. In the queue, 40% of the entities are sent again to the single process for rework and the rest of them leave the system through the departure process.

Furthermore in UML2.0 there are about 40 predefined activities (OMG, 2010b). The most important ones for this work are *CellBehaviorAction, TimeAction, AcceptEventAction, SendSignalAction, ReceiveSignalAction, readStructuralFeature* and *addStructuralFeatureValue.* Other activities are discussed in detail in various books (Weilkiens, 2008; Rumbaught et. al., 2004).

Figure 8. SysML actions

The *CellBehaviorAction* is represented as a usual activity using a rectangle with rounded corners; however, in addition it contains a fork symbol (see Figure 8). This action calls a behavior that is an interaction, a state machine or may again be an activity. Since only activity diagrams are used to model the behavior in this work, calling a *CellBehaviorAction* is limited to activities.

The *SendSignalAction* and *AcceptEventAction* are used for sending and receiving signals. The *SendSignalAction* is denoted as an arrow which symbolizes the transmission of signals. The *AcceptEventAction* is symbolized by a rectangle with an incoming arrow (see Figure 8). The *ReceiveSignalAction* receives a time signal such as a timeout.

As a signal the *TimeAction* calls an action after a specified time (rate). It is displayed as an hourglass (see Figure 8). All other actions as well as *addStructuralFeatureValue* are symbolized as a rectangle with rounded edges. The action *addStructuralFeatureValue* can set attributes, while *readStructuralFeature* can read attributes.

SysML extends the UML 2 activity diagrams by some components that are important for the modeling of production systems. Thus, temporal frequencies can be assigned to activity edges using rates, in which elements flow in or out (see Figure 7). The rate can be discrete or continuous and is put above the edge enclosed in curly braces (for example <discrete{rate=1/minute}>).

The decision elements have been extended in SysML as well and can regulate the use of tokens by usage of probabilities instead of Boolean conditions. To express probabilities, the key word <probability> followed by the appropriate value is used. Finally, the above mentioned type <optional> was introduced to SysML, which enables activities having multiple inputs to start even though some inputs do not have a token.

Different Levels of Granularity

The model of behavior can be classified into different levels of granularity. Pieper and Röttgers (2006, p. 46) describe how to classify the behavior of workflows into different levels. Also, Störrle (2005, p. 194) suggests that activity diagrams can describe different levels of granularity.

Now we show an example of a production scenario and how to describe its behavior in different levels of granularity. The first level, called "Process level," shows the order of the processes components. The example in Figure 9 shows an entity which arrives in the system through the arrival process, then it is processed, cools down and leaves the system through the departure process. For the most simulation tools this level of detail is enough (Anylogic, Flexsim, Simcron, etc.) but some simulation tools need a more detailed description.

Every process component on process level is an imaginary object (Arrival-/ Departure-Process, Queue or Process). In the next level of detail, called "Behavior level," we can define a set of behavior patterns for every process of the Process level. We describe how the process works in the above example. In the first step the process acquires the needed resources. In the next step the entity is processed. At the end the process frees the resources (see Figure 10).

The detailed behavior of the behavior patterns is described in the Execution level (see Figure 11). For this very detailed description the OMG has approx. 40 predefined actions which serve as a basis for a detailed description of behavior (Pieper & Röttgers, 2006, p. 47; Weilkiens & Oestereich, 2006, S 161 f). In the example we explain the behavior of acquiring resources. At first we compare the number of needed workers with the number of existing workers. Then the workers are reserved.

MODEL-TO-MODEL TRANSFORMATION

Due to the large number of publications on this topic, there are various definitions of model transformation. The OMG defines a model transformation as a "process of converting a model into another model of the same system" (cf. Miller & Murkerji,

Figure 9. Example on process level

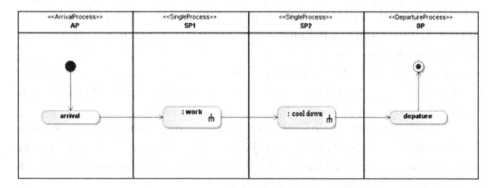

Figure 10. Example on behavior level

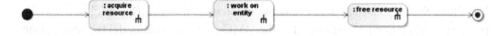

Figure 11. Example on execution level

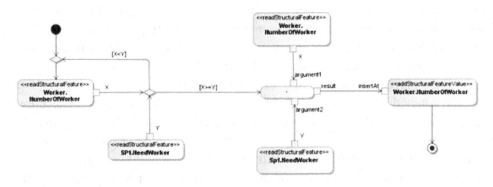

2003). A more detailed definition can be found in Kleppe et al. (Kleppe, Warmer, & Bast, 2003):

"A transformation is the automatic generation of a target model from a source model, according to a transformation definition. A transformation definition is a set of transformation rules that together describe how a model in the source language can be transformed into a model in the target language. A transformation rule is a description of how one or more constructs in the source language can be transformed into one or more constructs in the target language."

However, there are also model transformations which have more than one source model and/or target model. These do not even have to be described in the same modeling language (Mens, 2010; Biehl, 2010). If we extend the definition of Kleppe et al. to this aspect, the concept of model transformation can be defined as follows; the transformation definition is intentionally omitted in order to make the definition generally applicable.

Definition: A model transformation is the automatic generation of one or more target models from one or more source models, corresponding to a transformation definition.

For the model transformation, various methods are used. In the following sections, we will have a closer look at MOF2.0 QVT and its implementations, followed by some other approaches and technologies. In the end we will introduce the approach we deemed most appropriate for our project.

QVT (Query View Transformation)

QVT for a SysML based system is an obvious first candidate for a model transformation approach as QVT is a standard of the OMG for model-to-model transformation which was published in November 2005. QVT is based on the meta-models of the source and target models (see Figure 12 for its architecture). Both of them need to be described with the Meta Object Facility (MOF) to model a transformation with QVT. In a transformation we can create, delete, and replace model elements consistently using logs of previous changes. With QVT it is possible to transform unidirectionally and bidirectionally.

The QVT is a hybrid specification with an imperative and a declarative language part. The declarative part is based on QVT-Relations and QVT-Core. QVT-Relations is a declarative language which can specify unidirectional and bidirectional relations between models. QVT-Core is an abstract relational language which can - in theory - entirely map QVT-Relations. QVT-Core is too abstract for the user, so only QVT-Relations is relevant for practical applications.

QVT-Operational is an imperative language for model-to-model transformation. The language is based on existing imperative programming languages and on an extension of the Object Constrain Language (OCL). To define bidirectional transformations every direction must be implemented separately. In addition, QVT Black Box allows importing functions that have been user-implemented by means of .Net or Java.

For using standard QVT, there are free and proprietary tools. The commercial tool Borland Together is compatible to QVT-Operational. The transformation engine ModelMorf implements QVT-Relations. Free tools especially in the Eclipse world are Smart QVT from the France Telecom for QVT-Operational, and Medini QVT for QVT-Relational. Both have communities which became very quiet in recent years. On the other hand there is the Model to Model Transformation subproject (since 2012 MMT formerly M2M) of the Eclipse Modeling Project. MMT currently contains three major parts, Atlas Transformation Language (ATL) and two implementations of parts of the QVT standard. We will have a short look on ATL in the next section.

The QVT approaches of the MMT are QVTo and QVTd. QVTd is implementing QVT-Core and QVT-Relational and transformations between them. After some setbacks with an approach to utilize ATL for the transformations in QVTd it is still in development.

Figure 12. Architecture of QVT(cf. OMG 2007)

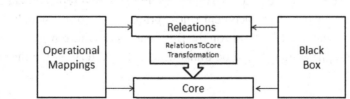

In contrast QVTo has reached a point where it seems to be a promising approach for model transformation. After some investigation and time to test its usefulness and usability for our project we see three major issues preventing us from currently using QVTo for our system.

The first challenge utilizing QVTo is the creation of meta-models of both modeling worlds from and to we want to transform. On the SysML side this poses no problem at all as there already is a SysML ECORE file for download. On the simulation tool side this is very different. Although there are some simulators based on Eclipse which even have public meta-models, for most simulation tools obtaining a full meta-model for their models in any format is a big problem. Currently most simulation tool makers still consider a closed proprietary format as a reasonable way to enforce customer loyalty; in some cases, even to a point where they officially declare the use of any other tool than their own one to manipulate or work on model files of their simulator as violation of rules of the EULA.

A second issue arises with respect to the team dynamic in our research group; as common with work involving students there is a high fluctuation of short term team members which bases the need for easy access to documentation and tutorials to any technology used. Currently good documentation and tutorials are very hard to come by, thereby almost limiting the information pool, to the specs and the user community. As the transformation is only a small part of the team members works; for our team afford and cost of training in QVT still outweighs its projected benefits.

Third, there are some minor issues with regard to completeness of the QVTo implementation. Due to some not yet implemented functionalities the recommended practices for workarounds sometimes stand in direct contrast to the QVT specs. Therefore we see a lack of maturity in the system which would already demand rework within the near future, as soon as these issues are removed.

In summary, QVT is a transformation standard for relational and imperative transformations. It is based on existing standards like MOF and OCL. QVT seems like a promising approach for future undertakings, but has in our opinion not yet reached a level of maturity where it is reasonable to be utilized to just do some supporting work.

Graph Based Transformation Model-to-Model

It is possible to describe the models as graphs and use graph replacement tools. A graph grammar consist of replacement rules (graph production), which have one graph on the left-hand side and one on the right-hand side; moreover, the grammar has an initial graph, which should be transformed. If a pattern on the initial graph matches, a rule is executed. If a match is found on the left-hand side, it is replaced with the right-hand side of the replacement rule. The rules are executed till the last match is found. If more than one rule matches, one of the matching rules is picked randomly. In addition the order of the execution of the rules is not specified. As a consequence graph grammars are not deterministic. There are special variants of graph grammars, like the Triple Graph Grammar (TGG), which are very suitable for model transformations. Transformation with graph grammars can become very difficult, especially for large and complex problems because it can be hard to describe the transformation rules with the given simple syntax. Although using graph grammars for the transformation did not seem to be a viable option, there are validation concepts which can be taken from graph grammar transformations and be applied to the imperative transformation.

Imperative Transformation

Imperative transformations are an alternative to declarative transformations. This applies especially to transformations which include very complex transformation rules which are hard to represent within formal transformation languages. At the beginning of our project in 2009, and still today we find the available transformation technologies not sufficient to be reasonably used in our system. This is mainly a consideration based on the maturity of these technologies and the unclear learning curve. As the transformation is not our main focus, these technologies would only be considered useful if the resulting total effort in training, development, and maintenance is reduced. Our current system is designed as a Java framework which uses imperative transformation implemented in Java code.

We developed a software environment that automatically generates models for simulation tools from given SysML models. To build an effective tool we use a multilayer architecture (see Figure 13). The process follows a five steps approach.

We will discuss the transformation based on a small example system and have a look on it throughout the transformation. The mini system contains a source, two processes where one needs a machine and a sink.

Step1: SysML Model Creation

In the first step the user creates a SysML representation of the system by using the common SysML diagrams. Based on the SysML meta-model for production systems (Figure 4), we create the following Block Definition Diagram to model the structural components of the system (Figure 14).

Figure 13. System architecture

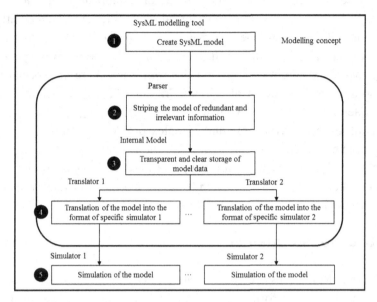

Using our stereotypes, all objects already have all the necessary attributes which only need to be filled with values. Multiplicities between objects are represented as in UML using associations or as done here as part properties.

The behavior of the system is represented with the Activity Diagram (Figure 15). This defines the course of action within the system and links all processes.

Step 2: Parser

SysML models do not only contain the system information we want to represent but they furthermore contain a lot of graphical information. This information is generated by SysML editors and stored within the model files, most of which is not at all necessary for the transformed model. For example positioning information of blocks, corners in associations and colors are important features during the creation of the model in SysML as they help the user to keep an overview on the model and increase readability for humans. As the model is transformed into another representation this data is of little to no use in the target system. The filtering is done with the help of a SAX parser. Currently we have implementations for the two SysML modeling tools MagicDraw and Topcased Engineer.

Figure 14. Structural model of the mini system

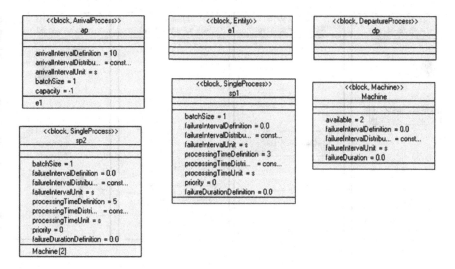

Step 3: Internal Model

The filtered bare core of the model is then stored within a java data structure. This data structure is based on the meta-model. This data structure represented in UML still looks almost exactly like the SysML diagrams. The internal model furthermore serves as an intermediate storage format to decouple modeling tools from simulators. Therefore new modeling tools can be addressed by creating a new parser. Hence, all simulation tools are still usable even with the new models.

Step 4: Translation to the Simulator Language

The second transformation step is the transformation of the model from the internal model to the actual simulation tool language. The design and technology used by these pieces of software is highly dependent on the target simulator and therefore differs significantly form simulator to simulator. Since models should generate the same result in all simulators the creating of these plugins is rarely just a matter of a mapping. For many simulators the creation of premade object blocks and code snippets is a good first approach. As most simulators are designed with a certain base behavior for their components in mind, it can be very complicated and time consuming to abuse library components in a way to obtain the expected behavior if

Figure 15. Activity diagram of the mini system

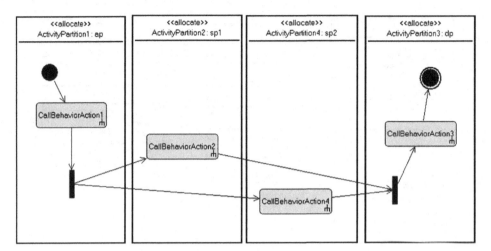

it conflicts with their base behavior. Usually the problem here lays not in just transforming information but in achieving behavior wanted by us instead of the behavior intended by the simulator designer. Currently we have complete implementations for the four commercial simulators Anylogic, Simcron Modeller, Factory Explorer, and Flexsim.

Step 5: Simulation

In a last step the transformed model can be simulated with the help of the chosen simulator. Transformation results for the previously introduced mini example can be seen in Figure 16.

As there is little knowledge gained by just being able to simulate models, future work will include the automated generation of analysis features to utilize knowledge gained by simulating the transformed models.

Validation and Verification

Model transformations are an active research field, especially since the model-driven software development gained importance. In addition to the development of approaches for describing such transformations the research is also concerned with the development of appropriate techniques for their validation and verification. These are necessary in order to validate the generated models transformations with respect to established criteria for correctness.

Figure 16. Generated Flexsim model

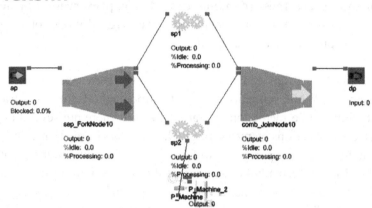

Verification and validation are two common terms in literature, which are often used synonymously; although they are generally pursuing different goals (Schatten et Al., 2010). In the literature the terms are defined differently. Without going into details of the many different forms of definitions available, we use the following definition: the validation of model transformations is a process which determines whether the specification of the transformation is sufficient for the requirements of the transformation. The verification of model transformations is a process which determines whether the implementation of the transformation satisfies its specification.

We define the two requirements for our development of transformations. The transformation should map SysML models into simulation models and be syntactically, functionally, and semantically correct. During validation a test is performed whether the rules and algorithms satisfy the requirements, whereas during verification it is tested whether the implementation is correct according to the rules and algorithms.

The validation and verification of a model transformation is used to test their correctness. To this end it is important which criteria are assessed. The following correctness criteria are necessary for model-to-model transformations.

- **Syntactical correctness:** The transformation produces a syntactically correct model or the transformation is syntactically correct with respect to the language of the target system.
- **Syntactic completeness:** The transformation accepts all elements of a syntactically correct source model.
- **Termination:** The transformation is complete after a finite amount of time.

- **Confluency, uniqueness:** The transformation produces always the same result/output independently from the order the transformation rules are applied.
- **Semantic correctness (dynamic consistency, preservation of behavior):** In the transformation, the semantics of the original model or its important semantic properties are preserved.

Model transformations can be described imperatively with relations or with graph-grammars. While validation and verification methods for model transformations using imperative methodologies are quite rare, there are several approaches for model transformations by means of graph grammars or relations. There are two fundamentally different approaches to formally verify model transformations. On the one hand it can formally be proven that the source and target models are semantically equivalent with respect to certain specified criteria. This equivalence is tested automatically at each transformation by a "checker." This approach is called checker-approach for formal model transformation verification. On the other hand, the rule-based approach or the meta-model level verification proves the general semantic correctness of a transformation for each input.

To show how to validate and verify the shown correctness criteria is a very complex topic. There is special literature available and we refer to it in the additional reading section. Typically particular methods are needed for imperative, relational, or graph-grammar- transformation and for every correctness criterion. Our main verification of structural correctness is based on the work of method for verification of model transformations with structural correspondences (Narayanan & Karsai, 2008), which is comparable to the approach of correspondence graphs for Triple Graph Grammars (Ehrig et Al., 2007). This approach was introduced for graph grammars, but can also be adapted to be used for the imperative transformation approach. It is based on a system of links between source and target model objects and proved to be very helpful.

SYSML MODELING TOOLS

There are several modeling tools for SysML. In this section we give an overview of some selected systems. For modeling using SysML, the modeling tool must provide all SysML modeling elements, an appropriate exchange format, and the possibility to model large models. It is a big advantage if XMI is supported which is based on the well-structured, hierarchical XML data format. With XML, data can be processed more easily. Also, the extensibility of the editor and the intuitive operation and easy access to graphical modeling are important criteria for a SysML modeling Tool. Because the tools are pretty similar, intuitive operation is given for all of them.

Enterprise Architect is developed by Sparx Systems. It is often used in software development with UML. Since version 9.0 of Enterprise Arcitect SysML 1.2 is supported. Sparx Systems also offers integration into Eclipse and Visual Studio. All necessary data exchange formats starting with XMI 2.0, XMI 2.1 to UML 2.x are supported. With 250000 registers users, it is one of the more popular UML modeling tools. Enterprise Architect supports many popular languages like C + +, C #, Java, Delphi, VB.Net, Visual Basic, ActionScript, PHP, Python, and via add-on also CORBA in generating and code return of software.

The SysML Toolkit from EmbeddedPlus is a plug-in for IBM Rational Software Development Platform (RSDP), which comes as a complete solution for software development. With version 2.5.1 SysML 1.1 is supported. An output of the models in XMI format is possible. A further feature of the EmbeddedPlus SysML Toolkit is the integration in Telelogic DOORS. The interface is based on Eclipse.

Telelogic Rhapsody and Telelogic Tau are a based on UML and SysML model-driven development environment (MDD) for embedded systems and software. Rhapsody enables code-centric workflow and facilitates the introduction of the MDD approach, since a manual report can be automatically converted into models. The Eclipse CDT integration allows developers to work in the Eclipse environment. Telelogic Tau is for enterprise IT applications and SOA environments.

Artisan Studio Uno is a free modeling tool for UML and SysML. There is a single-user version of Artisan Studio. Artisan Studio itself offers all the necessary components for the modeling of SysML models. The Artisan Studio is a commercial program for the development of software in a team. Interfaces to MATLAB/Simulink and IBM Rational DOORS are available.

MagicDraw is a modeling tool for UML. For the MagicDraw UML tool exists a SysML plug-in which supports SysML 1.2 in version 16.0 or later. Furthermore, it is possible to export models in XMI 2.1 format and validate SysML representation immediately. Magic Draw is a traditional UML development tool that offers many advanced features.

Papyrus 4 UML is an open source modeling tool for the creation of UML models. Papyrus 4 UML is an extension of the Eclipse development environment. For Papyrus 4 UML a SysML 1.1 extension exists. A special characteristic of Papyrus 4 UML is the extensible architecture that allows to add new diagrams and code generators. Papyrus can be used for free. The editor is still not mature, particularly with respect to the SysML features.

TOPCASED is an open source modeling tool mainly for the development of critical embedded systems. For TOPCASED there are many extensions, including TOPCASED-SysML. TOPCASED-SysML supports SysML 1.1 and the models are stored in XMI 2.1 format. The editor can be used in the TOPCASED development environment but also be integrated into the Eclipse development environment. TOP-CASED is an open source program, so it can be used freely and can be arbitrarily changed and further developed.

Usability of SysML for Systems Engineers

We analyzed the usability of SysML with some commercial modeling tools. In comparison to other modeling languages (example.g., MoogoNG, Jane) SysML provides the capability to model the complete scenario without restrictions or problems. Trained users can build complex models comfortably and rapidly. But only skilled users can use SysML adequately because modeling with SysML is very abstract (see Figure 17). Although there are good SysML modeling tools, they are not intuitively usable for discrete models. One reason for this is that these modeling tools were created for computer scientists and not for systems engineers. Usually systems engineers are not familiar with SysML. Modeling with SysML requires additional skills for the following reasons:

- SysML is very powerful and has a huge amount of modeling elements
- SysML is very abstract (which makes it powerful)

Therefore we decided to develop our own modeling tool which is customized to the requirements of systems engineers of production systems. SysML provides many more modeling possibilities than a production engineer would ever need. Therefore a customized tool has to support the modeler during the selection process.

The basic element of SysML is the block. A block is able to represent everything; for example, a machine, a worker, or a transporter. This is a very abstract way of

Figure 17. Complexity of SysML

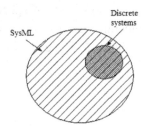

thinking which can be confusing. Even engineers whose tools generally have a fixed amount of defined elements can be confused. In SysML one can work with stereo-types which describe a defined element with attributes. So a suitable modeling tool is able to give a fixed and not too large number of modeling elements. To cover the modeling of all possible scenarios in the production, a significant number of ste-reotypes and stereotype attributes is necessary. In order to keep the overview, the engineer has to obtain only a preselection of stereotypes and stereotype attributes. To make this possible, the modeling tool needs to provide integrated, dynamically definable stereotypes.

We chose to develop our own modeling tool concept which is based on the open source project TOPCASED, a modeling tool, which receives large industrial support (example.g., Airbus, Continental, EADS). During the development of our tool, we adapted the usability specifically for systems engineers. The default setup is for the domain of production systems, but it is easily adaptable to other domains. The modeling concept is implemented in a profile of premade defined objects which significantly improve the ease to build a model, furthermore the reduction of options and elements within the graphical user interface significantly increased comprehensibility for system engineers in the test group. An impression on the currently used version is given in Figure 18.

FUTURE RESEARCH DIRECTIONS

The field of modeling with formal languages like SysML, model-to-model trans-formation and its verification and validation is a very recent topic. There have been many disputes about SysML during the short period of time since its publication. SysML is spreading very fast; today many of the most prominent developers of modeling tools like ARTiSAN, Telelogic, I-Logix, and Sparx Systems make use of SysML in their tools. In the future most UML tools will support SysML. But these tools are created for computer scientists and not for systems engineers. A systems engineer has another perspective on modeling. We hope that tool developers consider this in the future. Academia has to support this process by research on usability of modeling tools in a wide variety of engineering disciplines.

Another point is the approach to develop discrete systems with SysML. We tried to identify and structure the significant properties of discrete processes especially for production systems to give them a theoretical basis. With this theoretical basis it is easy to model discrete processes with SysML. Future work will extend our model to adapt it to discrete processes in many application domains.

Model transformation is an active research field, especially since the model-driven software development gained importance. Due to the large number of pub-

Figure 18. Topcased engineering with example

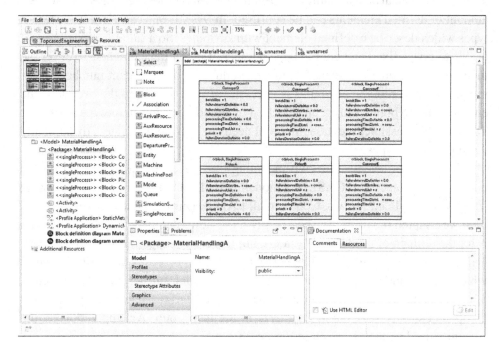

lications available, there are various approaches of model transformation, such as transformation with MOF2.0 QVT, transformation with OpenArchitectureWare and the transformation with graphs. But the question is whether it makes sense to use these methods for practical problems We think some work in this field is necessary to obtain methods which can be applied more easily and to test them for practical problems. QVT has a lot of potential but the whole QVT tool set is not fully implemented yet. In addition to the development of approaches for describing transformations research also has to deal with the development of appropriate techniques for their validation and verification.

CONCLUSION

In this chapter we have shown how to model discrete systems with SysML and how to translate these models for simulation tools. In the field of continuous processes Modelica has been established as a standard, but in the field of discrete processes there is no standard yet. There are only some quasi standards like petri nets, project networks or particular simulators. Thus, the field of discrete processes has a lack of an adequate modeling language. In contrast to the discrete modeling domain the continuous modeling domain benefits from several free and proprietary tools based on the modeling standard Modelica. Modelica is standardized by the Modelica Association and non-proprietary. Modelica is powerful and useful for modeling very complex scenarios. Furthermore by the modular concept of Modelica it is easy to model in domain specific problem space. As indicated in Section 1 SysML has the same attributes as Modelica and we think that it has the potential to become the first standard in the field of discrete processes.

We tried to identify and structure the significant properties of discrete processes to give them a theoretical basis. In the second section we show how to model discrete Systems with SysML. SysML separates between model and diagram and divides the model into a structural and a behavior part. The structural part describes the static structure, like the elements and their relationships. In the behavior part SysML describes the dynamic behavior at and between its elements. This concept is very clear and it provides the opportunity to build structured models. We also show that we are able model on different levels of granularity with SysML. A problem of modeling with SysML is the representation of large systems. It is obvious that modeling efforts as well as clarity can be problematic in these cases. But this is a principal problem of all graphical modeling languages. To solve the problem, modeling must be scalable. One approach would be to separate domain model and instance model. Another possible solution would be to prepare design patterns for recurring behavior.

Apart from the model development much research is performed on approaches for describing model transformations and the development of appropriate techniques for model and transformation validation and verification. For the model transformation, various methods are available. The most popular are transformation with MOF2.0 QVT, transformation with OpenArchitectureWare, imperative transformation and the transformation with graphs. There are techniques necessary to validate the developed model transformations with respect to established criteria for correctness. While verification and validation methods for model transformation using imperative methodology are quite rare there are several approaches for the model transformation with relations or graph grammars. For imperative, relational or graph-gramma transformation and for every correctness criteria, special methods are needed.

There are several modeling tools for SysML. A major problem of using SysML for discrete systems is that only skilled users can use SysML modeling tools adequately. Although there are good tools, they are not always optimal for discrete models. One reason for this is that these modeling environments were originally created for computer scientists and not for systems engineers. Therefore there is still a need for modeling tools for discrete systems with SysML, especially for engineers.

REFERENCES

Balzert, H. (2005). Lehrbuch der Objektmodellierung. [München, Germany: Spektrum Verlag.]. *Analyse und Entwurf mit der UML, 2*, 2.

Biehl, M. (2010). *Literature Study on Model Transformations. Royal Institute of Technology*. Retrieved March 20, 2012, from http://staffwww.dcs.shef.ac.uk/people/A.Simons/remodel/papers/BiehlModelTransformations.pdf

Ehrig, H., Ehrig, K., Ermel, C., Hermann, F., & Taentzer, G. (2007). Information Preserving Bidirectional Model Transformations. In *Fundamental Approaches to Software Engineering* (*Vol. 10*, pp. 72–86). Berlin, Germany: Springer-Verlag. doi:10.1007/978-3-540-71289-3_7.

Fowler, M. (2003). *UML Distilled: A Brief Guide to the Standard Object Modeling Language*. Reading, MA: Pearson Education.

Fritzon, P. (2011). *Introduction to Modeling and Simulation of Technical and Physical Systems*. Singapore: IEEE PRESS. doi:10.1002/9781118094259.

Hause, M. (2006). *The SysML Modelling Language*. Paper presented at the 15th European Systems Engineering Conference. Edinburgh, Scotland.

Huang, E., Ramamurthy, R., & McGinnis, L. (2007). System and simulation modeling using SysML. In *Proceedings of the 2007 Winter Simulation Conference.*(pp. 796-803). Tempe, Arizona: IEEE.

Kleppe, A., Warmer, J., & Bast, W. (2003). *MDA Explained: The Model Driven Architecture: Practice and Promise*. Boston, MA: Addison-Wesley.

Major, M. (2008). *Heuristik zur personalorientierten Steuerung von komplexen Montagesystemen*. Unpublished doctoral dissertation, University of Dresden, Dresden, Germany.

Mens, T. (2010). Model Transformation: A Survey of the State-of-the-Art. In Gerard, S., Babau, J., & Champeau, J. (Eds.), *Model Driven Engineering for Distributed Real-Time Embedded Systems* (pp. 18–36). New York: John Wiley & Sons.

Miller, J., & Murkerji, J. (2003). *MDA Guide Version 1.0.1. Object Management Group*. Retrieved March 20, 2012, from http://www.omg.org/news/meetings/workshops/UML_2003_Manual/00-2_MDA_Guide_v1.0.1.pdf

Narayanan, A., & Karasai, G. (2008). Verifying Model Transformations by Structural Correspondence. In, *Proceedings of the 7th International Workshop on Graph Transformation and Visual Modeling Techniques*. Retrieved March 20, 2012, from http://paperc.de/20384-verifying-model-transformations-by-structural-correspondence-9773186321795#!/pages/1

Neumann, K., & Schwindt, C. (1997). Activity-on-node networks with minimal and maximal time lags and their application to make-to-order production. [Berlin, Germany: Springer Verlag.]. *OR-Spektrum, 19*, 205–217. doi:10.1007/BF01545589.

Nikolaidou, M., Dalakas, V., Mitsi, L., Kapos, G.-D., & Anagnostopoulos, D. (2008). A SysML Profile for Classical DEVS Simulators. In Proceedings of Software Engineering Advances, 2008. ICSEA'08. Sliema, Malta.

Noche, B., & Wenzel, S. (2000*). The new simulation in production and logistics. Prospects, views and attitudes.* Paper presented at 9. ASIM-Fachtagung Simulation in Produktion und Logistik. Berlin, Germany.

Oestereich, B. (2006). *Analyse und Design mit UML 2.1.* München, Germany: Oldenbourg Verlag.

OMG. (2007). *Meta Object Facility (MOF) 2.0 Query/View/Transformation Specification.* Retrieved November 15, 2012, from http://www.omg.org/cgi-bin/doc?ptc/2007-07-07

OMG. (2010). *SysML Specification Version 1.2.* Retrieved March 20, 2012, from http://www.omg.org/spec/SysML/1.2/

Petri, C. A. (1962). *Kommunikation mit Automaten. Schriften des Reihnisch-Westfälischen Institut für Instrumentelle Mathematik an der Universität Bonn (Vol. 2).* Bonn, Germany: University of Bonn.

Pielok, T. (1995). *Prozesskettenmodulation – Management von Prozessketten mit Hilfe von Logistic Function Deployment.* Dortmund, Germany: Verlag Praxiswissen.

Piepper, D., Röttgers, C., & Gruhn, V. (2006). *MDA: effektives Software-Engineering mit UML 2 und Eclipse.* Berlin, Germany: Springer Verlag.

Pörnbacher, C. (2010). *Modellgetriebene Entwicklung der Steuerungssoftware automatisierter Fertigungssysteme.* Munich, Germany: Herbert Utz Verlag.

Reisig, W. (2010). *Petrinetze - Modellierung, Analyse, Fallstudien*. Wiesbaden, Germany: Vieweg-Teubner Verlag. doi:10.1007/978-3-8348-9708-4.

Rosenberg, D., & Mancarella, S. (2009). *Embedded Systems Development* using *SysML. Sparx Systtems*. Retrieved March 20, 2012, from http://www.sparxsystems.com/downloads/ebooks/Embedded_Systems_Development_using_SysML.pdf

Rumbaught, J., Jacobson, I., & Booch, G. (2004). *The Unifield Modeling Language Reference Manual*. Boston, MA: Addison-Wesley.

Schatten, A., Biffl, S., Demolsky, M., & Gostischa-Franta, E. A-Streicher, T., & Winkler, D. (2010). Best Practice Software-Engineering: Eine praxiserprobte Zusammenstellung von komponentenorientierten Konzepten, Methoden und Werkzeugen. Spektrum. Heidelberg, Germany: Akademischer Verlag.

Seemann, J., & Gudenberg, J. (2006). *Softwareentwurf mit UML 2.2*. Heidelberg, Germany: Springer-Verlag.

Seidel, U. A. (1998). *Verfahren zur Generierung und Gestaltung von Montageablaufstrukturenkomplexer Erzeugnisse*. Berlin, Germany: Springer-Verlag.

Sörrle, H. (2005). *UML 2 für Studenten*. München, Germany: Pearson Verlag.

Weilkiens, T. (2008). *Systems Engineering with SysML/UML*. Heidelberg, Germany: Dpunkt Verlag.

Weyprecht, P., & Rose, O. (2011) Model-driven development of simulation solution based on SysML starting with the simulation core. In *Proceedings of the 2011 Symposium on Theory of Modeling & Simulation: DEVS Integrative M&S Symposium* (pp. 189-192). Boston, MA: Society for Computer Simulation International.

ADDITIONAL READING

Baudry, B., Ghosth, S., Fleurey, F., France, R., Le Traon, Y., & Mottu, M. (2009). Barriers to systematic model transformation testing. *Communications of the ACM*, *53*, 139–143. doi:10.1145/1743546.1743583.

Biehl, M. (2010). *Literature Study on Model Transformations. Technical Report*. Stockholm, Sweden: Royal Institute of Technology.

Bock, C. (2006). SysML and UML 2.0 Support for Activity Modeling. *Journal of International Council of Systems Engineering*, *9*, 160–186.

Czarnecki, K., & Helsen, S. (2003). *Classification of Model Transformation Approaches*. Paper presented at the Workshop on Generative Techniques in the Context of Model-Driven. Anaheim, CA.

Czarnecki, K., & Helsen, S. (2006). Feature-based survey of model transformation approaches. *IBM Systems Journal - Model-Driven Software Development, 3*, 621-645.

Ehrig, H., Ehrig, K., Ermel, C., Hermann, F., & Taentzer, G. (2007). Information Preserving Bidirectional Model Transformations. In *Fundamental Approaches to Software Engineering* (*Vol. 10*, pp. 72–86). Berlin, Germany: Springer-Verlag. doi:10.1007/978-3-540-71289-3_7.

Ehring, H., & Ehring, K. (2006). Overview of Formal Concepts for Model Transformations Based on Typed Attributed Graph Transformation. *Electronic Notes in Theoretical Computer Science, 152*, 3–22. doi:10.1016/j.entcs.2006.01.011.

Friedenthal, S., Moore, A., & Steiner, M. (2011). A Practical Guide to SysML, Second Edition: The Systems Modeling Language. Boston, MA: The MK/OMG Press.

Hermann, F., Hülsbusch, M., & Köni, B. (2010). Specification and Verificationof Model Transformations. *Electronic Communications of the EASST, 30*, 15–35.

Holt, J., & Perry, S. (2008). *SysML for Systems Engineering*. London: Athenaeum Press Ltd. doi:10.1049/PBPC007E.

Johnson, T., Jobe, J., Paredis, C., & Burkhart, R. (2007). Modeling Continuous System Dynamics in SysML. In *Proceedings of the IMECE 2007*. Seattle, WA: ASME. Retrieved March 20, 2012, from http://www.srl.gatech.edu/publications/2007/JohnsonParedis-IMECE2007_DRAFT.pdf

Küster, J. (2004). *Systematic Validation of Model Transformations*. Paper presented at the Proceedings of 3rd UML Workshop in Software Model Engineering (WiSME 2004). Lisbon, Portugal.

Mens, T. (2010). Model Transformation: A Survey of the State-of-the-Art. In Gerard, S., Babau, J., & Champeau, J. (Eds.), *Model Driven Engineering for Distributed Real-Time Embedded Systems* (pp. 18–36). New York: John Wiley & Sons.

OMG. (2010a). *SysML Modelling Language explained*. Retrieved March 20, 2012, from http://www.omgsysml.org/SysML_Modelling_Language_explained-finance.pdf

OMG. (2010b). *SysML Specification Version 1.2*. Retrieved March 20, 2012, from http://www.omg.org/spec/SysML/1.2/

OMG. (2012). *What is OMG SysML*. Retrieved March 20, 2012, from http://www.omgsysml.org/

Rosenberg, D., & Mancarella, S. (2009). *Embedded Systems Development* using *SysML. Sparx Systems*. Retrieved March 20, 2012, from http://www.sparxsystems.com/downloads/ebooks/Embedded_Systems_Development_using_SysML.pdf

Schönherr, O., & Rose, O. (2010). Important Components for Modeling Production Systems with SysML. In *Proceedings of the 2010 IIE Annual Conference and Expo*. Cancun, Mexico: IIE.

Schönherr, O., & Rose, O. (2011). A General Model Description for Discrete Processes. In *Proceedings of the 2011 Winter Simulation Conference*. Phoenix, AZ: IEEE. Retrieved March 20, 2012, from http://www.informs-sim.org/wsc11papers/198.pdf

Weilkiens, T. (2008). *Systems Engineering with SysML/UML*. Heidelberg, Germany: Dpunkt Verlag.

KEY TERMS AND DEFINITIONS

Continuous Processes: Processes which lead to system state changes continuously over time.

Discrete Processes: Processes which lead to system state changes only at discrete points in time. These points in time are called events.

Meta-Meta-Model: A meta-meta model defines language constructs for defining meta-models.

Meta-Model: A meta-model is the syntactic and semantic description of a modeling language. In a meta-model is thus clearly defined which language elements are available for description of facts and what the concrete syntax and semantics look like.

Model: A model is a description of a specific scenario with language elements (for example, elements and relations) of a well-defined language.

Model-to-Model Transformation: A model-to-model transformation is the automatic generation of one or more target models from one or more source models, corresponding to a transformation definition.

Validation: The validation of model transformations is a process, which checks whether the specification of the transformation is sufficient for the requirements of the transformation.

Verification: The verification of model transformations is a process, which checks whether the implementation of the transformation satisfies its specification.

Chapter 10
An Integrated Framework to Simulate SysML Models Using DEVS Simulators

G. D. Kapos
Harokopio University of Athens, Greece

M. Nikolaidou
Harokopio University of Athens, Greece

V. Dalakas
Harokopio University of Athens, Greece

D. Anagnostopoulos
Harokopio University of Athens, Greece

ABSTRACT

System models validation is an important engineering activity of the system development life-cycle, usually performed via simulation. However, usability and effectiveness of many validation approaches are hindered by the fact that system simulation is not performed using a system model described by a standardized modeling language as SysML. This requires system simulation models to be recreated from scratch, burdening the engineer and introducing inconsistencies between system and validation models. In this chapter, the authors present how system engineers may effectively perform SysML system model validation utilizing the original SysML model and standards-based simulated related extensions. This is achieved by a framework that exploits MDA concepts and techniques, such as profiling, meta-modeling, and formal transformations. This way an open, standards-based, customizable approach for SysML models validation using DEVS simulators is formed. A simple battle system is used as an example throughout the chapter to facilitate the presentation of the proposed approach.

DOI: 10.4018/978-1-4666-4369-7.ch010

INTRODUCTION

Engineers from different fields usually resort to computer simulation in order to describe, understand, and predict the behavior of complex systems or systems of systems from various scientific fields. Discrete event simulation offers the means to evaluate some of these systems, not only in regular, but also under extreme circumstances in order to avoid errors. The majority of the engineers actually already resort to simulation in order to reduce risks. However, although the computational means are rapidly increasing and modern engineers are computer literate, there are no standardized manners to perform systems validation. Most of the engineers use specific computational environments that are usually expensive, commercial, de facto standards, or restricted in-house software tools.

In the last decade, there is a strong effort to standardize and unify frameworks and methodologies related to modeling and simulation, driven by international organizations such as ACM, SCS and/or OMG. Focus is set to extract additive value from standard languages and well-defined formalisms, in an open and hopefully more beneficial manner. A step towards the unification of the different approaches is the use of frameworks, based on open standards, which could bridge the gap, acting like an interface that allows useful information to transit among various tools. Let us, use here an example from the real world. One could see it as building bridges between islands. Although, these bridges should have foundations, solid enough, to carry the amount and types of information needed from both sides of the bridge, they should also be aesthetic and functional (i.e., the user should feel comfortable to use them without fear and without any further experience). The user should have only one consideration: source and destination.

Towards this effort, this chapter presents step-by-step a methodology for simulating system models with the aid of a working example. Emphasis is given on the benefits gained by the use of formal modeling and meta-modeling representations and standard transformations.

The goal of this chapter is to offer the reader the ability to:

- Perform a SysML model enrichment,
- Transform to DEVS executable models,
- Perform DEVS model execution,
- Expand, if interested the presented framework to other cases of interest.

More specifically the authors would try to illustrate how to create and enrich a model through MagicDraw or any other UML/SysML tool. Models are then transformed to DEVS models by means of open tools and standard languages such as QVT. Finally, these models may be executed in a simulation environment offered by a community outside OMG.

BACKGROUND

This section reviews the most important theoretical notions used throughout this chapter in order to facilitate the reader. The most interested reader should resort to literature. The approach followed here concerns theory related to the interconnection among SysML and simulation activity in brevity. On the contrary, people with deep knowledge of SysML, MDA, and/or DEVS may skip the whole section.

SysML Models Simulation

According to INCOSE, (Baker et al., 2000), model-based system engineering is utilized by a central system model, used to perform all engineering activities in the specification, design, integration, validation, and operation of a system. SysML (SysML, 2007) was proposed by the OMG as a general-purpose graphical modeling language for describing such models of a broad range of systems and systems-of-systems. SysML system models should be defined independently of specific implementations or tools. Specific activities may be accomplished either by the system engineer using a SysML modeling tool (example.g., system design) or by specific tools in an automated fashion (e.g., system validation) or even by a combination of both. In the case where specific tools are used, SysML models should be transformed to tool specific models, serving the specific engineering activity.

Since SysML became a standard, the need to integrate SysML modeling tools and simulation environments was evident. Apparently SysML supports a variety of diagrams describing system structure and states necessary to perform simulation; thus, there are a lot of efforts from both research and industrial communities to simulate SysML models (Huang, Ramamurthy, & McGinnis, 2007; Schonherr & Rose, 2009). In most cases, SysML models defined within a modeling tool are exported in XML format and, consequently, transformed into simulator specific models and forwarded to the simulation environment. Depending on the nature and specific characteristics of systems under study, there is a diversity of approaches on simulating models defined in SysML, which utilize different SysML diagrams. In (Peak et al., 2007), a method for simulating the behavior of continuous systems using mathematical simulation is presented, utilizing SysML parametric diagrams, which allow the description of complex mathematical equations. System models are simulated using composable objects (COBs) (Peak, Paredis, & Tamburini, 2005). It should be noted that in any case SysML models should be defined in a way which facilitates simulating them (Tamburini, 2006). In Kerzhner, Jobe, & Paredis (2011), simulation is performed using Modelica (Modelica Association, 2005). To ensure that a complete and accurate Modelica model is constructed using SysML, a corresponding profile is proposed to enrich SysML models with simulation-specific capabilities. These approaches are better suited for systems with continuous behavior.

Simulation of discrete event systems is utilized based on system behavior described in SysML activity, sequence or state diagrams. In McGinnis & Ustun (2009), system models defined in SysML are translated to be simulated using Arena simulation software. Model Driven Architecture (MDA) (OMG, 2003) concepts are applied to export SysML models from a SysML modeling tool and, consequently, transformed into Arena simulation models, which must be enriched with behavioral characteristics before becoming executable. In Wang & Dagli (2008), the utilization of Colored Petri Nets is proposed to simulate SysML models. If the system behavior is described using activity and sequence diagrams in SysML, it may be consequently simulated using discrete event simulation via Petri Nets. In both cases, although SysML system models are extracted and used, the system engineer must write large parts of the simulation code, especially concerning system behavior.

To the best of our knowledge, none of the frameworks presented to the research community so far enables fully automated translation to an existing simulation environment. Thus, engineers resort to simulation code composition. This chapter presents a framework that enables automated simulation execution of models already defined in SysML. To this end, MDA principles -commonly accommodated in such studies- are further exploited and only specific model enrichment with behavioral characteristics is required. A key advantage of such an approach is that focus remains on the model and all the work is conducted in the SysML modeling tool.

DEVS Formalism and Tools

DEVS formalism provides a conceptual framework for specifying discrete event simulation models executed on a variety of simulators (Zeigler, Praehofer, & Kim, 2000), as DEVS-C++, DEVSJava (Zeigler & Sarjoughian, 2003), cell-DEVS (Wainer & Giambiasi, 2001), DEVS/RMI (Zhang, Zeigler, & Hammonds, 2005) or even DEVS/SOA (Mittal, Risco-Martín, & Zeigler, 2009), which offers DEVS simulators as web services. Both SysML and DEVS follow the same principles regarding model structure (Nikolaidou, Dalakas, Mitsi, Kapos, & Anagnostopoulos, 2008). The main structural elements in SysML are blocks with properties and ports, which are very similar to DEVS components. Both support composite and simple models.

Containment and interconnection of SysML blocks through their ports is similar to composition and coupling in DEVS coupled blocks. These similarities facilitate the transformation of SysML models to valid executable DEVS simulation models.

Embedding DEVS formalism detailed description within SysML models provides the means to describe model behavior and enables the automated execution of these models on existing, popular, and effective simulation environments. Several DEVS simulation environments aim at XML-based DEVS modeling and interpretation in different programming languages (Hosking & Sahin, 2009; Risco-Mart´ın, Mittal, L´opez-Pen˜a, & Cruz, 2007; Meseth, Kirchhof, & Witte, 2009; Mittal, Risco-Mart´ın, & Zeigler, 2007; Risco-Mart´ín, De La Cruz, Mittal, & Zeigler, 2009). An XML data encapsulation is accomplished in Hosking & Sahin(2009) within the DEVS environment, as a unifying communication method among the entities in any Systems-of-Systems (SoS) architecture. In Mittal et al. (2007), the problem of model interoperability is addressed, with a novel approach of developing DEVSML as the transformation medium towards composability and dynamic scenario construction. The composed coupled models are then validated using atomic and coupled DTDs. In this case, model behavior is not emphasized. The approach presented in Risco-Mart´ın et al. (2009) supports the transformation of DEVSJava code into XML and vice versa for a subset of the DEVS formalism, FD-DEVS (Hwang & Zeigler, 2009). The latter DEVS-XML version is referred as XFD-DEVS and offers XSD definitions along with a tool for the transformation. In Meseth et al. (2009) an XML Schema is introduced for XLSC, a language for modeling atomic and coupled DEVS models. It was shown that a) XLSC can express a model's behavior as well as its structure, and b) an XLSC model can be simulated. An interpreter was prototypically implemented in Java and employed to directly execute the model's functions and update the model's state. In this case, atomic model behavior can be described in XML using a series of actions depicting specific instructions included in the simulation code. In any case, executable models are defined either in C++ or Java.

In all the aforementioned approaches, the XML representations proposed focused on the description of executable DEVS code taking into consideration the requirements imposed to describe DEVS model structure and behavior in a format incorporating implementation details, as for example the description of a DEVS atomic model function in C++ or Java including language commands and variable value assignments. In Risco-Mart´ın et al. (2007), DEVSXML was proposed as a platform-independent, XML-based format for describing DEVs models focusing on DEVS formalism, offering an upper level representation of DEVS behavior based on system state transitions. DEVSXML was proposed to establish DEVS model mobility and promote interoperability between discrete DEVS simulators, independently of the programming language they are implemented in (either C++ or Java) and the way they operate (either in a distributed or centralized fashion). DEVSXML may be consequently transformed into executable code for existing DEVS Simulators, using translators as the ones proposed in Risco-Mart´ın et al. (2007) for DEVSJava simulator, which was only implemented for DEVS coupled models.

Thus, DEVS behavior transformation is missing. Since DEVSXML targets an upper level representation of DEVS models suitable for describing them in an abstract fashion as in SysML, its adaptation as an intermediate format was explored. A few issues were raised as discussed in the following. First, DEVSXML does not incorporate the relation between state variable values and states. Second, in order to be implementation independent, DEVSXML is quite general and, therefore, does not handle complex expression values in a specific manner. Third, DEVSXML is -as implied by its name- the specification of a flat XML representation for DEVS models, rather than a meta-model for -conceptually richer- DEVS models. Fourth, in DEVSXML, XML attributes are rarely used, leading to element explosion and quite complex structure. Finally, actual testing and use of DEVSXML-compliant tools has been difficult.

In the following a meta-model for DEVS models and its corresponding XML representation that is (a) consistent with DEVS theory, (b) ready to be executed in DEVS simulation environments, and (c) fully compatible with SysML is used.

SYSML MODELS SIMULATION

Issues, Controversies, Problems

Automated executable simulation code generation from SysML system models is an appealing functionality. However, there is a series of issues that need to be addressed first, so that this process becomes open, standards-based, extensible, inter-operable, customizable and formally defined. Considering that the worlds of system engineering and simulation need to be interrelated in a concrete manner, lack of some of the above characteristics would hinder applicability and viability of such an approach.

- First, an important issue is the proper selection of methodology and language used for system modeling. These must:
    - Provide facilities to incorporate simulation-specific information,
    - Be supported by diverse modeling tools, and
    - Provide standard external representations for further use of the system models in simulation environments.
- Second, the simulation methodology and environment must be properly selected. Not all simulation methodologies are appropriate for all kinds of systems. In order to be able to utilize a simulation methodology in such an

approach, it should also provide a solid conceptual foundation. Furthermore, a set of extrovert simulation execution environments that are able to execute models following this foundation is necessary.

- Third, the simulation-aware system model should somehow be imported and executed in one or more simulation execution environments. Direct mappings to specific simulation execution environments code would result in redundant repetition of a process that involves correlating different aspects of a model (system description model and simulation system model), as well as different levels of abstraction (from a declarative, high-level model description to executable simulation code).

Such issues, as well as additional factors, like dealing with new version from both sides, render direct mapping cumbersome and impractical.

A Framework for Simulating SysML Models with DEVS

In the context of this chapter, MDA is considered as the most suitable framework for generating simulation models from SysML models, since focus is given on models defined for different domain activities in a formal, standards-based manner. The designer usually has the following considerations:

- How to obtain a central integrated system model
- How to transform it to executable code
- Which implementation tools to select

This section would offer solutions to these issues as well as the justification for the choices illustrated in the whole framework.

Introducing a Central System Model Using SysML

A framework for simulating SysML models with DEVS has been proposed in (Kapos, Dalakas, Nikolaidou, & Anagnostopoulos, n.d.) as depicted in Figure 1. Regarding the proposed modeling language, SysML/UML has been selected, as the emerging OMG standard for system modeling, supported by many modeling tools. Additionally, SysML/UML could be extended to handle simulation-related information via the profiling mechanism. A DEVS profile for SysML is used for this purpose.

In order to utilize the framework of Figure 1, the system engineer should enrich system models with DEVS-compliant simulation information, according to the DEVS-SysML profile. The profile constraints and extends SysML models, so that they are simulation enabled. It consists of a set of stereotypes and constraints. Ste-

Figure 1. Simulating system models with DEVS: step 1: enriching SysML system models; step 2: transforming DEVS-SysML models to DEVS models; step 3: executing DEVS models

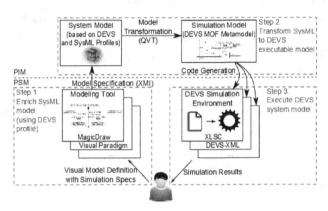

reotypes are used to characterize specific SysML model elements, while constraints specify how models should be created.

DEVS enriched SysML models can be automatically transformed to simulation code for specific DEVS simulators. Since DEVS formalism is supported by numerous implementations, the transformation includes an intermediate, yet autonomous and very important step, which is the generation of a pure DEVS representation of the system model, based on a DEVS MOF 2.0 meta-model. The MOF is an OMG standard for model-driven engineering that allows the definition of models representing specific domains, like the DEVS simulation formalism. Such models can be represented with XML, according to the XML Metadata Interchange (XMI) format. The existence of a DEVS meta-model independent of specific simulators enhances the usability of the proposed approach and facilitates simpler transformations for diverse simulation environments, as DEVSJava, cellDEVS, and so forth.

Transforming Meta-Models

Transformation of enriched SysML models to DEVS XMI representations should be specified and implemented using QVT, a standard set of languages for model transformation defined by the OMG. Specifically, QVT defines three transformation languages: QVT-Operational, QVT-Relations and QVT-Core. In this case, QVT-Relations, a declarative language for defining constraints on source and target model elements, has been used. QVT transformations can be applied on models that conform to MOF 2.0 meta-models (SysML and DEVS meta-models in our case).

OCL, another OMG standard language for defining constraints, is integrated and also extended in QVT with imperative features.

Regarding the transformation of DEVS-aware SysML models to DEVS models (according to the standard DEVS meta-model), QVT is ideal, as it is an OMG standard and provides powerful transformation facilities, like relational mappings and OCL with imperative features. It allows the definition of high-level, conceptual model transformations between different MOF meta-models.

Simulation Environment

Regarding the simulation environment, DEVS is appropriate for such an approach due to several of its attributes. First, there is remarkable similarity in structural characteristics of DEVS and SysML models. Also SysML offers modeling elements that could capture DEVS models behavior. Furthermore, there exist several approaches attempting to provide a high-level representation of DEVS executable models. This renders "DEVS world" mature-enough to define a standard meta-model for its models. A DEVS meta-model defined in terms of MOF would be ideal in this MDA approach. DEVS models defined in this standard representation could be transformed into execution environment-specific models and executed.

The transformation of DEVS MOF models to executable code for specific DEVS simulation environments is feasible, since all DEVS related information is clearly contained in the DEVS MOF models. However, the transformation depends on the target simulation environment. The XLSC DEVS (Meseth et al., 2009) was used as the simulation environment. The simulator accepts as input DEVS models described in XML and simulates them in a Java environment.

Building Bridges

From a software engineering perspective, according to the concepts of MDA (OMG, 2003), for each real-world domain, two kinds of discrete models should be defined: a Platform Independent Model (PIM), ensuring proper domain representation, and Platform Specific Model (PSM), corresponding to one or more executable versions of the PIM. In the DEVS simulation domain of Figure 1, the DEVS MOF meta-model is used to define a PIM, and consequently translated into code executed on a variety of DEVS simulators, as XLSC DEVSJava and DEVS/SOA, corresponding to PSM. In the SysML modeling domain, DEVS-SysML profile is used to define SysML models enriched with simulation capabilities. The UML meta-model and the SysML and DEVS-SysML profiles are used to define a PIM, while specific UML/

SysML modeling tools (e.g., MagicDraw, VisualPradigm), where model enrichment is conducted, correspond to PSM.

From an implementation perspective, the DEVS-SysML profile and a corresponding application programming interface (API) is implemented for MagicDraw (MG, 2007), which is a widely used UML modeling tool supporting SysML with a user-friendly programming interface. SysML models constructed using the DEVS-SysML profile and exported in XMI format are transformed into DEVS models (conforming to the DEVS MOF meta-model) via a QVT model transformation that has been defined for that purpose. The last part of the transformation (code generation) has been implemented for XLSC DEVS execution environment (Meseth et al., 2009). This is implemented in terms of XSLT ((W3C), 2007).

Profiles, Metamodels, and Transformations

Although the principles, notions and goals of the framework have been discussed, an overview of its fundamental parts are provided here, to facilitate comprehension of the case study presented in the rest of the chapter. Figure 2 (Kapos, Dalakas, Nikolaidou, & Anagnostopoulos, n.d.) provides a visual representation of the DEVS-SysML profile model elements, the DEVS meta-model and the transformation that has been implemented in terms of QVT. While standard QVT visual specification is appropriate for the representation of a single relation, a simpler notation was selected for Figure 2 due to clarity reasons. Nine model element-mapping groups are identified and shortly described in the following.

1. **The topmost part of the transformation:** The DEVS Model Block Definition Diagram (UML2 entity) contains all DEVS Atomic and DEVS Coupled blocks to be transformed into DEVS entities DEVS ATOMIC and DEVS COUPLED. It is implemented by a QVT relation, which finds all DEVS Model Block Definition Diagram entities in the UML2 XMI (normally there will be only one) and creates a DEVS MODEL for each one.
2. **DEVS common elements transformation:** This part transforms elements that are common in atomic and coupled DEVS models (i.e., model name and input/output ports).
3. **DEVS atomic state definition transformation:** Transforms the DEVS State Constraint blocks that define the state set.
4. **DEVS atomic state variable definition transformation:** Transforms the DEVS State Variable value properties to DEVS State Variables.
5. **DEVS atomic state association transformation:** Transforms the DEVS State Association Model to conditions attached to state set values.

Figure 2. Transforming DEVS-SysML models to DEVS models

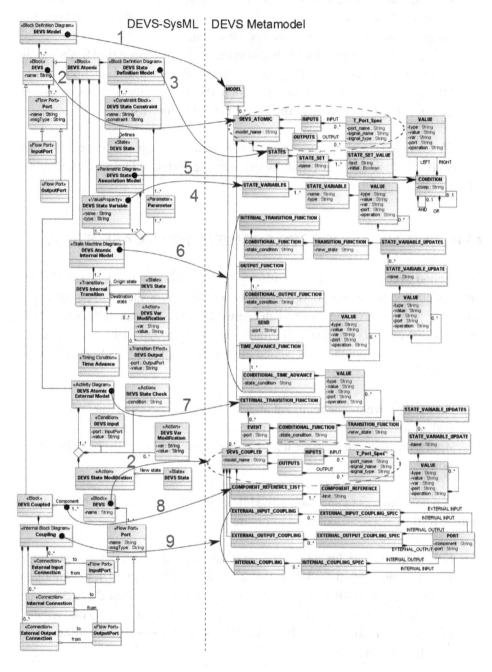

6. **DEVS atomic internal model transformation:** Transforms the DEVS Atomic Internal Model (State Machine Diagram) to Internal Transition Function, Output Function and Time Advance Function.
7. **DEVS atomic external model transformation:** Transforms the DEVS Atomic External Model (Activity Diagram) to External Transition Function.
8. **DEVS coupled components transformation:** Transforms the Component composition associations to the component reference list.

DEVS coupled coupling transformation: Transforms the port connections of the Internal Block Diagram to External Input Coupling, External Output Coupling and Internal Coupling.

APPLYING THE PROPOSED FRAMEWORK: A CASE STUDY

This section would present an application of the described approach by simulating a simple battle SysML model. In this example, a battle is considered to be conducted between a friendly division unit and an enemy unit. The division unit consists of a regiment that controls artillery and infantry units. Although focus is given on the presentation of the approach, the veiled aim of this application is to examine two strategies:

1. *Attack1by1*, where the regiment attacks the enemy first with the *artillery* unit and afterwards with the *infantry* unit, and
2. *AttackAll*, where the regiment attacks the enemy using all its available attack power.

The whole process of simulating SysML models with DEVS may be organized in three distinct steps, as indicated in Figure 1:

1. SysML model enrichment, where the system engineer adds the required information to the system model, so that it can be simulated in a DEVS simulator.
2. Transformation to DEVS executable model, where the enriched system model is transformed into a generic, but precise DEVS model that could be executed.
3. DEVS model execution, where the DEVS model is executed after proper adjustment, if necessary.

The battle simulation example will be presented according to this procedure.

SysML Model Enrichment

According to the proposed framework (Figure 1a) model enrichment is conducted by the designer following the DEVS-SysML profile. This profile defines a set of stereotypes and diagrams that must be used to characterize existing model elements and define simulation specification for the system. In the following, the main actions that need to be made in each diagram type are outlined. The tool selected for the purpose was MagicDraw. Starting with the creation of the appropriate model, the designer has to introduce two kinds of information:

- Structural information (DEVS separates its entities to Coupled/Atomic)
- Behavioral information regarding the case considered

Hence, there are some diagrams that need to be created/completed before any further action.

Block Definition Diagrams (Coupled)

The main structural elements in SysML -blocks- are used to define the required battle entities. All such blocks must be defined in one or more Block Definition Diagrams (bdds), as illustrated in Figure 3. In this case study we examine the behavior of specific passive components. Therefore, additional blocks for a simple experimental frame (*ef*) that control the simulation process are also introduced (Zeigler, Praehofer, & Kim, 2000). Thus, simulation scenarios may be created and executed. The blocks should be characterized as either *DEVS Atomic* or *DEVS Coupled*, depending on the complexity of their structure. For example, *efb* is the outer-most coupled element, containing the *ef* and *battle* models. On the other hand, components like *regiment*, *artillery*, *infantry* and *enemy* are atomic, where structure is simple, but behavior needs to be specified.

Internal Block Diagrams

Although model containment is displayed in bdds, port interconnection configuration of components contained in *DEVS Coupled* components is easily managed and displayed in Internal Block Diagrams (ibd). For example, ports *(Atack1by1* and *AttackAll)* of the *battle DEVS Coupled* component should be internally connected to ports of contained components *(division* and *enemy)*, as illustrated in the ibd of Figure 4. Contained components should also be interconnected.

Figure 3. Block definition diagram with the main entities in the battle example

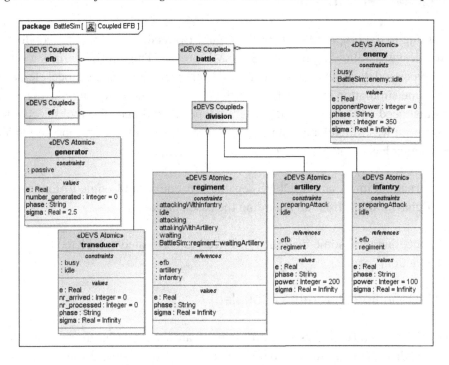

Thus, the designer must define internal connections of all *DEVS Coupled* components in the respective ibds. For example, internal connections of the *division* component should also be defined, as in Figure 5. Port direction is important for the connections. For contained components interconnections, only output-to-input port connections are allowed. On the contrary, when ports of the container component are connected to ports of the contained components, port direction must be the same, since incoming external events are delegated to contained components and outgoing external events are delegated to container output ports.

Figure 4. Internal block diagram of the battle DEVS coupled component

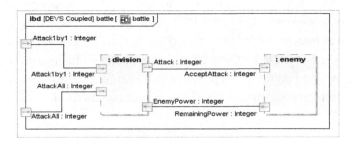

Block Definition Diagrams (Atomic)

Regarding *DEVS Atomic* components, a set of behavioral attributes (states, internal transition, time advance, output and external transition) should be defined. *Regiment DEVS* Atomic component is examined to describe how the attributes mentioned above are defined. States should be explicitly defined in an internal bdd named *States*. Figure 6 illustrates the *States* bdd of the *regiment* component. States are defined as *DEVS State Constraints*, where a parameter is constrained to a specific value.

Parametric Diagrams

The independent state constraints of the *States* bdd should somehow be correlated through one or more state variables. In the case of *regiment* the *phase* state variable should be defined and used. State constraints should be associated with the *phase* state

Figure 5. Internal block diagram of the division DEVS coupled component

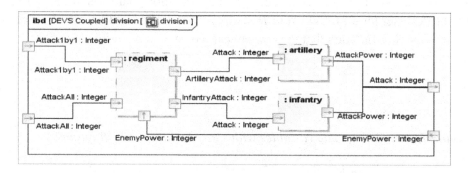

Figure 6. States definition in DEVS atomic components

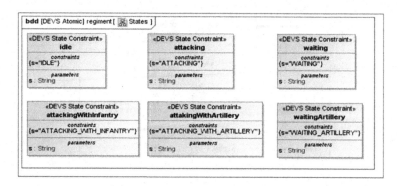

variable, as illustrated in the Parametric Diagram (par) of Figure 7. In our example, *phase* takes the place of the *s* parameter in each of the state constraints. When the active state is *attacking* then *phase* has the value *"ATTACKING"* and vice versa.

State Machine Diagrams

Information regarding internal transition, output, and time advance of a *DEVS Atomic* components is concentrated in a single State Machine Diagram (stm) named *Internal Transition*. Figure 8 displays this kind of diagram for the *regiment* component. A *DEVS State* must exist for each *DEVS State Constraint* defined in the bdd of Figure 6. An initial state (black-filled circle) is also used to indicate the initial state *(idle)*. All possible internal transitions must be defined with *DEVS State Transition* directed connections. For states that become active only after external events, no incoming connections must be defined (e.g., *attacking*, *attackingWithArtillery*, *attackingWithInfantry*). For states that do not transit to another state in the absence of external events, no outgoing connection should be defined (e.g., *idle*, *waiting*, *waitingArtillery*). No more than one outgoing *DEVS State Transitions* may be defined for each *DEVS* State, as imposed by DEVS formalism.

Time advance function is deduced from time duration guard conditions defined by the designer for all *DEVS State Transitions*. For each transition, this constraint defines the time duration that the component will stay in the originating state.

Figure 7. Associating state variables with states in parametric diagrams

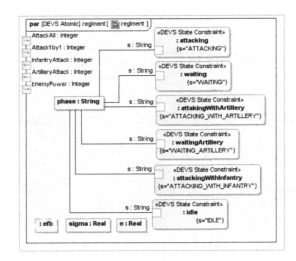

Figure 8. Defining internal transition, time advance and output in state machine diagrams

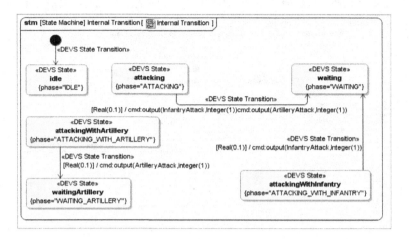

Output function is also defined via *DEVS State Transitions*, but in a rather operational manner. In the behavior body of each transition, output commands should be declared, indicating the output port name and the value (absolute or calculated) that must be sent.

Activity Diagrams

Finally, external transition function is defined via an Activity Diagram (act) for each *DEVS Atomic* component. Figure 9 illustrates such an act for *regiment DEVS Atomic* component. Input events from ports (e.g. *AttackAll, Attack1by1* and *EnemyPower*) should be combined with possible current (when the event occurs) states *(DEVS State Check)* in *DEVS Input State Join* nodes to define the resulting new states *(DEVS State Modification* actions*)*.

Figure 9 also illustrates how such DEVS-SysML model definition may be carried out in UML modeling tools, like MagicDraw. Use of required DEVS modeling elements may be facilitated by the respective custom GUI buttons. Additionally, model consistency checks may be based on Object Constraint Language (OCL) statements of the DEVS-SysML profile or directly implemented as tool plugins, using the provided tool API.

Other Considerations

During model enrichment, the designer is less prone to logical and syntactical errors, since the whole process is performed at a higher, visual layer, compared to

Figure 9. Defining external transitions in activity diagrams

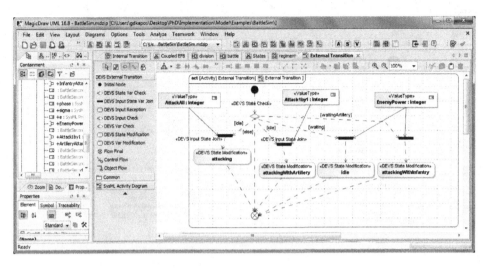

code composition. Moreover, the syntactical correctness of the enriched model is ensured by the constraints derived from the DEVS-SysML profile. Hence, only valid models may be translated and executed. Furthermore, logical errors introduced by the designer could be identified from the simulation results.

Normally, structural changes would not be required since the main system entities and their interconnections should have been already identified. Regarding any behavioral enrichment, a basic knowledge of the adopted simulation framework (i.e., DEVS) is required by the designer. However, as DEVS shares the same scope with SysML, namely describing a system of systems, this should not be a hinder. In addition, existing state machine diagrams and/or activity diagrams could be exploited, reducing the number of modifications needed.

In order to conduct an exact cost analysis, several factors should be previously considered. First, there is a dependency on the case study and the redundancy of the model elements. This may lead to a reusability of the enriched model elements, limiting the model enrichment cost. Second, model enrichment may be facilitated via custom plug-ins that can be developed for UML/SysML modeling tools. Such utilities may eliminate enrichment-related actions that may seem redundant. Finally, a usage of pre-existing simulation library components could further facilitate this process.

Model Transformation

The DEVS-SysML model, previously created, can now be utilized in the second step of the process, as indicated in Figure 1b. The model is transformed to a pure DEVS model representation that is execution-ready in the sense that it could be executed in a generic DEVS simulator or slightly transformed to be executed in specific DEVS simulators. Also, this step does not require much user effort, as the transformation is already defined and may be applied to any DEVS-SysML model.

DEVS-SysML is expressed in terms of the UML 2 meta-model, while a different, special purpose and simpler meta-model has been defined for DEVS models. A QVT-based transformation, composed of a series of QVT relations, is proposed for transforming DEVS-SysML models to DEVS models, since both meta-models are based on MOF. Medini QVT (http://projects.ikv.de/qvt/), a tool for model-to-model transformations, is used to perform the transformation. Figure 10 illustrates how the model generated in a UML modeling tool is presented in medini QVT. DEVS stereotypes and model components are clearly identified.

As already stated, the transformation outlined in Figure 2 consists of a set of QVT relations that are partially listed in Figure 11. Each relation associates specific aspects of the DEVS-SysML model to DEVS model elements, imposing constraints and post-conditions. This way, the whole set of QVT relations results in the appropriate, overall model transformation.

Exploiting the advantages of the proposed architectural scheme and methodology, this rather declarative and conceptual transformation can be executed in any QVT compliant tool, for any valid DEVS-SysML model, created in any UML modeling tool. Figure 12 depicts a part of the generated DEVS model in medini QVT.

After the completion of the second step, a pure DEVS representation of the system has been created. This representation contains the exact information required for the simulation model to be executed and to be used as an input for a specific DEVS simulator.

DEVS Model Execution

The third step of the process, as indicated in Figure 1c, constitutes of DEVS model execution, in this case in DEVS XLSC environment.

Figure 10. The source (DEVS-SysML) model in medini QVT

XLSC requires as input a slightly different, lower-level XML representation of DEVS models and acts as a translator for the DEVSJava simulator (Zeigler & Sarjoughian, 2003). Transformation of the DEVS model in XMI representation to the respective XLSC XML representation is performed using EXtensible Stylesheet Language Transformations (XSLT) (W3C), 2007), a World Wide Web Consortium (http://www.w3.org/), standard. A snapshot of this straight-forward XSLT, as shown in the free edition of the EditX tool (http://www.editix.com/), is depicted in Figure 13.

EditX is an XML tool that performs XSLT-based transformations. It should be mentioned here, that this last part of transformation is executed without the knowledge of the user with the help of a single script. Part of the outcome of the DEVS to XLSC transformation is shown in Figure 14. Compared to the DEVS model, represented in XMI format in Figure 12, it is properly adjusted so that it can be executed in the XLSC/DEVSJava environment.

Figure 15 provides a snapshot of the model being executed in the XLSC/DEVS-Java environment. The SimView component has been used for step-by-step graphical representation of the simulated model. In this snapshot the *regiment* component

Figure 11. The QVT relations implementing the DEVS-SysML to DEVS transformation in medini QVT

has received the *AttackAll* event and is concurrently forwarding *Attack* events to both *artillery* and *infantry* units, which have just got into the *preparingAttack* state.

Completion of the proposed steps in the simple Battle example provides a complete and clear picture of the methodology and its applicability. It also reveals how emphasis that has been given on formal, standardized methods and models, credited the methodology with several advantages, like interoperability, support by many tools, and openness.

Hence, the system engineer interferes only with the model via a standard graphical modeling language such as SysML and obtains valid simulation results through a DEVS simulator. The whole process is achieved without specialized knowledge, following the simple predefined steps of the proposed framework. The system engineer is not obliged to know how to create DEVS simulation models. As long as he/she is able to enrich system models with DEVS properties using standard notation, simulation code is created and executed automatically with no further programming effort, employing off-the-shelf tools.

Figure 12. The target (DEVS) model in medini QVT

Figure 13. Transforming DEVS models to XLSC XML representations with XSLT in EditX

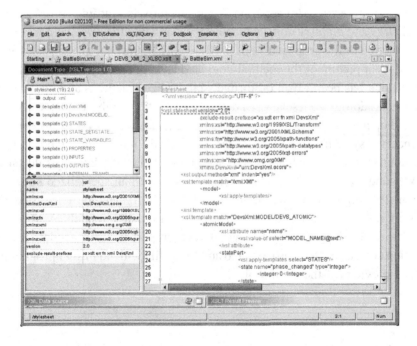

Figure 14. Target (XLSC) XML representation in EditX

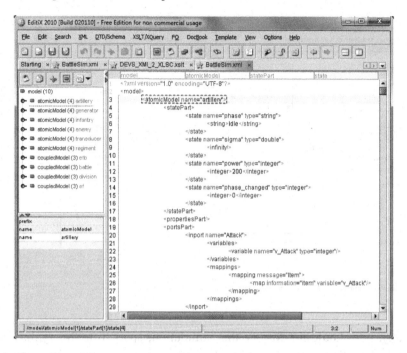

FUTURE RESEARCH DIRECTIONS

Integration of simulation-related information into a reference system model described using a standardized modeling language has been widely explored. These approaches are mainly based on standard modeling methodologies (like SysML) and formal simulation frameworks (like DEVS). Currently, such a standardization procedure is under development for SysML and Modelica (OMG, 2010), while ModelicaML (OSMC, 2009) is available from the Open Source Modelica Consortium (OSMC) as an extended subset of UML that enables the generation of executable Modelica code.

However, a factor critically affecting the wide adoption of such approaches besides standardization is their efficiency and ease of use. Standard system and simulation modeling couplings will lead to adoption from the majority of system modeling and simulation tools and, therefore, will dramatically change the landscape, from a practical perspective. System and simulation model integration should be extended to other simulation frameworks. Such extensions would prepare the ground for identifying common characteristics and developing a general approach for system and simulation model integration, independent of the simulation framework. This way, a system model with common extensions could be simulated in multiple, diverse simulation frameworks and tools.

Figure 15. Executing the model with XLSC/DEVSJava SimView component

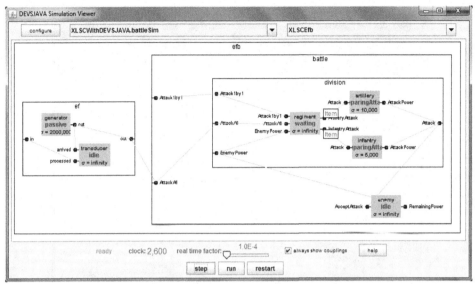

Finally, one should not foresee that simulation, apart from theory, has important implementation issues to deal with. Such issues are successfully confronted by commercial simulation environments (e.g., MATLAB/SimuLink (http://www.mathworks.com/products/simulink/) and, therefore, should be included in similar system and simulation model integration approaches. Now, the challenge is how a general approach that incorporates other simulation environments than DEVS should be formed utilizing the same MDA concepts.

CONCLUSION

This chapter provides a step-by-step approach to simulate SysML models via a DEVS simulator. The system engineer may simulate a SysML model by enriching it with DEVS-related properties, while the simulation code is generated automatically, ensuring the absence of inconsistencies between system and simulation models. The whole process is based on a framework that exploits MDA concepts, standards, and techniques, such as profiling, meta-modeling and formal transformations. It has been proven that automated simulation of system models is feasible. Moreover, since the employed tools support standards and formal approaches, the code generated and executed is trusted and the same stands for the obtained results. Therefore, complex system validation may be effectively performed using SysML models and standards-based extensions.

ACKNOWLEDGMENT

The authors would like to thank Nicolas Meseth, Patrick Kirchhof, and Thomas Witte for their valuable help. Not only they provided us with their XLSC prototype interpreter, but also they eagerly answered every question we posed.

REFERENCES

Baker, L., Clemente, P., Cohen, B., Permenter, L., Purves, B., & Salmon, P. (2000, July). *Foundational concepts for model driven system design*. [Computer software manual].

Hosking, M., & Sahin, F. (2009). An xml based system of systems discrete event simulation communications framework. In *Springsim '09: Proceedings of the 2009 Spring Simulation Multiconference* (pp. 1–9). San Diego, CA: Society for Computer Simulation International.

Huang, E., Ramamurthy, R., & McGinnis, L. F. (2007). System and simulation modeling using sysml. In *Wsc '07: Proceedings of the 39th Conference on Winter Simulation* (pp. 796–803). Piscataway, NJ: IEEE Press.

Hwang, M. H., & Zeigler, B. (2009, July). Reachability graph of finite and deterministic devs networks. *Automation Science and Engineering. IEEE Transactions on, 6*(3), 468–478.

Kapos, G. D., Dalakas, V., Nikolaidou, M., & Anagnostopoulos, D. (2012). (Manuscript submitted for publication). An Integrated Framework for Automated Simulation of SysML Models using DEVS. *Simulation*.

Kerzhner, A., Jobe, J., & Paredis, C. J. (2011). A formal framework for capturing knowledge to transform structural models into analysis models. *Journal of Simulation, 5*(3), 202–216. doi:10.1057/jos.2011.17.

McGinnis, L., & Ustun, V. (2009, December). A simple example of SysML-driven simulation. In *Proceedings of the 2009 Winter Simulation Conference* (pp. 1703–1710). Austin, TX. IEEE.

Meseth, N., Kirchhof, P., & Witte, T. (2009). Xml-based devs modeling and interpretation. In *Springsim '09: Proceedings of the 2009 Spring Simulation Multiconference* (pp. 1–9). San Diego, CA: Society for Computer Simulation International.

MG. (2007). *SysML Plugin for Magic Draw* [Computer software manual]. Magic Draw.

Mittal, S., Risco-Mart'ın, J. L., & Zeigler, B. P. (2007). Devsml: Automating devs execution over soa towards transparent simulators. In *DEVS Symposium, Spring Simulation Multiconference* (pp. 287–295). Norfolk, VA: ACIMS Publications.

Mittal, S., Risco-Mart'ın, J. L., & Zeigler, B. P. (2009). Devs/soa: A cross-platform framework for net-centric modeling and simulation in devs unified process. *Simulation, 85*(7), 419–450. doi:10.1177/0037549709340968.

Modelica Association. (2005). *Modelica language specification.* Linköping, Sweden.

Nikolaidou, M., Dalakas, V., Mitsi, L., Kapos, G.-D., & Anagnostopoulos, D. (2008). A sysml profile for classical devs simulators. In *Proceedings of the Third International Conference on Software Engineering Advances (ICSEA 2008)* (p. 445-450). Sliema, Malta: IEEE Computer Society.

OMG. (2003, June). *Model Driven Architecture. Version 1.0.1.* Retrieved from http://www.omg.org/cgi-bin/doc?omg/03-06-01.pdf

OMG. (2007, September). *Systems Modeling Language (SYSML) Specification. Version 1.0.*

OMG. (2010). *SysML and Modelica Integration.* Retrieved from http://www.omgwiki.org/OMGSysML/doku.php?id=sysml-modelica:sysml_and_modelica_integration

Open Source Modelica Consortium (OSMC). (2009). *ModelicaML - A UML Profile for Modelica.* Retrieved from http://www.openmodelica.org/index.php/developer/tools/134

Paredis, C. J. J., & Johnson, T. (2008). Using omg's sysml to support simulation. In *Wsc '08:Proceedings of the 40th Conference on Winter Simulation* (pp. 2350–2352). Miami, FL: WSC.

Peak, R., Burkhart, R., Friedenthal, S., Wilson, M., Bajaj, M., & Kim, I. (2007). Simulation-based design using sysml part 1: A parametrics primer. In *Incose International Symposium* (pp. 1–20). San Diego, CA: INCOSE.

Peak, R., Paredis, C. J., & Tamburini, D. R. (2005). *The composable object (cob) knowledge representation: Enabling advanced collaborative engineering environments (cees), cob requirements & objectives (v1.0) (Technical Report).* Atlanta, GA: Georgia Institute of Technology.

Risco-Mart'ın, J. L., De La Cruz, J. M., Mittal, S., & Zeigler, B. P. (2009). Eudevs: Executable uml with devs theory of modeling and simulation. *Simulation, 85*(11-12), 750–777. doi:10.1177/0037549709104727.

Risco-Mart'ın, J. L., & Mittal, S. L'opez-Pen˜a, M. A., & Cruz, J. M. de la. (2007). A w3c xml schema for devs scenarios. In *Springsim '07: Proceedings of the 2007 Spring Simulation Multiconference* (pp. 279–286). San Diego, CA: Society for Computer Simulation International.

Schonherr, O., & Rose, O. (2009). First steps towards a general SysML model for discrete processes in production systems. In *Proceedings of the 2009 Winter Simulation Conference* (pp. 1711–1718). Austin, TX: WSC.

Tamburini, D. R. (2006). *Defining Executable Design & Simulation Models using SysML*. Retrieved from http://www.pslm.gatech.edu/topics/sysml/

Wainer, G. A., & Giambiasi, N. (2001). *Timed cell-devs: modeling and simulation of cell spaces*. Retrieved from http://cell-devs.sce.carleton.ca/publications/2001/WG01b

Wang, R., & Dagli, C. (2008). An executable system architecture approach to discrete events system modeling using SysML in conjunction with colored petri nets. In *IEEE systems conference 2008* (pp. 1–8). Montreal, Canada: IEEE Computer Press. doi:10.1109/SYSTEMS.2008.4518997.

World Wide Web Consortium. (2007). *Extensible stylesheet language transformations (xslt)*. Retrieved from http://www.w3.org/TR/xslt20

Zeigler, B. P., Praehofer, H., & Kim, T. (2000). *Theory of modeling and simulation* (2nd ed.). Waltham, MA: Academic Press.

Zeigler, B. P., & Sarjoughian, H. S. (2003). *Introduction to DEVS modeling and simulation with JAVA. DEVSJAVA manual*. [Computer software manual]. Retrieved from www.acims.arizona.edu/PUBLICATIONS/publications.shtml

Zhang, M., Zeigler, B. P., & Hammonds, P. (2005). Devs/rmi-an auto-adaptive and reconfigurable distributed simulation environment for engineering studies. *International Test and Evaluation Association Journal, 27*(1), 49–60.

KEY TERMS AND DEFINITIONS

Discrete Event System Specification (DEVS): A modular and hierarchical formalism for modeling and analyzing discrete event systems. DEVS is a timed event system.

Meta-Model: A schema defining a set of concepts that can be used to create, exchange and transform models, conforming to the meta-model.

Meta-Object Facility (MOF): Provides the infrastructure for defining meta-models. It is, therefore, fundamental in MDA.

Model Driven Architecture (MDA): A software design approach for the development of software systems. It provides a set of guidelines for the structuring of specifications, which are expressed as models. Model driven architecture is a kind of domain engineering, and supports model driven engineering of software systems. It was launched by the Object Management Group (OMG) in 2001.

Object Constraint Language (OCL): A declarative language for describing rules that apply to models conforming to a MOF meta-model. It is a precise text language that provides constraint and object query expressions on any MOF model or meta-model that cannot otherwise be expressed by diagrammatic notation.

Object Management Group (OMG): A consortium, originally aimed at setting standards for distributed object-oriented systems. Now it focuses on modeling and model-based standards.

Query/View/Transformation (QVT): A standard set of languages for model transformation defined by the Object Management Group, with three model transformation languages (QVT-Operational, QVT-Relations, QVT-Core). All of them operate on models which conform to MOF 2.0 meta-models. The QVT standard integrates the OCL 2.0 standard and also extends it with imperative features.

Systems Modeling Language (SysML): A general-purpose modeling language for systems engineering applications. It supports the specification, analysis, design, verification and validation of a broad range of systems and systems-of-systems. SysML is defined as an extension of a subset of the Unified Modeling Language (UML) using UML's profile mechanism.

Unified Modeling Language (UML): A standardized general-purpose modeling language in the field of object-oriented software engineering by OMG. UML includes a set of graphic notation techniques to create visual models of object-oriented software-intensive systems.

XML Metadata Interchange (XMI): An OMG standard for exchanging model information via XML. It can be used for any model conforming to a meta-model expressed in MOF. The most common use of XMI is as an interchange format for UML models.

Chapter 11
Overview on Agent–Based Social Modelling and the Use of Formal Languages

Cristina Montañola-Sales
Universitat Politècnica de Catalunya - Barcelona Tech, Spain

José M. Cela-Espin
Barcelona Supercomputing Center, Spain

Xavier Rubio-Campillo
Barcelona Supercomputing Center, Spain

Josep Casanovas
Universitat Politècnica de Catalunya - Barcelona Tech, Spain

Adriana Kaplan-Marcusan
Universitat Autonoma de Barcelona, Spain

ABSTRACT

The use of agent-based modelling and simulation techniques in the social sciences has flourished in the recent decades. The main reason is that the object of study in these disciplines, human society present or past, is difficult to analyse through classical analytical techniques. Population dynamics and structures are inherently complex. Thus, other methodological techniques need to be found to more adequately study this field. In this context, agent-based modelling is encouraging the introduction of computer simulations to examine behavioural patterns in complex systems. Simulation provides a tool to artificially examine societies where a big number of actors with decision capacity coexist and interact. However, formal modelling in these areas has not traditionally been used compared to other fields of science, in particular in their use of formal languages during the modelling process. In this chapter, the authors aim to revise the most relevant aspects on modelling in social sciences and to discuss the use formal languages by social scientists.

DOI: 10.4018/978-1-4666-4369-7.ch011

INTRODUCTION

Computer modelling and complex systems simulation have dominated the scientific debate over the last decade, providing important outcomes in biology, geology and life sciences, and resulting in the birth of entirely new disciplines (e.g., bioinformatics, geoinformatics, health informatics, etc.). In the social sciences, the number of groups currently developing research programs in this direction is increasing. The results are extremely promising since simulation technologies have the potential to become an essential tool in the field (Gilbert, 2008).

However, some social scientists are sceptical about the idea of reproducing *in silico* population dynamics, because of the perceived complexity of social structures. This scepticism is understandable given the low number of projects that used this approach and the lack of experience of social scientists with these tools. Nevertheless, the research done in complexity science during recent years shows the way computer simulation can be applied to this field. Artificial intelligence portrays how the appropriate interconnection of very simple computational mechanisms is able to show extraordinary complex patterns, and access to distributed computing has become affordable. For this reason, agent-based simulation allows the implementation of experiments and studies that would not be viable otherwise (Pavon, Arroyo, Hassan, & Sansores, 2008).

Even though research in social complex systems is increasing, the number of social works using computer simulation in this area is not very substantial, according to the survey conducted by Leombruni and Richiardi (2006). Thus, efforts need to be made in order to give a boost in this multidisciplinary area of research, and provide tools suitable for this task. Collaboration among research groups becomes crucial, but the fact that social scientists and modellers use different languages is an issue that should be addressed in order to reach scientific advances. This is the reason why one of the main challenges of social simulation is to find a methodology capable of improving the communication channels between people related with the construction of the simulation model, who probably come from very different backgrounds. Only when there is a good communication between stakeholders simulation can be successful (Robinson & Pidd, 1998).

Formal languages are one of the possible solutions and probably the most suitable one. Here when we say *formal language* or *formalism* we refer to a language that is not ambiguous and can describe the behaviour of a system. An example of formal language can be mathematics or modelling languages such as Unified Modelling Language (UML), Petri Nets, Specification and Description Language (SDL) and those who are used as the basis for defining programming languages used in computer science. For instance, differential equations are used to describe the dynamic behaviour of complex systems in System Dynamics approach. The advantage of using formal languages is that they can explicitly describe the system to be modelled despite its complexity.

In that way, stakeholders could agree on how to define the simulation model, making the common work possible and helping in later stages of development such as verification and validation processes (Fonseca, 2008). However, social scientists and humanists usually are not trained on working with formalisms as in other disciplines of science. Moreover, there are no general conventions when modelling social processes.

The main question analysed in this chapter is how the use of formal languages can contribute to research in social fields. We aim to revise the most relevant aspects on modelling in social sciences. The remainder of this chapter is organised as follows. "Modelling Social Systems" summarises the current state of the art on the modelling process, in particular to these areas of research. In "Agent-Based Modelling In Social Sciences," components and needs of agent-based simulation models will be revised, and some applications of agent-based systems in different fields of humanities and social science will be shown. Finally, we will revise the characteristics of four different tools for social simulation studies in "Tools For Modelling In Social Simulation," and we will discuss some validation practises applied to these areas in "On Verifying And Validating Models" and some conclusions and remarks will be pointed out in "Conclusions."

MODELLING SOCIAL SYSTEMS

Social sciences and humanities are concerned with the study of human beings and their world. Using methods of empirical data collection and scientific analysis, the social sciences study human behaviour and society in a variety of fields such as sociology, psychology, political science, economics, or anthropology. The reason for having many specialised areas of research around human beings is that societal modelling is complex and can be studied from different approaches (Gilbert & Troitzsch, 2005). Social systems are complex in three different ways (Rossiter, Noble, & Bell, 2010):

- They are composed by many entities which interact between them with a high degree of interconnection. This interconnection can introduce internal feedbacks,
- Their structure and rules may vary over time so they have limited accuracy. This fact in turn makes validation difficult,
- They have limited available historic data to work with.

So how could social researchers tackle their questions about changes in social systems? As pointed by Kohler and van der Leeuw (2007) the fieldwork could be a place to start with but it is not enough to answer all questions. Therefore social scientists need to build models as possible explanations to contrast their theories and their data.

Computational modelling and analysis can handle systems with complex, dynamic, and interrelated parts, such as epidemics spread and extinction of an ethnic group, which occur within a context constrained by many socio-economic factors. It can also handle the emergence of social patterns from individual interactions. In that way, a part of computational modelling is committed to model a person as an agent and his social relationships as networks. In this chapter we want to show the nature of social simulation and why it is becoming so popular. We will also discuss modelling procedure and why simulation looks suitable for applications in social science and humanities.

A Brief History of Social Science Simulation

In the social sciences, the study of real world with simulation technologies started in the early 1960s with the advances and developments on computer (Troitzsch, 1997). In the beginning, the research on simulation focused mainly in discrete-event simulation and in System Dynamics which took advantage of the big calculus capacity of computers. System Dynamics approach uses big systems of differential equations to plot variables trajectories over time (Hanneman, 1988). Sterman (2000) describes it as "a powerful method to gain useful insight into situations of dynamics complexity and policy resistance" (pp. 38-39). However, System Dynamics is restricted to the social analysis at macro-level and it could only allow models that could be translated into equations.

In the early stages, simulation stressed more on the prediction of social systems than on their understanding (Gilbert & Troitzsch, 2005). To respond to policy concerns, another approach of the same period to model social behaviour appeared: Microsimulation (Orcutt, 1957). It aims to model the evolution of population dynamics over time through specifying a random sampling process for each individual at every simulation time point. Although microsimulation has no pretentions to explain but to predict as system dynamics, it is interesting that the unit of simulation is the individual with no attempt to model interactions between them. During many years, microsimulation was the only form of simulation which was widespread recognised by social scientists. Still today it is used in many countries for policy issues.

In the 1980s, advances came from mathematics and physics, especially those working in the artificial intelligence field. In these years, cellular automata (Von Neumann, 1966) start to be used to understand social interaction. Cellular automata are a mathematical kind of models that simulate dynamic systems which evolve in discreet steps. They consist of a grid where every square is known as a *cell*. Each cell has a concrete state in each moment of time and also a set of neighbours. In each step of time a transition function is applied homogeneously to each cell taking into account the cell state and also the neighbours' states, so a new state is assigned to that cell.

In the 1990s a new technique from the artificial intelligence domain which allows autonomous objective-driven movements in grids is born: Multi-agent based systems (Weiss, 1999). Artificial intelligence deals with the processes of life and how to better understand them by simulating them with computers. The field started with the beginning of computing, focusing in the modelling of individual cognition. Later, just until the computer capacity increased and the apparition of Internet, artificial intelligence researchers develop the distributed computing in form of autonomous independent entities able to interact, also called *agents*. From 1980s, artificial intelligence community also developed techniques of "machine learning" which are systems with the ability to learn from experience, adding the new information to their knowledge and procedural skills (Michalski, Carbonell, & Mitchell, 1985).

Not until the half of 1990s game theory is born, a discipline that includes models more directly related to our current simulations. Game theory is a set of mathematical models that study interactions and decisions of people in competing environments (Aumann, 1985). Also in the later half of the 20th century, new advances in computing allowed to combine cellular automata with game theory and to apply them to social sciences. One of the most well-known examples is the Life Game of Conway (Gardner, 1970) where just with four simple rules a cellular automata is built to simulate the life of a complex organisms society which interact between them.

Despite being relatively new, the agent-based simulation community is growing fast. This is due mainly to its potential, in particular to the domains where location (as social networks, where nodes and connections are essential [Wasserman, 1994]) and distribution (not centralised or organised by a hierarchy although it is possible to set some layers of organisation) are very important, in front of other equation-based models, more suitable for central systems that can be understood more by physical laws than by information processes (Menendez & Collado, 2007).

Why Model?

The concept of modelling is widely extended. It comes from the natural observation of the world and the curiosity or need to reproduce it. As Epstein (2008) says, "Anyone who ventures a projection, or imagines how a social dynamic—an epidemic, war, or migration—would unfold is running some model". The challenge is to write it down, to turn it from *implicit* where assumptions or data are hidden to *explicit*.

It does not matter if the model implies a mathematical formulation or any kind of graphical representation. Models are approximations to reality for an intended used (Pidd, 2010). Pidd proposes a graphical representation of a model as a box with inputs and outputs. The box will be black or grey depending on the purpose of the model. If one wished to perform controlled experimentation as in some areas of physical science, the box will be black since the model will be analysed through its outputs under defined inputs. On the contrary, if the box is grey that means we have some knowledge of the model's interior processes. That is the most suitable case when investigating case scenarios answering "what if" questions. The analyst part should be studied and it could display some unexpected emergent behaviour, a consequence of the internal dynamic interactions between the variables in the system.

In social sciences and humanities, the tradition to apply mathematical models is not very extended, with the exception of economy and sociology areas (Rubio, 2009). Common mathematical models in these fields are based on differential equations which are very useful to describe continuous systems but experience more difficulties in systems where the interest is on the interactions between discreet entities, as human beings can be. Moreover, to model individuals as discreet autonomous entities looks more natural. Given the difficulties to apply differential equations, statistical techniques have commonly been used as a powerful analysis tool (Stewart, 1990). They are able to extract general patterns from a set of data which does not appear to have a regular behaviour. However, statistical analysis provides models that indicate tendencies in a sample of values of variables. Therefore the information we can generate is very limited, particularly in forecasting and hypothesis testing.

Indeed, simulation is particularly suitable when we want to conduct experiments with a model in order to understand the behaviour of the system under study (Shannon, 1976). Therefore, simulation is one of the more powerful methodological approaches that a researcher can use to understand a complex system. Actually representation of reality through simulation models is often closer to reality processes than other mathematical models (Lozares Colina, 2004). Simulation not only includes the construction of a model to study the system dynamics of interest but also it can generate new knowledge that can have an impact on the model formulation itself. For instance, new hypothesis might arise which can turn on model refinement. The ultimate objective is to get closer to the answer of the initial formulated questions about the real world. According to Shannon, simulation process should start with the definition of a problem, analysing the important entities which play a role and the relations between variables, followed by a model formulation. At this stage it is important to decide the number of variables to take into account, since a balance is needed between simplicity and complexity. The model should have as many variables as needed to answer the initial questions. However, it is possible to refine it in later states of simulation process.

How to Model

It is not ventured to say that modelling is one of the keys to do research. A model has impact in all aspects of a simulation study. But which is the process of modelling? Law (2007) describes in the following way. When trying to simulate the real world we talk about *systems* of interest, which are a "collection of entities that act and interact together toward the accomplishment of some logical end" (pp. 3). To study them, modellers start from a set of thoughts in the stake-holder's mind around a problem or theory of interest. This set of ideas refers to the structure of the problem: Its objectives, the input and outputs of the system and its content (Robinson, 2008). In this process, some assumptions and simplifications are made. Robinson states that these assumptions help dealing with uncertainties or beliefs about the real world (the scope of the model), while simplifications help reducing the complexity of the model (its level of detail). According to Robinson, all these components form the *conceptual model*, which gives us an insight of the behaviour of the system. The process of building a model from a real or proposed system is called conceptual modelling. In Figure 1, Heath, Hill, and Ciarallo (2009) show how conceptual modelling is embedded in a simplified simulation development process. As we can see, previous steps of formalising a model include formulating a problem and defining the simulation study's objectives.

Despite the importance of the conceptual model in a simulation study, there is not agreement in the definition of what a conceptual model is. Onggo (2010) suggests it might be due to the wide variety of conceptual model representations which have been proposed in the literature. What seems clear is that conceptual modelling is very close to the notion of *abstraction*, which is related to computer science and has originated many specification languages (Roussopoulos & Karagiannis, 2009). To make this abstraction process effective an appropriate simplification of reality is needed (Pidd, 2003). That is, we need to set the boundaries of the real world's portion we want to model in an appropriate way which can give answer to the question we make. Moreover we need to remember that, despite this process of simplification, a model should be complex enough to answer the question raised (Banks, 1998). For example, a model that emulates a vehicle routing problem can answer questions on how a company should distribute its products in a given network. However, this model cannot answer questions on how this distribution will impact on the current traffic of the network. If we were interested on getting information on the traffic impact, we should enlarge our model to model the traffic flow to calculate how a given distribution of vehicles will affect it.

Thus, we need to find a balance between real world and the conceptualized system. If we directly consider the most complex model when performing a study we will encounter several problems, being the most important its credibility. How

Figure 1. Conceptual modelling in a simplified simulation development process by Heath et al. (2009)(©2012,JASSS Used with permission.)

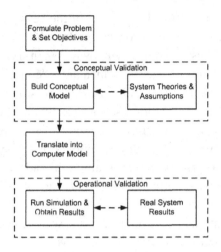

could we be certain that the non-necessary components in our model are not affecting the results? As Robinson (2008) states, simple models have many advantages, such as they are faster, require less data, are more flexible and, more importantly, better understanding means better interpretation of their results. That is why a good modelling design enhances the probability of simulation study success. Nevertheless, not in all research areas simplicity is seen as a positive value. For instance, in the social sciences, Leeuw (2004) states archaeologists cannot presume a simple behaviour until there is some evidence of it. As Davies, Roderick, and Raftery (2003) stay one should be careful to simplify certain natural processes since it presumes certain assumptions about how they operate, so one could miss some important facet to explain it. The tendency however is to build KISS (*Keep it simple, stupid*) models, an idea which stems from Occam's razor: Things should be kept as simple as possible and made as little more complex as explanation purposes demand (Axelrod, 1997). Applied to social simulation, KISS ideally seeks simple and abstract models that are general enough to be explanatory for multiple specific cases. Even so, in social sciences and humanities there is a particular difficulty when doing conceptual modelling: Sometimes data is not available or non-existent. Stakeholders need to proceed other ways by filling out the abstract social process or mechanism sufficiently to create a working implementation, focusing more on the instantiation of the desired mechanism than in being faithful to the observation of the real world process (Yang & Gilbert, 2008).

One important property of the conceptual model is that it is not oriented to any software, so stakeholders free from implementation concerns. Thus being able to represent the behaviour of a phenomenon or problem which can be later solved in the preferred computational methodology. Separating the modelling and coding process allow modellers to focus on developing the more appropriate ("right") model to perform the study of interest (Robinson, 2008), thus allowing all stakeholders to get integrated in a simulation project (Roussopoulos & Karagiannis, 2009). This condition makes it possible to easily communicate the model between them, to discuss different points of views, and to set common objectives. Therefore, a collaborative effort is needed since they might probably come from different domain knowledge and expertise (Chen et al., 2008). To do that, Nance (1994) states that stakeholders should pick up a standard representation to understand the concepts and ideas, keeping in mind that a good communication process enriches the simulation model.

Modelling with Formal Languages

In social sciences and humanities, models are often expressed through natural language, which is inherently ambiguous. This is due to the nature of systems involved in their studies, which are often very complex in reasoning and suppositions. Moreover, each research discipline has its own vocabulary and approach which causes more confusion. To avoid misunderstandings, scientists should express the phenomena and ideas under study in the same rigorous manner (Leeuw, 2004). That is, they should *formalise* their models, meaning they should describe the social system under study with a non-ambiguous language. With a formal language of that kind they can non-ambiguously describe their models which allow them to understand, specify, and analyse a system. As we said before, there is a clear advantage on doing so when teams are formed by experts from different areas of science. Formal models provide the way to make these interdisciplinary teams effectively work.

Between the natural language and a formal language, there are some alternative methods which can be used to describe social systems. For instance, Onggo (2010) points out at the use of diagrams for conceptual representation, which can show the information in two dimensions, being the activity cycle diagram, the process flow diagram, and the event relationship map the most widely used. Despite their usefulness, Onggo states it is not common that a single diagram could be used to represent completely a conceptual model.

In the area of social sciences an approximation to the idea of formalizing the conceptual model is the protocol *Overview, Design concepts and Details* (ODD), which goes beyond textual representation (Grimm et al., 2006). ODD is aimed for a description of individual-based models. It is meant to describe readable and completely the system of interest, through a structure for the description and guidelines for the content, so all important information is captured. In Polhill, Parker, Brown, and Grimm (2008), a more extensive description of ODD can be found along with an example of application to social simulation of land use change. An example of ODD structure of a case study on agent-based simulation applied to the study of hunter gatherers in India can be seen in Figure 2. The main limitation of ODD is that it is expressed in natural language, thus being subject to ambiguity. However, easily one can build a computational model from it and it helps make the theoretical foundations of large models more visible. Despite its potential and having reached certain popularity, more work and refinement of ODD should be done (Grimm et al., 2010).

The ideal would be to use formal methods to simulate social processes as other formalisms are commonly used in other applications of simulation, such as *Discrete Event System Specification* (DEVS) or *Petri Nets*, both mathematical kind modelling languages. Formalisms provide a technique for specify the characteristics of a system and its dynamics besides helping to the validation process. On one hand, specification is very useful to implement models, especially when working in multidisciplinary research. On the other hand, validation allows automatic verification and error checking of simulation systems. However, we have to take into account

Figure 2. ODD structure of on agent-based simulation of hunter gatherers persistence in arid margins in Gujarat (India) (©2012, Simulpast Project. Used with permission.)

**CS1: Hunter-Gatherer persistence in arid margins.
The case of N Gujarat (India).**

Table of Contents

that social simulation is quite a new area of research. Moreover, it mainly comes from social fields with poor traditions of mathematical modelling.

An example of the application of Petri Nets to social systems can be found in the work of Kohler et al. (2007) who used Petri Nets to model the Theory of Social Self-Organisation. Figure 3 shows their model.

Social scientists could also take advantage of other multifaceted representation to represent conceptual models. Multifaceted representations consist of a set of diagrams to represent different components in a model. One of the most used multifaceted representations is *Unified Modelling Language* (UML) (Fowler & Scott, 2000). As other simulation formalisms, this type of solution allows to verify the consistency of conceptual model components (Onggo, 2010). Bersini (2012) advocates for the use of UML in social simulation, particularly for modelling agent-based models, a type of social model that will be later discussed in this chapter. In his words, "we can only regret the minor diffusion of UML among researchers producing agent-based models and hope that this paper will improve the situation in the years to come." Richiardi, Leombruni, Saam, and Sonnessa (2006) propose to use at least part of UML in multiagent systems, specifically the static representation

Figure 3. Petri Nets example of a model to simulate the theory of social self-organisation by Köhler et al. (2007) (©2012,JASSS. Used with permission.)

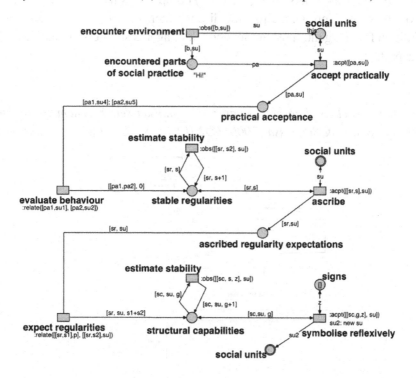

(Class Diagram) and the dynamic view (Sequence Diagram). An example of both types of diagrams from Richiardi et al. can be seen in Figure 4 and Figure 5.

Another type of multifaceted representation named *Specification and Description Language* (SDL) has been used to describe social systems. Some examples of the use and application of SDL include the modelling of a simple reflexive intelligent agent (Fonseca, 2008), some industrial planning and management applications (Fonseca, Casanovas, Monero, & Guasch, 2011) and modelling of an anaesthesia unit of a Chilean hospital (Leiva Olmos, Fonseca, & Ocana, 2011). An example of SDL of the later work can be seen in Figure 6. The advantage of using formalisms like SDL or UML is that they are meant for a distributed environment, thus being capable of reproducing large scale simulations.

AGENT-BASED MODELLING IN SOCIAL SCIENCES

Agent-based models come from the area of Artificial Intelligence (AI), which tries to artificially create systems that think and act as human beings (Russell & Norvig, 2010). In those terms, the unit of study is the agent. Unfortunately there is no standard definition of agent since different characteristics are important to different domains of applications. In spite of this fact, a commonly accepted one is from Huhns and Singh (1997): "active, persistent (software) components hat perceive, reason, act, and communicate" (pp. 1). Despite the disagreements of the AI community to find a definition for an agent, most authors consider agents should satisfied the following properties:

Figure 4. UML class diagram example of a market-seller system by Richiardi, Leombruni, Saam, & Sonnessa (2006) (©2012, JASSS. Used with permission.)

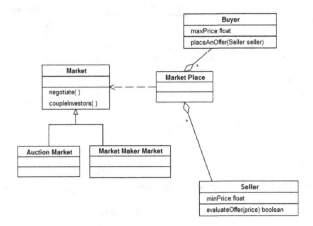

Figure 5. UML class diagram example of a market-seller system by Richiardi, Leombruni, Saam, & Sonnessa (2006) (©2012,JASSS. Used with permission.)

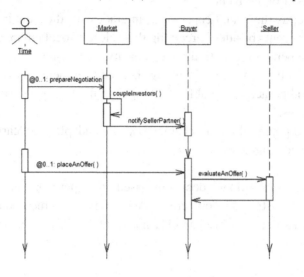

Figure 6. SDL example of an anaesthesia unit and surgical pavilions on a hospital by Leiva Olmos, Fonseca, & Ocaña (2011) (©2012, Fonseca, P. Used with permission.)

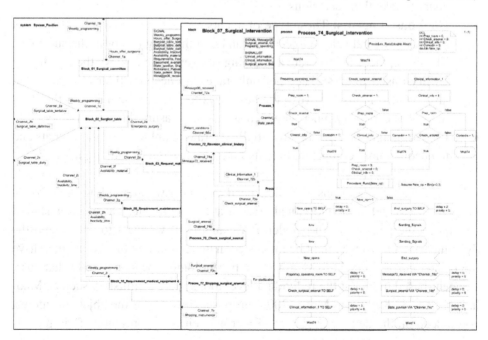

- Autonomy, understand as the capability to operate without the direct control of humans or other agents.
- Interactive, as the social capacity to interact with their environment and/or with other agents besides perceiving their closest local environment.
- Subjective perceptive, with limited capacity or reasoning.
- Reactive, in the sense of perceiving their environment and acting in consequence, and proactive, capable of taking the initiative with a behaviour based on objectives.
- Having the potential to add characteristics as adaptation, learning, complex planning and language.

Therefore an agent will take decisions based on its perceptions in its own environment where it exists and its objectives. According to the method through which the agent takes its decision, we can classify agents in four categories (Russell & Norvig, 2010):

- **Simple reflex agents:** Operate choosing an action from the perception of their environment. This type of agent has no memory and its behaviour is specified with if-then logical rules. Therefore, it is not really intelligent and will not be able to react to unexpected situations correctly.
- **Model-based reflex agents:** They operate also with individual logical rules but additionally have a model of the environment, whose rules take into account to take their decisions.
- **Goal-based agents:** These type of agents are designed with objectives, not only with logical rules. Objectives can be in the long run or in the short run. Therefore, these incorporate a planning so agents can achieve their goals.
- **Utility-based agents:** They not only take into account their objectives but also can distinguish between the best ways to achieve them. To do that they incorporate a utility function which serves to measure the best strategy.
- **Learning agents:** Are able to initially operate in unknown environments and to become more competent than its initial knowledge alone might allow.

One of the first questions modellers need to answer when building agent-based models is to model at the individual level or at the aggregate. The election should depend on the purpose of the model. For example, if we want to understand the dynamics of a crowd we might be interested in understanding the factors that drive the behaviour of every individual from a psychological perspective. In that case, an agent-based model at the individual level looks more promising, such as Madhavan, Papelis, Kady, and Moya (2009) propose. However, if the object of interest is too deep on the density evolution of a crowd, either a continuous-field models or aggregates of individuals could be possible (Goodchild, 2005). The size of the crowd could change our decision since the more variables intervene in a model the more difficulties researchers could encounter to understand them. Actually setting constraints is essential for agent-based models, since we cannot produce an unlimited number of models to generate an unlimited number of scenarios for social dynamics (Moss, 2001).

Simple observation of real world leads us to the idea of patterns. There are numerous patterns in reality. They are usually the result of the interactions of smaller pieces that somehow combine in not so expected ways to create a large-scale pattern (Wilensky, 2002). These patterns or phenomena arise out of interaction of numerous individuals (agents) at a micro-level. An example of emergent behaviour could be a flock of birds winging acting completely synchronised while there is no leader to follow. Agents might be a powerful tool to reproduce human behaviour in a shared environment with multiple agents. Simulation of agent-based models, also called agent-based simulation, is a technique which allows us to integrate complex decision making of human beings in an interactive context with other agents and with other variables that might be interesting for our model, such as geospatial factors. Agent-based simulation can be used to detect patterns of behaviour under the hypothesis that those patterns can emerge from the addition of individual decisions in a social model. The property of emergence is interesting in situations where the modeller suspects or detects that dependent and independent variables alternate their role intermittently, which is very common in social sciences (Menendez & Collado, 2007). Menendez and Collado also state that agent-based simulation helps on treating the problem of establishing causality directions between variables, which they say is very useful in social sciences since independent and the dependent variables can alter their role intermittently. For instance, they point out at the example of religiosity, where one could expect that religious change may vary in function of personal values but also the contrary could be correct.

Which is the goal of studying population dynamics with agent-based simulation? Based on the modeller level of understanding of the system under study, Heath et al. (2009) distinguish three types of purposes for simulation. When the level of understanding is high the simulation model can be used as a predictor, producing precise forecast of future behaviour under well defined conditions. When that level of understanding is in a medium stage, the simulator turns to a mediator providing insight into the system without offering a complete representation of its behaviour. Mediator simulation models can be used to test theories and their results can be used to improve the simulation. Finally, when low information about the model is available the use of simulation is as a generator, generating hypotheses and theories about the system behaviour. Concretely in social sciences, Menendez and Collado (2007) state there are two goals of simulation. First one is to verify if a social model is coherent and adjusts adequately. In fact, when data is non-existent, the parameter space should be explored to find the optimal adjust for unknown variables.

Once the simulation model behaves as expected, new hypothesis can be introduced, observing if the model reflects the real behaviour. This is especially useful when we have qualitative data and they do not know how to quantify it. With trial and error it is possible to modify parameters until observing the behaviour of interest. Through those parameters, relationships and mutual influence can be found. The second one is to virtually defy big limitations on experimenting in these areas, since some hypotheses cannot be tested otherwise by recreating empirical situations.

Therefore simulation can improve explanatory or even predictable capacities of models. However, if the knowledge of the model is poor, the results of simulation will be, resulting in simulation that's not useful at all.

Moss (2001) states that agent-based simulation can be useful in social sciences:

- To restate and assess existing theories, which are often sociological and anthropological
- To take advantage of sociological theories and concepts to inform simulation models
- As a formalise description of a system
- To analyse different scenarios
- To help in policy analysis and formation

Beyond these interests, Moss points out at the foundational purpose of agent based social simulation which is to develop a general social theory. Axtell, Axelrod, Epstein, and Cohen (1996) made an attempt to find out how general individual models might be by aligning some of them but Moss says it is far from being general. Simulation can provide insights and hypotheses on population dynamics but theories on social behaviour might be more relevant in the field (Bankes, 2002). That is the reason why Moss suggests there is no universally accepted theory of social process. Moreover, this fact explains why there has been very little use of agent-based models to recommend public policy.

A second reason for the importance of agent-based simulation in the field of social sciences and humanities is its naturalness as representational formalism in this field (Bankes, 2002). It provides a way to express the vast amount of data and knowledge about social agents' characteristics, including their behaviour, motivations, and relationships with other individuals or institutions. However, there are some areas of agent-based simulation that needs further attention, such as the calibration of models to data and the methodology to use these kind of models to answer specific questions or to solve problems.

Finally, agent-based approach to simulation are flexible since agents can be defined within any given system environment, and move on it freely (Castle & Crooks, 2006). In that way it is possible to define geospatial reference of agents through variables and parameters of the simulation. Moreover, agent interactions can be governed by space and networks, or a combination of the two, which will be more complicated to explain by mathematical formulation (Axtell, 2000).

Despite those advantages, agent-based simulation also has some limitations. In sociology, some researchers find difficulties on applying agent-based simulation models due to the lack of knowledge in some social phenomena. This lack might be not only be due to empirical evidence but also to limitations on sociological theory. An example of these type of problems can be found in Menendez & Collad, (2007), where they try to study religious evolution in Spanish society by the end of last century. As a conclusion of their study they point out that the need of finding more formal and documented models should be able to explain systematically social processes. Another disadvantage of this approach is the lack of full access to data relating to the phenomenon of interest, because the target of interest is not easy to access or simply data is non-existent. There is also a limit on the size of parameter space that can be checked for robustness when conducting agent-based simulation. If we increase the number variables we not only increase computational needs but also we compromise the credibility of the model, which is very difficult to validate against real data (Castle & Crooks, 2006).

Some Applications in Social Sciences

Among numerous applications of agent-based simulation to the social science, Schelling (1971) is credited with developing the first social agent-based model. In his work, he reproduced population dynamics in terms of segregation patterns. His work shows patterns can emerge from migratory movements of two different culture types of households, which were set to be quite tolerant. Later some other social models using the agent-based approached arose, such as Sugarscape (Epstein & Axtell, 1996), considered the first large scale agent model. Despite the simple behaviour of agents, Sugarscape results illustrate a variety of features of societies, including the emergence of social networks, trade and markets, and cultural differentiation and evolution. Another icon model of the agent-based modelling community is the Artificial Anasazi model (Dean et al., 2000; Epstein & Gang, 2006) which describes the population dynamics in the Long House Valley in Arizona between 800 and 1350. The model help to prove that simulation could reproduce settlements archaeological records on the occupation of the Anasazi in Long House Valley with simple household rules on choosing locations for farms. Moreover, the model showed that the abandonment of the valley around 1300 cannot be explained only by environmental variations.

In this section we do not pretend to revise the full range of agent-based simulation application but to point out some examples of interest. We can find examples in very different social areas. Archaeologists and anthropologists are also using agent-based simulations of ancient civilisations to help explain their growth and decline based on archaeological data. An example of that is Villatoro and Sabate-Mir (2008) who studied the Yamana indigenous of Tierra del Fuego (Patagonia) too deep in the factors which lead this hunter-gatherer society to extinction. In their study they provide that despite living in very hostile geographical conditions Yamana had a strong organisation and a set of norms that made possible a high interaction between different groups. To perform their study, they used an agent-based simulation where agents have a set of simple logical rules.

In economy, we can find numerous applications of agent-based simulation. An early example from Epstein and Axtell (1996) is the study on evolutionary trade network formation among strategically interacting buyers, sellers, and dealers. Another example to reproduce dynamics in queues, such as those of costumers in check-in desks, banks, or airports can be found in Gilbert and Troitzsch (2005). Also, economic factors are considered in the agent-based model of Balbi and Giupponi (2010) of adaptation to climate change. Tesfatsion (2002; 2006) give some more examples of agent-based modelling and simulation applications to economic systems.

Sociologists are also working on agent-based modelling. Cognitive science is starting to extend the idea of artificial agents to social settings (Bedau, 2003). In that sense, Gratch and Marsella (2001) use agent-based simulation to study the influence of emotion and cognition on social behaviour. As mentioned before, Menendez and Collado (2007) studied religious change in Spain by the end of last century and how it might be tied to values change.

If we add more intelligence to agents, such as orientating them rationally based on belief, desires and intentions aligned with psychological theory, we can find application in the simulation of traffic where drivers take their decisions based on their perceptions of traffic flow and characteristics (El Hadouaj, Drogoul, & Espie, 2001). Moreover, there are examples of simulation applied to emergency situations, such as fire emergency in an airport where agents need to decide their way to escape (Burmeister, Haddadi, & Mattilys, 1997). However, as Menendez and Collado (2007) state, sometimes it is not possible to precisely define desires and intentions which move human beings in the society to simulate them.

To conclude, we can say that although there is a lot of work done in agent-based simulation in social sciences, more effort needs to be done. In particular, the use of agent-based models for experimenting with geographical phenomena needs further work (Castle & Crooks, 2006). However, agent-based simulation has the potential to achieve remarkable goals in the areas of social sciences and humanities.

TOOLS FOR MODELLING IN SOCIAL SIMULATION

There is a lot of interest in developing agent-based modelling as a general technique to be applied to the study of societies. A numerous number of platforms exist to provide the means to study social phenomena. In this section, we will briefly describe some of them and compare them in terms of software capacity, architecture, and the type of applications they have been tested with. We have chosen the software platforms we currently believe to be of particular relevance to scientific modelling and simulation of societies. We do not intend to fully review them but just to revise their most important characteristics to help the reader picture the world of agent-based simulation tools. A more completed list on software platforms for agent-based modelling and simulation can be found in Nikolai & Madey (2011) and List of ABM tools (n.d.).

Agent-based systems are very complex applications to program, implement, and optimise, particularly when the size of the population to simulate is large. Actually, we can find two different situations when modelling and simulating social behaviour. On one hand, there is a computer scientist or someone with advanced skills in mathematical programming which faces the challenge to realise some research in a social domain. Unless he/she has the adequate knowledge in the sociological model, he/she will experience difficulties to build a valid model and later explain and communicate it to the social community. On the other hand, we could find a social scientist who wants to take advantage of simulation techniques to experiment with his/her theories and knowledge. Unless he/she has the programming experience to develop and implement his/her ideas, he/she will need to find someone to do that for him/her. The ideal case, therefore, would be the situation where the social scientist could autonomously use a tool to define his/her models and afterwards run them. Similarly when social scientists perform a multivariate analysis through a statistical tool without the need of programming skills or knowing in deep the mathematical algorithms involved, they should be able to test their hypothesis or theories. Thus, the need to give a boost in developing tools to help research community advance in the social simulation field.

Nowadays we can find numerous tools to experiment with social behaviour and dynamics. Moreover, as computer technology has advanced, the scale and sophistication of the software available for users has increased. Software toolkits might be difficult to handle, in particular when they use object oriented languages. In that sense, Nicolai and Madey (2009) point out that the use of object oriented languages is very extended: 42% use Java as their primary programming language, 17% uses C++, 11% uses, 8% uses a variant of Logo and the rest use a platform specific language which was designed to facilitate the modelling and simulation design. In fact, there is little consensus about the best general purpose programming language to use on simulation social behaviour (Gilbert & Bankes, 2002). Given the number of different programming languages that can be used, agent based modelling packages tend to be hard to understand for users who may have little or no programming experience, as social scientists generally are the case.

Apart from that, each tool has its own non-intuitive terminology so users should learn how to draw or write their models in each particular platform (Allan, 2010). This is due to the multidisciplinary nature of social agent-based modelling field, so easily there might be a conflict in the use of terms. Moreover, Nicolai and Madey (2009) state that there is no consistency in the use of terminology in some toolkits. For example, they point at the term "multi-agent system" which properly refers to a small system with heterogeneous agents that have artificial intelligence capabilities, it is in some cases used to refer to a large system of homogeneous agents (an agent-based system). This kind of slightly differences on the concepts' use can mislead the user or they can create difficulties in work teams. Depending on the user's background, the characteristics of the platform should be different. For instance, social scientists might be more concerned about how easily the interaction is with the interface to manage simulations and the degree of programming skills required, while computer scientists may consider if the tool is open source and its capability to be modified or extended for their own purposes. But no matter which type of user the tool should be meant for, they should have a good documentation. However, basic documentation is incomplete in general, albeit there are some exceptions (Allan, 2010). It mainly depends on how extended the community is using the tool and the community that supports its development.

Beyond that, there is no standard on how to specify agent based models not only in the social science and humanities community but also in the computer science, and specifically in artificial science fields. This issue makes difficult not only to address the issue on how defining the agents' characteristics but also the interactions between them and with the environment. As a consequence, the platforms we can find nowadays address that issue in their proper way, according to the type of applications they are meant for, their characteristics, and what the tool designers think can be more convenient for their type of users. Consequently, it is not surprising to see that several tools have their own language which is used specifically for that toolkit, as we mentioned before. Some of them, probably concerned about becoming simpler to learn and use, have support for visual programming (Nikolai & Madey, 2009).

There is another element that should be considered when modelling social dynamics. Sometimes models depend on the location of the phenomena being modelled, such that if one or more of those locations change the model results will also change (Wegener, 2000). Geographical location of agents is especially interesting for areas such as archaeology, history or ecology. Geographical Information Systems (GIS) are commonly used for representing data of geospatial nature. A GIS consist of a set of tools which allow users to interact and understand spatial information. GIS are meant for visualising, processing, and analysing spatial data presented as digital maps. In that sense, Wheatley and Gillings (2000) called it a spatial toolbox. A GIS can not only deal with data at an geographical scale but also with data not properly geographical such as culture, political ideology or religion since it this kind of information can be attached to an spatial reference (Rubio, 2009). A good revision of GIS techniques and capabilities can be found in Castle & Crooks (2006).

In the following subsections we will briefly describe the characteristics of four different tools which are most commonly used when simulating societies from the social scientist perspective. Those are: Swarm, Mason, Netlogo, and Repast. Although they were originally designed as general purpose tools, as an educational tool and as specific tool for social scientific use respectively, we can nowadays find applications in social simulation in all of them. These differences on the primary domain of application might not only affect the user interaction with the toolkit but also the fact some of them have become more popular among some specific areas of social studies and humanities. There is another aspect to consider in terms of characteristics of the software. In terms of use, some of them are open source while some others have a private license. Moreover, some tools support distributed environments and therefore can model large-scale populations. In this report, we decided to not include tools with education purpose, although there is a lot of interest in it (Serenko & B., 2002). Instead of that, we focus on platforms meant to develop and experiment simulation of social systems.

Swarm

Swarm is one of the oldest agent-based modelling toolkits developed in Santa Fe Institute (Minar, Burkhart, Langton, & Askenazi, 1996). It is intended for general purpose applications, particularly those related to artificial intelligence, to develop multi-agent models to simulate complex adaptive systems. Right now, Swarm development and management is under control of Swarm Development Group (Swarm Development Group, n.d.). In Swarm, users can not only implement their models but also observe and conduct experiments on the model in the virtual laboratory it provides. The design of models follows a schema of a hierarchy of swarms. A swarm is a group of agents and a schedule of actions that the agents execute. It is possible to design hierarchies of swarms whereby an agent can be composed of swarms of other agents in nested structures. When this happens, the agent behaviour at the higher level is defined by the emergent phenomena of the agents inside its swarm (Minar et al., 1996). Swarm separates the model from its observation. This property enables the model itself to remain unchanged if the observation code is modified. According to Allan (2010), the design philosophy appears aimed for many different models profiting Swarm's modelling concepts, not including specific tools to any particular domain.

Swarm simulations can be written mainly in Objective-C and some in Java, both object oriented languages. Therefore knowledge on object oriented programming is desirable. Swarm has a free source code form under the license GNU General Public License (GPL), which implies to make the source code for their entire model available to anyone who obtains a legitimate copy of the model's binary code. It runs in Windows, Linux, Mac and OS X operating systems. Swarm has no support for Geographical Information Systems (GIS) although there is an extension of Swarm simulation libraries named Kenge that provides functionalities to create cellular automata similar to raster GIS data layers, a surface upon which agents can act (Box, 2002). To date, it appears there is not any parallel implementation of Swarm.

Swarm has been applied to a variety of domains. We can find works in organisation management; for instance the work of Lin and Pai (2000) to simulate changing business processes to adapt to new business environments. Also there are several contributions to economics (Luna & Stefansson, 2000) and supply chains (Strader, Lin, & Shaw, 1998). In more technological areas, we can find applications in mobile technology (Lingnau & Drobnik, 1999) and in social networks of open source software development (Madey, Freeh, & Tynan, 2002). Terna (1998) shows how Swarm could be used in social science research and tries to approach Swarm terminology and work environment to social science community. To do that, he presents an application of Swarm to a negotiation and exchange system of consumers and vendors. Also Axelrod (1997) points out at how classical models, such as Game of Life or Prisoner's Dilemma, could be replicated with Swarm.

Traditionally, Swarm has been the most powerful and flexible simulation platform since it allows one to implement very intricate and complicated social mechanisms (Allan, 2010). However, since the modeller needs to have some experience in Objective-C and possible Java, Swarm has a steep learning curve. That is the reason why despite the efforts on disseminating Swarm, it has remained technically challenging for most social scientists to use. Consequently, it has not generated a broad-based community of practitioners of this methodology in social science. However, given its history, Swarm definitely contributed to make agent based modelling more visible to a large number of scientists (Janssen, Alessa, Barton, Bergin, & Lee, 2008).

Netlogo

Netlogo is an agent-based programming language and modelling environment for simulating complex phenomena. Netlogo derives from StarLogo (Resnick, 1994) and StarLogoT (StarLogoT, n.d.), an environment for experiment complex dynamics in parallel environments in Macintosh operating system. Netlogo was designed to provide a basic laboratory for teaching complexity concepts. To help doing that, it provides a graphical user interface to create models that control graphic agents that reside in a world in form of a grid of cells, which can be monitored. Since its ultimate goal is to be helpful in teaching agent-based simulation, the environment and the language in Netlogo is meant to be simple enough "to have a low threshold for beginners" (Tisue & Wilensky, 2004, pp. 19). Therefore, Netlogo includes a large number of example simulations to help beginning and experienced users alike. In Tisue & Wilensky (2004), the reader can find some useful information about Netlogo, including the history of its origins, a tour of its interface, an introduction to the Netlogo language, and the acceptance of Netlogo in the research community.

Netlogo uses a modified version of the Logo programming language (Harvey, 1997). This is a different approach from other toolkits such as Swarm and Repast which make simulation facilities available to programs written in a general-purpose language such as Java. Despite being free, Netlogo is not open source. Netlogo is written in Java so can be run on all major platforms, requiring Java version 1.4 to run the current Netlogo version 2.0. In principle, it can run in any operating system except for Windows 95 and MacOS 8 which were supported by previous Netlogo 1.3. According to Tisue and Wilensky (2004), the majority of users find Netlogo fast enough for most purposes, in particular when running simple code and large numbers of agents.

Although the Netlogo engine has no fixed limits on size, it is single-threaded, single processor based, thus being problematic to run large scale models. To fix that, there is an extension of Netlogo called BehaviorSpace which allows the user to run will the simulation in parallel, one per core in a multiple processor cores desktop computer or in cluster of processors. BehaviourSpace was specially design to explore the parameter space of a model, exploring possible behaviours to determine which combinations of settings cause the behaviours of interest. BehaviourSpace is also free and open source.

There are many applications of agent-based social simulation in Netlogo. In Damaceanu (2008), an agent-based computational model is built to simulate the distribution of wealth in social classes, taking into account economies based on renewable and non-renewable resources. They conclude that global economy must focus on using renewable resources because this approach may increase the global wealth. Another interesting simulation with Netlogo is the work of Zhao and Li (2008). They conducted a study on reputation evaluation mechanisms using Netlogo. Albiero et al. (2007) used Netlogo to test a power saving technique for mobile devices in a cooperative framework for the wireless domain. In Koper (2005), a learning network is modelled to study how social interactions might affect acquiring new learning competences. In Millington et al. (Millington, Romero-Calcerrada, Wainwright, & Perry, 2008) they used Netlogo to run an agent-based model of agricultural land-use decision-making to evaluate potential changes in wildfire risk for a Mediterranean landscape. Barcelo et al. (2010) used Netlogo to simulate the emergence of ethnicity and cultural differentiation in prehistoric huntergatherer groups in Patagonia (Argentina). Also Netlogo can be used to replicate models, as Janssen (2009) uses it to replicate the Artificial Anasazi model.

As we can see, Netlogo is probably the simulation platform most widely used in social sciences and humanities. The main reason is the smooth learning curve of the application, in particular if it is compared to other software packages. A social scientist without any skill in programming can easily start developing models with Netlogo following a short course or a tutorial, and it is a huge advantage over platforms that require expert programming skills. Unfortunately, this fact is at the same time a disadvantage. Netlogo forces the user to create a model following the concepts and constraints defined by the program itself and for this reason the researcher will run in trouble in case of creating a model that differs from the Netlogo approach. Moreover, the source code of this software is closed, so the possibilities of adapting the platform to other uses are weak.

In summary, Netlogo is a very popular tool in natural and social sciences community. Perhaps its success comes from its short learning curve and the extensive documentation and tutorials. Actually, Netlogo is known as being by far the most professional platform in its appearance and documentation (Allan, 2010). It is the perfect platform for prototyping the first versions of a model and exploring toy models, and an excellent tool to improve the understanding of social scientists regarding the process of modelling. However, it is not meant for large simulations with complex behaviour of agents and lots of interactions. For that, other alternatives should be explored.

Repast

The Recursive Porous Agent Simulation Toolkit (Repast) is a free open source toolkit that was developed by collaboration between the University of Chicago and the Argonne National Laboratory, and is under constant development and extension (Collier, 2001). Repast is a set of Java libraries that allows building simulation environments, creating agents in social networks, collect data automatically from simulation, and build user interfaces easily. Despite being designed for modelling social behaviour it is not limited to social simulation (North, Collier, & Vos, 2006). It has a wide variety of applications that range from social systems, to evolutionary systems, to market modelling, to industrial analysis.

According to Allan (2010), Repast has many similarities with Swarm, both in philosophy and appearance. Similarly it provides a library of code for designing, running, visualising and collecting data from simulations. Those similarities are due to the fact that Repast was initially a Java re-coding of Swarm. However, Repast does not actually implement swarms. Since Repast was aimed to support a social science domain, it includes specific tools for that field. Moreover, it was developed with the goal of being easy for inexperienced users. That could explain the development of different version of Repast: Repast-J in Java, Repast.Net in Microsoft .NET and Repast-Py in Python. However, currently these variants of Repast are no longer being developed; they have been replaced by Repast Symphony which provides all the core functionality of Repast-J or Repast.Net, although limited to implementation in Java. This last version improves primarily the Graphical User Interface (GUI), provides hierarchical and organisation support through contexts and designs a special space for defining agents' relationships (called projections) (North & Macal, 2005).

The Repast user community is large and active. Repast is available in both Java and Microsoft .NET forms. It is released under the Berkeley Software Distribution (BSD) license and therefore it is freely available for download with source code. In terms of architecture and computer capabilities, Repast Symphony has a concurrent and multi-threaded discrete event scheduler, it has available various numerical libraries such as random number generators and has distributed computing support using the Terracotta Enterprise Suite for Java. Point and click modelling in 2D and 3D is supported. In terms of documentation, although Repast provides some demonstration simulation models such as SugarScape, Swarm's Heatbugs and MouseTrap models, there are very few other simulation models generally available on the Internet. However, a mailing list of Repast can provide general support and discussion.

Tobias and Hofmann (2004) evaluated free Java-libraries for social scientific agent based simulation and found Repast to be the clear winner. For that evaluation they focused in general aspects of the toolkit such as license, documentation, support, user base and future viability, modelling and experimentation aspects such as support for modelling, simulation control, experimentation or installation, and modelling options such as inter-agent communication, networks, and spatial arrangements. Also, Allan (2010) points out Repast as being the agent-based modelling and simulation package with the greatest functionality.

Repast has many users involved in a variety of social domains. For example, we find applications in species explorations of landscape (Vidgen & Padget, 2009), reputation systems (Schlosser, Voss, & Bruckner, 2005; Wierzbicki & Nielek, 2011), dynamics of insurgencies (Bennett, 2008), social influence and decision-making (Altaweel, Alessa, & Kliskey, 2010) or evolutionary simulation (Edmonds, 2006). For other Repast application areas, such as evolution and ecosystems, artificial societies, and artificial biological systems, see North and Macal (2005).

Mason

Mason (Luke, Cioffi-Revilla, Panait, Sullivan, & Balan, 2005) is the newest entrant into the field of agent-based simulation toolkits from our list of toolkits for social simulation. It was developed by a joint effort of George Mason University's Computer Science Department and the George Mason University Center for Social Complexity. The limitations of Repast with computationally demanding models with many agents executed over many iterations inspired Mason design as a smaller and faster alternative. Therefore, Mason is being developed as a new platform with emphasis on efficient execution of the code, which is programmed in Java language. It contains a model library and a suite of visualisation tools in 2D and 3D, both running independently. As one of the newest software tools, it has migration options from others which is interesting for developers. The system is open source and free (Allan, 2010).

There are many applications of Mason in social science. An example of that is the work on Dunham (2005) on epidemiological simulation. Cioffi-Revilla (2010) used Mason to study the emergency and evolution of polities in Inner Asia. Cioffi-Revilla, along with Bigbee and Luke, also showed how the Sugarspace model could be replicated with Mason in Bigbee, Cioffi-Revilla, & Luke (2007). Luke and Ziparo (2010) used Mason to simulate virtual learning of automata. Other areas of application of Mason include climate change (Hailegiorgis et al., 2010), conflict (W. Kennedy et al., 2010; Rouleau et al., 2009), or nomad societies (Cioffi-Revilla, Rogers, & Latek, 2010). For a complete list of Mason applications, see their Website (http://cs.gmu.edu/~eclab/projects/mason/).

Allan (2010) points out at the wide range of multi-agent simulations that can be designed with Mason ranging from swarm robotics to machine learning to social complexity environments. For more information about the Mason system and its basic architectural design, see Luke et al. (2005).

Discussion

We have revised four widespread toolkits for agent-based simulations, including their needs, characteristics, and some of their shortages. We specifically focused on applications to social sciences and humanities and pointed out at some special needs. In summary, social scientists experience some specific difficulties when managing agent-based platforms:

- On managing the interaction with the tool, including the need for a good detailed documentation and usability.
- On designing agent-based models they generally have non-existing or basic programming skills.
- On defining the kind of features specific to social sciences and humanities (learning or reasoning capabilities of agents, emergent behaviour, interactions, social networks among others).

These difficulties should be taken into account not only when designing agent-based platforms with general broad purposes but also when improving the current tools that are nowadays in the market. Moreover, as social simulation field advances new features and needs will appear demanding for a reasonably fast adaptation of the current tools.

There are some issues that are not considered in the design of the software tools revised. First, in some areas of social sciences, such as archaeology, data used in specific case studies is often spatially referenced, and a need to track a huge volume of information arises. If the project is big enough a desktop computer or a small cluster can be insufficient to manage the amount of spatial information, being the result that some researchers can be forced to decrease the quality and quantity of raw data managed by the simulation. Second, as social simulation advances, the need to model and simulate a large number of agents and interactions between them increases. In some specific cases, those interactions can be extremely large, thus forcing the scientist to limit its number in order to execute the simulation in a standard computer. Although some of the existing ABM platforms try to fix these problems through the use of distributed systems, none of them are specifically designed for its execution in distributed supercomputers, probably the hardware architecture more suited to execute large-scale simulations (Rubio & Cela, 2010). Actually, this issue is also pointed at Greenough (2010) as a future challenge which must be faced in order to make agent based models a mainstream computational science technology.

As we pointed before, there are differences in terminology among software tools. Railsback et al. (2006) point out at some important differences to this respect between Mason, Netlogo, Repast and Swarm. Terminology differences can not only confuse the user of the platform but also they can lead to mistakes when working in multidisciplinary teams. Given that social simulation is a recognised multidisciplinary field, more attention should be paid to this issue. Probably the causes of using different terms in the field come from the same background difference of those who developed the software tool. Therefore, people working in social simulation should discuss and define each of these terms to avoid future misunderstandings among multidisciplinary teams and the whole social simulation community.

Agent-based models are being actively applied in many practical areas. The applications range from modelling adaptive behaviours and emergence of new ones in hunter-gathered prehistoric societies to understanding consumer behaviours in stock markets. The scope of the applications varies also from minimalist academic models meant to capture the most salient features of a system to decision support systems that want to answer world policy questions, with the difficulty of including real data and later validating the model. According to Allan (2010), in some areas of application it is not clear that minimalist applications can be sufficient, although they might contribute to detect difficulties and shortage in the design of models. What is clear is that there is still a lot of work to do in social simulation field, not only in the technical aspect but also in terms of definition and agreement on models that emulate population dynamics. In that sense, Allan also points at the need of a new generation of agent-based models including more advanced aspects on communication networks, conditional neighbour interaction rules, and a protocol for knowledge exchange.

ON VERIFYING AND VALIDATING MODELS

Validation and verification (V & V) is a significant element of any simulation study. As pointed by Robinson (1997), "without V & V there are no grounds on which to place confidence in a (simulation) study's results" (pp.53). In simulation, we often differentiate between verification and validation. Verification is a process to determine whether a conceptual model has been implemented correctly in its computerized form. To borrow the computer programming term, we debug the model. Validation is a process to determine whether the model is an accurate representation of the system being studied for a given set of modelling objectives. Moss (2001) sees the validation process as a a posteriori constraint and verification as a priori constraint. The reason is verification at the end limits the specification of the model, establishing some logic or theory limits before generating any output from simulation. However, validation aims to adjust the model (through simulation outputs) with observation. A failure on validating a verified model would imply to modify the model itself. As a consequence, either the model should be changed and separated somehow from the theory or formalism or this fact could indicate that the theory or formalism should be revised.

Although conceptually simple, verification can be challenging, especially when we are dealing with a relatively complex computer program. Law (2007) and Banks et al. (1999) lists a number of techniques that can be used in a verification process. Validation is neither easy job. Actually, Robinson states that it is not possible to prove that a model is valid in all contexts, because a model is only a simplified version of reality. Consequently, a model cannot describe all aspects of a real system. Hence, the main objective of validation is to prove that a model is sufficiently accurate for parts of the real world under study. Indeed, one of the key aspects of validation is to assess whether the outcomes of a model can explain the real phenomenon that is being studied (Ormerod & Rosewell, 2009). This can be fulfilled by performing as many validation methods as possible during a simulation study until we (and users) can gain enough confidence in the model and accept its results. Therefore, validation is a continuous process (Edmonds, 2000). Validation should also take into account the domain of the system under study (Sargent, 2005). Therefore, a validated model may not be valid for a set of different experimental conditions outside its domain.

Robinson identifies four different forms of validation in simulation modelling: Conceptual model validation, data validation, white-box validation and black-box validation (Robinson, 1997). Conceptual model validation deals with issues such as the level of detail of the model and determines if it is enough for the purpose it was developed. Data validation is needed to determine whether the data used in the simulation study is sufficiently accurate. The black-box validation concerns with the relationship between inputs to the model and its outputs, ignoring the elements inside a model. The objective is to determine if the output of the model reflects the real world observation for the same set of inputs. Finally, white-box validation tries to answer the question: does each element of the model and the structure of the model elements represent the real world with sufficient accuracy?

In the following subsections we will point at some specific issues of verification and validation processes in agent-based social models and the role of formal languages in these processes.

Verifying and Validating Agent-Based Models

In the area of agent-based simulation applied to social sciences and humanities, validation is a big issue of concern. Despite the increasing popularity of agent-based simulation in the last two decades, validation techniques are neither as widely used nor as formalised as one would expect. According to the survey conducted by Heath et al. (2009) on the articles related to agent-based models published between 1998 and 2008, 29% of the articles did not discuss the validation of their models. They further divide the validation reported in the articles into two categories: Conceptual (i.e. conceptual model validation) and operational (i.e., comparing the simulation result with the real observation). The researchers found that 17% of the articles used the conceptual validation only, 19% used the operational validation only, and 35% used both. They also noted the dominance of qualitative validation methods in the validation of agent-based models. They provide a conjecture that this issue might have its cause in the fact that many agent-based models are not conducive for quantitative validation methods.

Kennedy et al. (2006) suggest the lack of verification and validation for agent-based and social sciences could be attributed to agent-based modelling not being as mature as engineering modelling. Klügl (2008) noted that agent-based models often exhibit behaviour that can be problematic for validation purposes, such as non-linearity and multi-level properties. In addition, agent-based models often use significantly more assumptions which make the assessment of the validity of these assumptions more difficult. Agent-based models also require the finer level of model detail in which data at that level of detail may be difficult to obtain.

Duong (2010) also examines this issue and suggests that the greater uncertainty in social sciences compare to others, like physics simulations, the lack of consensus on how to represent social environment, and the lack of experimental controls in data collection might contribute to the difficulties in the validation of agent-based models. Windrum et al. (2007) examines a set of methodological problems in the empirical validation of agent-based models. The problems seem to have arisen due to, among other reasons, the lack of techniques to build and analyse these models and the lack of comparability between the ones which have already been developed.

A number of validation techniques have been proposed for agent-based simulation modelling. Klügl (2008) proposes a validation process for ABS models combining face validation and statistical methods. Arifin et al. in (2011) explain there are three ways to validate an agent-based simulation:

1. Through comparison of simulation output with real phenomena. Although simple, this method has disadvantages when real data is not complete.

2. Constructing mathematical models of the system under study and compare these models with the simulation results. However, it is not always possible to build a mathematical model of reality, particularly when formulating complex systems.

3. The third technique is docking (also known as alignment, replication, cross-model validation, or model-to-model comparison), a process of comparing two similar models which address the same question or problem with the objective of not only finding their similarities and differences but also to gain understanding of the phenomenon under study (Burton, 1998). When doing this comparison between independent simulation tools, docking might find differences of interpretation in the model specification and also in the implementations. Nevertheless finding a similar behaviour among multiple simulations will increase the validation confidence. Some examples of docking can be found in the literature. We will point at docking of the beer distribution game (North & Macal, 2002), of simulation of organisations (Ashworth & Louie, 2002) and of collaboration network (Xu, Gao, & Madey, 2003; Axtell et al., 1996).

Another technique is the validation at two levels, called cross-validation (Moss & Edmonds, 2003). It consists of a first qualitative validation at the agents' level, checking that the behaviour of the computational agents is similar to the target agents, and statistical validation of patterns of behaviour of the overall system. The concept of cross-validation comes from some ideas and theories from Physics, in particular on looking at systems with high volatility, and the social theories of social embeddedness.

The Use of Formal Languages in Verification and Validation

The use of formal methods, widely extended in engineering and computer science, can help in verification process of social simulation. The reason is that formal specification of models requires the designer to clearly, concisely, and unambiguously state what a system should do. The specification does not say how the model should do but what it does. In that way, the formalism specifies an abstract representation of the system under study. The ultimate goal is to validate this specification with experts from the domain of study (Black, Hall, Jones, Larson, & Windley, 1996), who should say if the specification express what they want.

After an agreement has been set up, there is no ambiguity on what the simulation model should perform. Later, the programmer will translate the specification to the implementation. Unless there is an automatic method to do this translation from the formalism to the code, verification should be performed. However, if this automatic mechanism exists, programmers will find it very helpful since one can take the formal language to verify that the code is performing as agreed.

In that sense, Moss et al. (1997) use a declarative formalism to address the validation and verification of ABM with cognitive agents. A similar approach is followed by Fonseca (2008) who takes advantage of SDL to specify agent-based social models, as we mentioned in "Modelling Social Systems." Fonseca (2010) also develops a tool to design simulation models with SDL language that automatically translates SDL to an implementation code. As said, this has the advantage to allow users to skip the verification process.

CONCLUSION

In this chapter, we have revised the concept and process of modelling in social science. We have seen why modelling is necessary in all disciplines of science and the characteristics of the modelling process. We focused our attention to the use of formal languages when modelling social systems. We saw the current alternatives that are being used in social fields and humanities, such as textual representation or the use of diagrams. The main drawback of describing a social system with natural language is its ambiguity. This issue has special significance when working in multidisciplinary teams or when trying to replicate models.

However, some advances have been made in social sciences. One example quite successful is the use of ODD protocol. Despite being ambiguous, it provides some ideas, concepts and organisation of models that have been very well accepted by practitioners (Grimm et al., 2010). But there is a long path to walk. Social sciences and humanities should profit from other available formal languages that are currently used in other applications of simulation to improve the description of their models. Perhaps increasing the interdisciplinary work in teams could advance this issue. Computer scientists are used to specify large complex systems through the use of mathematics, logical notation, or specification languages. Social systems are perhaps more complex in terms of interaction, structure, and emergent behaviour but nothing tells us it is not possible to go further, given the big advances made in the last 15 years. Formal languages can be the means to automatize the generation of computer code and to help in the verification process.

There is also still a lot of work to do in verification and validation applied to social agent based simulation. Ormerod and Bridget (2009) state that "no firm conclusions have been reached on the appropriate way to verify or validate such models" (pp.131). The process of validation requires a clear view of what the model is trying to explain and with which goals. Therefore, as Ormerod and Rosewell state, we need to answer the question "What are the key facts that the model needs to explain and how well must it do it?" (pp.133). Later, validation will show if the model outcomes explain the phenomenon under study.

REFERENCES

Albiero, F., Fitzek, F., & Katz, M. (2007). Cooperative power saving strategies in wireless networks: An agentbased model. In *4th International Symposium on Wireless Communication Systems, ISWCS 2007* (pp. 287–291). Trondheim, Norway: IEEE. doi: 10.1109/ISWCS.2007.4392347

Allan, R. (2010). *Survey of agent based modelling and simulation tools* (Tech. Rep.). Computational Science and Engineering Department, STFC Daresbury Laboratory, Warrington WA4 4AD.

Altaweel, M., Alessa, L. N., & Kliskey, A. D. (2010). Social influence and decision-making: Evaluating agent networks in village responses to change in freshwater. *Journal of Artificial Societies and Social Simulation, 13*(1), 15. Retrieved on July 16, 2012, from http://jasss.soc.surrey.ac.uk/13/1/15.html

Arifin, S., Davis, G., & Zhou, Y. (2011). A spatial agent-based model of malaria: Model verification and effects of spatial heterogeneity. [IJATS]. *International Journal of Agent Technologies and Systems, 3*(3), 17–34. doi:10.4018/jats.2011070102.

Ashworth, M. J., & Louie, M. A. (2002). *Alignment of the garbage can and NK fitness models: A virtual experiment in the simulation of organizations*. Pittsburgh, PA: Carnegie Mellon University.

Aumann, R. (1985). What is game theory trying to accomplish? In Arrow, K., & Honkapohja, S. (Eds.), *Frontiers of Economics*. Oxford, UK: Basil Blackwell.

Axelrod, R. (1997). Advancing the art of simulation in the social sciences. *Complexity, 3*(2), 16–22. doi:10.1002/(SICI)1099-0526(199711/12)3:2<16::AID-CPLX4>3.0.CO;2-K.

Axtell, R. (2000). *Why agents?: On the varied motivations for agent computing in the social Sciences.* Tech. Rep. No. 17. The Brookings Institution, Washington, DC. doi: 10.1002/(SICI)1099-0526(199711/12)3:2<16:AID-CPLX4>3.0.CO;2-K

Axtell, R., Axelrod, R., Epstein, J., & Cohen, M. (1996). Aligning simulation models: A case study and results. *Computational & Mathematical Organization Theory, 1*(2), 123–141. doi:10.1007/BF01299065.

Balbi, S., & Giupponi, C. (2010). Agent-Based Modelling of Socio-Ecosystems: A Methodology for the Analysis of Adaptation to Climate Change. [IJATS]. *International Journal of Agent Technologies and Systems*, 2(4), 17–38. doi:10.4018/jats.2010100103.

Bankes, S. C. (2002). Agent-based modeling: A revolution? *Proceedings of the National Academy of Sciences of the United States of America*, 99(Suppl 3), 7199–7200. doi:10.1073/pnas.072081299 PMID:11997445.

Banks, J. (1998). *Handbook of simulation: Principles, methodology, advances, applications, and practice*. New York: Wiley-Interscience.

Banks, J., Carson, J., Nelson, B., & Nicol, D. (1999). *Discrete-event system simulation*. Upper Saddle River, NJ: Prentice Hall.

Barcelo, J. A., Cuesta, J. A., Del Castillo, F., Galan, J. M., Mameli, L., Quesada, M., et al. (2010). Patagonian ethnogenesis: Towards a computational simulation approach. In *Proceedings of the 3rd World Congress on Social Simulation* (pp. 1–9). Kassel, Germany.

Bedau, M. A. (2003). Artificial life: Organization, adaptation and complexity from the bottom up. *Trends in Cognitive Sciences*, 7(11), 505–512. doi:10.1016/j.tics.2003.09.012 PMID:14585448.

Bennett, D. S. (2008). Governments, civilians, and the evolution of insurgency: Modeling the early dynamics of insurgencies. *Journal of Artificial Societies and Social Simulation, 11*(4), 7. Retrieved July 16, 2012, from http://jasss.soc.surrey.ac.uk/11/4/7.html

Bersini, H. (2012). UML for ABM. *Journal of Artificial Societies and Social Simulation, 15*(1), 9. Retrieved July 16, 2012, from http://jasss.soc.surrey.ac.uk/15/1/9.html

Bigbee, A., Cioffi-Revilla, C., & Luke, S. (2007). *Replication of sugarscape using MASON. Agent-Based Approaches in Economic and Social Complex Systems IV* (pp. 183–190). New York: Springer. doi:10.1007/978-4-431-71307-4_20.

Black, P., Hall, K., Jones, M., Larson, T., & Windley, P. (1996). A brief introduction to formal methods. In *Proceedings of the IEEE Custom Integrated Circuits Conference* (pp. 377–380). San Diego, CA: IEEE. doi: 10.1109/CICC.1996.510579

Box, P. (2002). Integrating geographic information systems and agent-based modeling techniques for simulating social and ecological processes. In Gimblett, H. R. (Ed.), *Spatial units as agents: Making the landscape an equal player in agent-based simulations* (pp. 59–82). Oxford, UK: Oxford University Press.

Burmeister, B., Haddadi, A., & Mattilys, G. (1997). Application of multi-agent systems in traffic and transportation. In *Software Engineering IEEE Proceedings* (Vol. 114, pp. 51–60). doi: 10.1049/ip-sen:19971023

Burton, R. (1998). Validating and docking: An overview. In Prietula, M., Carley, K., & Gasser, L. (Eds.), *Simulating Organizations: Computational Models of Institutions and Groups*. Menlo Park, CA: AAAI Press.

Castle, C., & Crooks, A. (2006). Principles and concepts of agent-based modelling for developing geospatial simulations. Working Paper Series, University College London, London, UK. Retrieved July 16, 2012, from http://discovery.ucl.ac.uk/3342/

Chen, D., Theodoropoulos, G., Turner, S., Cai, W., Minson, R., & Zhang, Y. (2008). Large scale agent-based simulation on the grid. *Future Generation Computer Systems, 24*(7), 658–671. doi:10.1016/j.future.2008.01.004.

Cioffi-Reilla, C. (2010). A methodology for complex social simulations. *Journal of Artificial Societies and Social Simulation, 13*(1), 7. Retrieved July 16, 2012, from http://jasss.soc.surrey.ac.uk/13/1/7.html

Cioffi-Revilla, C., Rogers, J. D., & Latek, M. (2010). The mason householdworlds of pastoral nomad societies. In C. C.-R. K. Takadama, & G. Deffaunt (Eds.), *Simulating interacting agents and social phenomena: The second world congress in social simulation*. Berlin, Germany: Springer. Retrieved July 16, 2012, from http://cs.gmu.edu/~eclab/projects/mason/publications/

Collier, N. (2001). Repast: An extensible framework for agent simulation. *Natural Resources and Environmental Issues, 8*(1), 4. Retrieved July 16, 2012, from http://digitalcommons.usu.edu/nrei/vol8/iss1/4

Damaceanu, R.-C. (2008). An agent-based computational study of wealth distribution in function of resource growth interval using Netlogo. *Applied Mathematics and Computation, 201*(1-2), 371–377. doi:10.1016/j.amc.2007.12.042.

Davies, R., Roderick, P., & Raftery, J. (2003). The evaluation of disease prevention and treatment using simulation models. *European Journal of Operational Research, 150*(1), 53–66. doi:10.1016/S0377-2217(02)00783-X.

Dean, J., Gumerman, G., Epstein, J., Axtell, R., Swedlund, A., Parker, M., et al. (2000). Understanding Anasazi culture change through agent-based modeling. *Dynamics in human and primate societies: Agent-based modeling of social and spatial processes* (pp. 179–205). Retrieved July 16, 2012, from http://www.santafe.edu/media/workingpapers/98-10-094.pdfdoi: 10.1002/(SICI)1099-0526(199711/12)3:2<16::AID-CPLX4>3.0.CO;2-K

Dunham, J. B. (2005). An Agent-Based Spatially Explicit Epidemiological Model in MASON. *Journal of Artificial Societies and Social Simulation, 9*(1), 3. Retrieved July 16, 2012, from http://jasss.soc.surrey.ac.uk/9/1/3.html

Duong, D. (2010). Verification, Validation, and Accreditation (VV&A) of Social Simulations. In *Spring Simulation Interoperability Workshop*. Orlando, FL. Retrieved July 16, 2012, from http://www.sisostds.org/DigitalLibrary.aspx?Command=Core_Download&EntryId=29024. Accessed 16 July 2012.

Edmonds, B. (2001). The Use of Models - Making MABS More Informative. In S. Moss., & P. Davidsson (Eds.), Multi-Agent-Based Simulation, Lecture Notes in Computer Science Vol. 1979, 269-282. Berlin, Germany: Springer. doi: doi:10.1007/3-540-44561-7_2.

Edmonds, B. (2006). The Emergence of Symbiotic Groups Resulting from Skill-Differentiation and Tags. *Journal of Artificial Societies and Social Simulation, 9*(1), 10. Retrieved July 16, 2012, from http://jasss.soc.surrey.ac.uk/9/1/10.html

El Hadouaj, S., Drogoul, A., & Espie, S. (2001). How to combine reactivity and anticipation: The case of conflicts resolution in a simulated road traffic. *Multi-Agent-Based Simulation*, 157–167. doi: 10.1007/3-540-44561-7_6

Epstein, G., & Gang, I. (2006). The Influence of Others on Migration Plans. *Review of Development Economics, 10*(4), 652–665. doi:10.1111/j.1467-9361.2006.00340.x.

Epstein, J. (2008). Why model? *Journal of Artificial Societies and Social Simulation, 11*(4), 12. Retrieved July 16, 2012, from http://jasss.soc.surrey.ac.uk/11/4/12.html

Epstein, J., & Axtell, R. (1996). *Growing artificial societies: Social science from the bottom up*. Cambridge, MA: The MIT Press.

Fonseca, P. (2008). SDL, a graphical language useful to describe social simulation models. In *Proceedings of the 2nd Workshop on Social Simulation and Artificial Societies Analysis (SSASA'08)*. Barcelona, Spain.

Fonseca, P. (2010). Using Specification and Description Language to define and implement discrete simulation models. In S*ummer Simulation Multiconference*. Ottawa, Canada. Retrieved July 16, 2012, from http://hdl.handle.net/2117/8341

Fonseca, P., Casanovas, J., Monero, J., & Guasch, A. (2011, July). Experiences of Simulation Use in Industrial Projects. In *SCS M&S Magazine*. Retrieved July 16, 2012, from http://scs.org/magazines/2011-07/index_file/Articles.htm

Fowler, M., & Scott, K. (2000). *UML distilled: a brief guide to the standard object modeling language* (2nd ed.). Boston, MA: Addison-Wesley.

Gardner, M. (1970). Mathematical games: The fantastic combinations of John Conway's new solitaire game 'Life'. *Scientific American, 223*(4), 120–123. doi:10.1038/scientificamerican1070-120.

Gilbert, G. (2008). *Agent-based models*. Thousand Oaks, CA: Sage Publications, Inc..

Gilbert, G., & Troitzsch, K. (2005). *Simulation for the social scientist* (2nd ed.). Milton Keynes, UK: Open University Press.

Gilbert, N., & Bankes, S. (2002). Platforms and methods for agent-based modeling. *Proceedings of the National Academy of Sciences of the United States of America, 99*(Suppl 3), 7197–7198. doi:10.1073/pnas.072079499 PMID:12011398.

Goodchild, M. (2005). GIS and Modeling Overview In D. Maguire, M. Batty, & M. (Eds.) GIS, spatial analysis, and modeling. Redlands, California: Esri Press. doi: 10.1.1.161.9550

Gratch, J., & Marsella, S. (2001). Tears and fears: Modeling emotions and emotional behaviors in synthetic agents. In *Proceedings of the fifth international conference on autonomous agents* (pp. 278–285). doi: 10.1145/375735.376309

Greenough, C. (2010, October). *Proposal to establish a UK Collaborative Computational Project in ABMS*. Retrieved July 16, 2012, from http://www.softeng.rl.ac.uk/abm_ccp

Grimm, V., Berger, U., Bastiansen, F., Eliassen, S., Ginot, V., & Giske, J. et al. (2006). A standard protocol for describing individual-based and agent-based models. *Ecological Modelling, 198*(1-2), 115–126. doi:10.1016/j.ecolmodel.2006.04.023.

Grimm, V., Bergerb, U., DeAngelisc, D. L., Polhill, J. G., Giskee, J., & Railsback, S. F. (2010). The ODD protocol: A review and first update. *Ecological Modelling, 221*, 2760–2768. doi:10.1016/j.ecolmodel.2010.08.019.

Hailegiorgis, A., Kennedy, W., Rouleau, M., Bassett, J., Coletti, M., Balan, G., et al. (2010). An agent based model of climate change and conflict among pastoralists in East Africa. In D. A. Swayne, W. Yang, A. A. Voinov, A. Rizzoli, & T. Filatova (Eds.), In *Proceedings of the International Congress on Environmental Modeling and Software (IEMSS2010)*. Ottawa, Canada.

Hanneman, R. (1988). *Computer-assisted theory building: Modeling dynamic social systems*. Newbury Park, CA: Sage.

Harvey, B. (1997). *Computer science logo style: Symbolic computing* (2nd ed., *Vol. 1-3*). Cambridge, UK: MIT Press.

Heath, B., Hill, R., & Ciarallo, F. (2009). A Survey of Agent-Based Modeling Practices (January 1998 to July 2008). *Journal of Artificial Societies and Social Simulation, 12*(4), 9. Retrieved July 16, 2012, from http://jasss.soc.surrey.ac.uk/12/4/9.html

Huhns, M., & Singh, M. (1997). *Readings in agents*. Burlington, MA: Morgan Kaufmann Publishers Inc..

Janssen, M., Alessa, L., Barton, M., Bergin, S., & Lee, A. (2008). Towards a community framework for agent-based modelling. *Journal of Artificial Societies and Social Simulation, 11*(2), 6. Retrieved July 16, 2012, from http://jasss.soc.surrey.ac.uk/11/2/6.html

Janssen, M. A. (2009). Understanding artificial Anasazi. *Journal of Artificial Societies and Social Simulation, 12*(4), 13. Retrieved July 16, 2012, from http://jasss.soc.surrey.ac.uk/12/4/13.html

Kennedy, R., Xiang, X., Madey, G., & Cosimano, T. (2006). Verification and validation of scientific and economic models.

Kennedy, W., Hailegiorgis, A., Rouleau, M., Bassett, J., Coletti, M., Balan, G., et al. (2010). An agent-based model of conflict in East Africa and the effect of watering holes. In *Proceedings of the 19th Conference on Behavior Representation in Modeling and Simulation (BRIMS)*. Columbia, SC

Klugl, F. (2008). A Validation Methodology for Agent-Based Simulations. In *Proceedings of the 23rd Annual ACM Sysmposium on Applied Computing* (pp. 39-43). New York: ACM. doi: 10.1145/1363686.1363696

Köhler, M., Langer, R., von Lüde, R., Moldt, D., Rölke, H., & Valk, R. (2007). Socionic multi-agent systems based on reflexive petri nets and theories of social self-organisation. *Journal of Artificial Societies and Social Simulation, 10*(1), 3. Retrieved July 16, 2012, from http://jasss.soc.surrey.ac.uk/10/1/3.html

Kohler, T., & van der Leeuw, S. (2007). *The model-based archaeology of socionatural systems*. Santa Fe, NM: SAR Press.

Koper, R. (2005). Increasing learner retention in a simulated learning network using indirect social interaction. *Journal of Artificial Societies and Social Simulation, 8*(2). Retrieved July 16, 2012, from http://jasss.soc.surrey.ac.uk/8/2/5.html

Law, A. M. (2007). *Simulation modeling and analysis* (4th ed.). New York: McGraw-Hill.

Leigh Tesfatsion. (n.d.). *General Software and Toolkits*. Retrieved July 16, 2012, from http://www2.econ.iastate.edu/tesfatsi/acecode.htm

Leiva Olmos, J., Fonseca, P., & Ocana, J. (2011). Modelling surgical pavilions and a unit of anaesthesia on a chilean hospital using specification and description language. In *Actas de la XIII conferencia española y III encuentro iberoamericano de biometría.* Retrieved July 16, 2012, from http://hdl.handle.net/2117/15525

Leombruni, R., & Richiardi, M. (2006). Laborsim: An agent-based microsimulation of labour supply–An application to Italy. *Computational Economics, 27*(1), 63–88. Retrieved July 16, 2012, from http://papers.ssrn.com/sol3/papers.cfm?abstract_id=868445

Lin, F., & Pai, Y. (2000). Using multi-agent simulation and learning to design new business processes. *Systems, Man and Cybernetics, Part A: IEEE Transactions on Systems and Humans, 30*(3), 380–384. doi:10.1109/3468.844361.

Lingnau, A., & Drobnik, O. (1999). Simulating mobile agent systems with Swarm. In *Proceedings of the First International Symposium on Agent Systems and Applications and Third International Symposium on Mobile Agents* (pp. 272–273). IEEE. doi: 10.1109/ASAMA.1999.805417

Lozares Colina, C. (2004). La simulacion social,¿una nueva manera de investigar en ciencia social? *Papers: revista de sociologia,* (72), 165–188.

Luke, S., Cioffi-Revilla, C., Panait, L., Sullivan, K., & Balan, G. (2005). Mason: A multiagent simulation environment. [from http://cs.gmu.edu/~eclab/projects/mason/]. *Simulation, 81*(7), 517. Retrieved July 16, 2012 doi:10.1177/0037549705058073.

Luke, S., & Ziparo, V. (2010). Learn to Behave! Rapid Training of Behavior Automata. In *Proceedings of Adaptive and Learning Agents Workshop at AAMAS* (pp. 61–68). Toronto, Canada: AAMAS.

Luna, F., & Stefansson, B. (2000). *Economic simulations in Swarm: Agent-based modelling and object oriented programming* (*Vol. 14*). New York: Springer. doi:10.1007/978-1-4615-4641-2.

Madey, G., Freeh, V., & Tynan, R. (2002). Agent-Based Modeling of Open Source using Swarm. In *Americas Conference on Information Systems* (pp. 1472–1475). Dallas, TX. Retrieved from http://www.nd.edu/~oss/Papers/amcis_swarm.pdf

Madhavan, P., Papelis, Y., Kady, R., & Moya, L. (2009). An agent-based model of crowd cognition. In *Proceedings of the 18th Conference on Behavior Representation in Modeling and Simulation* (pp. 139–140). Sundance, UT: Curran Associates, Inc. Retrieved July 16, 2012, from http://brimsconference.org/archives/2009/papers/BRIMS2009_014.pdf

Menendez, M., & Collado, S. (2007). Simulación de procesos sociales basada en agentes software. *EMPIRIA. Revista de Metodología de Ciencias Sociales, 14*, 139–161. Retrieved July 16, 2012, from http://dialnet.unirioja.es/servlet/articulo?codigo=2536607

Michalski, R., Carbonell, J., & Mitchell, T. (1985). *Machine learning: An artificial intelligence approach (Vol. 1)*. Burlington, MA: Morgan Kaufmann.

Millington, J., Romero-Calcerrada, R., Wainwright, J., & Perry, G. (2008). An agent-based model of mediterranean agricultural land-use/cover change for examining wildfire risk. *Journal of Artificial Societies and Social Simulation, 11*(4), 4. Retrieved July 16, 2012, from http://jasss.soc.surrey.ac.uk/11/4/4.html

Minar, N., Burkhart, R., Langton, C., & Askenazi, M. (1996). *The swarm simulation system: A toolkit for building multi-agent simulations*. Working Papers No. 96-06-042. Sante Fe, CA: Santa Fe Institute.

Moss, S. (2001). Messy Systems - The Target for Multi Agent Based Simulation. In Moss, S., & Davidsson, P. (Eds.), *Multi-Agent-Based Simulation (Vol. 1979*, pp. 1–14). Berlin, Germany: Springer. doi:10.1007/3-540-44561-7_1.

Moss, S., & Edmonds, B. (2003). *Sociology and simulation: Statistical and qualitative crossvalidation*. (Tech. Rep. No. 03105. Retrieved July 16, 2012, from http://cfpm.org/cpmrep105.html

Moss, S., Edmonds, B., & Wallis, S. (1997). V*alidation and Verification of Computational Models with Multiple Cognitive Agents*. Discussion Papers No. 97-25. Manchester Metropolitan University, UK. Retrieved July 16, 2012, from http://ideas.repec.org/p/wuk/mcpmdp/9725.html

Nance, R. (1994). The conical methodology and the evolution of simulation model development. *Annals of Operations Research, 53*(1), 1–45. doi:10.1007/BF02136825.

Nikolai, C., & Madey, G. (2009). Tools of the trade: A survey of various agent based modeling platforms. *Journal of Artificial Societies and Social Simulation, 12*(2), 2. Retrieved July 16, 2012, from http://jasss.soc.surrey.ac.uk/12/2/2.html

Nikolai, C., & Madey, G. (2011). *Comparison of agent-based modelling software*. Retrieved from http://en.wikipedia.org/wiki/Comparison_of_agent-based_modeling_software

North, M., Collier, N., & Vos, J. (2006). Experiences creating three implementations of the repast agent modeling toolkit. [TOMACS]. *ACM Transactions on Modeling and Computer Simulation, 16*(1), 1–25. doi:10.1145/1122012.1122013.

North, M., & Macal, C. (2002). *The beer dock: Three and a half implementations of the beer distribution game*. Swarmfest.

North, M., & Macal, C. (2005). In Komosinski, M. (Ed.), *Artificial life models in software* (pp. 115–141). Heidelberg, Germany: Springer. doi:10.1007/1-84628-214-4_6.

North, M., Sallach, D., & Macal, C. (Eds.). In Proceedings of Agent 2005: Generative Social Processes, Models, and Mechanism (pp. 177–192). Chicago, IL: Argonne National Laboratory.

Onggo, B. (2010). Methods for Conceptual Model Representation. In Brooks, R., Robinson, S., Kotiadis, K., & van der Zee, D.-J. (Eds.), *Conceptual modelling for discrete-event simulation* (pp. 337–354). Abingdon, UK: Taylor & Francis. doi:10.1201/9781439810385-c13.

Orcutt, G. (1957). A new type of socio-economic system. *The Review of Economics and Statistics*, *39*(2), 116–123. doi:10.2307/1928528.

Ormerod, P., & Rosewell, B. (2009). Validation and Verification of Agent-Based Models in the Social Sciences. In F. Squazzoni (Ed.), *Epistemilogical Aspects of Comuter Simulation in the Social Sciences, Second International Workshop, EPOS 2006* (Vol. 5466, pp. 130-140). Berlin, Germany: Springer-Verlag. doi: 10.1007/978-3-642-01109-2_10

Pavon, J., Arroyo, M., Hassan, S., & Sansores, C. (2008). Agent-based modelling and simulation for the analysis of social patterns. *Pattern Recognition Letters*, *29*(8), 1039–1048. doi:10.1016/j.patrec.2007.06.021.

Pidd, M. (2003). *Tools for Thinking: Modelling in Management Science* (2nd ed.). Chichester, UK: Wiley.

Pidd, M. (2010). Why modelling and model use matter. *The Journal of the Operational Research Society*, *61*(1), 14–24. doi:10.1057/jors.2009.141.

Polhill, J. G., Parker, D., Brown, D., & Grimm, V. (2008). Using the ODD Protocol for Describing Three Agent-Based Social Simulation Models of Land-Use Change. *Journal of Artificial Societies and Social Simulation, 11*(2), 3. Retrieved July 16, 2012, from http://jasss.soc.surrey.ac.uk/11/2/3.html

Railsback, S., Lytinen, S., & Jackson, S. (2006). Agent-based simulation platforms: Review and development recommendations. *Simulation*, *82*(9), 609–623. doi:10.1177/0037549706073695.

Resnick, M. (1994). *Turtles, Termites and Traffic Jams: Explorations in Massively Parallel Microworlds.* Cambridge, MA: MIT Press.

Richiardi, M., Leombruni, R., Saam, N. J., & Sonnessa, M. (2006). A common protocol for agent-based social simulation. *Journal of Artificial Societies and Social Simulation, 9*(1), 15. Retrieved July 16, 2012, from http://jasss.soc.surrey.ac.uk/9/1/15.html

Robinson, S. (1997). Simulation model verification and validation: Increasing the users' confidence. In *Proceedings of the 29th Conference on Winter Simulation* (pp. 53–59). Atlanta, GA: IEEE.doi: 10.1145/268437.268448

Robinson, S. (2008). Conceptual modelling for simulation Part I: Definition and requirements. *The Journal of the Operational Research Society, 59*(3), 278–290. doi:10.1057/palgrave.jors.2602368.

Robinson, S., & Pidd, M. (1998). Provider and customer expectations of successful simulation projects. *The Journal of the Operational Research Society, 49*(3), 200–209. doi: doi:10.1057/palgrave.jors.2600516.

Rossiter, S., Noble, J., & Bell, K. R. (2010). Social simulations: Improving interdisciplinary understanding of scientific positioning and validity. *Journal of Artificial Societies and Social Simulation, 13*(10), 1. Retrieved March 8, 2012, from http://jasss.soc.surrey.ac.uk/13/1/10.html

Rouleau, M., Coletti, M., Bassett, J., Hailegiorgis, A., Gulden, T., & Kennedy, W. (2009). Conflict in complex socio-natural systems: Using agent-based modeling to understand the behavioral roots of social unrest within the mandera triangle. In *Proceedings of the Human Behavior-Computational Modeling and Interoperability Conference 2009.* Oak Ridge, TN.

Roussopoulos, N., & Karagiannis, D. (2009). Conceptual modeling: Past, present and the continuum of the future. In Borgida, A., Chaudhri, V., Giorgini, P., & Yu, E. (Eds.), *Conceptual Modeling: Foundations and Applications* (*Vol. 5600*, pp. 139–152). Berlin, Germany: Springer. doi:10.1007/978-3-642-02463-4_9.

Rubio, X. (2009). *Modelitzacio i simulació aplicades a la recerca i interpretació de camps de batalla.* Unpublished doctoral dissertation, Universitat de Barcelona, Barcelona, Spain. Retrieved July 16, 2012, from http://hdl.handle.net/10803/1339

Rubio, X., & Cela, J. (2010). Large-scale agent-based simulation in archaeology: An approach using high-performance computing. In Computer Applications in Archaeology. Granada, Spain.

Russell, S., & Norvig, P. (2010). *Artificial intelligence: A modern approach*. Upper Saddle River, NJ: Prentice Hall.

Sargent, R. (2005). Verification and validation of simulation models. In *Proceedings of the 37th Winter Simulation Conference* (pp. 130–143). doi: 10.1109/WSC.2005.1574246

Schelling, T. (1971). Dynamic models of segregation. *The Journal of Mathematical Sociology, 1*(2), 143–186. doi:10.1080/0022250X.1971.9989794.

Schlosser, A., Voss, M., & Bruckner, L. (2005). On the simulation of global reputation systems. *Journal of Artificial Societies and Social Simulation, 9*(1), 4. Retrieved July 16, 2012, from http://jasss.soc.surrey.ac.uk/9/1/4.html

Serenko, A. & B., D. (2002). *Agent toolkits: A general overview of the market and an assessment of instructor satisfaction with utilizing toolkits in the classroom.* Working Paper No. 455. Hamilton, Canada: McMaster University.

Shannon, R. (1976). Simulation modeling and methodology. In *Proceedings of the 76 Bicentennial Conference on Winter Simulation* (pp. 9–15). Gaithersburg, MD. Retrieved July 16, 2012, from http://informs-sim.org/wsc76papers/prog76sim.html

Starlogo, T. (n.d.). Retrieved July 16, 2012, from http://ccl.northwestern.edu/cm/starlogot/

Sterman, J. (2000). *Business dynamics: Systems thinking and modeling for a complex world*. New York: McGraw-Hill.

Stewart, I. (1989). *Does god play dice? The new mathematics of caos*. Hoboken, NJ: Blackwell Publishing.

Strader, T., Lin, F., & Shaw, M. (1998). Simulation of order fulfillment in divergent assembly supply chains. *Journal of Artificial Societies and Social Simulation, 1*(2), 36–37. Retrieved July 16, 2012, from http://jasss.soc.surrey.ac.uk/1/2/5.html

Swarm development group. (n.d.). Retrieved July 16, 2012, from http://www.swarm.org/Terna, P. (1998). Simulation tools for social scientists: Building agent based models with swarm. *Journal of Artificial Societies and Social Simulation, 1*(2), 1–12. Retrieved July 16, 2012, from http://jasss.soc.surrey.ac.uk/1/2/4.html

Tesfatsion, L. (2002). Agent-based computational economics: Growing economies from the bottom up. *Artificial Life, 8*(1), 55–82. doi:10.1162/106454602753694765 PMID:12020421.

Tesfatsion, L. (2006). Agent-based Computational Economics: A Constructive Approach to Economic Theory. In L. Tesfatsion, & K. Judd (Eds.), *Handbook of Computational Economics: Agent-based Computational Economics* (pp. 831-880). Amsterdam, The Netherlands: North Holland. Retrieved July 16, 2012, from http://www.econ.iastate.edu/research/books-and-chapters/p7004 Accessed 16 July 2012.

Tisue, S., & Wilensky, U. (2004). Netlogo: A simple environment for modeling complexity. In *Proceedings of the International Conference on Complex Systems* (pp. 16–21). Boston, MA.

Tobias, R., & Hofmann, C. (2004). Evaluation of free java-libraries for social-scientific agent based simulation. *Journal of Artificial Societies and Social Simulation, 7*(1). Retrieved July 16, 2012, from http://jasss.soc.surrey.ac.uk/7/1/6.html

Troitzsch, K. (1997). Social science simulation - Origins, prospects, purposes. In R. Conte, H. R., & P. Terna (Eds.), Simulating Social Phenomena (Vol. 456, pp.41-54). Berlin, Germany: Springer- Verlag.

van der Leeuw, S. (2004). Why model? *Cybernetics and Systems, 35*(2-3), 117–128. doi:10.1080/01969720490426803.

Vidgen, R., & Padget, J. (2009). Sendero: An extended, agent-based implementation of Kauffman's NKCS model. *Journal of Artificial Societies and Social Simulation, 12*(4), 8. Retrieved July 16, 2012, from http://jasss.soc.surrey.ac.uk/12/4/8.html

Villatoro, D., & Sabater-Mir, J. (2008). Mechanisms for social norms support in virtual societies. In *Proceedings of the 5th conference of the European Social Simulation Association (ESSA08),* Brescia, Italy. Available from the author.

Von Neumann, J. (1966). *Theory of self-reproducing automata* (Burks, A., Ed.). Urbana, IL: University of Illinois Press.

Wasserman, S. (1994). *Social network analysis: Methods and applications*. Cambridge university press. doi:10.1017/CBO9780511815478.

Wegener, M. (2000). Spatial models and GIS. In Fotheringham, A., & Wegener, M. (Eds.), *Spatial Models and GIS: New Potential and New Models*. London: Taylor & Francis.

Weiss, G. (1999). *Multiagent systems: a modern approach to distributed artificial intelligence*. The MIT press.

Wheatley, D., & Gillings, M. (2000). Vision, perception and GIS: developing enriched approaches to the study of archaeological visibility. *Beyond the map: archaeology and spatial technologies*, 1–27. Available from the author.

Wierzbicki, A., & Nielek, R. (2011). Fairness emergence in reputation systems. *Journal of Artificial Societies and Social Simulation, 14*(1), 3. Retrieved July 16, 2012, from http://jasss.soc.surrey.ac.uk/14/1/3.html

Wilensky, U. (2002). Modeling nature's emergent patterns with multi-agent languages. In Proceedings of EuroLogo 2001 Linz (pp. 1–6).

Windrum, P., Fagiolo, G., & Moneta, A. (2007). Empirical Validation of Agent-Based Models: Alternatives and Prospects. *Journal of Artificial Societies and Social Simulation, 10*(2), 8. Retrieved July 16, 2012, from http://jasss.soc.surrey.ac.uk/10/2/8.html

Xu, J., Gao, Y., & Madey, G. (2003). A docking experiment: Swarm and repast for social network modeling. In *Seventh Annual Swarm Researchers Meeting*. South Bend, IN.

Yang, L., & Gilbert, N. (2008). Getting away from numbers: Using qualitative observation for agent-based modeling. *Advances in Complex Systems, 11*(2), 175–186. doi:10.1142/S0219525908001556.

Zhao, H., & Li, X. (2008). H-trust: A robust and lightweight group reputation system for peer-to-peer desktop grid. In *The 28th International Conference on Distributed Computing Systems Workshops* (pp. 235–240). Beijing, China: IEEE. doi: 10.1109/ICDCS.Workshops.2008.96

Chapter 12
Agent–Based Simulation Model Representation Using BPMN

Bhakti S. S. Onggo
Lancaster University Management School, UK

ABSTRACT

Conceptual modelling is the process of abstracting a model from a real or proposed system into a conceptual model. An explicit conceptual model representation allows the model to be communicated and analysed by the stakeholders involved in a simulation project. A good representation that can be understood by all stakeholders is especially essential when the project involves different stakeholders. The three commonly used paradigms in business applications are discrete-event simulation, agent-based simulation, and system dynamics. While the conceptual model representations in discrete-event simulation and system dynamics have been dominated by process-flow and stock-and-flow diagrams, respectively, research into the conceptual model representation in agent-based simulation is relatively new. Many existing representation methods for agent-based simulation models are less friendly to business users. This chapter advocates the use of Business Process Model and Notation (BPMN) diagrams for the agent-based simulation conceptual model representation in the context of business applications. This chapter also demonstrates how the proposed BPMN representation and other methods such as Petri Nets, DEVS, and UML are used to represent the well-known SugarScape model.

DOI: 10.4018/978-1-4666-4369-7.ch012

INTRODUCTION

Conceptual modelling is the process of abstracting a model from a real or proposed system into a conceptual model (Robinson 2010). There is a point in a simulation project where the conceptual modelling process occurs inside an individual modeller's mind. This 'thinking' process includes reflection on how to structure a problem and how the simulation model should be designed to help decision-makers solve the problem to hand, subject to certain constraints. At some point in the project, the conceptual model needs to be communicated to other stakeholders (users, domain experts, or other modellers). The importance of the quality of communication between stakeholders to make a simulation project successful makes the role of explicit conceptual model representation especially important (Robinson & Pidd 1998).

In the context of business applications, the representation of a conceptual model describes the problem domain (e.g., modelling objectives and the structure of business processes) and the model specifications which define the model's behaviour and enable the model's execution on a simulation tool. Explicit representation allows the model to be communicated and analysed by the stakeholders involved in a simulation project. When communication involves different types of stakeholders, a good representation that can be understood by all stakeholders is essential. In cases where critical decisions are involved, the risk of producing a wrong model (which may lead to wrong decisions) due to ineffective representation is even higher.

There are a number of modelling paradigms used in simulation. The three commonly used paradigms in business applications are discrete-event simulation (DES), agent-based simulation (ABS) and system dynamics (SD). Two of the key differences among the three paradigms are the way simulation modellers view the world and how the view is represented in a model. Readers interested in the differences between the three paradigms should refer to Brailsford et al. (2010), Macal (2010), Morecroft and Robinson (2006) and Siebers et al. (2010). From the perspective of conceptual model representation, most DES tools use a variant of the process-flow diagram. Similarly, tools dedicated to SD mostly use a variant of the stock-and-flow diagram. This may suggest that process-flow and stock-and-flow diagrams have been accepted as de-facto conceptual model representations in DES and SD, respectively. ABS is relatively younger than DES and SD. ABS has become popular partly due to the availability of high quality micro-data, increases in computing power, and advances in analytical behaviour modelling. Hence, research into conceptual model representation in ABS is relatively new.

Many existing methods used in ABS conceptual model representation are less friendly to business users who may not be familiar with software engineering or computer programming concepts. This is not surprising given ABS's origin in Artificial Intelligence (North & Macal 2007). The objective of this chapter is to propose the use of *Business Process Model and Notation (BPMN),* a standard designed for business users, for ABS conceptual model representation. The remainder of this chapter will be organised as follows. Section 2 explains conceptual modelling in the context of ABS. It also presents an overview of the selected existing methods for conceptual model representation in ABS. Section 3 explains the proposed BPMN-based conceptual model representation. This includes the proposed BPMN pattern for ABS model representation. Finally, the concluding remarks are given in Section 4.

REPRESENTATION METHODS FOR AGENT-BASED SIMULATION

An ABS model is a simulation model that is formed by a set of autonomous agents that interact with their environment and other agents through a set of internal rules to achieve their objectives (Onggo, 2010a). There is no universal agreement in the literature on ABS on the definition of an agent (North & Macal, 2007). Instead, we have observed, from the literature, a spectrum of complexity in the definition of an agent. At one extreme, an ABS model is composed of a set of homogeneous agents with a set of simple attributes (such as speed and direction) and simple behaviours (such as move and accelerate). This type of agent is referred to as a pseudo-agent in North and Macal (2007). At the other extreme, an ABS model is formed by a set of heterogeneous agents with various complex attributes (such as memory) and complex abilities (such as communication, perception, planning and learning). The lack of a universal agreement on what constitutes an agent results in various methods of representing an ABS model. This section provides an overview of the existing representation methods in agent-based simulation. Due to the limited space, it is virtually impossible to provide an extensive coverage of all existing methods in this section. Instead, we have selected representation methods that are generic and frequently used in the literature. These are flow charts, pseudo-code, Petri Nets, DEVS, and UML.

Flow Charts and Pseudo-Code

Flow charts and pseudo-code are commonly used to describe algorithms. The behaviour of agents in many ABS models is often expressed as logical rules. Hence, it is very common to see flow charts and pseudo-code (or even the computer code itself) used to represent agent behaviours in the literature. Figure 1 shows the pseudo-code of agent behaviours in one of the variants of the *SugarScape* wealth distribution model (Epstein & Axtell, 1996). In this model, agents live in a two-dimensional world that is divided into $n \times n$ grids. Each grid contains some sugar. The amount of sugar varies from grid to grid and grows over time until it reaches a pre-determined maximum amount (see SugarGrid.step).

The agents are created with different amounts of sugar in their possession. They have varying levels of vision quality and metabolism rate. Each agent will move to a grid with the highest amount of sugar and harvest all sugar in the grid. If there is a tie, a grid is chosen at random. An agent can only move to any unoccupied grid within the range of its vision. Each time, every agent consumes some of its sugar. The amount of sugar consumption depends on the metabolism rate of the agent. If the amount of sugar in its possession is not enough, the agent will die. Each agent will eventually die when it reaches its maximum age. When an agent dies, a new agent is created somewhere in the world to keep the figure of population constant but the sugar will not be passed on to the new agent (no sugar inheritance). The behaviour of the agent is shown in SugarPerson.step. The ABS representation in flow charts and pseudo-code tends to be closer to the computer code, which can be difficult for people without any knowledge of computer programming to read. On the flip side, flow charts and pseudo-code, if written properly, could be a very effective communication method for people who are familiar with computer programming to discuss the ABS model behaviour. Pseudo-code is a form of textual representation. Onggo (2010b) explained that the main advantage of using textual representation for a conceptual model is its flexibility, which explains why there is no single accepted standard for pseudo-code. Another advantage is that pseudo-code can be written relatively quickly using any text editor. The disadvantage of textual representation is that it presents information sequentially in comparison to a pictorial representation, such as a flow chart, that can show information in two dimensions.

Figure 1. SugarScape model in pseudo-code

```
SugarPerson.step()                          SugarGrid.step()
{                                           {
    // search new location                      sugar = max(maxSugar, sugar+growthRate)
    locations = all visible grids           }
    location = locations with max sugar
    move to location
    sugar = sugar + location.sugar

    // consume sugar
    sugar = sugar - metabolismRate

    // determine if the person will die
    if (sugar <= 0) or (age > maxAge) {
        create a new SugarPerson
        die
    }
}
```

DEVS (Discrete Event System Specification)

ABS models are often represented in DEVS and its variants. DEVS formal specification is applicable to a wide range of discrete-event models (Zeigler 1976). However, many researchers (for example, Zaft and Zeigler 2002, Onggo 2010a) have shown that DEVS can be used to represent ABS models by adding an extra layer to its core specification. The basic principle of DEVS is that a discrete-event system is defined as a tuple of seven components $<X, S, Y, \delta_{int}, \delta_{ext}, \lambda, ta>$ where:

- X is the set of events in the system.
- S is the state of the system.
- Y is the set of output variables.
- δ_{int} is the internal function that changes the current system state ($s \in S$) at time t to a new state $s' \in S$ at time $t+ta(s)$ provided there is no event $x \in X$ which occurs between time t and $t+ta(s)$.
- δ_{ext} is the external function that changes the current system state ($s \in S$) at time t to a new state $s' \in S$ because of the occurrence of an event $x \in X$ at time $t+\Delta t$ (where $0 \leq \Delta t \leq ta(s)$).
- λ is the output function that gives a set of output values (Y) given the current system state (S).
- Finally, ta is the time when the current system state ($s \in S$) is scheduled to change (see δ_{int}).

Figure 2 shows one of the possible DEVS representations of the Sugarscape model presented in Figure 1. The SugarPerson agents in this variant are autonomous rather than reactive. Hence, the model does not have any events (X) and the behaviour of agents is represented by the internal function (δ_{int}) alone. The states of the system (S) are formed by the amount of sugar in each grid in the world (GS), the grid location of the agents (PL), the amount of sugar owned by each agent (PS), and the age of each agent (PA). The model has one output variable (Y) (i.e., the Gini index), which is an economic measure of income equality in a society. A value of 0 equates to perfect income equality and 1 (or 100, depending on the equation) equates to the extremely skewed income distribution where one individual receives all income. The formula is calculated in the output function λ. The model uses the fixed-increment time-advancement (ta) method. At every time step, the internal function is triggered. The four components in the internal function correspond to the growth of sugar in each grid, the movement of agents, the harvest and consumption of sugar by agents, and the decision whether an agent will die and generate a new agent to replace it.

DEVS provides a mathematical representation of an ABS model. Hence, it provides the rigour and beauty of a mathematical representation. The representation can be validated mathematically and the simulator can be generated automatically from the mathematical representation. However, DEVS may not appeal to ABS modellers who are not familiar with the mathematics.

Petri Nets

Petri Nets and its variants are used to represent agents and agent behaviours in multi-agent systems (MAS). Although there are some differences between ABS and MAS (North & Macal, 2007), the representation of agents and agent behaviours is a topic common to the two fields. Similar to DEVS, Petri Nets is a formal language that can represent the static structure and the dynamic of behaviour of an ABS model. Holvoet (1995) is among the earliest who proposed the idea of representing agents in Petri Nets. In his proposal, each agent is represented using a net. In other words, the behaviour of an agent is encapsulated within its net. A net is formed by a set of places (drawn as circles) and transitions (drawn as rectangles). Figure 3 shows the SugarScape model represented in the Timed Coloured Petri Nets. The left net represents a SugarPerson and the right net represents a grid. The dashed line between the transition "Move" and the net SugarGrid signifies the existence of a communication channel between the SugarPerson and SugarGrid. This is where the function getGrid finds the grid with the highest amount of sugar within the agent's visible region. Similarly, there is a communication channel between the transition "Harvest" and the net SugarGrid where the agent will consume the sugar on the grid.

As shown in Figure 3, the Petri Nets has the advantage of offering a graphical representation on top of its precise semantics. However, the Petri Nets has a number

Figure 2. SugarScape model in DEVS

$$X = \{\}$$
$$S = GS \cup PL \cup PS \cup PA$$

$GS = \{ gs_{i,j} \mid 1 \le i, j \le n \}$ where the world is divided into $n{\times}n$ grids and gs_{ij} is the amount of sugar at grid (i, j)

$PL = \{ (px_i, py_i) \mid 1 \le i \le m \}$ where (ps_i, py_i) are the grid location of person i and m is the number of people $(m < n{\times}n)$

$PS = \{ ps_i \mid 1 \le i \le m \}$ where ps_i is the amount of sugar owned by person i

$PA = \{ pa_i \mid 1 \le i \le m \}$ where pa_i is the age of person i

$Y = \{ g \}$ where $0 \le g \le 1$ is the Gini index

$\delta_{int}(S) = \{gs_{i,j} \mid \forall_{1 \le i,j \le n} \, gs_{i,j} = \max(gs_{i,j}^{max}, gs_{i,j} + gr_{i,j})\} \cup$

$\{(px_i, py_i) \mid \forall_{1 \le i \le m} (px_i, py_i) = move(px_i, py_i, v_i, GS)\} \cup$

$\{ps_i, pa_i, gs_{j,k} \mid \forall_{1 \le i \le m} ps_i = ps_i + gs_{px_i,py_i} - met_i \wedge pa_i = pa_i + 1 \wedge \exists!_{1 \le j,k \le n} \ (j = px_i \wedge k = py_i) \rightarrow (gs_{j,k} = 0)\} \cup$

$\{px_i, py_i, ps_i, pa_i \mid \exists_i (pa_i \ge pa_i^{max} \vee ps_i \le 0) \rightarrow (pa_i = 0 \wedge (px_i, py_i) = newloc() \wedge ps_i = newsugar())\}$

where $gs_{i,j}^{max}$ is the maximum amount of sugar at grid (i, j), gr_{ij} is the sugar growth rate at grid (i, j), $move$ is a function that returns the coordinate of a grid with the highest amount of sugar (including the tie breaker), v_i is the vision of agent i, met_i is the metabolism rate of agent i, pa_i^{max} is the maximum age of agent i, $newloc$ is a function that returns a random unoccupied grid location, and $newsugar$ is a function that returns a random amount of sugar.

$\delta_{ext} = \{\}$

$\lambda(\forall_i ps_i) = \frac{1}{2m^2 \overline{ps}} \Sigma_{i=1}^{m} \Sigma_{j=1}^{m} |ps_i - ps_j|$ where $\overline{ps}$ is the average sugar owned by SugarPerson agents

$ta(S) = dt$

of limitations when it is used to represent agent-based systems such as the lack of specification for inter-agent communications, the static nature of the net and the lack of specification for intelligence. Since the initial work by Holvoet (1995), there have been significant advances in the research that address these limitations. One of the notable works was produced by Moldt and Wienberg (1997) who extended the Coloured Petri Nets to include intelligent behaviours and specifications of agent communications. A more recent example is the work of van der Zee (2009) who used the Timed Coloured Hierarchical Petri Nets in the representation of ABS models in the context of manufacturing systems.

UML (Unified Modelling Language)

In his survey, Allan (2010) finds that the majority of popular ABS frameworks and tools are based on Object Oriented principles, i.e. they use classes and methods to represent agents and agent behaviours. Hence, it is not surprising to find many articles use the UML diagrams (or their variants), which are commonly used in Object Oriented design, to represent agents and agent behaviours. Bauer (1999) and Odell et al. (2000) propose the Agent UML (AUML) which extends the UML to make it more suitable for modelling agents and agent-based systems in general. The AUML website (http://www.auml.org) lists a number of articles demonstrating the use of UML diagrams and their variants in representing the structure of agents and their behaviours. UML has a number of diagrams and each of the diagrams is suitable for representing a particular aspect of the model. For example, the internal structure of an agent (e.g., its attributes and list of activities) can be represented using the class

Figure 3. SugarScape model in petri nets

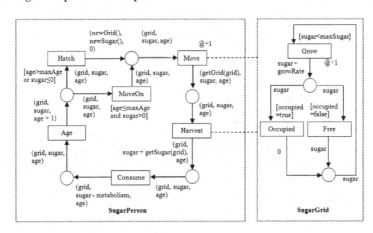

diagram. The interactions between agents and agent behaviours can be represented using the sequence diagram, collaboration diagram, or activity diagram. UML also provides notations that support the representation of agents with multiple roles. The detailed specification for UML can be found from www.uml.com.

Figure 4 shows the AUML sequence diagram that describes a partial snapshot of the interactions between a SugarPerson and a grid with the highest amount of sugar in its visible region in the Sugarscape model. The SugarPerson starts the communication by enquiring into the amount of sugar the grid has. After asking all the grids within its visibility, if the SugarPerson finds out that the grid has the highest amount of sugar, it will ask whether the grid is available. If the grid is not available, the SugarPerson will ask the grid with the next highest amount of sugar. On the other hand, if the grid is available, the SugarPerson will move to the grid and harvest the sugar in the grid. The sequence diagram does not show the internal activities (i.e., activities that do not have any interaction with other agents or another environment) such as consumption of sugar by the SugarPerson or the growth of sugar in the grid. The internal activities are best represented using the UML activity diagram.

UML provides a multi-faceted representation of an ABS model using various UML diagrams and annotations. Hence, it has the advantage of providing a more complete representation of an ABS model. UML has another advantage as a standard supported by various organisations, especially in the software industry. It can be extended and tailored for specific domain, as demonstrated by the AUML. The main

Figure 4. Interactions between agents in SugarScape model in AUML sequence diagram

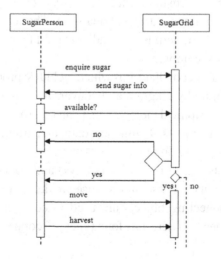

disadvantage of UML is its closeness to the software systems. Although it can be used outside software systems, most reported UML applications are related to software systems (Dobing & Parsons, 2006).

BPMN-BASED MODEL REPRESENTATION

The previous section shows four of the existing representation methods for ABS models. The main issue with these methods is that they are less friendly to business users who may not be familiar with software engineering or computer programming concepts. For this we propose the use of BPMN-based model representation. This section starts with an introduction to the Business Process Model and Notation (BPMN). It is followed by a discussion on how BPMN can be used to represent ABS models. Finally, we propose a BPMN pattern based on the DEVS' internal and external functions.

BPMN

BPMN is a business process modelling language standard controlled by the Object Management Group (OMG). The most recent BPMN specification document states that the objective of the standard is "to provide a notation that is readily understandable by all *business users*, from the *business analysts* that create the initial drafts of the processes, to the *technical developers* responsible for implementing the technology that will perform those processes, and finally, to the business people who will manage and monitor those processes" (OMG 2010). This objective clearly indicates the two key parts of BPMN: a *business view* and a *technical view*. The business view is used by the business analysts to create descriptive business process models which can be communicated and analysed. The technical view is used by the technical developers who will need to add detailed formal specifications to the models to make them executable.

BPMN supports a number of diagrams which includes: process diagram, collaboration diagram, choreography diagram and conversation diagram. These diagrams use a collection of core graphical elements that can be grouped into five categories: flow objects, connecting objects, swimlanes, data, and artefacts. Table 1 shows the general shape of the core components.

Flow objects (events, activities, and gateways) and connecting objects are the most essential components because they are used to define the structure and behaviour of a process. Connecting objects are used to connect flow objects to each other or to other elements. There are four types of connection: sequence flows,

Table 1. BPMN core graphical components – adapted from OMG (2010)

Element	Notation
Event	
Activity	
Gateway	
Sequence flow	
Message flow	
Association	
Data association	
Pool	
Lane	
Data object	
Data input	
Data output	
Data store	
Group	
Text annotation	Descriptive Text Here

message flows, association and data association. Swimlanes, which comprise pools and lanes, are used to group a number of elements. For example, an organisation can be represented as a pool and each department within the organisation can be represented as a lane inside the pool. Subsequently, a process inside a specific lane represents a process internal to the department. The remaining graphical component categories (data and artefact) can be used to add details to the model. BPMN provides various data annotations, such as data objects, data input, data output, and data stores, to specify links to externally defined data structures. This is because BPMN does not have elements to describe the structure of the data used in the model. Instead, BPMN shows how the data is used in the model. Finally, artefacts are used to provide additional information to a model. This can be in the form of group annotation or text annotation. OMG (2010) provides a detailed specification of all BPMN core elements.

The *process diagram* is used to represent two categories of business processes: private and public. A private (or internal) process model describes activities internal to a participant (such as an organisation or business entities within the same organisation). A public process model describes the interactions between activities internal to a participant and the activities of one or more other participants. In a public process model, internal activities that do not interact directly with other participants are not shown.

The *collaboration diagram* is used to model the interactions between two or more participants. The collaboration model appears similar to a set of interacting public process models except that all private activities may be shown, including those that do not interact directly with other participants. A collaboration diagram allows a public process to be represented as a black box when we cannot see (or are not interested in) the internal activities of the process. Figure 5 shows an example of a collaboration diagram that describes what happens when an applicant submits an online credit card application to a bank. The bank will check his/her credit rating from a credit agency. When the credit rating is received, the bank will decide whether to accept or decline the application and send the result to the applicant. This simple example does not show the detail because it is only meant to show how a collaboration diagram looks like for readers who are not familiar with BPMN. The figure shows that three participants are involved and they interact through messages.

Similar to the collaboration diagram, the *choreography diagram* is used to define the interactions between participants. The main difference lies in the focus. The collaboration diagram focuses more on the participants while the choreography diagram focuses more on the relationships between participants. Figure 6 (left) shows the choreography diagram for the same process shown in the collaboration diagram in Figure 5. The interactions are shown as choreography activities. The notation for a choreography activity is similar to that for the collaboration diagram but with two or more bands. The non-shaded band in a choreography activity is the sending participant and the shaded band is the receiving participant. The message is attached to the choreography activity as an association. For example, the leftmost

Figure 5. Collaboration diagram

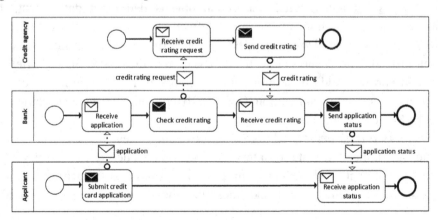

choreography activity in Figure 6 shows that an applicant submits a credit card application to the bank. This activity is followed by the bank checking his/her credit rating from the credit agency. Finally, the rightmost choreography activity shows that the bank will send the application status to the applicant.

The *conversation diagram* provides the high level overview of the interactions between participants in the model as shown in Figure 6 (right). The diagram shows the participants as pools and the detailed interactions between participants are encapsulated within the hexagon. It summarises the interactions between participants shown in the choreography diagram (Figure 6 left).

BPMN-Based Model Representation

Onggo and Karpat (2011) are the first who proposed the use of BPMN to represent ABS models. As mentioned earlier, BPMN is a standard designed for business users. This is the main advantage of using BPMN in representing ABS models in the context of business applications. Furthermore, BPMN is supported by big vendors such as IBM, Oracle, SAP, Unisys, and others. Hence, the number of software tools that support BPMN is likely to grow. The main disadvantage of BPMN is that it is designed for a process-oriented modelling tool. Onggo (2012) addresses this issue and demonstrates that BPMN can be used to represent ABS models. His arguments will be explained in more detailed in this section. Unless otherwise stated, ABS models in this section onwards refer to ABS models in the context of business applications.

Macal and North (2010) showed the wide range of ABS applications. Given the vast number of ABS applications, they discussed a small sample. They identified business-related applications such as the artificial society, economics and market analysis. Bonabeau (2002) discussed the application of ABS to modelling human systems, specifically in the business context. He divided the business applications into four areas: flows (e.g., customer flow management, traffic management), market (e.g., stock market, ISP market), organisation (e.g., organisational behaviour, risk analysis, business operations) and diffusion (e.g. adoption of new products, viral

Figure 6. Choreography diagram (left) and conversation diagram (right)

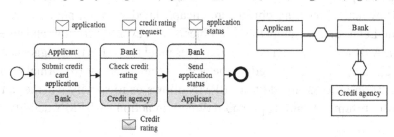

marketing). Typical agents in business applications are individuals (such as consumers and investors) and organisations (such as firms and government institutions). These agents plan and execute their plan to achieve their objectives. They are intelligent because they can learn by comparing the result of their actions to their objectives. They can also learn by analysing the information they receive from other agents and their environment. They may change their beliefs, plans or actions based on what they have learned from other agents or their environment. The behaviour of these agents is shown from their actions including their interactions with other agents and their environment over time. The interactions may lead to an emerging behaviour such as the formation of markets (labour market, financial market, etc.). Each agent has a unique identity and a set of attributes or characteristics. These attributes can be static (such as birthdate), relatively static (such as an organisation's vision and mission and type of individual decision making) or dynamic (such as memory and wealth). The attributes of an agent can have a significant influence on its behaviour.

The examples given in Macal and North (2010) and Bonabeau (2002) suggest that a method for ABS model representation need to support the representation of agents, agent behaviours, agent interactions, and the environment. The following discussion shows that BPMN can be used to represent those elements.

The concept of participants in the BPMN collaboration diagram is similar to the concept of agents in ABS. Hence, a BPMN pool can be used to represent an agent and this has at least three advantages. First, the pool provides a visual boundary of an agent which encapsulates the attributes and behaviour of the agent. Hence, it is easy to identify an agent, its attributes and its behaviour. The second advantage is that a pool can be divided into a number of lanes. This allows us to implement an agent who has multiple roles. Since the lanes within a pool can be organised into a hierarchical structure, we can represent the role hierarchy that an agent may have, such as departments within a division and divisions within a firm (see Figure 7). Finally, a BPMN pool implies the existence of domain control within the pool. This is in line with the notion of agent autonomy in ABS.

BPMN data annotations can be used to represent the attributes of an agent. This representation allows us to specify activities that use the attributes and how the attributes are used (example.g., as an input, output or both). The behaviour of an agent can be specified using a combination of flow objects and connecting objects. These flow and connecting objects are encapsulated within a pool that represent the agent. Let us discuss about the flow objects (i.e., events, activities and gateways) in detail. A BPMN event can be used to represent (1) an event that triggers an agent to act, (2) an event that is raised by the action of an agent, or (3) a final event that ends a certain process. In addition, BPMN allows us to specify whether an event will pause, resume, or interrupt (and redirect) an action. A BPMN activity can be

Figure 7. Agents in BPMN

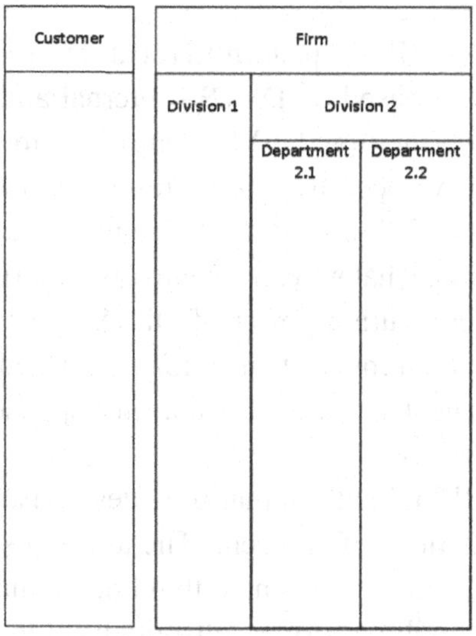

used to represent an action done by an agent. It is important to note that a BPMN activity represents a step or action (not a state) in the process. A BPMN gateway can be used to represent various decision types such as branching, selection and merging. The BPMN connecting objects are used to connect the BPMN flow objects. Experienced modellers may appreciate that the combinations of flow objects and connecting objects in BPMN can be used to represent various complex agent behaviours.

Next, we need to show that BPMN can be used to represent environment. Environment in ABS models can be passive or active depending on its behaviour. Environment is passive if it reacts only as a response to an action done by an agent. In the absence of actions from agents, the environment will remain the same. On the other hand, an active environment can change its states even in the absence of any actions by agents. This shows that environment behaves very much like an agent. Consequently, the same BPMN constructs we use for the agent can be applied to environment.

Finally, BPMN imposes that the communications between participants must be conducted via messages and signals. Messages are sent to specific recipients while signals are broadcast and it is up to the participants to decide whether they are interested in the signals. The communication via message passing and broadcast are consistent with the interactions between agents in ABS. Hence, this section has shown that BPMN has the ability to represent the core components of an ABS model (i.e., agents and their attributes, behaviour, environment, and interactions).

A BPMN-Pattern for ABS Model Representation

Onggo (2012) proposes a BPMN pattern that can be used to represent an ABS model. The pattern is built based on DEVS's internal and external functions and provides their visual representation. DEVS is one of the most elegant formal specification languages that have been used to represent various ABS models (Dávila & Uzcátegui, 2000; Zaft & Zeigler, 2002; Hocaoglu et al., 2002; Gonçalves et al., 2004). This has an advantage that we can tap into the significant body of knowledge that proves the general computing power of DEVS. An *internal function* and an *external function* are used to represent an action performed by an agent based on a condition internal to the agent and an action done in response to an action performed by another agent, respectively.

Figure 8 shows the BPMN pattern that provides a visual representation of the internal and external functions of an agent. The top part shows that a start event, which is represented as a circle with single thin line boundary, activates an agent. Once activated, the agent will perform a self-initialisation action. This is followed by a sub-process called 'Activate agent' that represents the main actions that will be performed by the agent throughout its lifetime. The sub-process can be expanded as shown in the bottom part of Figure 8. It encapsulates the two types of actions (or functions) that an agent can perform: internal and external.

The internal function in Figure 8 has a loop icon indicating that it will be repeated until the simulation ends. If necessary, modellers can add logical rules to specify the condition for the execution of certain internal functions. The external functions are represented as non-interrupting BPMN event sub-processes. A non-interrupting event sub-process is activated as a response to an event external to the agent and its execution will not terminate the execution of the currently active internal and other external functions. BPMN uses a dashed-line boundary to indicate that a sub-process is a non-interrupting. If the agent needs to interrupt the execution of its internal function, the modeller needs to specify this explicitly in the BPMN diagram. Semantically, the structure of sub-process 'Activate agent' means that when the simulation ends, the agent will wait until all actively running internal and external functions end before executing the activity 'Finalise agent'. When this task is complete an end event (represented as a circle with a single thick line boundary) is raised and the agent dies.

Figure 9 shows the representation of the internal function and external functions of a grid location (SugarGrid) in the SugarScape model using the BPMN pattern. These functions are specified inside the 'Activate agent' sub-process (see Figure 8). The sugar in each grid will grow up to its maximum carrying capacity. This is

Figure 8. BPMN pattern for a generic agent

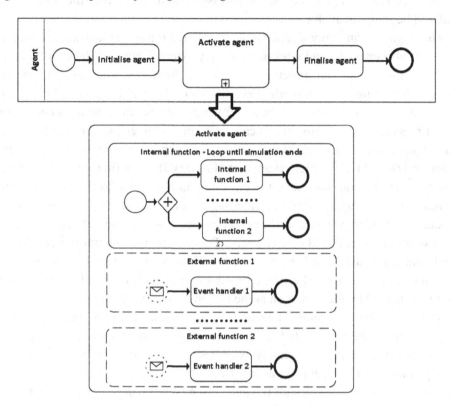

represented as an internal function because its execution is not triggered by any external event. The model specifies that each iteration takes one unit of simulation time. The model specifies three external functions. The first external function responds to any sugar enquiry message sent by a SugarPerson. A non-shaded icon in BPMN denotes adjective 'catching' (or receiving) and a shaded icon denotes adjective 'throwing' (or sending). In this example, when the external function receives the 'sugar enquiry' message, it will send the 'sugar info' message to the sender. The second external function is executed when a SugarPerson sends a message to indicate its intention to enter the grid. If the grid has been occupied by another SugarPerson, the request will be declined. Otherwise, the grid will send a message to grant the permission and set its status to 'occupied'. Subsequently, the grid will wait for the harvest request from the SugarPerson. When the harvest request is received, the grid will send the amount of the harvested sugar and reset its sugar to zero. The last external function is executed when the current occupier is leaving the grid. The grid will check whether the sender is the current occupier. If the sender is not the current occupier, the request will be ignored. Otherwise, the status of the grid will be set to 'available'.

The SugarPerson is not a reactive agent. Hence it has one internal function to represent his behaviour and does not have any external function. The BPMN representation for its internal function is shown in Figure 10. The internal function starts with the SugarPerson sending enquiries to grids within its visibility region. The parallel bar at the bottom of the activity indicates that the activity is performed a few times on a list of items, in this case, a list of visible grids. The next few components show that the SugarPerson is sending an intention to enter the best available SugarGrid (i.e., it has the highest amount of sugar). If it can find such a SugarGrid then the SugarPerson will leave the current grid and move to the new grid and harvest the grid's sugar. Otherwise, the SugarPerson will stay in the current grid. Regardless of the movement, the SugarPerson needs to consume its sugar and if its sugar is zero or less, it will die. The SugarPerson will also die when it reaches its maximum age. If the SugarPerson is alive at this stage, its age will be increased by one simulation time unit. The whole process will be repeated until the simulation ends as indicated by the loop icon at the bottom of the sub-process.

The inter-agent communications and the interactions between an agent and its environment can be represented using the message flows. An interaction between two agents can be represented simply by connecting the relevant flow object (except for a gateway) in one agent to another flow object (except for a gateway) in the other agent. The same applies for the interaction between an agent and its environment. In the examples given in Figure 9 and Figure 10, we simply connect each throwing event to its corresponding catching event.

As mentioned earlier, BPMN also allows us to view the interactions at the higher abstraction level using the choreography and conversation diagrams. In these two diagrams, the detailed behaviour is hidden. The top diagram in Figure 11 shows the choreography diagram that represents the interactions between the SugarPerson and one of the candidate grids. The interaction is started by the SugarPerson when it enquires about the amount of sugar the SugarGrid has. If the SugarPerson decides to enter this SugarGrid, the SugarPerson will continue the interaction by sending its intention to enter to the SugarGrid. If the SugarGrid grants the permission, the SugarPerson will continue the interaction by sending the harvest request message. The SugarGrid will respond with the amount of sugar that can be harvested. The interactions between the SugarPerson with its current SugarGrid location (i.e., intention to leave) can be represented in the same way. The conversation diagram at the bottom of Figure 11 shows the summary of the interactions between the SugarPerson and the SugarGrid.

Figure 9. SugarGrid's internal and external functions in BPMN

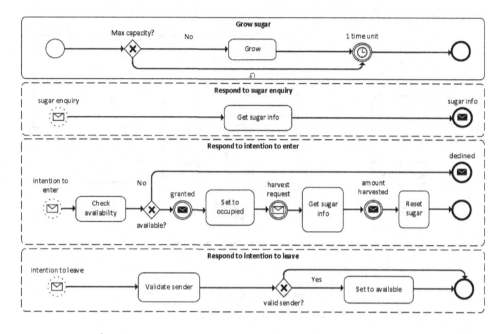

Figure 10. SugarPerson's internal function in BPMN

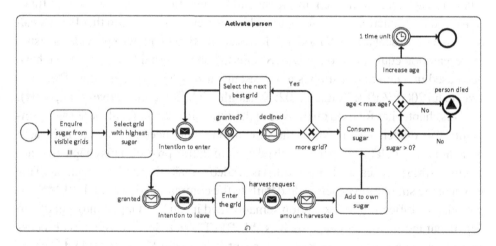

CONCLUSION

Although BPMN is designed as a process-oriented modelling language, this chapter has shown that BPMN can be used as an agent-oriented modelling language. This chapter has demonstrated that a BPMN pattern can be used to represent ABS models

Figure 11. SugarScape model in BPMN choreography diagram (top) and conversation diagram (bottom)

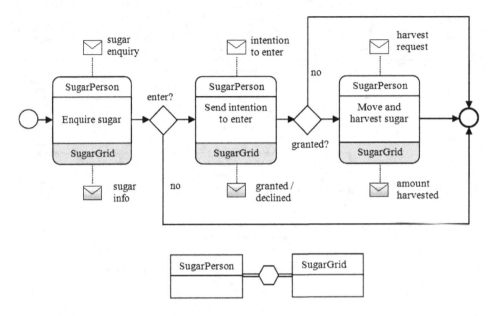

where the agents and their environment can be specified as a set of internal functions, external functions and attributes. This chapter does not claim that BPMN can be used to represent all ABS models. However, the BPMN pattern provides a visual representation equivalent to the DEVS' internal and external functions which have been used in a number of studies to represent various ABS models (e.g., Davila & Uzcátegui 2000; Zaft & Zeigler 2002; Hocaoglu et al., 2002; Gonçalves et al., 2004).

This chapter has focused on the role of the simulation conceptual model as a communicative model. This is where the simulation model needs to be communicated with the non-simulation experts involved in a simulation project. This chapter has not discussed the specification language that is needed to make the model executable. This is where the simulation experts add details to the communicative model. BPMN 2.0 provides specification for execution semantic and it can be mapped into a platform dependent modelling language such as WS-BPEL (Web Service-Business Process Execution Language). As a proof-of-concept Onggo and Karpat (2011) develop a web-based simulation tool called Agent-based Model and Notation Designer (ABMN Designer). It provides the visual interactive modelling tool where users can draw ABS models using BPMN graphical elements. In practice, this conceptual model can be used as a communication tool between business users and simulation modellers. It also helps with the conceptual model validation process. The conceptual model (diagram) can be saved as an XML document. Subsequently, simulation modellers can add detailed specifications to each element in the diagram to model behaviour using a simple specification language called Agent-based simulation language (ABSL). Readers interested in ABSL should refer to Onggo and Karpat (2011).

The proposed ABS model representation using BPMN has some limitations that need to be addressed in future research to make it applicable to a wider range of ABS models. The first limitation is that the ability to represent environment that cannot be easily represented as a set of internal and external functions is limited. The second limitation is caused by the fact that BPMN assumes an implicit queuing for each activity. Hence, the explicit representation of the resources needed for an activity to start is lacking. Since the structure of agents represented in BPMN is static, it leads to the third limitation, i.e. it is difficult to represent the change of structure in the model (for example, adding new BPMN activities or remove the existing activities) while the model is running. Finally, historically, BPMN does not provide detailed representation for data. Hence, it limits the ability to represent complex attributes of an agent (such as memory, beliefs, and perceptions).

ACKNOWLEDGMENT

This chapter is an extended version of Onggo, B.S.S. (2012) 'BPMN pattern for agent-based simulation model representation' in the Proceedings of the 2012 Winter Simulation Conference and Onggo, B.S.S. and Karpat, O. (2011) 'Agent-based conceptual model representation using BPMN' in the Proceedings of the 2011 Winter Simulation Conference.

REFERENCES

Alan, R. J. (2010) *Survey of agent-based modelling and simulation tools*. Science and Technology Facilities Council. Retrieved September 20, 2011, from http://epubs.stfc.ac.uk

Bauer, B., Müller, J. P., & Odell, J. (2001). Agent UML: A formalism for specifying multiagent interac-tion. In Ciancarini, P., & Wooldridge, M. (Eds.), *Agent-Oriented Software Engineering*. Berlin, Germany: Springer-Verlag. doi:10.1007/3-540-44564-1_6.

Bonabeau, E. (2002). Agent-based modeling: Methods and techniques for simulating human systems. *Proceedings of the National Academy of Sciences of the United States of America*, 99(Suppl 3), 7280–7287. doi:10.1073/pnas.082080899 PMID:12011407.

Brailsford, S. C., Desai, S. M., & Viana, J. (2010). Towards the holy grail: Combining system dynamics and discrete-event simulation in healthcare. In *Proceedings of the 2010 Winter Simulation Conference* (pp. 2293-2303). Los Alamitos, CA: IEEE Computer Society Press.

Dávila, J., & Uzcátegui, M. (2000). GALATEA: A multiagent simulation platform. In *Proceedings of the International Conference on Modeling, Simulation and Neural Networks*. IEEE. Retrieved September 20, 2011, from http://iies.faces.ula.ve/Amse2000/papers/simulation/MSNN-JDMU00.pdf

Dobing, B., & Parsons, J. (2006). How UML is used. *Communications of the ACM, 49*(5), 109–113. doi:10.1145/1125944.1125949.

Epstein, J. M., & Axtell, R. (1996). *Growing artificial societies: Social science from the bottom up*. Washington, DC: Brookings Institution Press.

Gonçalves, A. S., Rodrigues, A., & Correia, L. (2004). *Multi-agent simulation within geographic information systems*. Paper presented in the 5th Workshop on Agent-Based Simulation. Lisbon, Portugal. Retrieved September 20, 2011, from: http://www.lnec.pt/organizacao/dha/nti/estudos_id/pdfs/AGoncalvesetal_ABS2004.PDF

Hocaoglu, M. F., Firat, C., & Sarjoughian, H. S. (2002). DEVS/RAP: Agent-based simulation. In *Proceedings of the 2002 AI, Simulation and Planning in Highly Autonomous Systems Conference*. Lisbon, Portugal: IEEE.

Holvoet, T. (1995). Agents and Petri Nets. In O. Herzog, W. Reisig, & R. Valk (Eds.), Petri Nets Newsletters, 49, 3-8.

Macal, C. M. (2010). To agent-based simulation from system dynamics. In *Proceedings of the 2010 Winter Simulation Conference* (pp. 371-382). Los Alamitos, California: IEEE Computer Society Press.

Macal, C. M., & North, M. J. (2010). Tutorial on agent-based modelling and simulation. *Journal of Simulation, 4*, 151–162. doi:10.1057/jos.2010.3.

Moldt, D., & Wienberg, F. (1997). Multi-agent systems based on coloured Petri Nets. In Azéma, P., & Balbo, G. (Eds.), *LNCS 1248: Application and theory of Petri Nets* (pp. 82–101). Berlin, Germany: Springer. doi:10.1007/3-540-63139-9_31.

Morecroft, J., & Robinson, S. (2006). Comparing discrete event simulation and system dynamics: Modelling a fishery. In *Proceedings of the 2006 OR Society Simulation Workshop* (pp. 137-148). Birmingham, UK: OR Society.

North, M. J., & Macal, C. M. (2007). *Managing business complexity: Discovering strategic solutions with agent-based modeling and simulation*. Oxford, UK: Oxford University Press.

Object Management Group. (2010). *Business Process Model and Notation (BPMN) version 2.0*. Retrieved September 20, 2011, from http://www.bpmn.org

Odell, J., Parunak, H., & Bauer, B. (2000) Extending UML for agents. In *Proceedings of the Agent-Oriented Information Systems Workshop* (pp. 3–17).

Onggo, B. S. S. (2010a). Running Agent-Based Models on a Discrete-Event Simulator. In *Proceedings of the 24th European Simulation and Modelling Conference* (pp. 51-55). Hasselt, Belgium: Eurosis-ETI.

Onggo, B. S. S. (2010b). Methods for Conceptual Model Representation. In Robinson, S., Brooks, R., Kotiadis, K., & van der Zee, D.-J. (Eds.), *Conceptual Modelling for Discrete-Event Simulation* (pp. 337–354). Boca Raton, FL: Taylor and Francis. doi:10.1201/9781439810385-c13.

Onggo, B. S. S. (2012). BPMN pattern for agent-based simulation model representation. In *Proceedings of the 2012 Winter Simulation Conference*. Berlin, Germany. IEEE Computer Society Press.

Onggo, B. S. S., & Karpat, O. (2011). Agent-based conceptual model representation using BPMN. In *Proceedings of the 2011 Winter Simulation Conference* (pp. 671-682). Phoenix, AZ: IEEE Computer Society Press.

Robinson, S. (2010). Conceptual modelling for simulation: Definition and requirements. In Robinson, S., Brooks, R., Kotiadis, K., & van der Zee, D.-J. (Eds.), *Conceptual Modelling for Discrete-Event Simulation* (pp. 235–256). Boca Raton, FL: Taylor and Francis. doi:10.1201/9781439810385-c1.

Robinson, S., & Pidd, M. (1998). Provider and customer expectations of successful simulation projects. *The Journal of the Operational Research Society*, *49*(3), 200–209.

Siebers, P. O., Macal, C. M., Garnett, J., Buxton, D., & Pidd, M. (2010). Discrete-event simulation is dead, long live agent-based simulation! *Journal of Simulation*, *4*, 204–210. doi:10.1057/jos.2010.14.

Van der Zee, D. J. (2009). Building insightful simulation models using formal approaches – A case study on Petri Nets. In *Proceedings of the 2009 Winter Simulation Conference* (pp. 886-898). Austin, TX: IEEE Computer Society Press.

Zaft, G., & Zeigler, B. P. (2002).Discrete event simulation of social sciences: The XeriScape artificial society. In *Proceedings of the 6th World Multiconference on Systemics, Cybernetics and Informatics*. Orlando, FL: International Institute of Informatics and Systemics.

Zeigler, B. P. (1976). *Theory of modeling and simulation*. New York: John Wiley.

KEY TERMS AND DEFINITIONS

Agent-Based Simulation: A simulation model that is formed by a set of autonomous agents that interact with their environment and other agents through a set of internal rules to achieve their objectives (Onggo 2010a).

BPMN Pattern: A generic model structure represented using BPMN diagrams that can be used for a specific purpose.

Business Process Model and Notation (BPMN): A business process modelling language standard controlled by the Object Management Group.

Conceptual Model: A non-software specific description of the computer simulation model describing the objectives, inputs, outputs, content, assumptions and simplifications of the model (Robinson 2010).

Conceptual Modelling: The process of abstracting a model from a real or proposed system into a conceptual model.

Conceptual Model Representation: An explicit representation of a conceptual model. It can be in the form of textual representation, pictorial representation or multi-faceted representation (Onggo 2010b).

External Function: In BPMN pattern, it is a function that represents an action done in response to an action performed by another agent.

Internal Function: In BPMN pattern, it is a function that represents an action performed by an agent based on a condition internal to the agent.

Compilation of References

(2003). InDong, J. S., & Woodcock, J. (Eds.). Lecture Notes in Computer Science: *Vol. 2885. A Relational Model for Formal Object-Oriented Requirement Analysis in UML.* New York: Springer.

Ajmone Marsan, M., Balbo, G., Bobbio, A., Chiola, G., Conte, G., & Cumani, A. (1985). On Petri nets with stochastic timing. In *Proceedings of the International Workshop on Timed Petri Nets.* Torino, Italy. IEEE Computer.

Ajmone Marsan, M., Balbo, G., Conte, G., Donatelli, S., & Franceschinis, G. (1995). *Modeling with generalised stochastic Petri nets.* New York: Wiley.

Alan, R. J. (2010) *Survey of agent-based modelling and simulation tools.* Science and Technology Facilities Council. Retrieved September 20, 2011, from http://epubs.stfc.ac.uk

Albiero, F., Fitzek, F., & Katz, M. (2007). Cooperative power saving strategies in wireless networks: An agentbased model. In *4th International Symposium on Wireless Communication Systems, ISWCS 2007* (pp. 287–291). Trondheim, Norway: IEEE. doi: 10.1109/ISWCS.2007.4392347

Ali, M., Ben-Abdallah, H., & Gargouri, F. (2005). Towards a Validation Approach of UP Conceptual Models. In *Proceedings of the Workshop Consistency in Model Driven Engineering in European Conference on Model Driven Architecture-Foundations and Applications* (pp. 143–154).

Ali, M. (2010). *Verification and validation of UML models: approaches and tools.* Editions Universitaires Europeennes.

Alla, H., Ladet, P., Martinez, J., & Silva, M. (1984). Modeling and validation of complex systems by coloured Petri nets. In *Proceedings of 5th European Workshop on Applications and Theory of Petri Nets* (pp. 122-140).

Allan, R. (2010). *Survey of agent based modelling and simulation tools* (Tech. Rep.). Computational Science and Engineering Department, STFC Daresbury Laboratory, Warrington WA4 4AD.

Altaweel, M., Alessa, L. N., & Kliskey, A. D. (2010). Social influence and decision-making: Evaluating agent networks in village responses to change in freshwater. *Journal of Artificial Societies and Social Simulation, 13*(1), 15. Retrieved on July 16, 2012, from http://jasss.soc.surrey.ac.uk/13/1/15.html

Andersen, D., Richardson, G., & Vennix, J. (1997). Group model building: adding more science to the craft. *System Dynamics Review*, *13*(2), 187–201. doi:10.1002/(SICI)1099-1727(199722)13:2<187::AID-SDR124>3.0.CO;2-O.

ArgoUML tool. (2006). Retrieved from www.argouml.org.

Arifin, S., Davis, G., & Zhou, Y. (2011). A spatial agent-based model of malaria: Model verification and effects of spatial heterogeneity.[IJATS]. *International Journal of Agent Technologies and Systems*, *3*(3), 17–34. doi:10.4018/jats.2011070102.

Ashworth, M. J., & Louie, M. A. (2002). *Alignment of the garbage can and NK fitness models: A virtual experiment in the simulation of organizations*. Pittsburgh, PA: Carnegie Mellon University.

Aumann, R. (1985). What is game theory trying to accomplish? In Arrow, K., & Honkapohja, S. (Eds.), *Frontiers of Economics*. Oxford, UK: Basil Blackwell.

Axelrod, R. (1997). Advancing the art of simulation in the social sciences. *Complexity*, *3*(2), 16–22. doi:10.1002/(SICI)1099-0526(199711/12)3:2<16::AID-CPLX4>3.0.CO;2-K.

Axtell, R. (2000). *Why agents?: On the varied motivations for agent computing in the social Sciences.*Tech. Rep. No. 17. The Brookings Institution, Washington, DC. doi: 10.1002/(SICI)1099-0526(199711/12)3:2<16:AID-CPLX4>3.0.CO;2-K

Axtell, R., Axelrod, R., Epstein, J., & Cohen, M. (1996). Aligning simulation models: A case study and results. *Computational & Mathematical Organization Theory*, *1*(2), 123–141. doi:10.1007/BF01299065.

Baker, L., Clemente, P., Cohen, B., Permenter, L., Purves, B., & Salmon, P. (2000, July). *Foundational concepts for model driven system design*. [Computer software manual].

Balbi, S., & Giupponi, C. (2010). Agent-Based Modelling of Socio-Ecosystems: A Methodology for the Analysis of Adaptation to Climate Change.[IJATS]. *International Journal of Agent Technologies and Systems*, *2*(4), 17–38. doi:10.4018/jats.2010100103.

Ballard, S. M., & Kuhl, M. E. (2006). The use of simulation to determine maximum capacity in the surgical suite operating room. In *Proceedings of Winter Simulation Conference*. Monterey, CA: WSC.

Balmelli, L., Brown, D., Cantor, M., & Mott, M. (2006). Model-driven systems development. *IBM Systems Journal*, *45*(3), 569–585. doi:10.1147/sj.453.0569.

Balzert, H. (2005). Lehrbuch der Objektmodellierung.[München, Germany: Spektrum Verlag.]. *Analyse und Entwurf mit der UML*, *2*, 2.

Bankes, S. C. (2002). Agent-based modeling: A revolution? *Proceedings of the National Academy of Sciences of the United States of America*, *99*(Suppl 3), 7199–7200. doi:10.1073/pnas.072081299 PMID:11997445.

Banks, J. (1998). *Handbook of simulation: Principles, methodology, advances, applications, and practice*. New York: Wiley-Interscience.

Banks, J., Carson, J., Nelson, B., & Nicol, D. (1999). *Discrete-event system simulation*. Upper Saddle River, NJ: Prentice Hall.

Banks, J., Carson, J., Nelson, B., & Nicol, D. (2001). *Discrete-Event System Simulation*. Upper Saddle River, New Jersey: Prentice Hall.

Compilation of References

Barcelo, J. A., Cuesta, J. A., Del Castillo, F., Galan, J. M., Mameli, L., Quesada, M., et al. (2010). Patagonian ethnogenesis: Towards a computational simulation approach. In *Proceedings of the 3rd World Congress on Social Simulation* (pp. 1–9). Kassel, Germany.

Barendregt, J., Van Oortmarssen, G., Vos, T., & Murray, C. (2003). A Generic Model for the assessment of disease epidemiology: the computational basis of DisMod II. *Population Health Metrics, 1*(4). PMID:12773212.

Barlas, Y. (1996). Formal aspects of model validity and validation in system dynamics. *System Dynamics Review, 12*(3), 183–210. doi:10.1002/(SICI)1099-1727(199623)12:3<183::AID-SDR103>3.0.CO;2-4.

Barlas, Y. (2002). System dynamics: Systemic Feedback Modeling for Policy Analysis. In *UNESCO, Knowledge for Sustainable Development - An Insight into the Encyclopedia of Life Support Systems* (pp. 1131–1175). Oxford: UNESCO-Eolss Publishers, Paris, France.

Barros, F. J. (1995). Dynamic structure discrete event system specification: A new formalism for dynamic structure modeling and simulation. In Proceedings of the 27th conference on Winter simulation (pp. 781-785). Miami, FL: WSC.

Barton, R., & Schruben, L. (2001). Simulating Real Systems. *In submission*.

Bauer, B., Müller, J. P., & Odell, J. (2001). Agent UML: A formalism for specifying multiagent interac-tion. In Ciancarini, P., & Wooldridge, M. (Eds.), *Agent-Oriented Software Engineering*. Berlin, Germany: Springer-Verlag. doi:10.1007/3-540-44564-1_6.

Baumgart, A., Zoeller, A., Denz, C., Bender, H.-J., Heinzl, A., & Badreddin, E. (2007). Using Computer Simulation in Operating Room Management: Impacts on Process Engineering and Performance. In *Proceedings of International Conference on System Sciences*. Waikoloa, HI: IEEE.

Bedau, M. A. (2003). Artificial life: Organization, adaptation and complexity from the bottom up. *Trends in Cognitive Sciences, 7*(11), 505–512. doi:10.1016/j.tics.2003.09.012 PMID:14585448.

Bennett, D. S. (2008). Governments, civilians, and the evolution of insurgency: Modeling the early dynamics of insurgencies. *Journal of Artificial Societies and Social Simulation, 11*(4), 7. Retrieved July 16, 2012, from http://jasss.soc.surrey.ac.uk/11/4/7.html

Bersini, H. (2012). UML for ABM. *Journal of Artificial Societies and Social Simulation, 15*(1), 9. Retrieved July 16, 2012, from http://jasss.soc.surrey.ac.uk/15/1/9.html

Bézivin, J., & Muller, P. A. (1999). *A Formal Approach to Use Cases and Their Relationships* (Vol. 618). New York: Springer. Retrieved from http://citeseer.ist.psu.edu/overgaard99formal.html

Biehl, M. (2010). *Literature Study on Model Transformations. Royal Institute of Technology*. Retrieved March 20, 2012, from http://staffwww.dcs.shef.ac.uk/people/A.Simons/remodel/papers/BiehlModelTransformations.pdf

Bigbee, A., Cioffi-Revilla, C., & Luke, S. (2007). *Replication of sugarscape using MASON. Agent-Based Approaches in Economic and Social Complex Systems IV* (pp. 183–190). New York: Springer. doi:10.1007/978-4-431-71307-4_20.

Black, P., Hall, K., Jones, M., Larson, T., & Windley, P. (1996). A brief introduction to formal methods. In *Proceedings of the IEEE Custom Integrated Circuits Conference* (pp. 377–380). San Diego, CA: IEEE. doi: 10.1109/CICC.1996.510579

Bocciarelli, P., D'Ambrogio, A., & Fabiani, G. (2012). A model-driven approach to build hla-based distributed simulations from sysml models.[Rome, Italy: SciTePress.]. *Proceedings of SIMULTECH, 12*, 49–60.

Bonabeau, E. (2002). Agent-based modeling: Methods and techniques for simulating human systems. *Proceedings of the National Academy of Sciences of the United States of America, 99*(Suppl 3), 7280–7287. doi:10.1073/pnas.082080899 PMID:12011407.

Bontkes, T. E. (1993). Dynamics of rural development in southern Sudan. *System Dynamics Review, 9*(1), 1–21. doi:10.1002/sdr.4260090102.

Boutayeb, A., Twizell, E., Achouayb, K., & Chetouani, A. (2004). A mathematical model for the burden of diabetes and its complications. *Biomedical Engineering Online, 3*(20). PMID:15222886.

Box, P. (2002). Integrating geographic information systems and agent-based modeling techniques for simulating social and ecological processes. In Gimblett, H. R. (Ed.), *Spatial units as agents: Making the landscape an equal player in agent-based simulations* (pp. 59–82). Oxford, UK: Oxford University Press.

Bozga, M., Graf, S., Mounier, L., Kerbrat, A., Ober, I., & Vincent, D. (2000). SDL for Real-Time: What Is Missing? SAM'2000. Grenoble, France.

Bozga, M., Graf, S., Mounier, L., Ober, I., Roux, J.-L., & Vincent, D. (2001). Timed Extensions for SDL. In Proceedings of SDL-Forum'01. Copenhagen, Denmark: SDL.

Brade, D. (2000). Enhancing modeling and simulation accreditation by structuring verification and validation results. In J. A. Joines, R. R. Barton, K. Kang, & P. A. Fishwick (Eds.), In *Proceedings of Winter Simulation Conference*. Orlando, FL: ACM.

Brailsford, S. C., Desai, S. M., & Viana, J. (2010). Towards the holy grail: Combining system dynamics and discrete-event simulation in healthcare. In *Proceedings of the 2010 Winter Simulation Conference* (pp. 2293-2303). Los Alamitos, CA: IEEE Computer Society Press.

Braun, T., Gotzhein, R., & Wiebel, M. (2011). Integration of FlexRay into the SDL-Model-Driven Development Approach. In Kraemer, F., & Herrmann, P. (Eds.), *System Analysis and Modeling: About Models* (pp. 56–71). Berlin, Germany: Springer. doi:10.1007/978-3-642-21652-7_4.

Bumiller, E. (2010, 4 26). We have Met the Enemy and He is Powerpoint. *The New York Times*.

Burmeister, B., Haddadi, A., & Mattilys, G. (1997). Application of multi-agent systems in traffic and transportation. In *Software Engineering IEEE Proceedings* (Vol. 114, pp. 51–60). doi: 10.1049/ip-scn:19971023

Burton, R. (1998). Validating and docking: An overview. In Prietula, M., Carley, K., & Gasser, L. (Eds.), *Simulating Organizations: Computational Models of Institutions and Groups*. Menlo Park, CA: AAAI Press.

Cantor, M. (2003, May). Rational Unified Process for Systems Engineering, RUP SE Version 2.0, IBM Rational Software white paper [Computer software manual].

Cardoen, B., Demeulemeester, E., & Beliën, J. (2010). Operating room planning and scheduling: A literature review. *European Journal of Operational Research*, *201*(1), 921–932. doi:10.1016/j.ejor.2009.04.011.

Cardoen, B., Demeulemeester, E., & Bel, J. (2006). *Optimizing a multiple objective surgical case scheduling problem*. Katholieke Universiteit Leuven, Leuven-Belgium.

Carrie, A. (1992). *Simulation of manufacturing systems*. New York: Wiley.

Carson, E. R., & Flood, R. L. (1990). Model Validation: Philosophy, Methodology and Examples. *Trans Inst MC*, *12*(4), 178–185. doi:10.1177/014233129001200404.

Casas, F. I. (2010). Using Specification and Description Language to define and implement discrete simulation models. In Proceedings of the 2010 Summer Simulation Multiconference. Ottawa, Canada: SCS.

Castle, C., & Crooks, A. (2006). Principles and concepts of agent-based modelling for developing geospatial simulations. Working Paper Series, University College London, London, UK. Retrieved July 16, 2012, from http://discovery.ucl.ac.uk/3342/

Castro, R., Kofman, E., & Wainer, G. A. (2008). A formal framework for stochastic DEVS modeling and simulation. In Proceedings of the 2008 Spring Simulation Multiconference (pp. 421-428). Ottawa, Canada: ACM.

Centers for Disease Control and Prevention. (n.d.). Retrieved February 25, 2010, from http://www.cdc.gov/diabetes/statistics/incidence

Cerda, E. De pablos, L., & Rodríguez, M. (2001). La gestión de las listas de espera quirúrgica en España. Ministry of Economy and Finance Institute of Fiscal Studies, Spain.

Chen, D., Theodoropoulos, G., Turner, S., Cai, W., Minson, R., & Zhang, Y. (2008). Large scale agent-based simulation on the grid. *Future Generation Computer Systems*, *24*(7), 658–671. doi:10.1016/j.future.2008.01.004.

Chick, S. E. (2006). Six ways to improve a simulation analysis. *Journal of Simulation*, *1*, 21–28. doi:10.1057/palgrave.jos.4250006.

Chow, A. C. H., & Zeigler, B. P. (1994). Parallel DEVS: a parallel, hierarchical, modular, modeling formalism. In Proceedings of the 26th conference on Winter Simulation (pp. 716–722). Orlando, FL: Society for Computer Simulation International.

CINDERELLA SOFTWARE. (2007). Cinderella SDL. Retrieved March 31, 2009, from http://www.cinderella.dk

Cioffi-Reilla, C. (2010). A methodology for complex social simulations. *Journal of Artificial Societies and Social Simulation, 13*(1), 7. Retrieved July 16, 2012, from http://jasss.soc.surrey.ac.uk/13/1/7.html

Cioffi-Revilla, C., Rogers, J. D., & Latek, M. (2010). The mason householdworlds of pastoral nomad societies. In C. C.-R. K. Takadama, & G. Deffaunt (Eds.), *Simulating interacting agents and social phenomena: The second world congress in social simulation*. Berlin, Germany: Springer. Retrieved July 16, 2012, from http://cs.gmu.edu/~eclab/projects/mason/publications/

Coello, C. C., van Veldhuizen, D. A., & Lamont, G. B. (2002). Evolutionary Algorithms for Solving Multi-Objective Problems. *Genetic Algorithms and Evolutionary Computation, 5*.

Collier, N. (2001). Repast: An extensible framework for agent simulation. *Natural Resources and Environmental Issues, 8*(1), 4. Retrieved July 16, 2012, from http://digitalcommons.usu.edu/nrei/vol8/iss1/4

Damaceanu, R.-C. (2008). An agent-based computational study of wealth distribution in function of resource growth interval using Netlogo. *Applied Mathematics and Computation, 201*(1-2), 371–377. doi:10.1016/j.amc.2007.12.042.

Danaei, G., Friedman, A., Oza, S., Murray, C., & Ezzati, M. (2009). Diabetes prevalence and diagnosis in US states: analysis of health surveys. *Population Health Metrics, 7*(16). PMID:19781056.

Davies, R., Roderick, P., & Raftery, J. (2003). The evaluation of disease prevention and treatment using simulation models. *European Journal of Operational Research, 150*(1), 53–66. doi:10.1016/S0377-2217(02)00783-X.

Dávila, J., & Uzcátegui, M. (2000). GALATEA: A multiagent simulation platform. In *Proceedings of the International Conference on Modeling, Simulation and Neural Networks*. IEEE. Retrieved September 20, 2011, from http://iies.faces.ula.ve/Amse2000/papers/simulation/MSNN-JDMU00.pdf

De la Fuente, P. (n.d.). *Universidad de Valladolid*. Retrieved, from http://jair.lab.fi.uva.es/-pablfue/leng_simulacion/materiales/v_v_0405.pdf

Dean, J., Gumerman, G., Epstein, J., Axtell, R., Swedlund, A., Parker, M., et al. (2000). Understanding Anasazi culture change through agent-based modeling. *Dynamics in human and primate societies: Agent-based modeling of social and spatial processes* (pp. 179–205). Retrieved July 16, 2012, from http://www.santafe.edu/media/workingpapers/98-10-094.pdfdoi: 10.1002/(SICI)1099-0526(199711/12)3:2<16::AID-CPLX4>3.0.CO;2-K

Denton, B., Rahman, A., Nelson, H., & Bailey, A. (2006). Simulation of a multiple operating room surgical suite. In *Proceedings of Winter Simulation Conference*. Monterey, CA: WSC.

Dexter, F., Blake, J., Penning, D., Sloan, B., Chung, P., & Lubarsky, D. (2002). Use of linear programming to estimate impact of changes in a hospital's operating room time allocation on perioperative variable costs. *Anesthesiology, 96*(3), 718–724. doi:10.1097/00000542-200203000-00031 PMID:11873050.

Dexter, F., Macario, A., Lubarsky, D., & Burns, D. (1999). Statistical method to evaluate management strategies to decrease variability in operating room utilization: Application of linear statistical modeling and Monte Carlo simulation to operating room management. *Anesthesiology, 91*(1), 262–274. doi:10.1097/00000542-199907000-00035 PMID:10422952.

Compilation of References

Dexter, F., Macario, A., & O'Neill, L. (2000). Scheduling surgical cases into overflow block time - Computer simulation of the effects of scheduling strategies on operating room labor costs. *Anesthesia and Analgesia, 90*, 980–988. doi:10.1213/00000539-200004000-00038 PMID:10735811.

Dexter, F., Macario, A., & Traub, R. (2003). Operating room utilization alone is not an accurate metric for the allocation of operating room block time to individual surgeons with low caseloads. *Anesthesiology, 98*(5), 1243–1249. doi:10.1097/00000542-200305000-00029 PMID:12717148.

Dijkstra, E. W. (1971). Hierarchical ordering of sequential processes. *Acta Informatica, 1*, 115–138. doi:10.1007/BF00289519.

Dobing, B., & Parsons, J. (2006). How UML is used. *Communications of the ACM, 49*(5), 109–113. doi:10.1145/1125944.1125949.

Doldi, L. (2001). *Sdl illustrated - Visually design executable models*. TRANSMETH SUD OUEST.

Doldi, L. (2003). *Validation of Communications Systems with SDL: The Art of SDL Simulation and Reachability Analysis*. New York: John Wiley & Sons, Inc. doi:10.1002/0470014156.

Dudley, R. (2008). A basis for understanding fishery management dynamics. *System Dynamics Review, 24*(1), 1–29. doi:10.1002/sdr.392.

Dunham, J. B. (2005). An Agent-Based Spatially Explicit Epidemiological Model in MASON. *Journal of Artificial Societies and Social Simulation, 9*(1), 3. Retrieved July 16, 2012, from http://jasss.soc.surrey.ac.uk/9/1/3.html

Duong, D. (2010). Verification, Validation, and Accreditation (VV&A) of Social Simulations. In *Spring Simulation Interoperability Workshop*. Orlando, FL. Retrieved July 16, 2012, from http://www.sisostds.org/DigitalLibrary.aspx?Command=Core_Download&EntryId=29024. Accessed 16 July 2012.

Edmonds, B. (2001). The Use of Models - Making MABS More Informative. In S. Moss., & P. Davidsson (Eds.), Multi-Agent-Based Simulation, Lecture Notes in Computer Science Vol. 1979, 269-282. Berlin, Germany: Springer. doi: doi:10.1007/3-540-44561-7_2.

Edmonds, B. (2006). The Emergence of Symbiotic Groups Resulting from Skill-Differentiation and Tags. *Journal of Artificial Societies and Social Simulation, 9*(1), 10. Retrieved July 16, 2012, from http://jasss.soc.surrey.ac.uk/9/1/10.html

Ehrig, H., Ehrig, K., Ermel, C., Hermann, F., & Taentzer, G. (2007). Information Preserving Bidirectional Model Transformations. In *Fundamental Approaches to Software Engineering* (Vol. *10*, pp. 72–86). Berlin, Germany: Springer-Verlag. doi:10.1007/978-3-540-71289-3_7.

El Hadouaj, S., Drogoul, A., & Espie, S. (2001). How to combine reactivity and anticipation: The case of conflicts resolution in a simulated road traffic. *Multi-Agent-Based Simulation*, 157–167. doi: 10.1007/3-540-44561-7_6

Engels, G., Küster, J. M., Heckel, R., & Groenewegen, L. (2001). *A methodology for specifying and analyzing consistency of object-oriented behavioral models* (Vol. 26). New York: ACM. DOI http://doi.acm.org/10.1145/503271.503235

Engels, G., Kuester, J., & Groenewegen, L. (2002). Consistent interaction of software components. *Journal of Integrated Design & Process Science*, 6(4), 2–22.

Epstein, J. (2008). Why model? *Journal of Artificial Societies and Social Simulation*, 11(4), 12. Retrieved July 16, 2012, from http://jasss.soc.surrey.ac.uk/11/4/12.html

Epstein, G., & Gang, I. (2006). The Influence of Others on Migration Plans. *Review of Development Economics*, 10(4), 652–665. doi:10.1111/j.1467-9361.2006.00340.x.

Epstein, J. M., & Axtell, R. (1996). *Growing artificial societies: Social science from the bottom up*. Washington, DC: Brookings Institution Press.

Espinoza, H., Cancila, D., Selic, B., & Gérard, S. (2009). Challenges in combining SysML and MARTE for model-based design of embedded systems. In *ECMDA-FA (Vol. 5562*, pp. 98–113). New York: Springer. doi:10.1007/978-3-642-02674-4_8.

Esteban Sastre, D. (2010). *Introducción a SDL*. Retrieved December 2010, from http://pegaso.ls.fi.upm.es/~lmengual/telelogic/INTRODUCCION_SDL.pdf

Estefan, J. A. (2008, June). Survey of model-based systems engineering (MBSE) methodologies - revision b [Computer software manual].

Fei, H., Meskenst, N., & Chu, C. (2006). An operating theatre planning and scheduling problem in the case of a block scheduling strategy. In *Proceedings of International Conference on Service Systems and Service Management*. Shanghai, China: IEEE.

Fischer, J., Kühnlenz, F., Ahrens, K., & Eveslage, I. (2009). Model-based Development of Self-organizing Earthquake Early Warning Systems. In I. Troch, & F. Breitenecker (Eds.), Proceedings of MATHMOD 2009. Vienna, Austria: ARGESIM.

Fishman, G. S. (2001). *Discrete-Event Simulation: Modeling, Programming and Analysis*. Berlin, Germany: Springer-Verlag. doi:10.1007/978-1-4757-3552-9.

Fonseca i Casas, P. (2008). SDL distributed simulator. In *Proceedings of Winter Simulation Conference*. Miami, FL: INFORMS.

Fonseca i Casas, P., Colls, M., & Casanovas, J. (2010). Towards a representation of environmenal models using specification and description language. In Proceedings on the International Joint Conference on Knowledge Discovery, Knowledge Engineering and Knowledge Management. Valencia, Spain: Springer.

Fonseca i Casas, P., Colls, M., Casanovas, J., & Josep, C. G. (2010). *Representing Fibonacci function through cellular automata using specification and description language*. Ottawa, Canada.

Fonseca, P. (2008). SDL, a graphical language useful to describe social simulation models. In *Proceedings of the 2nd Workshop on Social Simulation and Artificial Societies Analysis (SSASA'08)*. Barcelona, Spain.

Fonseca, P. (2010). Using Specification and Description Language to define and implement discrete simulation models. In *Summer Simulation Multiconference*. Ottawa, Canada. Retrieved July 16, 2012, from http://hdl.handle.net/2117/8341

Compilation of References

Fonseca, P., Casanovas, J., Monero, J., & Guasch, A. (2011, July). Experiences of Simulation Use in Industrial Projects. In *SCS M&S Magazine*. Retrieved July 16, 2012, from http://scs.org/magazines/2011-07/index_file/Articles.htm

Fonseca, P., Colls, M., & Casanovas, J. (2011). A novel model to predict a slab avalanche configuration using m:n-CAk cellular automata. *Computers, Environment and Urban Systems*, 35(1), 12–24. doi:10.1016/j.compenvurbsys.2010.07.002.

Forrester, J. (1961). *Industrial Dynamics*. Massachutses: Pegasus Communications.

Forrester, J., & Senge, P. (1980). Tests for Building Confidence in System Dynamics Models. In Legasto, A., Forrester, J., & Lyneis, M. (Eds.), *System Dynamics*. Amsterdam: North-Holland.

Fowler, M. (2003). *UML Distilled: A Brief Guide to the Standard Object Modeling Language*. Reading, MA: Pearson Education.

Fowler, M., & Scott, K. (2000). *UML distilled: a brief guide to the standard object modeling language* (2nd ed.). Boston, MA: Addison-Wesley.

Fritzon, P. (2011). *Introduction to Modeling and Simulation of Technical and Physical Systems*. Singapore: IEEE PRESS. doi:10.1002/9781118094259.

Gardner, M. (1970). Mathematical games: The fantastic combinations of John Conway's new solitaire game 'Life'. *Scientific American*, 223(4), 120–123. doi:10.1038/scientificamerican1070-120.

Gilbert, G. (2008). *Agent-based models*. Thousand Oaks, CA: Sage Publications, Inc..

Gilbert, G., & Troitzsch, K. (2005). *Simulation for the social scientist* (2nd ed.). Milton Keynes, UK: Open University Press.

Gilbert, N., & Bankes, S. (2002). Platforms and methods for agent-based modeling. *Proceedings of the National Academy of Sciences of the United States of America*, 99(Suppl 3), 7197–7198. doi:10.1073/pnas.072079499 PMID:12011398.

Gogolla, M., Büttner, F., & Richters, M. (2007). USE: A UML-Based Specification Environment for Validating UML and OCL. *Science of Computer Programming*, 69(1-3), 27–34. doi:10.1016/j.scico.2007.01.013.

Gonçalves, A. S., Rodrigues, A., & Correia, L. (2004). *Multi-agent simulation within geographic information systems*. Paper presented in the 5th Workshop on Agent-Based Simulation. Lisbon, Portugal. Retrieved September 20, 2011, from: http://www.lnec.pt/organizacao/dha/nti/estudos_id/pdfs/AG-oncalvesetal_ABS2004. PDF

Goodchild, M. (2005). GIS and Modeling Overview In D. Maguire, M. Batty, & M. (Eds.) GIS, spatial analysis, and modeling. Redlands, California: Esri Press. doi: 10.1.1.161.9550

Gratch, J., & Marsella, S. (2001). Tears and fears: Modeling emotions and emotional behaviors in synthetic agents. In *Proceedings of the fifth international conference on autonomous agents* (pp. 278–285). doi: 10.1145/375735.376309

Greenough, C. (2010, October). *Proposal to establish a UK Collaborative Computational Project in ABMS*. Retrieved July 16, 2012, from http://www.softeng.rl.ac.uk/abm_ccp

Grieskamp, W., & Lepper, M. (2000). *Using Use Cases in Executable Z*. Washington, DC: IEEE Computer Society.

Grimm, V., Bergerb, U., DeAngelisc, D. L., Polhill, J. G., Giskee, J., & Railsback, S. F. (2010). The ODD protocol: A review and first update. *Ecological Modelling, 221*, 2760–2768. doi:10.1016/j.ecolmodel.2010.08.019.

Grimm, V., Berger, U., Bastiansen, F., Eliassen, S., Ginot, V., & Giske, J. et al. (2006). A standard protocol for describing individual-based and agent-based models. *Ecological Modelling, 198*(1-2), 115–126. doi:10.1016/j.ecolmodel.2006.04.023.

Guasch, A., Piera, M. À., Casanovas, J., & Figueras, J. (2002). *Modelado y simulación*. Barcelona, Spain: Edicions UPC.

Hailegiorgis, A., Kennedy, W., Rouleau, M., Bassett, J., Coletti, M., Balan, G., et al. (2010). An agent based model of climate change and conflict among pastoralists in East Africa. In D. A. Swayne, W. Yang, A. A. Voinov, A. Rizzoli, & T. Filatova (Eds.), In *Proceedings of the International Congress on Environmental Modeling and Software (IEMSS2010)*. Ottawa, Canada.

Hanneman, R. (1988). *Computer-assisted theory building: Modeling dynamic social systems*. Newbury Park, CA: Sage.

Harvey, B. (1997). *Computer science logo style: Symbolic computing* (2nd ed., *Vol. 1-3*). Cambridge, UK: MIT Press.

Hause, M. (2006). *The SysML Modelling Language*. Paper presented at the 15th European Systems Engineering Conference. Edinburgh, Scotland.

Heath, B., Hill, R., & Ciarallo, F. (2009). A Survey of Agent-Based Modeling Practices (January 1998 to July 2008). *Journal of Artificial Societies and Social Simulation, 12*(4), 9. Retrieved July 16, 2012, from http://jasss.soc.surrey.ac.uk/12/4/9.html

Hekimoglu, M., & Barlas, Y. (2010). Sensitivity Analysis of System Dynamics Models by behavior Pattern Measures. *Proceedings of the 28th International Conference of the System Dynamics Society*. Seul.

Hennessy, J. L., Patterson, D. A., & Arpaci-Dusseau, A. C. (2007). *Computer Architecture: A Quantitative Approach*. Burlington, MA: Morgan Kaufmann.

Hocaoglu, M. F., Firat, C., & Sarjoughian, H. S. (2002). DEVS/RAP: Agent-based simulation. In *Proceedings of the 2002 AI, Simulation and Planning in Highly Autonomous Systems Conference*. Lisbon, Portugal: IEEE.

Holvoet, T. (1995). Agents and Petri Nets. In O. Herzog, W. Reisig, & R. Valk (Eds.), Petri Nets Newsletters, 49, 3-8.

Horner, J., & Hirsch, G. (2006). *American Journal of Public Health*, (96): 452–458. PMID:16449591.

Hosking, M., & Sahin, F. (2009). An xml based system of systems discrete event simulation communications framework. In *Springsim '09: Proceedings of the 2009 Spring Simulation Multiconference* (pp. 1–9). San Diego, CA: Society for Computer Simulation International.

Compilation of References

Huang, D., & Sarjoughian, H. (2004). Software and Simulation Modeling for Real-Time Software-Intensive Systems. In Proceedings of the 8th IEEE International Symposium on Distributed Simulation and Real-Time Applications (pp. 196-203). Budapes, Hungary: IEEE.

Huang, E., Ramamurthy, R., & McGinnis, L. (2007). System and simulation modeling using SysML. In *Proceedings of the 2007 Winter Simulation Conference.*(pp. 796-803). Tempe, Arizona: IEEE.

Huhns, M., & Singh, M. (1997). *Readings in agents*. Burlington, MA: Morgan Kaufmann Publishers Inc..

Hwang, M. H., & Zeigler, B. (2009, July). Reachability graph of finite and deterministic devs networks. *Automation Science and Engineering. IEEE Transactions on, 6*(3), 468–478.

IBM. (2009). *TELELOGIC*. Retrieved March 31, 2009, from http://www.telelogic.com/

ISO. (2009, October). *Information technology –open distributed processing– use of UML for ODP system specifications*. Retrieved from ISO/IECCD19793.

ITU-T. (1999). Specification and Description Language (SDL). Retrieved April 2008, from http://www.itu.int/ITU-T/studygroups/com17/languages/index.html

ITU-TS. (1997). *ITU-TS Recommendation Z.120: Message Sequence Chart (MSC)*. Geneva, Switzerland: ITU-TS.

ITU-TS. (2004). *ITU-TS Recommendation Z.120: Message Sequence Chart (MSC)*. Geneva, Switzerland: ITU-T.

Izukura, S., Yanoo, K., Osaki, T., Sakaki, H., Kimura, D., & Xiang, J. (2011). Applying a model-based approach to IT systems development using SysML extension. In *MoDELS* (*Vol. 6981*, pp. 563–577). New York: Springer. doi:10.1007/978-3-642-24485-8_41.

Jacobson, I., Booch, G., & Rumbaugh, J. (1999). *The unified software development process*. Boston, MA: Addison-Wesley.

Jan Pels, H., & Goossenaerts, J. (2007). A Conceptual modeling technique for discrete event simulation of operational processes. In Olhager, J., & Persson, F. (Eds.), *IFIP International Federation for Information Processing* (*Vol. 246*, pp. 305–312). Boston: Springer.

Janssen, M. A. (2009). Understanding artificial Anasazi. *Journal of Artificial Societies and Social Simulation, 12*(4), 13. Retrieved July 16, 2012, from http://jasss.soc.surrey.ac.uk/12/4/13.html

Janssen, M., Alessa, L., Barton, M., Bergin, S., & Lee, A. (2008). Towards a community framework for agent-based modelling. *Journal of Artificial Societies and Social Simulation, 11*(2), 6. Retrieved July 16, 2012, from http://jasss.soc.surrey.ac.uk/11/2/6.html

Jeang, A., & Chiang, A.-J. (2010). Economic and Quality Scheduling for Effective Utilization of Operating Rooms. *Journal of Medical Systems, 34*. PMID:20814721.

Jebali, A., Hadj Alouaneb, A., & Ladeta, P. (2006). Operating rooms scheduling. *International Journal of Production Economics, 99*, 52–62. doi:10.1016/j.ijpe.2004.12.006.

Jensen, K. (1997). *Coloured Petri nets: Basic concepts, analysis methods and practical use* (*Vol. 1-3*). Berlin, Germany: Springer-Verlag. doi:10.1007/978-3-642-60794-3.

411

Kacem, M. H., Jmaiel, M., Kacem, A. H., & Drira, K. (2006). *A UML-based approach for validation of software architecture descriptions* (pp. 158–171). TEAA.

Kahn, R. (2003). Dealing with Complexity in Clinical Diabetes. *Diabetes Care*, 26(11), 3168–3171. doi:10.2337/diacare.26.11.3168 PMID:14578256.

Kapos, G. D., Dalakas, V., Nikolaidou, M., & Anagnostopoulos, D. (2012). (Manuscript submitted for publication). An Integrated Framework for Automated Simulation of SysML Models using DEVS. *Simulation*.

KDeb, K., Pratap, A., Agarwal, S., & Meyarivan, T. (2002). A Fast and Elitist Multi-Objective Genetic Algorithm: NSGA-II. *Evolutionary Computation*, 6.

Kendall, D. (1953). Stochastic Processes Occurring in the Theory of Queues and their Analysis by the Method of the Imbedded Markov Chain. *Annals of Mathematical Statistics*, 24(3), 338–354. doi:10.1214/aoms/1177728975.

Kennedy, R., Xiang, X., Madey, G., & Cosimano, T. (2006). Verification and validation of scientific and economic models.

Kennedy, W., Hailegiorgis, A., Rouleau, M., Bassett, J., Coletti, M., Balan, G., et al. (2010). An agent-based model of conflict in East Africa and the effect of watering holes. In *Proceedings of the 19th Conference on Behavior Representation in Modeling and Simulation (BRIMS)*. Columbia, SC

Kerzhner, A. A., Jobe, J. M., & Paredis, C. J. J. (2011). A formal framework for capturing knowledge to transform structural models into analysis models. *Journal Simulation*, 5(3), 202–216. doi:10.1057/jos.2011.17.

Kerzhner, A. A., & Paredis, C. J. J. (2010). Model-based system verification: A formal framework for relating analyses, requirements, and tests. In *Models in software engineering - Workshops and symposia at MODELS 2010* (pp. 279–292). Berlin, Germany: Springer-Verlag.

Kleppe, A., Warmer, J., & Bast, W. (2003). *MDA Explained: The Model Driven Architecture: Practice and Promise*. Boston, MA: Addison-Wesley.

Klugl, F. (2008). A Validation Methodology for Agent-Based Simulations. In *Proceedings of the 23rd Annual ACM Sysmposium on Applied Computing* (pp. 39-43).New York: ACM. doi: 10.1145/1363686.1363696

Knight, F. (1921). *Risk, Uncertainty, and Profit*. Boston: Houghton Mifflin.

Kofman, E. (2004). Discrete Event Simulation of Hybrid Systems. *SIAM Journal on Scientific Computing*, 25(5), 1771–1797. doi:10.1137/S1064827502418379.

Köhler, M., Langer, R., von Lüde, R., Moldt, D., Rölke, H., & Valk, R. (2007). Socionic multi-agent systems based on reflexive petri nets and theories of social self-organisation. *Journal of Artificial Societies and Social Simulation, 10*(1), 3. Retrieved July 16, 2012, from http://jasss.soc.surrey.ac.uk/10/1/3.html

Kohler, T., & van der Leeuw, S. (2007). *The model-based archaeology of socionatural systems*. Santa Fe, NM: SAR Press.

Koper, R. (2005). Increasing learner retention in a simulated learning network using indirect social interaction. *Journal of Artificial Societies and Social Simulation, 8*(2). Retrieved July 16, 2012, from http://jasss.soc.surrey.ac.uk/8/2/5.html

Kraemer, F., Slåtten, V., & Herrmann, P. (2009). Model-Driven Construction of Embedded Applications Based on Reusable Building Blocks – An Example. In Reed, R., Bilgic, A., & Gotzhein, R. (Eds.), *SDL 2009: Design for Motes and Mobiles (Vol. 5719,* pp. 1–18). Berlin, Germany: Springer. doi:10.1007/978-3-642-04554-7_1.

Kruchten, P. (1998). *Rational Unified Process: An Introduction.* Boston, MA: Addison-Wesley.

Kruchten, P. (1999). *The Rational Unified Process: An introduction.* Boston, MA: Addison-Wesley.

Kusters, R., & Groot, P. (1996). Modelling resource availability in general hospitals – Design and implementation of a decision support model. *European Journal of Operational Research, 88,* 428–445. doi:10.1016/0377-2217(95)00201-4.

Law, A. M. (2007). *Simulation modeling and analysis* (4th ed.). New York: McGraw-Hill.

Law, A. M., & Kelton, W. D. (2000). *Simulation Modeling and Analysis.* New York: McGraw-Hill.

Leigh Tesfatsion. (n.d.). *General Software and Toolkits.* Retrieved July 16, 2012, from http://www2.econ.iastate.edu/tesfatsi/acecode.htm

Leiva Olmos, J., Fonseca, P., & Ocana, J. (2011). Modelling surgical pavilions and a unit of anaesthesia on a chilean hospital using specification and description language. In *Actas de la XIII conferencia española y III encuentro iberoamericano de biometría.* Retrieved July 16, 2012, from http://hdl.handle.net/2117/15525

Leombruni, R., & Richiardi, M. (2006). Laborsim: An agent-based microsimulation of labour supply–An application to Italy. *Computational Economics, 27*(1), 63–88. Retrieved July 16, 2012, from http://papers.ssrn.com/sol3/papers.cfm?abstract_id=868445

Lin, F., & Pai, Y. (2000). Using multi-agent simulation and learning to design new business processes. *Systems, Man and Cybernetics, Part A: IEEE Transactions on Systems and Humans, 30*(3), 380–384. doi:10.1109/3468.844361.

Lingnau, A., & Drobnik, O. (1999). Simulating mobile agent systems with Swarm. In *Proceedings of the First International Symposium on Agent Systems and Applications and Third International Symposium on Mobile Agents* (pp. 272–273). IEEE. doi: 10.1109/ASAMA.1999.805417

Litvak, B., Tyszberowicz, S., & Yehudai, A. (2003). *Behavioral Consistency Validation of UML Diagrams* (Vol. 00). Los Alamitos, CA: IEEE. DOI http://doi.ieeecomputersociety.org/10.1109/SEFM.2003.1236213

Liu, Z., & Araki, K. (2005). *Theoretical Aspects of Computing - ICTAC 2004, First International Colloquium.* Guiyang, China: Springer.

Lo, A., & Mueller, M. (2010). *Cornell University Library.* Retrieved July 20, 2011, from WARNING: Physics Envy May Be Hazardous To Your Wealth!: http://www.arxiv.org/abs/1003.2688

Lowery, J., & Davis, J. (2009). Determination of operating room requirements using simulation. In *Proceedings of Winter Simulation Conference*. Austin, TX: IEEE.

Lozares Colina, C. (2004). La simulacion social,¿una nueva manera de investigar en ciencia social? *Papers: revista de sociologia*, (72), 165–188.

Lucas, C., Buechter, K., Coscia, R., Hurst, J., Meredith, J., & Middleton, J. et al. (2001). Mathematical modeling to define optimum operating room staffing needs for trauma centers. *Journal of the American College of Surgeons*, *192*(5), 559–565. doi:10.1016/S1072-7515(01)00829-8 PMID:11333091.

Luke, S., & Ziparo, V. (2010). Learn to Behave! Rapid Training of Behavior Automata. In *Proceedings of Adaptive and Learning Agents Workshop at AAMAS* (pp. 61–68). Toronto, Canada: AAMAS.

Luke, S., Cioffi-Revilla, C., Panait, L., Sullivan, K., & Balan, G. (2005). Mason: A multiagent simulation environment.[from http://cs.gmu.edu/~eclab/projects/mason/]. *Simulation*, *81*(7), 517. Retrieved July 16, 2012 doi:10.1177/0037549705058073.

Luna, F., & Stefansson, B. (2000). *Economic simulations in Swarm: Agent-based modelling and object oriented programming (Vol. 14)*. New York: Springer. doi:10.1007/978-1-4615-4641-2.

Macal, C. M. (2010). To agent-based simulation from system dynamics. In *Proceedings of the 2010 Winter Simulation Conference* (pp. 371-382). Los Alamitos, California: IEEE Computer Society Press.

Macal, C. M., & North, M. J. (2010). Tutorial on agent-based modelling and simulation. *Journal of Simulation*, *4*, 151–162. doi:10.1057/jos.2010.3.

Madey, G., Freeh, V., & Tynan, R. (2002). Agent-Based Modeling of Open Source using Swarm. In *Americas Conference on Information Systems* (pp. 1472–1475). Dallas, TX. Retrieved from http://www.nd.edu/~oss/Papers/amcis_swarm.pdf

Madhavan, P., Papelis, Y., Kady, R., & Moya, L. (2009). An agent-based model of crowd cognition. In *Proceedings of the 18th Conference on Behavior Representation in Modeling and Simulation* (pp. 139–140). Sundance, UT: Curran Associates, Inc. Retrieved July 16, 2012, from http://brimsconference.org/archives/2009/papers/BRIMS2009_014.pdf

Major, M. (2008). *Heuristik zur personalorientierten Steuerung von komplexen Montagesystemen*. Unpublished doctoral dissertation, University of Dresden, Dresden, Germany.

Martin, G., & Rogardt, H. (2004). Lecture Notes in Computer Science: *Vol. 3273. From Informal to Formal Specifications in UML*. New York: Springer.

McDonald-Maier, K., & Muhammad Yasir, Q. (2009). Data Cache-Energy and Throughput Models: Design Exploration for Embedded Processors. *EURASIP Journal on Embedded Systems*, *2009*, 7.

McGarvey, B., & Hannon, B. (2004). *Modeling Dynamic Systems*. Springer.

McGinnis, L. F., & Ustun, V. (2009). A simple example of SysML-driven simulation. In *Proceedings of Winter Simulation Conference* (pp. 1703–1710). Austin, TX: WSC.

Compilation of References

Menendez, M., & Collado, S. (2007). Simu-lación de procesos sociales basada en agentes software. *EMPIRIA. Revista de Metodología de Ciencias Sociales, 14*, 139–161. Retrieved July 16, 2012, from http://dialnet.unirioja.es/servlet/articulo?codigo=2536607

Mens, T. (2010). Model Transformation: A Survey of the State-of-the-Art. In Gerard, S., Babau, J., & Champeau, J. (Eds.), *Model Driven Engineering for Distributed Real-Time Embedded Systems* (pp. 18–36). New York: John Wiley & Sons.

Meseth, N., Kirchhof, P., & Witte, T. (2009). Xml-based devs modeling and interpretation. In *Springsim '09: Proceedings of the 2009 Spring Simulation Multiconference* (pp. 1–9). San Diego, CA: Society for Computer Simulation International.

Meyer, B. (1992). *Applying Design by Contract (Vol. 25)*. Washington, DC: IEEE.

MG. (2007). *SysML Plugin for Magic Draw* [Computer software manual]. Magic Draw.

Michalski, R., Carbonell, J., & Mitchell, T. (1985). *Machine learning: An artificial intelligence approach (Vol. 1)*. Burlington, MA: Morgan Kaufmann.

Miller, J., & Murkerji, J. (2003). *MDA Guide Version 1.0.1. Object Management Group.* Retrieved March 20, 2012, from http://www.omg.org/news/meetings/workshops/UML_2003_Manual/00-2_MDA_Guide_v1.0.1.pdf

Millington, J., Romero-Calcerrada, R., Wainwright, J., & Perry, G. (2008). An agent-based model of mediterranean agricultural land-use/cover change for examining wildfire risk. *Journal of Artificial Societies and Social Simulation, 11*(4), 4. Retrieved July 16, 2012, from http://jasss.soc.surrey.ac.uk/11/4/4.html

Minar, N., Burkhart, R., Langton, C., & Askenazi, M. (1996). *The swarm simulation system: A toolkit for building multi-agent simulations.* Working Papers No. 96-06-042. Sante Fe, CA: Santa Fe Institute.

Ministerio de Salud de Chile. (2009). *Compromisos de Gestión.* Viña del Mar.

Ministerio de Salud de Chile. (2009). *Producción Anual.* Hospital Dr. Gustavo Fricke, Viña del Mar.

Mittal, S., Risco-Mart'ın, J. L., & Zeigler, B. P. (2007). Devsml: Automating devs execution over soa towards transparent simulators. In *DEVS Symposium, Spring Simulation Multiconference* (pp. 287–295). Norfolk, VA: ACIMS Publications.

Mittal, S., Risco-Mart'ın, J. L., & Zeigler, B. P. (2009). Devs/soa: A cross-platform framework for net-centric modeling and simulation in devs unified process. *Simulation, 85*(7), 419–450. doi:10.1177/0037549709340968.

Modelica Association. (2005). *Modelica language specification.* Linköping, Sweden.

Moldt, D., & Wienberg, F. (1997). Multi-agent systems based on coloured Petri Nets. In Azéma, P., & Balbo, G. (Eds.), *LNCS 1248: Application and theory of Petri Nets* (pp. 82–101). Berlin, Germany: Springer. doi:10.1007/3-540-63139-9_31.

Molloy, M. K. (1981). *On the integration of delay and throughput measures in distributed processing models.* PhD thesis, University of California, Los Angeles.

Morecroft, J., & Robinson, S. (2006). Comparing discrete event simulation and system dynamics: Modelling a fishery. In *Proceedings of the 2006 OR Society Simulation Workshop* (pp. 137-148). Birmingham, UK: OR Society.

Morecroft, J. (2007). *Strategic Modelling and Business Dynamics. A feedback systems approach*. Chichester: John Wiley & Sons Inc..

Moss, S., & Edmonds, B. (2003). S*ociology and simulation: Statistical and qualitative crossvalidation*. (Tech. Rep. No. 03105. Retrieved July 16, 2012, from http://cfpm. org/cpmrep105.html

Moss, S., Edmonds, B., & Wallis, S. (1997). *Validation and Verification of Computational Models with Multiple Cognitive Agents*. Discussion Papers No. 97-25. Manchester Metropolitan University, UK. Retrieved July 16, 2012, from http://ideas.repec.org/p/wuk/mcpmdp/9725.html

Moss, S. (2001). Messy Systems - The Target for Multi Agent Based Simulation. In Moss, S., & Davidsson, P. (Eds.), *Multi-Agent-Based Simulation* (*Vol. 1979*, pp. 1–14). Berlin, Germany: Springer. doi:10.1007/3-540-44561-7_1.

Nance, R. (1994). The conical methodology and the evolution of simulation model development. *Annals of Operations Research*, *53*(1), 1–45. doi:10.1007/BF02136825.

Narayanan, A., & Karasai, G. (2008). Verifying Model Transformations by Structural Correspondence. In, *Proceedings of the 7th International Workshop on Graph Transformation and Visual Modeling Techniques*. Retrieved March 20, 2012, from http://paperc.de/20384-verifying-model-transformations-by-structural-correspondence-9773186321795#!/pages/1

Neumann, K., & Schwindt, C. (1997). Activity-on-node networks with minimal and maximal time lags and their application to make-to-order production.[Berlin, Germany: Springer Verlag.]. *OR-Spektrum*, *19*, 205–217. doi:10.1007/BF01545589.

Nikolai, C., & Madey, G. (2009). Tools of the trade: A survey of various agent based modeling platforms. *Journal of Artificial Societies and Social Simulation*, *12*(2), 2. Retrieved July 16, 2012, from http://jasss. soc.surrey.ac.uk/12/2/2.html

Nikolai, C., & Madey, G. (2011). *Comparison of agent-based modelling software*. Retrieved from http://en.wikipedia.org/wiki/Comparison_of_agent-based_modeling_software

Nikolaidou, M., Dalakas, V., & Anagnostopoulos, D. (2010). Integrating Simulation Capabilities in SysML using DEVS. In *IEEE International Systems Conference (SysCon 2010)*. San Diego, CA: IEEE Computer Society.

Nikolaidou, M., Dalakas, V., Mitsi, L., Kapos, G.-D., & Anagnostopoulos, D. (2008). A SysML Profile for Classical DEVS Simulators. In Proceedings of Software Engineering Advances, 2008. ICSEA'08. Sliema, Malta.

Nikolaidou, M., Kapos, G.-D., Dalakas, V., & Anagnostopoulos, D. (2012). Basic Guidelines for Simulating SysML Models: An Experience Report. In *Proceedings Of 7th International Conference on System of Systems Engineering*. Genova, Italy: IEEE.

Nikolaidou, M., Tsadimas, A., Alexopoulou, N., & Anagnostopoulos, D. (2009). Employing Zachman Enterprise Architecture Framework to systematically perform Model-Based System Engineering Activities. *Proceedings of*, *HICSS-42*, 1–10.

Niu, Q., Peng, Q., ElMekkawy, T., Tan, Y. Y., Bryant, H., & Bernaerdt, L. (2007). Performance analysis of the operating room using simulation. *The Canadian Design Engineering Network (CDEN) and the Canadian Congress on Engineering Education (CCEE)*, *38*. Winnipeg, Canada.

Compilation of References

Noche, B., & Wenzel, S. (2000). *The new simulation in production and logistics. Prospects, views and attitudes*. Paper presented at 9. ASIM-Fachtagung Simulation in Produktion und Logistik. Berlin, Germany.

Nolan, B., Brown, B., Balmelli, L., Bohn, T., & Wahli, U. (2008). Model driven systems development with rational products [Computer software manual].

NoMagic. (2013). *MagicDraw UML*. Retrieved January 2013 from http://www.magicdraw.com

North, M., Sallach, D., & Macal, C. (Eds.). In Proceedings of Agent2005: Generative Social Processes, Models, and Mechanism (pp. 177–192). Chicago, IL: Argonne National Laboratory.

North, M. J., & Macal, C. M. (2007). *Managing business complexity: Discovering strategic solutions with agent-based modeling and simulation*. Oxford, UK: Oxford University Press.

North, M., Collier, N., & Vos, J. (2006). Experiences creating three implementations of the repast agent modeling toolkit. [TOMACS]. *ACM Transactions on Modeling and Computer Simulation, 16*(1), 1–25. doi:10.1145/1122012.1122013.

North, M., & Macal, C. (2002). *The beer dock: Three and a half implementations of the beer distribution game*. Swarmfest.

North, M., & Macal, C. (2005). In Komosinski, M. (Ed.), *Artificial life models in software* (pp. 115–141). Heidelberg, Germany: Springer. doi:10.1007/1-84628-214-4_6.

Nutaro, J. J. (2011). *Building Software for Simulation: Theory and Algorithms with Applications in C*. Hoboken, NJ: John Wiley & Sons.

Object Management Group. (2010). *Business Process Model and Notation (BPMN) version 2.0*. Retrieved September 20, 2011, from http://www.bpmn.org

OCL language. (2003). http://www.omg.org

Odell, J., Parunak, H., & Bauer, B. (2000) Extending UML for agents. In *Proceedings of the Agent-Oriented Information Systems Workshop* (pp. 3–17).

Oestereich, B. (2006). *Analyse und Design mit UML 2.1*. München, Germany: Oldenbourg Verlag.

OMG. (2003). *UML specification*. Retrieved from http://www.omg.org

OMG. (2003, June). *Model Driven Architecture. Version 1.0.1*. Retrieved from http://www.omg.org/cgi-bin/doc?omg/03-06-01.pdf

OMG. (2007). *Meta Object Facility (MOF) 2.0 Query/View/Transformation Specification*. Retrieved November 15, 2012, from http://www.omg.org/cgi-bin/doc?ptc/2007-07-07

OMG. (2007, September). *Systems Modeling Language (SYSML) Specification. Version 1.0*.

OMG. (2007). *UML Superstructure Specification, Version 2.1.2*.

OMG. (2007). *XML Metadata Interchange*. Retrieved January 2013 from http://www.omg.org/spec/XMI/2.1.1/PDF/index.htm.

OMG. (2009). *UML profile for MARTE: Modeling and analysis of real-time embedded systems specification, version 1.0*.

OMG. (2010). *SysML and Modelica Integration*. Retrieved from http://www.omgwiki.org/OMGSysML/doku.php?id=sysml-modelica:sysml_and_modelica_integration

OMG. (2010). *SysML Specification Version 1.2*. Retrieved March 20, 2012, from http://www.omg.org/spec/SysML/1.2/

OMG. (2010). *Systems Modeling Language (SYSML) Specification, Version 1.2.*

Onggo, B. S. S. (2010). Running Agent-Based Models on a Discrete-Event Simulator. In *Proceedings of the 24th European Simulation and Modelling Conference* (pp. 51-55). Hasselt, Belgium: Eurosis-ETI.

Onggo, B. S. S. (2012). BPMN pattern for agent-based simulation model representation. In *Proceedings of the 2012 Winter Simulation Conference*. Berlin, Germany. IEEE Computer Society Press.

Onggo, B. S. S., & Karpat, O. (2011). Agent-based conceptual model representation using BPMN. In *Proceedings of the 2011 Winter Simulation Conference* (pp. 671-682). Phoenix, AZ: IEEE Computer Society Press.

Onggo, B. S. S. (2010). Methods for Conceptual Model Representation. In Robinson, S., Brooks, R., Kotiadis, K., & van der Zee, D.-J. (Eds.), *Conceptual Modelling for Discrete-Event Simulation* (pp. 337–354). Boca Raton, FL: Taylor and Francis. doi:10.1201/9781439810385-c13.

Open Source Modelica Consortium (OSMC). (2009). *ModelicaML - A UML Profile for Modelica*. Retrieved from http://www.openmodelica.org/index.php/developer/tools/134

OpenModelica. (2013). *OpenModelica*. Retrieved January 2013 from http://www.openmodelica.org/index.php/developer/tools/134

Orcutt, G. (1957). A new type of socio-economic system. *The Review of Economics and Statistics, 39*(2), 116–123. doi:10.2307/1928528.

Ormerod, P., & Rosewell, B. (2009). Validation and Verification of Agent-Based Models in the Social Sciences. In F. Squazzoni (Ed.), *Epistemilogical Aspects of Comuter Simulation in the Social Sciences, Second International Workshop, EPOS 2006* (Vol. 5466, pp. 130-140). Berlin, Germany: Springer-Verlag. doi: 10.1007/978-3-642-01109-2_10

Owre, S., Shankar, N., Rushby, J. M., & Stringer-Calvert, D. W. J. (2001). *PVS System Guide 2.4*. Menlo Park, CA: SRI International.

Paci, G., F. P., Benini, L., & Marchal, P. (2007). Exploring temperature-aware design in low-power MPSoCs. *International Journal of Embedded Systems, 3.*

Paige, R. F., Jonathan, S. O., & Phillip, J. B. (2002). *Checking the Consistency of Collaboration and Class Diagrams using "PVS*. London: British Computer Society.

Paredis, C. J. J., & Johnson, T. (2008). Using OMG'S SYSML to support simulation. In S. J. Mason, R. R. Hill, L. Mönch, O. Rose, T. Jefferson, & J. W. Fowler (Eds.), *Proceedings of Winter Simulation Conference* (pp. 2350–2352). Miami, FL: IEEE.

Paredis, C. J. J., Bernard, Y., Koning, R. M. B. H.-D., & Friedenthal, S. (2010). An overview of the SysML-Modelica transformation specification. *Jet Propulsion, 2*, 14.

Pavon, J., Arroyo, M., Hassan, S., & Sansores, C. (2008). Agent-based modelling and simulation for the analysis of social patterns. *Pattern Recognition Letters, 29*(8), 1039–1048. doi:10.1016/j.patrec.2007.06.021.

Peak, R., Burkhart, R., Friedenthal, S., Wilson, M., Bajaj, M., & Kim, I. (2007). Simulation-based design using sysml part 1: A parametrics primer. In *Incose International Symposium* (pp. 1–20). San Diego, CA: INCOSE.

Compilation of References

Peak, R., Paredis, C. J., & Tamburini, D. R. (2005). *The composable object (cob) knowledge representation: Enabling advanced collaborative engineering environments (cees), cob requirements & objectives (v1.0) (Technical Report)*. Atlanta, GA: Georgia Institute of Technology.

Pelánek, R. (2008). Fighting state space explosion: Review and evaluation. *Proc. of Formal Methods for industrial Critical Systems*.

Persson, M., & Persson, J. (2009). Health economic modelling to support surgery management at a Swedish hospital. *Omega, 37*(4). doi:10.1016/j.omega.2008.05.007 PMID:20161166.

Peterson, J. L. (1980). A note on colored Petri nets. *Information Processing Letters, 11,* 40–43. doi:10.1016/0020-0190(80)90032-0.

Petri, C. A. (1962). *Kommunikation mit Automaten*. PhD Thesis, University of Bonn, Germany.

Pidd, M. (2003). *Tools for Thinking: Modelling in Management Science* (2nd ed.). Chichester, UK: Wiley.

Pidd, M. (2010). Why modelling and model use matter. *The Journal of the Operational Research Society, 61*(1), 14–24. doi:10.1057/jors.2009.141.

Pielok, T. (1995). *Prozesskettenmodulation – Management von Prozessketten mit Hilfe von Logistic Function Deployment*. Dortmund, Germany: Verlag Praxiswissen.

Piepper, D., Röttgers, C., & Gruhn, V. (2006). *MDA: effektives Software-Engineering mit UML 2 und Eclipse*. Berlin, Germany: Springer Verlag.

Polhill, J. G., Parker, D., Brown, D., & Grimm, V. (2008). Using the ODD Protocol for Describing Three Agent-Based Social Simulation Models of Land-Use Change. *Journal of Artificial Societies and Social Simulation, 11*(2), 3. Retrieved July 16, 2012, from http://jasss.soc.surrey.ac.uk/11/2/3.html

Pons, C., Giandini, R., Baum, G., Garbi, J. L., & Mercado, P. (2003). *Specification and checking of dependence relations between UML models*. Hershey, PA: IGI Global.

Pörnbacher, C. (2010). *Modellgetriebene Entwicklung der Steuerungssoftware automatisierter Fertigungssysteme*. Munich, Germany: Herbert Utz Verlag.

PragmaDev SARL. (2006). *SDL-RT standard V2.2*. Paris: Standard, PragmaDev SARL.

PragmaDev SARL. (2012). Retrieved from http://www.pragmadev.com/product/code-Generation.html

Railsback, S., Lytinen, S., & Jackson, S. (2006). Agent-based simulation platforms: Review and development recommendations. *Simulation, 82*(9), 609–623. doi:10.1177/0037549706073695.

Reed, R. (2000). Re: SDL-News: Request for Help: Initialisation of Pids. Retrieved April 2009, from http://www.sdl-forum.org/Archives/SDL/0032.html

Reed, R. (2000). SDL-2000 form New Millenium Systems. Telektronikk 4.2000, 20-35.

Reed, R. (2000). SDL-2000 new presentation. Retrieved June 18, 2012, from http://www.sdl-forum.org/sdl2000present/index.htm

Reggio, G., Cerioli, M., & Astesiano, E. (2001). *Towards a Rigorous Semantics of UML Supporting Its Multiview Approach.* London: Springer-Verlag. doi:10.1007/3-540-45314-8_13.

Reisig, W. (2010). *Petrinetze - Modellierung, Analyse, Fallstudien.* Wiesbaden, Germany: Vieweg-Teubner Verlag. doi:10.1007/978-3-8348-9708-4.

Resnick, M. (1994). *Turtles, Termites and Traffic Jams: Explorations in Massively Parallel Microworlds.* Cambridge, MA: MIT Press.

Richardson, G. P. (1976). Problems with Causal Loop Diagrmas. *System Dynamics Review, 2*(2), 158–170. doi:10.1002/sdr.4260020207.

Richiardi, M., Leombruni, R., Saam, N. J., & Sonnessa, M. (2006). A common protocol for agent-based social simulation. *Journal of Artificial Societies and Social Simulation, 9*(1), 15. Retrieved July 16, 2012, from http://jasss.soc.surrey.ac.uk/9/1/15.html

Richmond, B. (1994). System Dynamics/Systems Thinking: Let's Just Get On With It. *International Systems Dynamics Conference.* Sterling.

Rico, R., & Martínez, S. (2008). *Gestiopolis. com.* Retrieved July 1, 2010, from http://www.gestiopolis.com/administracion-estrategia/lenguaje-de-modelacion-en-sistemas.htm#mas-autor

Risco-Mart'ın, J. L., & Mittal, S. L'opez-Pen˜a, M. A., & Cruz, J. M. de la. (2007). A w3c xml schema for devs scenarios. In *Springsim '07: Proceedings of the 2007 Spring Simulation Multiconference* (pp. 279–286). San Diego, CA: Society for Computer Simulation International.

Risco-Mart'ın, J. L., De La Cruz, J. M., Mittal, S., & Zeigler, B. P. (2009). Eudevs: Executable uml with devs theory of modeling and simulation. *Simulation, 85*(11-12), 750–777. doi:10.1177/0037549709104727.

Robinson, S. (1997). Simulation model verification and validation: Increasing the users' confidence. In *Proceedings of the 29th Conference on Winter Simulation* (pp. 53–59). Atlanta, GA: IEEE.doi: 10.1145/268437.268448

Robinson, S. (2008). Conceptual modelling for simulation Part I: Definition and requirements. *The Journal of the Operational Research Society, 59*(3), 278–290. doi:10.1057/palgrave.jors.2602368.

Robinson, S. (2010). Conceptual modelling for simulation: Definition and requirements. In Robinson, S., Brooks, R., Kotiadis, K., & van der Zee, D.-J. (Eds.), *Conceptual Modelling for Discrete-Event Simulation* (pp. 235–256). Boca Raton, FL: Taylor and Francis. doi:10.1201/9781439810385-c1.

Robinson, S., & Pidd, M. (1998). Provider and customer expectations of successful simulation projects. *The Journal of the Operational Research Society, 49*(3), 200–209.

Rodríguez-Cayetano, M. (2011). Design and Development of a CPU Scheduler Simulator for Educational Purposes Using SDL. In *System Analysis and Modeling: About Models (Vol. 6598,* pp. 72–90). Oslo, Norway: Springer. doi:10.1007/978-3-642-21652-7_5.

Rosenberg, D., & Mancarella, S. (2009). *Embedded Systems Development* using *SysML. Sparx Systtems.* Retrieved March 20, 2012, from http://www.sparxsystems.com/downloads/ebooks/Embedded_Systems_Development_using_SysML.pdf

Compilation of References

Rossiter, S., Noble, J., & Bell, K. R. (2010). Social simulations: Improving interdisciplinary understanding of scientific positioning and validity. *Journal of Artificial Societies and Social Simulation, 13*(10), 1. Retrieved March 8, 2012, from http://jasss.soc.surrey.ac.uk/13/1/10.html

Rouleau, M., Coletti, M., Bassett, J., Hailegiorgis, A., Gulden, T., & Kennedy, W. (2009). Conflict in complex socio-natural systems: Using agent-based modeling to understand the behavioral roots of social unrest within the mandera triangle. In *Proceedings of the Human Behavior-Computational Modeling and Interoperability Conference 2009*. Oak Ridge, TN.

Roussopoulos, N., & Karagiannis, D. (2009). Conceptual modeling: Past, present and the continuum of the future. In Borgida, A., Chaudhri, V., Giorgini, P., & Yu, E. (Eds.), *Conceptual Modeling: Foundations and Applications* (*Vol. 5600*, pp. 139–152). Berlin, Germany: Springer. doi:10.1007/978-3-642-02463-4_9.

Rubio, X. (2009). *Modelitzacio i simulació aplicades a la recerca i interpretació de camps de batalla*. Unpublished doctoral dissertation, Universitat de Barcelona, Barcelona, Spain. Retrieved July 16, 2012, from http://hdl.handle.net/10803/1339

Rubio, X., & Cela, J. (2010). Large-scale agent-based simulation in archaeology: An approach using high-performance computing. In Computer Applications in Archaeology. Granada, Spain.

Rudolph, E., Grabowski, J., & Graubmann, P. (1999). Towards a Harmonization of UML-Sequence Diagrams and MSC. In Dssouli, R., Bochmann, G. V., & Lahav, Y. (Eds.), *SDL'99 - The Next Millenium*. Bochum, Germany: Elsevier. doi:10.1016/B978-044450228-5/50014-X.

Rumbaught, J., Jacobson, I., & Booch, G. (2004). *The Unifield Modeling Language Reference Manual*. Boston, MA: Addison-Wesley.

Russell, S., & Norvig, P. (2010). *Artificial intelligence: A modern approach*. Upper Saddle River, NJ: Prentice Hall.

Saaltink, M. (1997). *The Z/EVES System* (pp. 72–85). Berlin, Germany: Springer-Verlag.

Sánchez, M. A. (2011). Using System Dynamics to Assess the Role of Socio-economic Status in Tuberculosis Incidence. In B. Gilles, A. Pardo, & G. Schneider (Ed.), *Lecture Notes in Computer Science: 9th International Conference on Software Engineering and Formal Methods, Special Track on Modelling for Sustainable Development. 7041*, pp. 464-475. Berlin/Heidelberg: Springer-Verlag.

Sargent, R. (2005). Verification and validation of simulation models. In *Proceedings of the 37th Winter Simulation Conference* (pp. 130–143). doi: 10.1109/WSC.2005.1574246

Sargent, R. G. (2007). Verification and validation of simulation models. In S. G. Henderson, B. Biller, M.-H. Hsieh, J. Shortle, J. D. Tew, & R. R. Barton (Eds.), *Proceedings of the 2007 Winter Simulation Conference*. Washinton, DC: IEEE.

Saucier, R. (2000). *Computer Generation of Statistical Distributions*. Retrieved from http://ftp.arl.mil/random/

Schatten, A., Biffl, S., Demolsky, M., & Gostischa-Franta, E. A-Streicher, T., & Winkler, D. (2010). Best Practice Software-Engineering: Eine praxiserprobte Zusammenstellung von komponentenorientierten Konzepten, Methoden und Werkzeugen. Spektrum. Heidelberg, Germany: Akademischer Verlag.

Schelling, T. (1971). Dynamic models of segregation. *The Journal of Mathematical Sociology, 1*(2), 143–186. doi:10.1080/002 2250X.1971.9989794.

Schlosser, A., Voss, M., & Bruckner, L. (2005). On the simulation of global reputation systems. *Journal of Artificial Societies and Social Simulation, 9*(1), 4. Retrieved July 16, 2012, from http://jasss.soc.surrey.ac.uk/9/1/4.html

Schonherr, O., & Rose, O. (2009). First steps towards a general SysML model for discrete processes in production systems. In *Proceedings of the 2009 Winter Simulation Conference* (pp. 1711–1718). Austin, TX: WSC.

Schruben, L. W. (1980). Establishing the Credibility of Simulations. *Simulation, 34*(3), 101–105. doi:10.1177/0037549780 03400310.

Seemann, J., & Gudenberg, J. (2006). *Softwareentwurf mit UML 2.2.* Heidelberg, Germany: Springer-Verlag.

Seidel, U. A. (1998). *Verfahren zur Generierung und Gestaltung von Montageablaufstrukturen komplexer Erzeugnisse.* Berlin, Germany: Springer-Verlag.

Senge, P. (1990). *The fifth discipline: the art and practice of the learning organization.* New York: Doubleday/Curency.

Serenko, A. & B., D. (2002). *Agent toolkits: A general overview of the market and an assessment of instructor satisfaction with utilizing toolkits in the classroom.* Working Paper No. 455. Hamilton, Canada: McMaster University.

Shannon, R. (1976). Simulation modeling and methodology. In *Proceedings of the 76 Bicentennial Conference on Winter Simulation* (pp. 9–15). Gaithersburg, MD. Retrieved July 16, 2012, from http://informs-sim.org/wsc76papers/prog76sim.html

Shaw, B., & Marshall, A. (2007). Modelling the flow of congestive heart failure patients through a hospital system. *The Journal of the Operational Research Society, 58*, 212–218.

Sibbel, R., & Urban, C. (2001). *Agent-Based Modeling and Simulation for Hospital Management.* Dordrecht, The Netherlands: Kluwer Academic Publishers.

Siebers, P. O., Macal, C. M., Garnett, J., Buxton, D., & Pidd, M. (2010). Discrete-event simulation is dead, long live agent-based simulation! *Journal of Simulation, 4*, 204–210. doi:10.1057/jos.2010.14.

Silva, M., & Valette, R. (1989). Lecture Notes in Computer Science: *Vol. 424. Petri nets and flexible manufacturing* (pp. 374–417).

Soon-Kyeong, K., & David, C. (2004). A Formal Object-Oriented Approach to defining Consistency Constraints for UML Models. In *Proceedings of Australian Software Engineering Conference (ASWEC'2004)*. Melbourne, Australia. IEEE.

Sörrle, H. (2005). *UML 2 für Studenten.* München, Germany: Pearson Verlag.

Spivey, J. M. (1992). *The Z Notation: A Reference Manual.* Upper Saddle River, NJ: Prentice Hall.

Starlogo, T. (n.d.). Retrieved July 16, 2012, from http://ccl.northwestern.edu/cm/starlogot/

Compilation of References

Steins, K., & Persson, F. (2010). Increasing Utilization in a Hospital Operating Department Using Simulation Modeling. *Simulation*, *86*(8-9), 463–480. doi:10.1177/0037549709359355.

Sterman, J. (2000). *Business dynamics: Systems thinking and modeling for a complex world*. New York: McGraw-Hill.

Stewart, I. (1989). *Does god play dice? The new mathematics of caos*. Hoboken, NJ: Blackwell Publishing.

Strader, T., Lin, F., & Shaw, M. (1998). Simulation of order fulfillment in divergent assembly supply chains. *Journal of Artificial Societies and Social Simulation, 1*(2), 36–37. Retrieved July 16, 2012, from http://jasss.soc.surrey.ac.uk/1/2/5.html

Su, Y., & Shen, N. (2010). Modeling the Effects of Information Quality on Process Performance in Operating Room. In *Proceedings of 12th International Conference on Computer Modelling and Simulation*. Cambridge, UK: IEEE.

Swarm development group. (n.d.). Retrieved July 16, 2012, from http://www.swarm.org/ Terna, P. (1998). Simulation tools for social scientists: Building agent based models with swarm. *Journal of Artificial Societies and Social Simulation, 1*(2), 1–12. Retrieved July 16, 2012, from http://jasss.soc.surrey.ac.uk/1/2/4.html

Tamburini, D. (2006). *Defining executable design & simulation models using sysml*. Paper presented at Frontiers in Design & Simulation Research Workshop. Atlanta, GA.

Tamburini, D. R. (2006). *Defining Executable Design & Simulation Models using SysML*. Retrieved from http://www.pslm.gatech.edu/topics/sysml/

Telecommunication standardization sector of ITU. (1999). *Specification and Description Language (SDL)*. Retrieved April 2010, from http://www.itu.int/ITU-T/studygroups/com17/languages/index.html

Tesfatsion, L. (2006). Agent-based Computational Economics: A Constructive Approach to Economic Theory. In L. Tesfatsion, & K. Judd (Eds.), *Handbook of Computational Economics: Agent-based Computational Economics* (pp. 831-880). Amsterdam, The Netherlands: North Holland. Retrieved July 16, 2012, from http://www.econ.iastate.edu/research/books-and-chapters/p7004 Accessed 16 July 2012.

Tesfatsion, L. (2002). Agent-based computational economics: Growing economies from the bottom up. *Artificial Life*, *8*(1), 55–82. doi:10.1162/106454602753694765 PMID:12020421.

Thompson, K., & Duintjer Tebbens, R. (2008). Using system dynamics to develop policies that matter: global management of poliomyelitis and beyond. *System Dynamics Review*, *24*(4), 433–449. doi:10.1002/sdr.419.

Tisue, S., & Wilensky, U. (2004). Netlogo: A simple environment for modeling complexity. In *Proceedings of the International Conference on Complex Systems* (pp. 16–21). Boston, MA.

Tobias, R., & Hofmann, C. (2004). Evaluation of free java-libraries for social-scientific agent based simulation. *Journal of Artificial Societies and Social Simulation, 7*(1). Retrieved July 16, 2012, from http://jasss.soc.surrey.ac.uk/7/1/6.html

Topçu, O., Adak, M., & Oguztüzün, H. (2008). A metamodel for federation architectures. *ACM Transactions on Modeling and Computer Simulation, 18*(3), 10:1–10:29.

Troitzsch, K. (1997). Social science simulation - Origins, prospects, purposes. In R. Conte, H. R., & P. Terna (Eds.), Simulating Social Phenomena (Vol. 456, pp.41-54). Berlin, Germany: Springer- Verlag.

Tsadimas, A., Nikolaidou, M., & Anagnostopoulos, D. (2009). Handling non-functional requirements in information system architecture design. In ICSEA '09 (p. 59-64).

Tsadimas, A., Nikolaidou, M., & Anagnostopoulos, D. (2012). Extending SysML to explore non- functional requirements description and verification: The case of information system design. In *Requirements Engineering Track - 27th ACM Symposium on Applied Computing - SAC12*. Trento, Italy. ACM.

Tsadimas, A., Nikolaidou, M., & Anagnostopoulos, D. (2010). Evaluating software architecture in a model- based approach for enterprise information system design. In *SHARK '10* (pp. 72–79). New York: ACM. doi:10.1145/1833335.1833346.

Tutorial, S. D. L. (n.d.). IEC International Engineering Consortium. Retrieved January 2009, from http://www.iec.org/online/tutorials/sdl/

UK Prospective Diabetes Study Group. (1998). Effect of intensive blood glucose control policy with metformin on complications in type 2 diabetes patients. *Lancet, 352,* 864–865.

United Nations Environment Programme (2009). Buildings and Climate Change: Summary for Decision Makers.

van der Leeuw, S. (2004). Why model? *Cybernetics and Systems, 35*(2-3), 117–128. doi:10.1080/01969720490426803.

Van der Zee, D. J. (2009). Building insightful simulation models using formal approaches – A case study on Petri Nets. In *Proceedings of the 2009 Winter Simulation Conference* (pp. 886-898). Austin, TX: IEEE Computer Society Press.

Vangheluwe, H. (2000). DEVS as a common denominator for multi-formalism hybrid systems modelling. In Proceedings of IEEE International Symposium on Computer-Aided Control System Design (pp. 129–134). Anchorage, AK: IEEE.

Vidgen, R., & Padget, J. (2009). Sendero: An extended, agent-based implementation of Kauffman's NKCS model. *Journal of Artificial Societies and Social Simulation, 12*(4), 8. Retrieved July 16, 2012, from http://jasss.soc.surrey.ac.uk/12/4/8.html

Villatoro, D., & Sabater-Mir, J. (2008). Mechanisms for social norms support in virtual societies. In *Proceedings of the 5th conference of the European Social Simulation Association (ESSA08),* Brescia, Italy. Available from the author.

Compilation of References

Von Neumann, J. (1966). *Theory of self-re-producing automata* (Burks, A., Ed.). Urbana, IL: University of Illinois Press.

Wainer, G. A., & Giambiasi, N. (2001). *Timed cell-devs: modeling and simulation of cell spaces*. Retrieved from http://cell-devs.sce.carleton.ca/publications/2001/WG01b

Wainer, G. A. (2009). *Discrete-Event Modeling and Simulation: A Practitioner's Approach*. Boca Raton, FL: CRC Press. doi:10.1201/9781420053371.

Wainer, G. A., & Mosterman, P. J. (2011). *Discrete-Event Modeling and Simulation: Theory and Applications*. Boca Raton, FL: CRC Press.

Walden, K., & Nerson, J.-M. (1995). *Seamless Object-Oriented Software Architecture*. Upper Saddle River, NJ: Prentice Hall.

Wang, R., & Dagli, C. (2008). An executable system architecture approach to discrete events system modeling using SysML in conjunction with colored petri nets. In *IEEE Systems Conference 2008* (pp.1–8). Montreal, Canada: IEEE Computer Press.

Wang, J. (2007). Petri nets for dynamic event-driven system modeling. In Fishwick, P. (Ed.), *Handbook of Dynamic System Modeling*. CRC Press. doi:10.1201/9781420010855.ch24.

Wasserman, S. (1994). *Social network analysis: Methods and applications*. Cambridge university press. doi:10.1017/CBO9780511815478.

Wegener, M. (2000). Spatial models and GIS. In Fotheringham, A., & Wegener, M. (Eds.), *Spatial Models and GIS: New Potential and New Models*. London: Taylor & Francis.

Weigert, T., Weil, F., Marth, K., Baker, P., Jervis, C., & Dietz, P. … Mastenbrook, B. (2007). Experiences in Deploying Model-Driven Engineering. In E. Gaudin, E. Najm, & R. Reed (Eds.), SDL 2007: Design for Dependable Systems (Vol. 4745, pp. 35-53). Berlin, Germany: Springer. doi: doi:10.1007/978-3-540-74984-4_3.

Weilkiens, T. (2008). *Systems Engineering with SysML/UML*. Heidelberg, Germany: Dpunkt Verlag.

Weiss, G. (1999). *Multiagent systems: a modern approach to distributed artificial intelligence*. The MIT press.

Weyprecht, P., & Rose, O. (2011) Model-driven development of simulation solution based on SysML starting with the simulation core. In *Proceedings of the 2011 Symposium on Theory of Modeling & Simulation: DEVS Integrative M&S Symposium* (pp. 189-192). Boston, MA: Society for Computer Simulation International.

Wheatley, D., & Gillings, M. (2000). Vision, perception and GIS: developing enriched approaches to the study of archaeological visibility. *Beyond the map: archaeology and spatial technologies*, 1–27. Available from the author.

Wierzbicki, A., & Nielek, R. (2011). Fairness emergence in reputation systems. *Journal of Artificial Societies and Social Simulation, 14*(1), 3. Retrieved July 16, 2012, from http://jasss.soc.surrey.ac.uk/14/1/3.html

Wild, S., Roglic, G., Green, A., Sicree, R., & King, H. (2004). Global Prevalence of Diabetes. Estimates for the year 2000 and projections for 2030. *Diabetes Care, 27*, 1047–1053. doi:10.2337/diacare.27.5.1047 PMID:15111519.

Wilensky, U. (2002). Modeling nature's emergent patterns with multi-agent languages. In Proceedings of EuroLogo 2001 Linz (pp. 1–6).

Windrum, P., Fagiolo, G., & Moneta, A. (2007). Empirical Validation of Agent-Based Models: Alternatives and Prospects. *Journal of Artificial Societies and Social Simulation, 10*(2), 8. Retrieved July 16, 2012, from http://jasss.soc.surrey.ac.uk/10/2/8.html

Wong, C. Y., Dillon, T. S., & Forward, K. E. (1985). Timed places Petri nets with stochastic representation of place time. In *Proceedings of the International Workshop on Timed Petri Nets* (pp. 66-103). Torino, Italy. IEEE Computer Society.

World Health Organization. (2008). *World Health Statistics 2008*.

World Wide Web Consortium. (2007). *Extensible stylesheet language transformations (xslt)*. Retrieved from http://www.w3.org/TR/xslt20

Xu, J., Gao, Y., & Madey, G. (2003). A docking experiment: Swarm and repast for social network modeling. In *Seventh Annual Swarm Researchers Meeting*. South Bend, IN.

Yang, J., Long, Q., Liu, Z., & Li, X. (2004). *A Predicative Semantic Model for Integrating UML Models*. New York: Springer.

Yang, L., & Gilbert, N. (2008). Getting away from numbers: Using qualitative observation for agent-based modeling. *Advances in Complex Systems, 11*(2), 175–186. doi:10.1142/S0219525908001556.

Yeager, K. C. (1996). The MIPS R10000 Superscalar Microprocessor. *IEEE Micro, 16*.

Zaft, G., & Zeigler, B. P. (2002). Discrete event simulation of social sciences: The XeriScape artificial society. In *Proceedings of the 6th World Multiconference on Systemics, Cybernetics and Informatics*. Orlando, FL: International Institute of Informatics and Systemics.

Zagonel, A., Rohrbaugh, J., & Andersen, D. (2004). Using simulation models to address "What if" questions about welfare reform. *Journal of Policy Analysis and Management, 23*(4), 890–901. doi:10.1002/pam.20054.

Zeigler, B. P., & Sarjoughian, H. S. (2003). *Introduction to DEVS modeling and simulation with JAVA. DEVSJAVA manual*. [Computer software manual]. Retrieved from www.acims.arizona.edu/PUBLICATIONS/publications.shtml

Zeigler, B. P. (1976). *Theory of modeling and simulation*. New York: John Wiley.

Zeigler, B. P. (1984). *Multifacetted Modelling and Discrete Event Simulation*. London: Academic Press.

Zeigler, B. P. (1984). *Theory of Modelling and Simulation*. Malabar, FL: Krieger Publishing Company.

Zeigler, B. P., Kim, T. G., & Praehofer, H. (2000). *Theory of Modeling and Simulation*. New York: Academic Press.

Zervos, C. R. (1977). *Coloured petri nets: Their properties and applications*. PhD thesis, University of Michigan, Michigan.

ZETA. (1999). *Zeta referential guide*. Technical report

Compilation of References

Zhang, M., Zeigler, B. P., & Hammonds, P. (2005). Devs/rmi-an auto-adaptive and reconfigurable distributed simulation environment for engineering studies. *International Test and Evaluation Association Journal*, *27*(1), 49–60.

Zhao, H., & Li, X. (2008). H-trust: A robust and lightweight group reputation system for peer-to-peer desktop grid. In *The 28th International Conference on Distributed Computing Systems Workshops* (pp. 235–240). Beijing, China: IEEE. doi: 10.1109/ICDCS. Workshops.2008.96

Zheng, Q., Chen, S., Shen, J., Liu, Z., Fang, K., & Xiang, W. (2010). Simulation Modeling of the Operating Room Based on SIMIO. *Applied Mechanics and Materials*, *37-38*, 1162–1166. doi:10.4028/www.scientific.net/AMM.37-38.1162.

Zimmermann, A., Dalkowski, K., & Hommel, G. (1996). A case study in modeling and performance evaluation of manufacturing systems using colored Petri nets. In *Proceedings of the 8th European Simulation Symposium (ESS '96)* (pp. 282-286). Society for Computer Simulation.

About the Contributors

Pau Fonseca i Casas is a Professor of the Department of Statistics and Operational Research of the Polytechnic University of Catalonia, teaching in statistics and simulation areas. He obtained his Master's degree in Computer Engineering in 1999 and his PhDin 2007 from Polytechnic University of Catalonia. He also works in the InLab FIB as a head of the Environmental Simulation area, developing simulation projects since 1998. He is member of LogiSim group, dedicated to the research and development of simulation tools and projects. His website is http://www-eio.upc.es/~pau/. His research interests are discrete simulation applied to industrial, environmental, and social models, and the formal representation of such models.

* * *

Mouez Ali is a doctor and assistant of computer science in the Higher Institute of Computer science and Multimedia (Sfax, Tunisia). She received her master's (in 2004) and her doctorate degrees (in 2010) from the University of Sfax (Faculty of Economics and Managment of Sfax-Tunisia). She is a member of the research laboratory MIRACL. Her research interests focus on formal methods and their application, model based testing, model verification and validation (V&V) and specification of functional and non-functional requirements.

Dimosthenis Anagnostopoulos is a professor in the Department of Informatics and Telematics at Harokopio University of Athens. He holds a PhD and Bachelor's degree in Computer Science from the Department of Informatics and Telecommunications at the University of Athens. He has published more than 100 papers in international journals and conferences. His research interests include discrete event simulation, faster-than-real-time simulation, modeling, and simulation of distributed information systems. He has actively participated in numerous projects related to simulation, e-government, and information systems.

Joaquín Aranda received the Licentiate degree from the UCM (1983), and the PhD degree from the UNED (1989). He served as a teaching assistant in the Computer Science and Automatic Control Department in the UCM. Since 1988 he has been with the Computer Science and Automatic Control Department in the UNED where he is currently a full professor and previously he was an assistant professor and associate professor. He was Deputy Director of the University School of Computer of UNED (1997-2001), and Director of Computer Science High School (2001-2005). He leads the research group about industrial computing (1997-...), and he is the Head of the Computer Science and Automatic Control Department of UNED (2007-...). He is the author or co-author of more than 120 publications. His scientific activities cover various aspects within the control engineering field: controller design, robust control, computer control, modeling and simulation, and application of control and simulation to high speed craft, marine systems, airplane, and robotic. He has been involved in 34 research projects relating to these topics (public competitive projects, private company projects, special actions, etc.); in 18 projects he was the main researcher, coordinator, or group leader. He was the advisor of seven PhD theses and co-advisor of four PhD theses. Now he is the main researcher of the project "System for surveillance, search and rescue in the sea by means of collaboration of autonomous marine and air vehicles" and advisor of 3 PhD theses.

Hanene Ben-Abdallah is a Professor of Computer Science in the Department of Computer Science at FSEG, University of Sfax, Tunisia. She received her Master's and PhD in CIS from the University of Pennsylvania, Philadelphia, USA in 1996. Her research focuses on quality assurance of software and business process models through the application of reuse techniques, formal methods, and quality metrics.

Eva Besada-Portas is an assistant professor of the Department of Computer Architecture and Automatic Control of the Complutense University of Spain, Madrid, since 2005. She has also been a post post-doctoral visiting researcher of the Department of Computer Science of the University of New Mexico, USA, from 2006 to 2010. Her research interests are in optimal control, bio-inspired optimization algorithms, UAVs, path planning, multisensor fusion systems and estimation techniques, and machine learning.

Josep Casanovas, received a PhD in Computer Science (1983),Industrial Engineer, and a MSc in Economics. He is the Director of inLab.FIB at Barcelona School of Informatics. He is a full professor in the Statistics and Operations Research Department at UPC. His main research areas are modeling and simulation, future Internet, and information systems. He is the author of research articles and other publications and has collaborated in many projects for the EU and different companies and institutions. He is the Vice-Rector for the University Policy of UPC-BarcelonaTech (2006-2011), responsible for ICT policies at UPC and director of the Centre for Cooperation to Development. He has been leading relevant research and applied-oriented projects in modeling and simulation areas, including project NAT, the complete model building and simulation of the new Airport Terminal Hub of Barcelona, and Clinical Trials modeling. Now he is coordinating the Severo Ochoa research program in the Barcelona Supercomputing Center (BSC-CNS) focused in HPC simulation based in Next generation Exascale supercomputers.

Jose María Cela-Espín is the director of the Computer Applications in Science & Engineering Department at the Barcelona Supercomputing Center (BSC). He is also an associated professor of the Universitat Politècnica de Catalunya (UPC). He has participated in more than 20 R+D projects and he has published more than 40 papers in international journals and conferences. His research is related with the parallelization and optimization of numerical simulations, mainly in PDEs solvers, inverse problem simulations, ab-initio molecular dynamics codes, plasma physics codes, and different types of optimization codes (nonlinear optimization, stochastic optimization, etc.).

Vassilis Dalakas is currently working as a network and system administrator at Harokopio University of Athens. He is also a Research Fellow in the Department of Informatics and Telematics at the same institution. He obtained his BSc in Physics and a MSc degree in Digital Signal Processing with honours, both at National Kapodistrian University of Athens from the Physics and Informatics & Telecommunications Departments, respectively. His PhD in Informatics was obtained from the same institution, in cooperation with the Institute for Space Applications and Remote Sensing of the National Observatory of Athens. His research interests include signal processing for satellite communications systems and modeling and simulation standardization methods. He is a member of the European Satellite Communications Network of Excellence (SatNEx) and of IEEE.

Luis de la Torre is an assistant professor of the Department of Computer Sciences Automatic and Control of the UNED (Open University of Spain), Madrid, where he began his PhD degree in Systems Engineering and Automatic Control in 2008. He previously joined the Department of Computers Architecture and Automatic Control of the UCM as a research fellow in 2007, while he was finishing his MSc degree. His research interests are in evolutionary algorithms, UAVs, path planning, remote and virtual laboratories, and distance education.

Jaume Figueras i Jové (MSc in Computer Science) He is an assistant professor at UPC in the Automatic Control Department. He is also head of GIS projects at inLab FIB. His research is focused in automatic control and computer simulation where participated and has lead different research and industrial projects. He was the designer of CORAL, an optimal control system for sewer networks, applied at Barcelona; PLIO, an optimal control system and planner for drinking water, applied at Santiago de Chile and Múrcia. He also participates in mobile devices tracking projects such as the power consumption optimization of tramway in Barcelona with TRAM and SIEMENS; SportTraces and SkiTraces smartphone and Web apps to monitor sport races and skiers. He is also winner of the Living Labs Global Award 2012 for the application CityWalking for the city of Terrassa. He is also the local contact person of OSM in Catalonia and participates in different FOSS projects.

Faïez Gargouri is a Professor of Computer Science at the Higher Institute of Computer Science and Multimedia (Sfax-Tunisia), where he was the Dean from 2007 to 2011. He has received his maitrise diploma in Computer Management in the Faculty of Economics and Management of Sfax (1988), his Master's in Computer Science from the Paris 6 University (1990) and his PhD thesis at the Paris-5 University. He got his Habilitation Degree in Computer Science from the Faculty of Sciences of Tunis (2002). He is interested in the field of information systems: design, quality measurement, verification, decision-making, multimedia, Ontology, and knowledge management. He has been the director of the research laboratory MIRACL (ISIM, Sfax) since 2011 and is responsible for the Information Systems Engineering Team, where he supervisse several theses works (5 defunded yet). He is the author of more than 100 papers in journals, conferences, and books. He is member of the Scientific and Steering Committees of various international conferences.

Rhys Goldstein is a Simulation Researcher at Autodesk Research. His work aims to help designers use simulation to predict and ultimately reduce energy consumption in buildings. He is currently investigating the use of a modeling formalism known as the Discrete Event System Specification (DEVS) to help researchers collaborate in the development of simulation software. Rhys received a BSc in Engineering Physics at the University of British Columbia in 2003, and a MSc in Biomedical Engineering at Carleton University in 2009. His master's thesis was on the simulation of small-scale deformable biological structures, an example being vesicle clusters that self-assemble inside nerve cells. Rhys also worked in mineral exploration for several years, leading geophysical surveys in Tasmania, Cyprus, Oman, and many sites in North America.

Antoni Guasch is a research engineer focusing on modelling, simulation, and optimization of dynamic systems. He received his PhD from the UPC in 1987. After a postdoctoral period at the State University of California (USA), he became a professor of the UPC (www.upc.edu). He is now a professor in the department of Ingeniería de Sistemas, Automática e Informática Industrial in the UPC and head of Simulation and Industrial Optimization at inLab FIB (http://inlab.fib.upc.edu/). Since 1990, Prof. Guasch has lead more than 40 industrial and research projects related to modelling, simulation, and optimization of nuclear, textile, transportation, car manufacturing, water and steel industrial processes. Prof. Guasch's current research project,sponsored by Agbar, is related to the development of optimization algorithms for agricultural land irrigation.

George-Dimitrios Kapos is currently performing research for his PhD thesis on automated simulation execution from standards-based system models at the Department of Informatics and Telematics, Harokopio University of Athens. In parallel, he works as an analyst and software developer at the IT Department of the Greek Consignment Deposit & Loans Fund, also participating in efforts for realization of e-Government in Greece. He obtained his BSc in Informatics and a MSc degree in Advanced Information Systems, both with honors from Informatics & Telecommunications Department, National Kapodistrian University of Athens. His research interests include model-based systems validation, distributed-object systems dynamic behavior and distributed, heterogeneous databases homogenization.

Azam Khan is the head of the Environment & Ergonomics Research Group at Autodesk Research. Starting in the field of human-computer interaction, Azam focused on advanced 3D camera navigation interaction techniques, large displays, visualization, and pen-based interaction. More recently, Azam has been exploring modeling and simulation including physics-based generative design, air flow and occupant flow in an architectural context, and simulation visualization and validation based on sensor-networks. In 2009, Azam founded and chaired SimAUD, the Symposium on Simulation for Architecture and Urban Design to foster cross-pollination between the simulation research and the architecture research communities. Azam is also the Principal Investigator of the Parametric Human project and, in 2010, Azam became a founding member of the International Society of Human Simulation.

Adriana Kaplan Marcusán is Director of the Chair in Knowledge Transfer Research Park / UAB, in the Department of Social and Cultural Anthropology at UAB. She is the principal investigator of the Interdisciplinary Group for the Study and Prevention of Harmful Traditional Practices (GIPE-PTP). She has been a collaborator researcher at the Medical Research Council, advisor at the Women's Bureau in the Gambia, and consultant for various international agencies including UNFPA, UNDP, UNICEF, and EU. Her research career is in the study of migration in Sub-Saharan African and anthropological analysis of the processes of acculturation and social integration in the field of sexual and reproductive health. Her research focus is on the study and prevention of female genital mutilation (FGM) from a gender perspective, longitudinal, circular and transnational.

Cristina Montañola-Sales is a PhD student in the Statistics and Operations Research Department at Universitat Politècnica de Catalunya (UPC). She is currently doing her research in the Barcelona Supercomputing Center and working as research assistant at inLab Barcelona School of Informatics in UPC. She holds a MSc in Computer Science from UPC. Her research interests include agent-based modelling, computer simulation, and high-performance computing, focusing in their applications to the social sciences and humanities. She is part of SimulPast (http://www.simulpast.es), a project designed to explore the dynamics of human-environment interaction from an archaeological perspective.

Alejandro Moreno has been a research personnel of the Department of Computer Science and Automatic Control of the UNED, Spain, since 2008. Currently, he is finalizing his PhD in Systems Engineering and Automatic Control. His academic studies comprehend a Bachelor's degree in Computer Science at the UAM, Master's degree in Geographic Information Systems (GIS) at the UPSAM, and Master's degree in Artificial Intelligence (AI) at the UPM. His research interests focus on modeling, parallelizing, and distributing simulations within Discrete Event Systems Specification (DEVS) of Artificial Intelligence based methods of optimization.

Mara Nikolaidou is a professor in the Department of Informatics and Telematics at Harokopio University of Athens. She holds a PhD and Bachelor's degree in Computer Science from the Department of Informatics and Telecommunications at University of Athens. Her research interests include software and information system engineering, service-oriented architectures, e-government, and digital libraries. Over the years she has actively participated in numerous projects on service-oriented architectures, digital libraries, and e-government. She has published more than 100 papers in international journals and conferences.

Jorge Leiva Olmos is head of the Department of Data Information and Communication Management of Hospital Dr. Gustavo Fricke, Viña del Mar, Chile (working at the hospital since 1999) and a professor at the Department of Mathematics of the University of Playa Ancha, Valparaíso, Chile, teaching in statistics. Titled in statistic in 1999 (University of Playa Ancha, Chile), Master's degree in statistical in 2007 (University of Valparaíso, Chile), Master's degree in Statistics and Operations Research in 2011 (Polytechnic University of Catalonia and University of Barcelona, Spain) and a current student in PhD Statistics and Operations Research at the Polytechnic University of Catalonia.

Bhakti Satyabudhi Stephan Onggo is a lecturer in Business Process Modelling and Simulation at the Department of Management Science at the Lancaster University Management School. He completed his PhD in Computer Science from the National University of Singapore and his MSc in Management Science from the Lancaster University. His research interests are in the areas of simulation methodology (modelling paradigms and conceptual modelling), simulation technology (parallel and distributed simulation), and business process modelling and simulation applications.

Falk Stefan Pappert is a PhD student at the Universität der Bundeswehr München, Germany. He is a member of the scientific staff of Prof. Dr. Oliver Rose at the Chair of Modeling and Simulation. He received his M.S. degree in Computer Science from Dresden University of Technology. His research interests are model validation, simulation-based scheduling, and optimization of production systems. He is a member of GI.

Jordi Ocaña Rebull is a professor at the Department of Statistics of the University of Barcelona (UB). He obtained his PhD in 1981 from the UB. His teaching and research activities are centered mainly in two statistical areas: Computer Intensive Methods and Biostatistics. He is the director of the Summer School of the Interuniversity Master in Statistics and Operations Research, an UB/Technical University of Catalonia joint venture (http://meioupcub.masters.upc.edu/Summer-School). His research interests include simulation and computer intensive methods in statistics, equivalence testing (bioequivalence, equivalence in simulation models validation, data integration in bioinformatics), and formal aspects of statistical software (object orientation, design patterns in statistical software). He is a member and co-founder of the research group in Multivariate Analysis and Computational Statistics of the UB.

José L. Risco-Martín is associate professor at the Computer Architecture and Automation Department of Complutense University of Madrid (UCM), Spain. His research interests focus on design methodologies for integrated systems and high-performance embedded systems, including new modeling frameworks to explore thermal management techniques for Multi-Processor System-on-Chip, novel architectures for logic and memories in forthcoming nano-scale electronics, dynamic memory management and memory hierarchy optimizations for embedded systems, Networks-on-Chip interconnection design, and low-power design of embedded systems. He is also interested on theory of modeling and simulation, with emphasis on Discrete Event Systems Specification (DEVS), and the application of Bio-inspired optimization techniques in Computer Aided Design (CAD) problems.

Oliver Rose holds the Chair for Modeling and Simulation at the Institute of Technical Computer Science of the Universität der Bundeswehr München, Germany. He received an MS in applied mathematics and a PhD in Computer Science from Würzburg University, Germany. His research focuses on the operational modeling, analysis, and material flow control of complex manufacturing facilities, in particular, semiconductor factories. He is a member of IEEE, INFORMS Simulation Society, ASIM, and GI.

Xavier Rubio-Campillo holds a degree in Computer Science from the University Pompeu Fabra, and a PhD in Heritage from the University of Barcelona. He is a postdoctoral researcher at Barcelona Supercomputing Center. His research interests are focused on the use of high-performance computer simulation in social sciences and the humanities. He is also a member of DIDPATRI research group in University of Barcelona that deals with an interdisciplinary approach to the study of past societies. He is part of SimulPast (http://www.simulpast.es), a project designed to explore the dynamics of human-environment interaction from an archaeological perspective.

Marisa Analía Sánchez received a PhD in Computer Science from Universidad Nacional del Sur in Bahía Blanca, Argentina. She is currently a lecturer of undergraduate and graduate courses at the Department of Management Sciences at Universidad Nacional del Sur. From 1994 to 2004 she had been on the faculty at the Departments of Computer Science and Electrical Engineering. Her research interests include business intelligence with focus on simulation. Her main field of application is business problems.

Oliver Schönherr is a PhD student at the Universität der Bundeswehr München, Germany. He is a member of the scientific staff at the Chair for Modeling and Simulation. He received his MS in Computer Science from the Dresden University of Technology, Germany.

Anargyros Tsadimas was born in Lamia in 1979. He received his BSc in Applied Informatics from the University of Macedonia in 2002, his MSc in Advanced Information Systems from the Department of Informatics & Telecommunications of the National and Kapodistrian University of Athens in 2005, and since 2008 he is working on his PhD which has the title of Integration of Discrete Design Activities of Model-Based Enterprise Information System Engineering. His research interests lie in the areas of modeling & simulation of systems, distributed systems, and enterprise information systems engineering. He has 12 publications in international conference proceedings. He has participated in R&D projects founded by the European Union and the Greek State.

Gabriel A. Wainer received the MSc (1993) and PhD degrees (1998, with highest honors) from the University of Buenos Aires, Argentina, and Université d'Aix-Marseille III, France. In July 2000, he joined the Department of Systems and Computer Engineering, Carleton University (Ottawa, ON, Canada), where he is now a full professor. He is the author of three books and numerous research articles, has edited four other books, and helped organize various conferences in the field of modeling and simulation, including being one of the founders of SIMUTools, SimAUD, and the Symposium on Theory of Modeling and Simulation. He is Vice-President Conferences, and was Vice-President Publications, and a member of the Board of Directors of SCS. He is the head of the Advanced Real-Time Simulation lab, located at Carleton University's Centre for advanced Simulation and Visualization (V-Sim). He has been the recipient of various awards, including the IBM Eclipse Innovation Award, SCS Leadership Award, and various best paper awards. He has been awarded the First Bernard P. Zeigler DEVS Modeling and Simulation Award, and the SCS Outstanding Professional Award (2011).

Index